# AMERICAN HEROINES

KAY BAILEY HUTCHISON

# AMERICAN
# HEROINES

*The Spirited Women*

*Who Shaped Our Country*

William Morrow  *wm*  *An Imprint of* HarperCollins*Publishers*

920.7209
Hut

HarperCollins books may be purchased for educational, business, or sales promotional
use. For information please write: Special Markets Department, HarperCollins Publishers Inc., 10 East 53rd Street, New York, NY 10022.

FIRST EDITION

Printed on acid-free paper

Library of Congress Cataloging-in-Publication Data

Hutchison, Kay Bailey, 1943–
    American heroines : the spirited women who shaped our country /
Kay Bailey Hutchison.—1st ed.
    p.   cm.
    ISBN 0-06-056635-3 (alk. paper)
    1. Heroes—United States—Biography.   2. Women heroes—United States—
Biography.   3. Women—United States—Biography.   4. United States—Biography.
I. Title.

CT3260.H87     2004
920.72'0973—dc22
[B]                                                                    2004056677

04 05 06 07 08 DIX/RRD 10 9 8 7 6 5 4

*This book is dedicated to my family,*

*without whom I couldn't do half of what I do:*

*my husband of twenty-six years, Ray,*

*his daughters Brenda and Julie,*

*our grandchildren Travis, Camille, Hailey, Ashton, and Aaron,*

*and the lights of my life,*

*Kathryn Bailey Hutchison and Houston Taylor Hutchison,*

*our children.*

# CONTENTS

# ACKNOWLEDGMENTS

This book was a team effort. So many wonderful people contributed to it, for which I feel blessed and appreciative.

Claire Wachtel, my editor, was nothing short of fabulous. She helped from the germ of the idea to the very end. Howard Cohn, the researcher and draft writer, put so much of himself into the book. He was the easiest person with whom to work.

Jan Benson, my able and trusted assistant, loved the book as much as I did and volunteered more hours to it than anyone besides Howard and me, even through a heart attack! I love her for it.

Two law firms were great. Bob Barnett of Williams and Connolly was my agent—and did so much more. My husband's law firm, Vinson and Elkins, offered us office space for a week to finish the book. Attorneys Rob Walters and Jeff Chapman, along with office manager Bill Evans, made us feel welcome. Administrative assistants Dinah Crim and Ida Perryman pitched in to help so much.

Lindsey Howe Parham, David Beckwith, Kevin Cooper, Jenifer Sarver, Jordan Byrne, Cramer Miller, and Bethany Smith all volunteered to help with facts and suggestions.

T. R. Fehrenbach, Texas's most distinguished historian, also made valuable suggestions. Former Texas lieutenant governor Bill Hobby provided wonderful background for the chapter on his mother, and Hally Ballinger Bryan Clements, Stephen F. Austin's great-great-niece, offered sources for the chapter on Mary Austin Holley. Wick and Christine Allison added several key concepts. And finally, Dr. Linda Sundquist-Nassie has written a beautiful biography of my great-great-grandmother Mary Shindler and allowed me to use some of the material she had found for this book. She was very generous and I hope her full biography is published in its totality.

# INTRODUCTION

*... if I were asked ... to what the singular*
*prosperity and growing strength of that people*
*ought mainly to be attributed, I should reply: to*
*the superiority of their women.*

ALEXIS DE TOCQUEVILLE, *Democracy in America,* 1835

I N HIS TRAVELS across America, Alexis de Tocqueville observed
something special, something inherently different in American
women compared to Europeans. Their spunk and independence
struck him as key ingredients in the success of this upstart nation with its
bold experiment in democracy.

The role women played as equal partners in settling and taming the
land, made them tough and capable. When the men were off writing
the Constitution and preparing our country for a government of the
people, women such as Abigail Adams took care of the farms to make
ends meet. While the men were establishing colleges, women such as
Emma Willard were teaching the children to read and write. When borders pushed westward, the women drove the wagons, endured the elements, and helped run the family businesses, from grocery stores to vast
ranches. Because of the loss of a father or husband, it was not uncommon for a woman to be the sole proprietor of a business—keeping the

books, trading goods, or selling animals. If they were out in the country, they fought the Indians to protect their homesteads.

When my great-great-grandfather Charles S. Taylor rode off on horseback 157 miles to Washington-on-the-Brazos to sign the Texas Declaration of Independence in 1836, my great-great-grandmother Anna Maria took their four young children to Louisiana to escape the Mexican army and the Indians they feared would attack. The mass exodus of women and children from Texas during the war with Mexico was called the Runaway Scrape. The ravages of disease plus cold and rainy weather made for a treacherous journey. Anna Maria Taylor lost all four of her children to diseases during that time. But the triumph of spirit over adversity brought her back to her home in Nacogdoches, where she rejoined her husband, stood with him as he helped lead the newly independent nation, the Republic of Texas, and, oh, by the way, produced nine more children! They and thousands of brave pioneers built the land that became the state of Texas, annexed by the United States in 1846.

My mother grew up in that same historic town, Nacogdoches. My grandmother, aunt and uncle, and cousins all lived in the family home there. So my brothers and I were frequently piled into the car to ride the back roads from La Marque to East Texas to visit them.

We learned Texas history through osmosis. The Old Stone Fort, which was used as a gathering place before Texas was a republic, is a block away from Grandmother's house. The historic cemetery, Oak Grove, where many heroes of the fight for Texas independence lie, is three blocks in the other direction. My great-great-grandfather Charles S. Taylor is buried there, along with Thomas J. Rusk, one of the two U.S. senators first elected from Texas to the seat I now hold. The two were friends and business partners. My mother and father are buried there, too.

Perhaps this early introduction to our unique heritage made me love Texas with a passion. I appreciate the toughness and sacrifice of the early pioneers. They could have had easier lives back east but chose to clear the deep forests to create their own communities.

As an example, our family has a letter from my great-great-grandmother on my grandfather's side, Martha Hall Sharp, dated May 1,

1849. She was the daughter of Governor William Hall of Tennessee, the man who succeeded Sam Houston in that position. She wrote her sister from her new two-room log house in San Augustine, Texas: "Out in this new country I see no one but strangers, but they are the kindest people I have ever met with. The society is as good as in any portion of Tennessee. There is no such thing as fine houses or furniture. We are too far from navigation to get such things. If I had been in Tennessee, I would have thought the house we occupy would not do at all . . . but with all these inconveniences, we are getting along finely."

What touched me about this letter was its upbeat, positive attitude. I have always had a sense of hope and optimism, too. Like so many of the hearty women before me, I didn't know I couldn't run for public office and win. So I did—perhaps inspired by those before me. Or maybe I ventured into public life just because the spirit of these women was in my genes. The indomitable spirit of American women is the focus of this book. It has been a thread in our culture that runs throughout the life of our nation. No history can be written appropriately without acknowledging the part women have played in building the greatness of our country.

Perhaps because we have only been a republic for 228 years, the thread continues. These stories of our grandmothers and those before are still passed down—mother to daughter. We learned much of our nation's travails through their chronicles and diaries. We see their determination and contribution . . . and we are inspired by it. Building their lives and our fledgling democracy through obstacles and hardships, while keeping their spirit and resilience, they set an example succeeding generations have followed; and so the torch is passed. Each adds another layer in the fabric of our nation—something new, something better. Pioneers led the way, running the family businesses and opening schools; then came Rosie the Riveter and the WASP, who flew ferry missions in World War II for no credit; now we are doctors, mayors, generals, admirals, and CEOs of Fortune 500 companies.

There are those who think the role of women in our country has been too slow in evolving, but let's look at the big picture. I believe America is the best place in the world to be a woman. Our opportunities are boundless. Our predecessors put building blocks in place, and each decade our place in society improves. That indomitable optimism will be passed on, and we must assure that it is. This book is written to make one small contribution to that goal . . . that the spirit of women that has defined our country since its inception will remain alive and continue to shape the future of America.

## Women of Today

I CHOSE pioneer women in different fields. After each chapter on an early leader, I interviewed contemporary women who are still breaking barriers in the same general arena. Through their stories I hope to show the contributions women have made to America, and some of the experiences and traits these incredible women possess, as well as what drove them to struggle through prejudice to do important work that helped move our country to become the most powerful on earth.

# CHAPTER ONE

# PIONEERS AND
# PRESERVATIONISTS

## Mary Austin Holley

MARY AUSTIN DIDN'T grow up dreaming of a life in Texas. As a child in New Haven, Connecticut, during the closing years of the eighteenth century, this daughter of a prominent mercantile family may have imagined faraway places but probably expected to spend a comfortable life close to home. Mary was born in 1784, the fourth of Elijah and Esther Phelps Austin's eight children. Her father helped develop the lucrative shipping trade between the young Republic and China, but when Mary was ten years old, Elijah Austin died of yellow fever. Although the Austins weren't plunged into poverty, Esther Austin couldn't afford to keep her family together, so Mary was sent to live with her uncle, Timothy Phelps, another prosperous New Haven merchant, and his family.

In 1805, Mary Austin married Horace Holley, a Yale graduate from Salisbury, Connecticut, who turned his back on a promising legal career in New York to return to Yale and study divinity. His first posting, at a Congregational church in the small Connecticut town of Greenfield Hill, left Mary feeling isolated from the cultural life she craved. In 1808, Rev. Holley was invited to serve as minister of Boston's Hollis Street Congregational Church, and Mary and Horace jumped at the chance to become part of Boston's vibrant social and intellectual world. Mary, whose first child, Harriette, was born that same year, found the cultural atmosphere bracing, while Horace, whose religious ideas were growing increasingly liberal, quickly found himself quite at home among Boston's philosophers and politicians.

A serious thinker and impassioned speaker, Horace rapidly gained a place for Mary and himself among New England's intellectual elite. He was invited to join the Harvard University Board of Overseers, quite an accomplishment for a "mere" Yale graduate, and when the Hollis Street church closed down during the construction of a larger building, William Emerson, father of the philosopher Ralph Waldo Emerson and minister of First Church, arranged for Horace to alternate as preacher there until Hollis Street reopened. At one dinner party that included, among other guests, John Quincy Adams, Horace engaged the former president in an argument about religion. In his memoirs, Adams recalled, "[T]he table-talk was almost engrossed by us, and the attention of the whole table turned to us, much to my disadvantage, the topic being one upon which he was much more exercised and better prepared than I was. Mr. Webster, Mr. A. H. Everett, and one or two others occasionally relieved me by asking a question; but Holley was quite a match for us all."

The intellectual life may have been rich, but the Holleys were always short of money. So when tiny Transylvania University in Lexington, Kentucky, asked Rev. Holley to become president of the institution in 1818, he accepted. Mary was opposed to leaving New England, but she was pregnant with their second child, and the promise of a substantially higher salary proved an irresistible lure. Besides, Horace had ideas about education that he was eager to try out on a large scale, and the trustees' plans to establish Lexington as the "Athens of the West" meshed perfectly with Rev. Holley's own aspirations. In Lexington, he would be able to put his theories to work in ways that a minister could not easily do. Despite some resistance from conservative Presbyterian clergy, support from Henry Clay and other prominent Kentuckians assured Rev. Holley's appointment.

Under its new president, Transylvania attracted more students, added a law school and medical school to its undergraduate program, and gained prominence in the South and beyond. But even as Transylvania grew in size and importance, so did opposition to Rev. Holley's liberal views. After he delivered a eulogy at the funeral of Colonel James Morrison, who had been chairman of Transylvania's board of trustees, praising his friend for "taking truth wherever he found it and giving the hand of fellowship to all good men of every country and denomination," a group of conservative clergymen waged a campaign to drive Rev. Holley from the presidency. One ploy was to reduce his salary, money always being a difficult matter for the Holleys, and when Kentucky governor Joseph Desha also withdrew his personal support in 1827, Rev. Holley resigned and moved to New Orleans.

The family connection to Lexington endured, however. The Holleys' daughter, Harriette, married William Brand, a Transylvania graduate and son of a wealthy Lexington businessman. A link to New Orleans existed as well; many Louisianians sent their sons to Transylvania to study, some of them as young as ten, and a number of the Louisianians had boarded with the Holleys while attending classes in Lexington. Drawing on this experience, Holley formed a plan: to found a "traveling academy" for the children of wealthy planters from the region, who would pursue their educations while touring Europe under his tutelage—very likely the first "study abroad" program conceived in the United States. Rev. Holley finally scrapped the idea when he discovered that parents weren't prepared to send their young sons so far from home.

Discouraged, Horace considered starting a local college in the city, but before getting down to serious planning, the Holleys took a brief vacation in New York. On board the *Louisiana,* husband and wife came down with yellow fever, the same disease that had claimed Mary's father's life. This time, it was Horace Holley who succumbed to the illness, and he was buried at sea. Yellow fever, which had made Mary Austin Holley fatherless when she was ten, now left her, at the age of forty-three, a widow with a young son to support.

Without close ties to a place or a community, Mary was adrift. Her first concerns were to make arrangements for young Horace's education and to find a fitting way to memorialize her husband. To that end she went to Boston, where members of the Hollis Street church had already begun collecting a fund for Horace's support. She found a school for him in Cambridge, one whose students included boys from the German Coast of Louisiana, and then returned to the South to write the biography of her husband. *A Discourse on the Genius and Character of the Rev. Horace Holley, LL.D.* was published in Boston in the summer of 1828, and received good reviews in a number of newspapers from New England to Kentucky. To drum up interest in the memoir, she traveled up the East Coast and back, making sure that all subscribers to the book received their copies and urging booksellers to stock the volume.

Mary was now at a crossroads faced by many women without independent means: she could live with her daughter and son-in-law in Lexington or find some way to earn her own living. Returning to Lexington to become part of Harriette and William Brand's growing household (the Brands eventually had ten children) didn't appeal to Mary. She might have felt different if her memories of Lexington had been more agreeable, or if the Brands' social and religious views had been closer to hers. So when the wealthy Labranches, Hermogene and Elizabeth, invited Mary to live at Good Hope Plantation in Louisiana as governess to their young daughter, Melazie, in 1829—and to bring Horace with her—Mary seized the opportunity to avoid becoming dependent on her daughter and son-in-law and to provide a comfortable environment for her son. Horace, often sickly and unpredictable, never got along well with William Brand. The Good Hope Plantation would prove to be the best situation for Mary Austin Holley and even more so for Horace. He spent much of the rest of his life there, even at times when his mother was not employed by the Labranches, and eventually became the plantation's carpenter.

Mary's brother, Henry Austin, obtained a large grant of land in the Austin colony in Texas, which had been established by their uncle

Moses, father of Stephen F. Austin, but was administered by the son following Moses Austin's death in 1821. In 1830, Henry was preparing for his wife and children to join him in Bolivar, on the Brazos River, where he had built a small house and founded a town, though its entire population at that time consisted of himself and his gardener. At about that time, he encouraged his sister Mary to apply for a land grant of her own from their cousin Stephen, before a new Mexican law prohibiting further immigration from the United States took effect.

Henry's letter arrived at the right time. Perhaps more than anything else, Mary was searching for a way to assure a secure future for Horace, but she may also have wished for stronger ties to her family. She had been living at a great distance from her brothers since 1818, when she moved to Lexington, and hadn't seen Stephen Austin since he was a boy at boarding school in Connecticut. Still, her letter to him was remarkably frank and open. "I have been left alone," she wrote, "to mark out the future destiny of myself and my son. More particularly with regard to my son, I have thought I would write to you and renew our acquaintance, in order to learn what prospect Texas would offer him, looking some distance ahead; whether it would be an object for me to take any steps with such views—securing land, etc."

Mary was also thinking about securing her own independence, joining the brother who had already settled in Texas and persuading others to follow his example. "I have thought too if my brothers could make it their interest to move to Texas, we could there together build up our fallen family in new hopes and happiness. I am happily and usefully situated where I am but I am *alone,* and think—I am sure—I should prefer a place of tolerable comfort, *entirely my own,—a permanent home* to all this luxury, with dependence in the least possible sense."

Besides Mary's brother Henry, Stephen Austin's younger brother, James Elijah Brown Austin (known simply as Brown), had joined Stephen in Texas in the mid-1820s, and his married sister Emily Perry and her family were about to move to the Austin colony as well, also at Stephen's fervent urging. Brown had died just two years earlier, at the age of twenty-six, leaving his older brother bereft. He had been Stephen's closest confidant and his chief lieutenant, managing administrative matters for Stephen, especially when the elder Austin traveled to

San Antonio, Saltillo, Mexico City, and elsewhere to deal with political and legal issues affecting the future of his colony. Brown's death had left a void in Stephen's life that made the prospect of Mary Austin Holley's joining his small community all the more appealing.

For some reason, Mary's letter never reached Stephen, but he heard from her brother Henry that Mary had written to him about settling in Texas, and in mid-1831 Stephen wrote—as he himself realized—with uncharacteristic effusiveness: "I never received a line from you, and have now written as though a month, and not twenty-five years had intervened since we met or had any communication. I hope you will follow my example, for it will be my greatest pleasure to hear from you."

Whatever the reason—loneliness, recollections of the intellectual ferment that surrounded the Holleys in New England, or even (as some have speculated) infatuation with his fine-featured, charming cousin—Stephen's enthusiasm was limitless: "I shall be happy to see you here . . . the idea of your removal here, and of the society that will of course spring up under your wand gives me more real pleasure than anything which has occurred in some years. . . . May we not form a little world of our own where neither the religious, political, or *money-making* fanaticism, which is throwing the good people of our native country into all sorts of convulsions, shall ever obtain admission? . . . Let us unite a few choice families and make a neighborhood, as we say in this country. . . . I will set apart a league [4,428 acres] of land for you and hold it in reserve until next winter or spring. . . . Besides which, should you fancy a situation for settlement in any of my own land you shall have one, for the land you get from the government can be settled by a tenant." The grant of land was standard procedure for families who settled in the Austin colony, but Stephen's impassioned invitation to Mary to settle nearby in Peach Point reveals an intensity of feeling that is rare in Stephen's other letters.

Mary visited Texas for the first time that fall, and was particularly impressed by the resourcefulness of the women she encountered. "[L]iving in a wild country under circumstances requiring constant exertion, forms the character to great and daring enterprise," she later wrote in her second book about Texas:

It is not uncommon for ladies to mount their mustangs and hunt with their husbands [to ride long distances on horseback to attend a ball] with their silk dresses . . . in their saddle-bags. Hardy, vigorous constitutions, free spirits, and spontaneous gaiety are thus induced, and continued a rich legacy to their children, who, it is to be hoped, will sufficiently value the blessing not to squander it away in their eager search for the luxuries and refinements of polite life. Women have the capacity for greatness, but they require occasions to bring it out. They require, perhaps, stronger motives than men—they have stronger barriers to break through of indolence and habit—but, when roused, they are quick to discern and unshrinking to act. . . . Many a wife in Texas has proved herself the better half, and many a widow's heart has prompted her to noble daring.

Noting the conditions under which the settlers were living and the spirit of good fellowship that persisted, and fascinated by the unfamiliar topography, vegetation, and climate of the area, she began forming the idea of writing a book about Texas even before she and Henry departed from Brazoria for his home in Bolivar. From Brazoria, she sent a letter to Stephen, asking him whether he thought a book about Texas and its settlement by mainly Anglo-Americans from the neighboring United States would be useful, as well as whether he would consent to having her tell the story of his role in colonizing the area. Mary was probably trying to cast herself in a more challenging role than that of governess to the children of a wealthy sugar planter. She had been comfortable in the Labranche household and was genuinely fond of the family, not to mention grateful for the way they welcomed her eccentric son into their midst, but she was also keen to construct a more substantial life for herself than was possible on Louisiana's privileged, isolated German Coast.

Ten years after his father's death, the Austin colony, of which Stephen was impresario, counted only about 5,000 settlers. Under the terms of his contracts with the Mexican government, Stephen had the title to vast expanses of land in Texas, but he was still broke. He believed that a book about Texas might well encourage settlers in numbers far beyond those that had so far been attracted by the promise of fertile land—free, or nearly free—and a benevolent climate. Further, he realized that Mary Austin Holley's talents—aided by Henry Austin's encyclopedic knowledge of the local flora and folklore and his own familiarity with the region's political history and topography—might be ideally suited to the task.

In fact, Stephen was so enthusiastic about his cousin's idea that, despite an illness from which he hadn't yet recovered, he arrived, unannounced, on horseback at Henry's three-room house in Bolivar from his home in San Felipe. The place was in great confusion, for Henry's wife (also named Mary) and their six young children had just debarked after sailing from New York with as much of their furniture as they could manage to bring. Somehow, Stephen and Mary Austin Holley found a corner in which to plot a book, whose main purpose was to entice as many Americans and Europeans as possible to settle in the territory that was encompassed by Stephen's impresario contracts with Mexico. At the same time, he recounted the history of this region of Mexico, his personal adventures, his ideas about colonization, and his experience with the political leaders in the state capital, Saltillo (Texas was at the time part of the state of Coahuila), and Mexico City, the seat of the national government. Mary took feverish notes, and the narrative she formed out of these conversations, together with her own observations and experiences and her brother's copious knowledge of local life and nature, became the heart of the first historical treatment of the region, *Texas: Observations, Historical, Geographical, and Descriptive,* published in Baltimore in 1833.

Stephen spoke freely to Mary about his hopes for Texas and also about the difficulties of trying to mediate between the large plantation owners who were vital to the colony's economic prosperity and the Mexican government. Mexico had outlawed slavery, although slave owners were permitted to bring their existing slaves to Texas with them. How long it would be possible to maintain the delicate balance between the opposing economic and political pressures, Stephen was unsure, but the questions troubled him so deeply that before Mary left Texas on Christmas Day, he sent her a statement to be included in the book, one that expressed disapproval of slavery but also suggested that Texas might ultimately separate from Mexico.

Stephen later thought better of those politically risky opinions and asked Mary to delete them from the manuscript, which she did. They reveal, however, a passionate side to Stephen Austin that he ordinarily kept under wraps but that seemed to emerge when he wrote or spoke to his cousin. Thanking Mary for coming to Texas, he wrote, "I need a social circle—a few friends of congenial tastes, the want of which has left a void. That void is being filled. My sister's family and Henry's . . . and you, my friend, you—how shall I ever thank you for venturing into this wilderness: how express the happiness of the ten days visit at Henry's? . . . Before you came I had begun to change the opinion that I was laboring here solely for others and posterity and am now convinced that I shall enjoy some of the fruits of my planting." For her part, Mary seems to have returned the favor. In Texas, she promised that she would write his biography, and she dedicated *Texas* to him, with extravagant praise of his "judicious, disinterested, and generous management, of the affairs of your Colony."

Late in 1831, however, Mary received sad news from Texas. Henry Austin's wife and eldest daughter had died of cholera early in the summer. Henry was personally bereft, of course, and he was unprepared to care for his five surviving children, ranging in age from five to fifteen. Henry had also grown increasingly pessimistic about the future in Texas, where some Anglo-American settlers had staged a short-lived revolt to protest Mexico's restrictive laws, which limited the colonists' rights to trade and self-government.

Henry was probably Mary's closest family member, after her own children, and she was to take on more and more responsibility for his children's care and education. With the risks of civil unrest and epidemics of disease so high, there was no question of Mary's returning to Texas for the time being, but she was heartened when she heard from Stephen. In his view, the political prospects, at least, were getting brighter. When the Mexican generals Antonio López de Santa Anna and José Antonio Mexia led a bloodless coup against the increasingly antidemocratic central government, Stephen sided with them and persuaded the settlers that the new regime would be more sympathetic to their interests. Meanwhile, he redirected attention to peaceful means of seeking redress, in venues such as the coming October convention, where the settlers planned to pressure the government to grant their desire for separate statehood within the Mexican federation.

Owing to delays in finding a publisher, Mary was able to include Stephen's lengthy account of the changes in the status of Mexico and Texas in the first edition. As with many books of the time, the publication costs were paid for by the author, who offset them in part by soliciting subscriptions (i.e., advance orders) from friends and interested persons. She had trusted her brother-in-law, Orville Holley, to arrange for publication, but Orville had neglected to follow through. Finally, Mary decided to ask her brother Charles, a minister in Garrison Forest, near Baltimore, to find a printer for the manuscript, and the book finally appeared in 1833.

When Melazie Labranche, her Louisiana tutee, married, Mary moved back to Lexington and packed Horace off for a trip to Louisiana under the supervision of a friend. Occupied with matters ranging from the distribution of *Texas* to overseeing the care and education of four of Henry Austin's children, whom he hoped to place in her care, Mary abandoned any hopes of settling in Texas in the near future. From Lexington, she avidly followed developments in Texas in the press, and even subscribed to a Texas paper. Stephen Austin, however, who had been Mary's main source of news about developments in Texas, was silent for more than a year. Arrested for treason after proposing that Texans prepare for separate statehood within the Mexican federation before it was authorized by the central government, he spent nearly a year in prison in Mexico City and was able to return to Texas only in mid-1835, when Santa Anna, now the autocratic president of Mexico, declared a general amnesty.

In May 1835, before Stephen's release, Mary made another visit to Texas, ostensibly to see about the welfare of Henry's children, but while there she eagerly made sketches and recorded the abundant signs of growth and change that had taken place. Henry gave Mary the news that her return to the Austin colony coincided with Stephen's long-awaited release from imprisonment in the Mexican capital. Nevertheless, Mary acceded to Henry's anxious pleas when he urged her to take his four youngest children out of Texas before the advent of the summer cholera season. Materially, Henry was finally showing signs of prosperity, but he could not, on his own, look after his motherless children properly.

That Stephen was finally a free man again was momentous news in itself, but Mary probably had no inkling that the summer of 1835 would be a true turning point in Texas history. When Stephen's first letter after two years of silence reached her in Lexington, however, he revealed how dramatically his views of Mexico-Texas relations had changed. Able to observe the Santa Anna government at close range between the time he was released from prison and when he was permitted to leave Mexico City, he saw that the concentration of power in the president meant that the government would never loosen the reins on trade, taxation, and self-determination to a degree that would satisfy the American settlers in Texas. Texas and Mexico were on a collision course, and Stephen—who had long been the "peace party's" standard-bearer—was now at the head of those who clamored for independence.

Stephen's letter was as frank as usual. He did not confront the question of independence directly but couched his program in terms of "Americanizing" Texas. He preferred to leave unanswered the question of whether Texas could continue to be part of Mexico after it had been successfully "Americanized." In his letter to Mary, he clearly tailored his arguments to an audience of Americans, and he urged her to put her literary talents and journalistic contacts to good use by spreading his message as widely as possible across Kentucky and the other states. "Texas," he wrote, "should be effectually, and fully, Americanized—that is, settled by a population that will harmonize with their neighbors on the *East,* in language, political principles, common origin, sympathy, and even interest." For the first time, despite his own reservations about slavery, he acknowledged that it was expedient to bend to the desires of the large agricultural landowners in Texas to exploit slave labor as their American counterparts did, and declared, "Texas must be a slave country."

Stephen's letter is extraordinary for several reasons. Not only was it his boldest statement to date on the urgent questions of the future of Texas, but the reader can actually watch him working out his ideas as he writes to his cousin and favored confidante. At first, he seems to be arguing for special treatment of Texas *within* the Mexican federation. "Being fully Americanized under the Mexican flag would be the same thing in effect, and ultimate result, as coming under the United States flag."

Within a few sentences, however, we see a new idea emerge: that Texas should become a *part* of the United States, whether through political means or purchase. Mexico's abrupt retreat from constitutional, democratic government in 1834 had precipitated Stephen's own harsh, year-long imprisonment as well as independence movements in California and other parts of the country, including the state of Zacatecas in central Mexico. When Santa Anna, whom Stephen had once counted as a personal friend and a friend to Texas, brutally suppressed the Zacatecas uprising, Stephen and others were convinced that accommodation with Mexico was no longer possible. "The fact is," he continued, "we must, and ought to become a part of the United States. Money should be no consideration." He appears to have believed then that Mexico might be amenable to selling the territory of Texas to the United States, since that solution would be preferable to the revolution that would otherwise inevitably follow, costing many lives on both sides. "A gentle breeze shakes off a ripe peach. Can it be supposed that the violent political convulsions of Mexico will not shake off Texas so soon as it is ripe enough to fall?"

He saw massive American immigration to Texas as the means of tipping the balance in the settlers' favor, and he hoped that Mary would put her pen to work to help bring it about. "I wish a great immigration this fall and winter from Kentucky, Tennessee, *every where,* passports, or no passports, *any how.*" The patient, prudent politician had finally given way to the passionate patriot: "For fourteen years I have had a hard time of it, but nothing shall daunt my courage or abate my exertions to complete the main object of my labors—*to Americanize Texas.* This fall, and winter, will fix our fate—a great immigration will settle the question."

Mary did her best to keep up with the rapid changes taking place in Texas and to share what she learned with the public. Through her efforts, articles and advertisements encouraging Americans to emigrate to Texas appeared in newspapers in Kentucky and the neighboring states and territories. Volunteers and potential settlers began to answer the call, and by September 1835 the hints of revolution were evident across the breadth of the territory, from the Louisiana border to San Antonio. The central government attempted to intimidate the independence-minded Texans by sending reinforcements into the region, but an army of volunteers under Stephen's command kept the Mexican troops hemmed in around San Antonio.

From the remote safety of Lexington, Mary struggled to keep abreast of the news, but word reached her slowly. As well as her information allowed, she spread the word of what was going on in Texas in the press and traced developments for her new history. But cut off as she was from the action, she in fact could learn relatively little that was current and was left wondering about how her brother, cousins, and other friends and relatives were faring.

Nearly six peaceful months lay ahead for Texas, but the stage was already set for the gradual march toward independence. In November 1835, representatives of the settlers met to consider the political future of Texas. They voted to accept Texas as a separate state within the Mexican federation, as long as Mexico was governed by the Constitution of 1824, which Santa Anna had abandoned when he assumed autocratic powers. Looking ahead, the delegates asserted that they had the authority to become independent of Mexico if circumstances warranted, as they fully expected they would. To seek support for their cause, they appointed Stephen Austin, Branch T. Archer, and William Wharton commissioners to the United States and made Sam Houston, a former governor of Tennessee, general of the army.

The commissioners' plan was to travel to Washington, D.C., to garner support—material and political—for Texas as an independent nation or, perhaps, as a state within the United States. Opinion was divided on both sides of the American border about whether or not Texas should be annexed, with much of the disagreement stemming from the fact that Texas, were it to enter the Union, would inevitably be a slave state. A speech of Stephen's, delivered in Louisville on March 7, 1836 (the news of the Alamo massacre did not arrive in the United States until April), made the case for Texas as "the cause of light and liberty" in the tradition of the American Revolution. Stephen was unable to repeat the speech when he stopped in Lexington, but he gave a copy to Mary, who planned to include it in the new edition of *Texas*. When Julius Clarke, her publisher, saw the speech, however, he decided the urgent question of the future of Texas justified publishing the speech separately, as a pamphlet.

The goal of Stephen's speech was to elicit sympathy and support for Texas from an audience that was both American and Southern. To appeal to the former, it was enough simply to declare that the people of Texas were the sons and daughters of Americans and valued the same liberties that all "free born and enterprising men naturally expect and require." To win the support of people in states that were the new republic's close neighbors, he portrayed the emancipation of Texas as (1) opening an expanse of land that offered "enterprise, wealth, and happiness" to Americans who wished to settle there, (2) spreading the principles of civil and religious freedom to another portion of the North American continent, and (3) protecting the exposed southwestern border of the United States from invasion or "intervention in the domestic concerns of the South." In other words, Stephen was reassuring his audience that Texas would be sympathetic to the institution of slavery on which the economy of the South depended.

To Mary, Stephen's political concerns were important, but since she had not settled her Texas land, as a practical matter they were somewhat remote from her. But for people living in Texas, these issues soon turned into matters of survival as well as principle. My great-great-grandfather, Charles Taylor, was one of them. In 1836, he was a land commissioner in East Texas, responsible for issuing titles and collecting fees, and *alcalde* (the equivalent of mayor) of Nacogdoches County. As such, he was the representative of the Mexican government at the easternmost edge of the country, and he witnessed firsthand the widening rift between Texans and the dictatorship. As the movement for independence from Mexico began to grow, he sided with Texas in the dispute with the central government over taxation. Thomas Rusk, the secretary of war for the Texan insurgents, asked him to allow the fees entrusted to him to be used to purchase weapons for the Texas army. He agreed, believing that the people who paid the taxes wanted freedom to govern themselves. Charles S. Taylor and Thomas Rusk were two of the four delegates elected from Nacogdoches to the convention that produced the Texas Declaration of Independence. Together with the other fifty-seven delegates to the convention at Washington-on-the-Brazos, they signed the declaration on March 2, 1836.

The fortified Alamo was the first line of defense on Texas's western border with Mexico. After it fell on March 6 and the Mexican army won another quick victory at nearby Goliad, the eastward flight of American settlers trying to escape the approaching Mexican army grew into a human stream of women, children, and aged and infirm men, in wagons, on horseback, and on foot, alarmed by reports of the massacre in San Antonio. Most able-bodied men had left to join the army that was forming under Sam Houston's command, so the refugees were in large measure unarmed and unprotected. As Houston's army commenced its own retreat—first to the Colorado River and then even farther east, to the Sabine—Texans, hoping to use their army as a shield from the approaching troops and hostile Indian tribes, continued to abandon settlement after settlement in an effort to reach the safety of Galveston Island, or even Louisiana.

The Runaway Scrape, as Texans call this flight of refugees, caught nearly every family in Central and East Texas in its flood. The eastern border towns of Nacogdoches and San Augustine, and their neighboring settlements, joined the masses of the displaced just before mid-April. My great-great-grandmother Anna Maria Taylor was one of the thousands of refugees fleeing from the Mexican advance and the threat of Indian raids. With her husband, Charles Taylor, attending the convention of delegates at Washington-on-the-Brazos, Anna Maria (known as Mary by her family), like other mothers in the Runaway Scrape, struggled on foot or in wagons that were likely to get stuck in the muddy trails, tried to feed her children despite acute shortages of food, and shielded them as well as she could from spring rains and disease. And like many of those mothers, she didn't manage to save any of her four children.

Anna Maria Taylor left no written account of her experience in the Runaway Scrape. I have only the family stories that have been passed down to me across five generations. We do know the stuff she was made of, though, because after the War of Independence ended, she and her

husband went back to Nacogdoches, where she bore nine more children. My son, Houston Taylor Hutchison, is named for them and for
their friend and fellow revolutionary Sam Houston. Her ordeal undoubtedly had much in common with the recollections of other Runaway Scrape participants like Kate Terrell and Ann Raney Coleman.

## Ann Raney Coleman

L IKE MY GREAT-GREAT-GRANDFATHER, Ann Raney was born
in England and arrived in Texas in the early 1830s. Her family settled near Brazoria, where her father, John Raney, had received a
grant of land in the Austin colony. According to Ann Raney Coleman's
journal, written late in her life, the original land grant expired before
John Raney could claim it (the grants usually bore a one-year deadline),
but Stephen Austin offered him a second grant after meeting the twenty-
two-year-old Ann at a ball in Brazoria, where she told Stephen of her
father's predicament. Because John Thomas, Ann's first husband, had
broken his arm in the first Texas rebellion in 1832, he was exempt from
military service and stayed on his farm when the War of Independence
started. As the Mexican army approached, the families on neighboring
farms fled, but Thomas planned to remain on his land as long as possible. He was determined to protect his farm, livestock, and cotton crop—
"four or five hundred head of cattle, four or five hundred head of hogs,
one hundred bales of cotton . . . five hundred head of chickens." When
a neighbor reported that Mexican troops were preparing to cross the

Brazos River, the Thomases joined the many other families fleeing eastward toward the Sabine River, at the border between Mexican Texas
and American Louisiana.

To reduce the risk of attack by hostile Indian tribes, families traveled
in groups. Ann estimated that their group consisted of about one hundred families. Still, there were dangers. On the first evening, hearing that
"Indians were killing families going the lower route to the Sabine," the
men rode off to investigate and left the women, children, and slaves behind in the camp. When what sounded like an "Indian yell" was heard in
the vicinity of the campground, everyone hid in the nearby woods until
the men returned the next morning.

Ann reports in her journal that the group traveled during the day
but stayed awake at night, "as either the Indians or the Mexicans were
on the lookout for our horses." She and her husband "never slept, only
at noon when the Negroes got dinner and the horses were turned out to
graze." She would nap until the company started up again, taking her
food with her and eating on horseback. Her young son rode with her,
but "sometimes I found myself fast asleep on my horse, and only when I
was nearly over the horse's head, I awoke to the sense of danger with my
little boy in my lap."

Besides living through the Runaway Scrape, Ann Raney Coleman
earned notoriety late in life because of her protracted campaign to secure a military pension from the state of Texas for her service during the
War of Independence. Before the battle of Velasco, Ann "took ammunition on horseback 15 miles half way to Velasco for the Battle of Velasco
and placed it in the hollow of a tree for Captain Brown to go after or
send for it, and on my return home I was followed by two Mexican spies
and it was a race for life. Had I not had the best horse they would have
caught me." Widowed twice and destitute in her old age, Ann had her
petition refused on the grounds that her second marriage made her ineligible for a pension for services performed before she remarried.

Ann freely admitted that her treatment at the hands of the state
angered her. She criticized as "unjust" the law that permits a man to
"marry as many times as he wants to, and they allow him his pension.
But woman, the weaker vessel, if she marries again is deprived of a living
the balance of her days." Far from a "weak vessel" herself, Ann caused a

Union soldier to wonder, during the Civil War, whether she was "a Union lady," since she showed no fear of the Northerners. "That word *afraid* is not in my vocabulary, sir," she told the soldier. "I am one of the old Revolutioners of Texas." "I thought you were something uncommon," he told her, "you are so spunky."

Ann's love of her adopted land was undiminished despite poverty and her conviction that the state had failed to treat her justly. When she returned to Texas in 1866, she wrote, "that state that holds the bones of my dear parents and one brother—that state I love, for in her land I found friends; in her land I saw joy and sorrow, for here my parents breathed their last sigh; here I cheered the heart of our veteran soldiers as they went to battle for independence, who cried victory or death. They are men, true to duty, and her women lovely emblems of virtue and beauty, the vernal aspect of nature, the voluptuous foliage, terraced banks and Jesamine covered lattice, the balmy zephyrs and the Italian sky all tend to sublime."

If the spunk of the women who settled Texas was much in evidence throughout the period of colonization, during the Runaway Scrape it was put to perhaps its most difficult test. Kate Terrell, another participant, wrote of the ingenuity and fearlessness with which mothers loaded their bedding and their infants onto anything with wheels—carriages, wagons, or carts, which were sometimes pulled by cows rather than horses or oxen—and hurried from their houses, leaving food on the table for the next family to eat. "It was an unwritten law," she recalled, "that smoke-houses were to be left open for the hungry to supply their wants, but nothing was to be wasted." She wrote of a mother and her newborn baby kept dry and warm by other women in the camp who "gathered around the sick woman and held blankets over her" while the rain fell. Resourcefulness and courage were commonplace among the women. As Thomas Rusk, whose own wife, Mary, helped ensure the calm evacuation of Nacogdoches, observed, "The men of Texas deserved much credit, but more was due the women. Armed men facing a foe could not but be brave; but the women, with their little children around them, without means of defense or power to resist, faced danger and death with unflinching courage."

# *Jane Long*

BESIDES THE RUNAWAY SCRAPE, women faced—and passed—other dramatic tests in preindependence Texas as well. Jane Long, who settled in Nacogdoches with her husband, Dr. James Long, in 1819, lived through the Mexican defeat of Spanish colonial rule in 1821. Her husband was captured before the birth of the couple's second child in December of that year. Jane, who earned the sobriquet "Daughter of Maryland, Wife of Mississippi, Mother of Texas," helped spread the legend that her daughter, called Ann James, was the first child born to an English-speaking woman in Texas. Census records show that other children had been born earlier, but Jane was nonetheless a staunch Texas patriot who played a crucial supporting role in the region's early history. After James Long was accidentally killed in Mexico City in April 1822, Jane remained in Texas. She raised her daughter, became one of Stephen Austin's early colonists in 1824, and in 1832 bought a boardinghouse in Brazoria, where Stephen Austin delivered his pivotal proindependence address at the 1835 convention held there.

Mary Austin Holley was forced to follow the dramatic developments of the war from the safety of distant Lexington, Kentucky, but her contribution to the cause was no less noteworthy. She considered herself one of the revolutionaries—a Texan and a settler, and an Austin, to boot—so it was natural for her to see her own fate mingled with that of her relatives and compatriots who endured those harrowing months in Texas. She helped rally Kentucky volunteers to the war by making sure that newspapers gave prominent coverage to military developments and the settlers' plight. As the state's military contingent prepared to depart for Texas, Mary organized the local women to sew uniforms for them— a "sacred charity," in her words, on behalf of the "holy cause" of independence.

After April 21, 1836, when the Texans sealed their victory by defeating the Mexican army at San Jacinto and capturing General Santa Anna, Mary redoubled her efforts on behalf of the new republic. The new edition of *Texas,* published in July 1836, appeared to excellent reviews. It sold well in the United States and Texas, and was even quoted on the floor of the Texas Congress and said to be "better than any speech on the subject." Mary must have been disappointed when Stephen was passed over for the presidency and settled instead for the post of secretary of state. But with the government's composition set, she turned her attention and energy to American recognition of the republic, with a campaign supporting passage of a resolution in support of the Republic of Texas in the Kentucky legislature. Quick annexation was out of the question; President Andrew Jackson and others were concerned that Mexico or England might declare war on the United States if Texas were granted statehood. For the time being, then, Mary lobbied state senators and informed them about the subject on which she was now recognized as an authority. She was so persistent that the bill was nicknamed "Mrs. Holley's Resolutions."

Buoyed by her success in influencing the legislators in Kentucky, Mary imagined a new career for herself—as lobbyist in Washington for Texas interests—and wrote to Stephen, on January 14, 1837, laying out the germ of her idea for his consideration. A month after sending her letter she learned that Stephen had died of pneumonia in Columbia, the new state capital, on December 27, 1836, nearly three weeks before she had written to him. His last words, uttered in feverish delirium, were "Texas recognized . . . Did you see it in the papers?"

Henry Austin had written to Mary, telling her of Stephen's death and also that President Houston was moving the national capital to a new town, named for himself, not far from the site of his victory over Santa Anna at San Jacinto. Thus ended Mary's hopes of a political career. Even more, the news probably ended her dream of starting life over in Texas. She continued to call herself a Texan and returned to visit Henry and other friends and relatives at the end of the year, but not even when she was in the country did she feel as close to Texas as when Stephen was alive.

Sam Houston himself, despite his own ambitions, always acknowledged Stephen Austin's vital role in the making of Texas. In 1844, when Mary was working on her planned biography of her cousin, she spoke briefly with Houston, who was then president of the republic (one year later, following annexation, he would be one of Texas's first U.S. senators; the other was Thomas J. Rusk). He professed affection and admiration for "General Austin, the Father and Foundation of the country. There would have been nothing here but for him." Houston further defended Stephen from accusations that his motives in his dealings in the colony and with Mexico had been to enrich himself, and he called Austin "a real patriot—not a mere politician," who was still not well understood.

For the rest of her life, Mary worked intermittently on Stephen's biography, but she never managed to finish the book. Curiously, she delayed visiting Peach Point, where Stephen had lived and where his papers—essential to writing an authoritative life of her cousin—were preserved by his sister, until 1838. Her visit gave her an opportunity to make copies of some of the papers, and it also helped her reach closure about his death. After visiting his grave, she wrote in her diary, "High weeds weep in solitude over it. My poor cousin sleeps in peace," and two weeks later she recorded her thoughts after riding on horseback past the sloping land where Stephen had hoped to build his own house: "[W]e passed his chosen spot on this Earth, where he and I were to have our paradise—beautiful indeed it is, diversified with copse and lawn; but how changed to me!" (In 1910, Stephen F. Austin's remains were moved from his sister's farm near Brazoria to the Texas State Cemetery in Austin.)

For the next several years, Mary continually made plans to settle in Texas permanently, only to postpone them for one reason or another. Her brother-in-law Edward Holley declined her offer of part of her Texas land to farm, in return for helping Horace to get started in farming as well. Edward explained that he was too old to move to the frontier. But after finding a buyer—at a very low price—for 1,500 acres of her land, she immediately made plans for another trip to Texas.

When Mary arrived in Galveston in 1841, she noticed political changes that seemed to her good signs. Mirabeau B. Lamar was now president and had moved the capital from Columbia to the newly founded town of Austin, named, of course, for Stephen and located on the Colorado River on land that had been within the boundaries of the original colony. That change buoyed Mary's spirits, but she was troubled by the military and commercial expedition to Santa Fe that Lamar was promoting. The president hoped to inspire New Mexicans to follow the example of Texas, declare independence from Mexico, and join the republic. The quixotic effort failed, and many of those who made the voyage were killed or captured and imprisoned in Mexico. Among the victims of the ill-fated scheme was James Austin, Henry's seventeen-year-old son; he was killed at Mier, in one of the expedition's last skirmishes.

From Texas, Mary returned to Louisiana and eventually made her way back to Lexington. When James Knox Polk, running on a pro-annexation platform, defeated Henry Clay for the presidency, Mary—who favored annexation—fretted that statehood would cast an even greater shadow over Stephen's achievements than had already occurred, and she resumed work on the Austin biography. In her manuscript, she progressed as far as her own first meeting with Stephen in Texas in 1831, before being forced to put the work aside and return to the Labranches in Louisiana in late 1845. Her son-in-law, William Brand, who suffered from severe rheumatism, found it impossible to live with Mary's son, Horace. As William's condition worsened, so did the atmosphere in the Brands' otherwise comfortable household in Lexington. On the Labranche plantation, there would always be room for Horace, whose carpentry skills made him a valuable member of the community, and he remained there until his death in 1853.

Mary was accorded the honors due her as a beloved teacher, and in fact, after her former charge, Melazie, gave birth, Mary moved into the New Orleans house of the Donatien Augustins, helping to look after the new baby and tutoring the family's two older children. In the summer of

1846, when the Augustins decided to remain in New Orleans despite the risk of disease, Mary contracted yellow fever. She died on August 2. She had not completed her biography of Stephen Austin, nor—despite the advantages of education and friendship with political and intellectual leaders—had she overcome the obstacles to establishing a life as an independent woman. But she had done more, most likely, than any other woman to focus the attention of the world on the struggle of Texas's early settlers for their rights and independence.

The establishment of the republic did not settle once-and for all the questions about Texas's identity and history. Shortly before and after the turn of the twentieth century, descendants of families who had been allies in the earlier struggle fought ideological battles that seemed nearly as fierce as the military struggles that had given birth to the republic in 1836.

## Adina De Zavala

ADINA EMILIA DE ZAVALA, one of the protagonists of a bitter controversy over the future of the Alamo as a historic site, helped to establish an accurate historical picture of Texas in the nineteenth century and even earlier, in particular with respect to the contributions of its important and sizable Tejano population. She was born at her family's home on Buffalo Bayou on November 28, 1861, not far from the site of the Battle of San Jacinto. Lorenzo de Zavala, her grandfather, who served as the first vice president of the Republic of

Texas, had settled there before the War of Independence. Twice governor of the state of Mexico and a former Mexican ambassador to France,
de Zavala had helped draft Mexico's liberal Constitution of 1824. He
supported Antonio López de Santa Anna when the general was elected
Mexico's president in 1833, but joined the movement for Texas independence the next year after Santa Anna seized dictatorial powers.

Adina was the eldest of Augustine and Julia (Tyrrell) De Zavala's six
children (Augustine capitalized the *De* in the family name). She spent
her childhood in Galveston, where she graduated from the Ursuline
Academy with distinction. In 1873, her family moved to a ranch near
San Antonio, and in 1879, she enrolled in the first class at Sam Houston
Normal Institute in Huntsville, Texas. After receiving her teaching cer-
tificate in 1881, Adina taught school in Terrell and San Antonio until
1907. From then on, she devoted all of her time to historical and preservation activities.

In San Antonio, Adina became deeply involved in the cultural life of
her city and region. By 1889, she and other San Antonio women had
begun to meet to pursue their collective interest in Texas history. They
called themselves the De Zavala Society (in honor of Adina's illustrious
grandfather) and set themselves the goal of discovering and preserving
San Antonio's historic sites. The ruins of five Franciscan missions were
located in the city and its surrounding areas; the San Antonio de Valero
Mission (known as the Alamo) was one of them. A Catholic, a Mexican-
American, and a Texan, Adina dedicated her energies to creating a historical consciousness in Texas that reflected the cultural richness of its
past: Indian and Spanish, Tejano and Anglo.

Several years later, in Houston, a second group—which included
Hally Bryan, granddaughter of Stephen F. Austin's sister Emily; her
cousin Betty Ballinger; and Mary Jane Harris Briscoe, widow of a signer
of the Texas Declaration of Independence—founded the Daughters of
the Republic of Texas. This group, also devoted to Texas history, was especially concerned with the Texas Revolution, the Republic of Texas,
and the people who contributed to the cause of Texas independence. In
1893 the DRT invited the De Zavala Society to become the seventh
chapter of its two-year-old organization. The state of Texas had acquired
the chapel of the Alamo mission in 1883 and appointed the city to care

for it, but nothing had been done to restore the building in the ensuing ten years. The De Zavala chapter's initial focus was on preserving the buildings other than the chapel that had also been part of the Franciscan mission, especially the convent, originally the main building of the complex. That structure was at the time owned by a wholesale grocery (and perhaps liquor) firm, Hugo & Schmeltzer, which had purchased it in 1886.

The San Antonio de Valero Mission was founded in 1718 by Fray Antonio de Olivares. It consisted of a group of buildings dotting two courtyards on an area of nearly three acres—a chapel, a *convento* (friary), workshops, a granary, storerooms, and rooms in which Indians lived. The complex was protected by walls and stockades. The oldest surviving buildings, of which the convent was the first, most likely date from the 1720s. The Spanish Baroque chapel, which was used as a church only briefly, if at all, was begun in 1744 and completed in 1757. In 1762, the domed roof collapsed, "on account of the stupidity of the builder," according to contemporary records, and the church was still unrepaired when all missions in Texas were secularized in 1793.

Throughout most of the next century, the buildings were used almost exclusively for military purposes, even after the Republic of Texas returned all the missions within its territory to the Catholic church in 1841. Spanish, Mexican, Texan, and then American troops occupied the compound from 1801 or 1802 on. They made occasional repairs to the buildings or altered them to serve their needs better. In fact, the Franciscans had almost certainly been the first to fortify the compound, especially after a massacre at the nearby San Saba Mission in 1758. The walls were thick and turreted, and an irrigation ditch—crossed by a narrow bridge leading to the single carriage entrance cut through the granary (also called the low barracks) that formed part of the south wall— provided additional protection. Jean-Louis Berlandier, a French botanist who visited the Alamo as a member of a Mexican exploration party in 1828, wrote in his notebook: "An enormous battlement and some barracks are found there, as well as the ruins of a church which could pass for one of the loveliest monuments of the area, even if its architecture is overloaded with ornamentation like all the ecclesiastical buildings of the Spanish colonies."

The ruined chapel remained untouched until midcentury. The U.S. Army made repairs and additions in the 1840s—filled in the convent's second story and built a gabled roof to replace the old flat one. Initially the army left the chapel unimproved, but about 1847 it rebuilt the chapel's facade to a uniform height, put a roof on the building, and created a second floor. It cut new windows in the chapel's front wall and designed the now-famous parapet that was inconsistent with the original Spanish Baroque design. Edward Everett, a talented draftsman who sketched the building for the army in 1847–48, said of the alterations, "[T]asteless hands have evened off the rough walls, as they were left after the siege, surmounting them with a ridiculous scroll, giving the building the appearance of the headboard of a bedstead."

Long before the army finally left the compound in 1876, the integrity of the site had been compromised. Before the Civil War, the outer walls and the Indians' adobe dwellings vanished. New city streets cut through part of the property, and the granary (which the city had bought in 1871 to use as a jail) was torn down to enlarge the plaza. In the words of William Corner, a local historian, "piecemeal, 'here a little, there a little,' the old mission has been improved off the face of the earth." Of the buildings that were standing in 1836, only two remained: the convent and the church.

The state of Texas bought the chapel from the Roman Catholic church in 1882 and made San Antonio responsible for its upkeep. The city made a start at restoring the building to its original condition by removing the second story the army had added, but its efforts ended there. The convent remained in private hands. This was the status quo that faced Adina De Zavala when her society was formed. In 1892 she received verbal assurance from Gustav Schmeltzer (of Hugo & Schmeltzer, the owners) that his firm would give the De Zavala Society the right of first refusal when and if the convent building was put on the market. At regular intervals, she reminded Schmeltzer of his promise, and in 1900 she informed him that her society planned to launch a campaign to raise the money to buy the convent. They agreed on a purchase price of $75,000; at the same time, Hugo & Schmeltzer pledged $10,000 to the campaign.

# *Clara Driscoll*

A DINA HERSELF WAS a person of modest means, but she probably expected (or hoped) that wealthy members of other DRT
chapters would help raise the money. The campaign struggled
until Clara Driscoll arrived on the scene. When Clara saw the Alamo
chapel upon returning from France in 1899, she was moved by its forlorn state. Fresh from a finishing-school education at the fashionable
Chateau Dieudonne near Paris, the eighteen-year-old was shocked by
America's indifference to its historic monuments. In Europe, she wrote
in a letter to the *San Antonio Express* in 1901, "every respect and deference is shown to any edifice that boasts of historic interest." The Alamo,
in contrast, was an abject ruin, although "[t]here does not stand in the
world today a building or monument which can recall such a deed of
heroism or bravery, such sacrifice and courage, as that of the brave men
who fought and fell inside those historic walls." The patriotic daughter
of Robert Driscoll, Sr., a prosperous Corpus Christi banker and rancher,
she had been the first Queen of the San Antonio Fiesta in 1896, a celebration of the Texans' victory at the decisive battle of San Jacinto (still an
important social event in the city each spring). Now a young woman,
Clara wanted to preserve the "sacred ruins and picturesque antiquity"
that were being threatened by commerce.

The problem was that the chapel that stirred Clara Driscoll's passions was not where the siege and sacrifice took place at the Alamo on
March 6, 1836. The women and children had taken refuge in a few

rooms of the chapel that were not in ruins. The fighting, especially the hand-to-hand combat, occurred inside the plain, two-story convent and in the courtyard in front of it. When Clara first looked at that building, it was hidden behind a garish superstructure emblazoned with the logo of the Hugo & Schmeltzer wholesale grocery firm. What she saw indeed appeared to be an "unsightly obstruction" that "should be torn away," and she proposed that the convent be demolished so that the chapel could be appreciated "for what it is . . . the Grandest Monument in the History of the World."

By early 1903, Clara had joined the De Zavala Chapter of the DRT and was working side by side with Adina to buy the convent building, "in order," as Clara wrote to Charles Hugo, "to make a park about the old ruins." It is thanks to their efforts that the Alamo site was largely preserved as a historic monument and not razed to make room for a parking lot or hotel in downtown San Antonio. The two women met with the owners to discuss the terms of the sale, and Clara paid $500 for a thirty-day option to buy the property, at the end of which they promised to pay the rest of the down payment and the balance over five years. There was no longer any mention of Hugo & Schmeltzer's $10,000 contribution. Clara was chairman and treasurer of the finance committee, whose aim was to raise the purchase price by means of a large number of small donations.

The finance committee also petitioned the Texas legislature for funds to cover the option to purchase, if not the full purchase price. Thanks to the efforts of Hal Sevier (who married Clara Driscoll in 1906), an amendment was tacked on to the general appropriations bill, but Governor S. W. T. Lanham struck the item from the budget. At the April deadline and when other payments fell due, Clara made up the difference between the amounts raised and what was due out of her personal funds. She made it clear, however, that she was purchasing the property for the DRT and had no commercial plans for the Alamo.

Whether or not Clara intended her philanthropic gesture to shame the people and politicians of Texas into taking responsibility for the Alamo, she succeeded in doing just that. The public voiced its approval of using state funds to purchase the property, and even Governor Lanham, who had refused the earlier $5,000 appropriation on a technicality, switched sides. In 1905, the legislature approved $65,000 for the Alamo purchase, thanked Clara and Adina for their efforts on behalf of the historic site, and in October turned over to the DRT the two buildings that made up the Alamo property, which Governor Lanham described as the state's "most sacred and historic possession."

In acknowledgment of the fact that Clara had initially committed her own money to purchase the convent, the DRT executive committee appointed her custodian. In late 1907, Adina got wind of Clara's plans to demolish the convent, which she thought obstructed the view of the chapel, and there were suits and countersuits on both sides. Two separate chapters—the De Zavala and the Alamo Mission—contested for recognition as the DRT's presence in San Antonio. In 1908, while Clara was out of town, Adina got possession of the keys from city officials and refused to return them. She had three men guard the building, with instructions to let no one in. When the sheriff arrived with an injunction that charged her with occupying the building without authorization, Adina barricaded herself inside for three days. Local officials refused to allow food or drink to be brought to her, but a contemporary account reported that "[a] sister patriot, Miss Lytle, poured coffee through a pipe which she slipped under a window, and in this way the young woman sustained strength to resist the invaders until Governor Campbell took a hand." As long as she remained inside, the local law enforcement officers kept their distance.

Adina's dramatic act of civil disobedience won the public to her side. She agreed to relinquish control of the convent to the state superintendent of buildings. The DRT said it would not tear down the building, although the organization had filed papers stating that, because the convent was not part of the original mission, they proposed to "remove this unsightly building and place in lieu thereof a park, museum, or something else." A public solicitation issued by Clara Driscoll Sevier euphemistically referred to plans "for the beautifying of the Alamo Mission grounds adjoining the Chapel of the Alamo, more generally known as the Hugo-Schmeltzer property," but did not explicitly state that the convent building was to be torn down. The letter envisioned "a beautiful park filled with swaying palms and tropical verdure, enclosed by a low way, with arched gateway of Spanish architecture," and mentioned only that the chapel roof would be restored and "a replica of the original doors of the church" installed.

A few years earlier, Clara's largesse in purchasing the convent had won her acclaim as "the Savior of the Alamo." After Adina's efforts to save the building from destruction in 1908, a new popular song, "Remember the Alamo," was dedicated to her, and she was called "the Heroine of the Alamo." Ironically, each of the women desired to commemorate the heroes of the siege, but they disagreed about how best to do so. Adina, who saw the landmark with a historian's eyes, wanted to preserve its past as a Franciscan mission and the place where William Travis, Davy Crockett, Jim Bowie, and others had given their lives in the cause of Texas independence. Since the last stages of the battle had taken place in the courtyard in front of the convent and inside the building itself, she saw no conflict between the two.

Clara Driscoll (she dropped "Sevier" after divorcing her husband in 1937), who was, like Adina, a Roman Catholic, had no interest in the Alamo's missionary past. Her focus—like that of most DRT members— was on the 1836 revolution. Moreover, Clara, who wrote a novel, a collection of short stories, and a comic opera, apparently saw the Alamo through a more imaginative filter: the tragic deaths of the heroes of the Alamo deserved to be commemorated in a setting that evoked emotion, like the chapel, not in a squat, plain building like the convent. Clara, of course, was not alone in her belief. Many people agreed that if tearing down the convent would enhance appreciation of the chapel—and the events it symbolized—so be it. It was at all times an emotional debate, one that recurred at intervals until well after the Texas Centennial in 1936.

The new governor, Oscar B. Colquitt, tried to resolve the dispute by meeting with both factions in San Antonio in 1911. Adina, who had done her homework thoroughly, submitted building plans and maps showing that during the siege of the Alamo the chapel itself was a ruin, and that the convent served as the Texans' fortress and was the place where the final bloodshed occurred. The Driscoll group countered that the convent walls were of no significance and that it was preferable to tear them down in order to make room for the proposed park and monument. Governor Colquitt sided with Adina. "The walls which were then standing, we want to preserve," he insisted, and ruled that the 1870s-era wooden frame should be removed and the structure restored to its 1836 state. He also ordered the building of a one-story stone arcade, designed by a professor of architecture at the University of Texas, along the east courtyard wall.

The early-twentieth-century controversy over what to do about the Alamo was surprisingly heated, especially considering that the mission buildings had been ignored, or worse, for most of the seventy-five years following the siege. The DRT went back to court to try to stop the work Governor Colquitt had prescribed. Insisting that "the Alamo chapel is the real Alamo," and "the Hugo & Schmeltzer building [that is, the convent] is not historically sacred," the debate came down to the feeling, as Clara expressed it, that "I don't think the Alamo should be disgraced by this whiskey house, which obscures the most remarkable relic in the world."

Adina had succeeded in swaying public opinion and influencing the thinking of history-minded people like Governor Colquitt, but the DRT continued to prefer Clara's more photogenic and evocative vision. Before the work the governor had ordered could be completed, the available money ran out, and while he was out of the state in 1913, his lieutenant governor allowed the convent's second story (parts of which had been built before 1836) to be torn down. The ground floor of the building survived. Adina, who broke with the DRT in 1913 but continued her efforts to restore the original mission, noted in a 1935 article, "Historically, the church of the Alamo is not of such great importance. It was the building adjoining the long barracks [the convent], which witnessed the slaughter of our Texas heroes. But we still have the lower walls of the long barracks and of the arcades facing the patio."

Adina's vocal opposition to what she considered a conception of the Alamo that falsified both history and architecture estranged her from the DRT. But the "Second Battle for the Alamo," as historians have called the bitter feud, was just one of her efforts to bring to light and preserve the historic sites and history of Texas. In 1901, for example, she discovered Enrique Esparza, who as an eight-year-old had taken refuge in the Alamo with his mother and his four siblings. Gregorio Esparza, Enrique's father, was one of the Texan soldiers; he and one of his sons were killed in the battle or executed immediately afterwards. Enrique, who was interviewed about his experiences at the Alamo at least three other times (in 1902, 1907, and 1911), talked of waiting with the other surviving women and children to be seen by Santa Anna. In this group were Susanna Dickinson and her daughter, Angelina, who for many years were said to have been the only survivors (the *San Antonio Light* of November 10, 1901, states, "No Texas history mentions the escape of anyone from the Alamo but Mrs. Dickinson and child . . ."). But Enrique named several Mexican or Tejana women and their children as well, including Juana Melton, who sent her brother to ask Anita Esparza, Enrique's mother, not to reveal to the general that Melton's husband was American. Melton evidently feared that Santa Anna might suspect that she favored Texas independence and treat her harshly. In fact, Santa Anna released all the surviving women and children.

Until Adina went to work to shed light on the Tejano presence at the Alamo and elsewhere, the prevailing nineteenth-century view was that only three "Mexicans" had fought on the side of Texas, but of the thirteen Texas natives among the men inside the fort during the siege, eleven were of Mexican ancestry. At least eight Tejanos lost their lives there. A ninth, Brigido Guerrero, may have survived by convincing his Mexican captors that he'd been taken prisoner by the Texans, and three, including Juan Seguín, were sent out as messengers before the final attack. Seguín was the son of Texas Declaration of Independence signer Erasmo Seguín, a captain in the Texas army, and later one of the heroes of the Battle of San Jacinto. He left the Alamo on February 25 with a message for Houston and returned with twenty-five Tejano volunteers to rendezvous with James Fannin and return to the fort. Fannin never appeared; he surrendered and was executed. Seguín was generally ignored by historians until his bravery was exposed through his portrayal in John Wayne's film *The Alamo* (1960).

Unable to reconcile with the DRT, Adina founded the Texas Historical and Landmarks Association (THLA) in 1912 and continued her work of identifying and drawing attention to the places where Texas history had been made and the people who made it. The THLA charter makes clear that the Alamo controversy continued to be very much on her mind.

The organization's mission was "to work for the repair, restoration, and preservation of all the missions in Texas; and [to promote] the use of the main building of the Alamo—the long two-story Fort (north of the Church of the Alamo [the Hugo-Schmeltzer property])—as a Texas Hall of Fame and a Museum of History, Art, Relics, and Literature."

The scars of the "Second Battle for the Alamo" did not heal in the lifetimes of Adina and Clara Driscoll, who died in 1955 and 1945, respectively. Neither subsequently mentioned the other when writing about the Alamo. On balance, it was the Driscoll camp whose view of the Alamo prevailed. Although part of the convent structure was finally preserved, the building was never restored to its 1836 state. Equally significant is the fact that plans for the site did not attempt to reclaim the western portion of the original mission plaza that had been excised by city streets that bisected it. Nor was any archaeological research done on the site for many years, not even during the extensive preparations for the 1936 centennial. When archaeological excavations were finally undertaken in 1966, the findings coincided with many of the claims Adina had made based on her historical inquiries.

One of the chief successes of the THLA was the preservation of the Spanish Governors' Palace, on the Plaza de Armas in San Antonio. Adina's efforts brought the palace to public attention and persuaded the city to acquire the building in 1928 and restore it. A largely self-taught historian and folklorist, Adina made numerous and significant contributions to Texas history and ethnography. She was a charter member of the Texas State Historical Association and a member of its executive council, and her research led to the identification of many of the sites of the earliest Catholic missions established in the territory of Texas when it was still part of New Spain. Her accomplishments made her a logical choice in 1923 for inclusion on the first Texas Historical Board. In the following decade, she was appointed to the San Antonio Bicentennial Commission, which planned the celebration of the city's two hundredth anniversary, and she contributed to the observance of the state centennial through her membership on the Committee of One Hundred and the advisory board of the Texas Centennial Committee.

Her contributions to folklore scholarship were also notable. A longtime member and officer of the Texas Folklore Society, she presented a number of papers and published them in the society's journal. Her book, *History and Legends of the Alamo and Other Missions in and around San Antonio* (1917), is a contribution to both history and folklore. She wrote several pamphlets as well, including *The Story of the Siege and Fall of the Alamo: A Résumé* (1911) and *Margil Vine, the Legend of the First Christmas at the Alamo* (1916). She was a contributor to the first edition of the *Handbook of Texas* (1952), almost certainly the only Tejana writer in the first edition, and has been acknowledged as the first Tejano historian.

## *Women of Today*

THE EARLIEST WOMEN LEADERS had no role models or mentors. They charted new waters. The women breaking ground today have had more acceptance in their fields and have realized many successes. The woman who showed me the ropes and has become my mentor and friend is Anne Armstrong. She makes her home on a remote ranch in South Texas, in a county that has more cows than people. In 1976, she left that 50,000 acres of sandy prairie to serve as America's first woman ambassador to Great Britain, our country's most coveted foreign diplomatic post.

In 1971, when I was a television news reporter in Houston, Texas, I interviewed Anne just after she had been elected cochair of the Republican National Committee. I was very impressed with her. She called me the next week to ask if I would like to move to Washington, D.C., to be her press secretary. I thought about it for a couple of weeks and decided to do it. I learned more in the first six months I worked for her than I could have learned getting an MBA! Since then, I haven't made a major decision in my career without consulting Anne first.

## ANNE LEGENDRE ARMSTRONG

BORN IN NEW ORLEANS in 1927, Anne Legendre graduated Phi Beta Kappa from Vassar College in 1949. She worked briefly as a journalist before marrying Tobin Armstrong in 1950 and moving to the Armstrong cattle ranch in Texas. Anne and Tobin have five children. She got her start in politics campaigning door-to-door for Eisenhower, was elected cochair of the Republican National Committee in 1971, and was the first woman keynote speaker at a Republican National Convention in 1972. President Gerald Ford appointed her the first woman ambassador from the United States to the Court of St. James's (1976–77). She held many advisory and cabinet-status positions in Washington from 1972 on, including that of chairman of the President's Foreign Intelligence Advisory Board from 1981 to 1990. In 1987, Ronald Reagan awarded her the Presidential Medal of Freedom. She currently serves as the chairman of the Executive Committee of the Board of Trustees at the Center for Strategic and International Studies in Washington, D.C.

### IMPORTANT TRAIT FOR SUCCESS

ANNE ARMSTRONG: I was born with energy, so I didn't have anything to do with that, but I was also born in an era that suddenly, with World War II, was opening for women. That, too, was luck. And I had parents who were determined that I get the best education possible. I've always gone for the best people too. I want the best. I've never been afraid of being overshadowed by people. For instance, on the President's Foreign Intelligence Advisory Board, I wanted Alan Greenspan and Kissinger and Brzezinski and people of that ilk, all of whom were twice as intelligent as I about intelligence, but that's why we did a good job. I tried to gather around me wonderful people. One of the main reasons I valued you as a staffer was that even in your twenties, you would always level with me and stand up to me when I was wrong.

BIGGEST OBSTACLE

AA: Well, at the time it was that I was female. But in my past, my parents didn't have my brother until ten years after me, so I was treated sort of like a boy by them and expected to go into any job or take any course and go for the stars. But when I was first in politics way back in the sixties and even the seventies, there were still lots of barriers that women had to face.

For instance, in the White House, little things there were demeaning: for instance, women weren't allowed to wear pantsuits and we didn't have access to the males-only gym. As for major barriers, both Presidents Nixon and Ford were wise enough—I was the first woman counselor with cabinet rank—not to give me just the traditional feminine responsibilities. I sat on the foreign policy board; I sat on the economic board. It took courage for President Ford to appoint me ambassador to England and for President Reagan to make me chairman of his intelligence board. They set examples to old-style CEOs and old-style politicos.

KAY BAILEY HUTCHISON: One thing you didn't mention, but I would—I am amazed that you did so much from where you lived. Isolation, the inability to just hop on a plane and get to Washington in two and a half hours like I do. You have to drive two hours to the Corpus Christi airport, connect in Dallas, so it is a full day trip to Washington or New York. You have to spend three days for a one-day meeting.

AA: Right. Well, one thing was having a husband like Tobin. Ranchers can be with their families so much more than somebody who's working for a regular company. Our five children, who were all born within five years, had a father who was a super parent and had time to help with them. We were a very, very close family partly because we were so isolated, and when I started being away for long times in the 1970s, Tobin was able to stay close to the kids at home. We don't have a high school in our county, and the kids all went off to high school, mainly in San Antonio. There were so many lucky things in my life that enabled me to have a wonderful family life and also get ahead in what I wanted to do and what I hoped was making the country and even the world a better place.

## BEST PREPARATION FOR ROUGH-AND-TUMBLE OF LIFE

AA: My early childhood. I played football with my father. I learned to keep fit. I had kind of a protected childhood, but I just have a competitive nature and a determined character.

## BEST NEGOTIATING STRATEGY

AA: Learn as much as you can about the person you're negotiating with, and then look at things from his or her point of view. I learned a lot from you, Kay, for you had friendships with many political competitors. Figure out the ways where you can both win. Be very, very patient. I know some people find it's good to rant and rave in negotiating, but that isn't the way I do it. Learn what your negotiating friend needs, and see where you can come to a stance that will end up benefiting both of you.

## HELPFUL CHILDHOOD MEMORY

AA: My family expected me to do anything, never held me back. I worked every summer after I was fourteen because it was World War II. I worked in a hospital. Fine parents and fine education. That is what I would wish for every young person. For those days, mine was a fabulous education, and I got it with the help of some scholarships.

KBH: Well, you were such an academic star.

AA: You know, Tobin had the grandfather who was a famous ranger who captured the number one bad man, John Wesley Hardin. But what amazes me about Major Armstrong is the fact that he lived out in this wild horse desert, and he certainly wasn't rich, but he managed to send every one of his six children, even the women, to top schools—to UT [University of Texas] and Newcomb [Sophie Newcomb, the women's college of Tulane University] and the sons to Princeton, Yale, etc. They all turned out fantastic. And again, nothing can replace a fine education.

BEST ADVICE

AA: My mother and father would say, "Tell the truth and go for the stars," and what I admire most about Texas A&M in having served as a regent there is its insistence on values: "Aggies do not lie, cheat, steal, nor tolerate those who do." They follow the Golden Rule, they work hard, they value close families, and they love their country. That's it.

CHAPTER TWO

# WOMEN OF FAITH

*Elizabeth Seton*

IN A SENSE, ELIZABETH SETON had two lives. The first was as the privileged but somewhat neglected daughter of a prominent Episcopalian family. Her father, Richard Bayley, was a surgeon in New York City and the first professor of anatomy at King's College (now Columbia University). In 1794, she married William Seton, a merchant. Elizabeth's father-in-law, also William Seton, was one of Alexander Hamilton's business associates and served as cashier of the Bank of New York for the first ten years after its founding. Her second life began in 1803, when her husband died of tuberculosis in Italy, where she was drawn to Catholicism. A young widow with five children, she converted to Catholicism, became a nun not long afterward, and founded the American Sisters of Charity.

It is Elizabeth Seton's second life, of course, that makes her an exception among the thousands of eighteenth- and nineteenth-century

American women whose husbands' early deaths forced them to search for ways to support themselves and their children. Many of those who, like her, were educated tried to earn their livelihoods by teaching. As her contemporary Mary Austin Holley had done, Elizabeth started a school for young children in her house in New York, but after her conversion and that of her sister-in-law Cecilia, anti-Catholic prejudice in the city made it difficult for the school to succeed there.

Long before she converted, Elizabeth held strong moral and religious beliefs. After her marriage, she and other wealthy, upper-class women started the Society for the Relief of Poor Widows with Small Children. Perhaps the first organized charity of its kind in the country, it earned the women who started it the title "the Protestant Sisters of Charity."

The Setons had gone to Pisa, where William's friends and business associates Antonio and Filippo Filicchi lived. They hoped that the change of climate would help him recover from tuberculosis, but he died on December 27, 1803, shortly after the Setons' arrival, and was buried in the English cemetery at Leghorn (Livorno). Elizabeth and her oldest daughter, Anna Maria (whom the Filicchis nicknamed Anina), were unable to sail back to the United States for nearly six months. Storms forced the cancellation of several planned crossings, and then Anina contracted scarlet fever and the ship's captain refused to allow them to board. While she waited in Pisa, Elizabeth began to attend Mass regularly and found, among other things, that the Catholic custom of daily services answered her spiritual needs more fully than the weekly Episcopal worship had done. She was also moved by the depth of faith that she observed at Mass. A devoted and eloquent letter writer, she often wrote to Rebecca Seton, William's half sister, who was also her close friend. In April 1804, she observed about the churchgoers in Pisa: "I don't know how anybody can have any trouble in this world who believes all these dear souls believe. If I don't believe it, it shall not be for want of praying. Why they must be as happy as angels almost."

The pious Filicchis encouraged Elizabeth's growing interest in their faith, and when she and Anina finally returned to New York, Antonio Filicchi traveled with them. His motives were twofold: to keep an eye on the still-bereft Elizabeth and to have a firsthand look at the Filicchis' numerous commercial interests in the northeastern United States. When Elizabeth landed in New York in early June, she found her sister-in-law Rebecca Seton gravely ill. Rebecca's death, within a month, deepened her grief and strengthened her inclination toward conversion. Through Filicchi, Elizabeth made contact with the leading Catholic churchmen in America, including Bishop John Carroll and Louis William DuBourg in Baltimore. Maryland was an important center for Catholicism, in large measure because the Calvert family, aristocratic English Catholics, had founded their colony on principles of broader religious tolerance than were practiced in most of the rest of the country at the time. For months, Elizabeth vacillated about whether to convert, while Bishop Carroll, John Hobart (later Episcopal bishop of New York), and other theologians literally competed for her allegiance. In January 1805, she wrote, "The controversies on it I am quite incapable of deciding, and as the strictest Protestant allows salvation to a good Catholick, to the Catholicks I will go, and try to be a good one, may God accept my intention and pity me." She formally converted in March 1805; not too many months later, Cecilia Seton also became a Catholic.

DuBourg, aware that Elizabeth's educational efforts in New York were foundering, invited her to open a school under the auspices of his order, the Sulpicians, in Baltimore. St. Mary's, a boys' school and seminary just outside the city proper, was already in operation; DuBourg proposed opening a girls' school next door. Elizabeth moved to Baltimore in 1808, installed her household and boarding school in a medium-size brick house, and welcomed her first students in September. The program put more emphasis on piety and good behavior than on academics, not surprising in light of its mission and the nearly total absence of rigorous education for girls in the United States at the time. In Elizabeth's own words, the routine followed this pattern: "In the chapel at six until light, school at nine, dine at one, school at three, chapel at six-thirty, examination of conscience and Rosary, sometimes at the chapel also at three— and so it goes day after day without variation." By December, she had ten students, including her own three daughters, Anina, Catherine (Kit), and Rebecca (Bec). Elizabeth's dual roles of mother and schoolmistress kept her so busy, as she herself wrote, that "from half-past-five in the morning until nine at night every moment is full, no space even to be troubled."

It is not known precisely when Elizabeth formed plans to found a new order of nuns. She did not formally become a nun herself until March 1809, but she had written to Filippo Filicchi months earlier: "I have long since made vows which as a Religious I could only renew, and the thirst and longing of my soul is fixed on the Cross alone." Throughout the time she spent in Baltimore, however, she pursued her spiritual labors assiduously and developed a strong bond with Pierre Babade, a priest who became her principal confessor. It was Father Babade who predicted that Elizabeth was destined to become "the mother of many children."

A few months later, in June, she left for Emmitsburg, Maryland, forty miles west of Baltimore, accompanied by thirteen-year-old Anina; her sisters-in-law, Harriet and Cecilia; and Maria Murphy, one of the original members of the Sisters of Charity of St. Joseph, as the new order was called. The habit, adapted from Elizabeth's own widow's outfit, was a simple black dress and matching bonnet. Over the next month, this group was joined by Kit and Bec; Elizabeth's two sons, William and Richard; five other nuns, Maria Murphy, Susan Clossy, Mary Ann Buttler, Rose White, and Catherine Mullen; and two students from the school in Baltimore, Julia La Britton and Isabella O'Conway, the daughter of one of the nuns.

In Emmitsburg, the group waited to move into a building being constructed on a farm purchased for the order by Samuel Cooper, a wealthy recent convert to Catholicism who was studying at the Sulpicians' Mount St. Mary's Seminary, located nearby. Elizabeth was to be the head of what she described as "a community which will live under the strictest rules of order and regularity but I shall not give those laws nor have any care of compelling others to fulfill them. If any person embraces them and afterward chooses to infringe them they will only find in me a friend to admonish." As an order under the protection of the Sulpicians, the sisters would be subject to their rule.

This arrangement was to become a point of contention before many more months had passed. The original Sisters of Charity had been founded by Saint Vincent de Paul in France in the seventeenth century, and it was proposed that the American group adopt the rules governing the French order. In France, the Sisters of Charity were devoted to the care of the sick and of orphans, whereas the Americans' central activity was their school, and they depended on its income for their sustenance. The issue of whether the rules should be applied wholesale or adapted to suit the situation of the American Sisters of Charity was unsettled for some time. One of the original regulations prohibited a woman with children of her own from being Mother Superior of the order. If it were applied in Emmitsburg, it would mean, of course, that Elizabeth would have to step down as head.

She corresponded with now Archbishop John Carroll about the problem, and also wrote to George Weis, a layman who was a personal friend and benefactor. To Weis, she wrote: "The only word I have to say to every question is, *I am a Mother.* Whatever providence awaits me consistent with that plea I say Amen to it." In other words, she would not abandon her role as mother to her natural children in order to be spiritual mother to the Sisters of Charity. Archbishop Carroll supported her, for his own reasons: He wanted to maintain as much local control as possible over the American institution. The American Sisters of Charity would be governed by rules that considered their particular situation. In addition to allowing Elizabeth to continue as head, education was made one of the community's explicit purposes.

Throughout the months of germination, Elizabeth bore up patiently in the face of conflicts that were as often political as theological—for example, a disagreement over whether the sisters could continue to choose their own confessors, correspond with priests whom they had consulted in the past, or receive visits from those priests. A number of the nuns, like Elizabeth herself, were devoted to Pierre Babade, but they were told not to continue writing to him. The theological point at stake was a subtle one—whether the individual souls of the sisters were part of the work of the order or something private to themselves—but the psychological issue was whether and to what degree the women would be allowed to govern their own fates.

As one of Elizabeth's biographers expressed it, this was "merely the beginning of Elizabeth Seton's trials in Emmitsburg." Others struck much closer to home, as when her elder son, William, was suddenly taken ill in October 1809 and was thought to be dying. He recovered, as suddenly and as mysteriously as he had gotten sick, but Elizabeth's sister-in-law Harriet died a month later and was buried in the shroud originally intended for William. Writing to her dear friend Julia Scott a few days after Harriet's death, Elizabeth said, "Tribulation is my element—if only it carries me home at last, never mind the present." The crises continued throughout the winter, in the drafty, still unfinished White House. Anina and two of the sisters, Susan and Martina Quinn, suffered from an unidentified pulmonary ailment, and Cecilia's tuberculosis got so bad that the effort of trying to stand made her faint.

While waiting for their own building to be habitable, the group had lived on the grounds of the Sulpician settlement, in a structure called the Stone House. In fact, it was a primitive log house, four rooms on two floors, with the upper floor more a garret than a finished story. Somehow, sixteen people, including nine adults, squeezed into the Stone House. One room was used as a chapel, and there was no pump for water, which was carried from a spring on the property.

Finally, in late February 1810, they were able to move into the White House. By then Cecilia was so weak that she had to be carried. She died a week after Easter. When the White House was finally completed, Elizabeth—who had previously been accustomed to considerable luxury—was pleased. She described the place as an "elegant little chapel, thirty cells holding a bed, chair, and table each, a large infirmary, a very spacious refectory besides parlor school room, my working room, etc." Despite the lack of amenities and the remoteness of the place, women flocked to join the new order.

John Baptist David, who was for a while installed as director of the Sisters of Charity, showed himself insensitive and indifferent to what Elizabeth or the other nuns might think. When he was developing rules for the girls' school, he told her he would send them to her for "revision" only after his order had approved them. When Elizabeth wrote Archbishop Carroll to object, he advised her to disengage from earthly matters—in other words, submit to authority. Inside the order, there was talk that Sister Rose Landry White, a widow like Elizabeth but also a protégée of David's, would replace her as head, or that the order would be split in two, one charitable, led by Sister Rose and based in Baltimore, and one educational, with Elizabeth at its head, in Emmitsburg. Finally, Archbishop Carroll stepped in to defuse the controversy. To Elizabeth he wrote that if she were not the Mother Superior, "my hope for the continuance of the establishment would be very much weakened." David left, a new director, John Dubois, arrived, and any internal dissension was healed. About her differences with Sister Rose, Elizabeth wrote, "Our reserve is of the mind, not of the heart; her affectionate kindness to my children binds me by gratitude independent of our spiritual connections."

Despite Elizabeth's devotion to her calling, nothing could displace her devotion to her children. Anina had never been truly well since she was taken ill in Italy, and in Emmitsburg her health grew continually worse. Around New Year, 1812, Elizabeth wrote to Julia Scott: "My precious comfort and friend is undergoing all the symptoms which were fatal to our Cecilia and so many of the family." In January 1812, Anina was made a sister of St. Joseph's, as she had desired to be for some time. Afterward she said, "Now it is done, that I may become a sister and be numbered among the children of the blessed Saint Vincent."

Anina died on March 12, 1812. Elizabeth, whose grief after her husband's death almost certainly influenced her desire to convert, was bereft a second time. She wrote to her friend Eliza Sadler: "The remembrance of my lovely one now forces itself in every moment—her singular modesty and grace of action, the lifting of her eyes from the ground to cast the rays of her soul into mine."

Her emotional depths notwithstanding, Elizabeth had been able to accommodate to the deaths of others, like her sisters-in-law, to whom she had been extremely close. As she wrote to Julia Scott in 1810: "After ten minutes it [the soul] returns to its usual motion and all goes on as if nothing had happened. This same effect has followed the death of all so dear. While Faith lifts the staggering soul on one side, Hope supports it on the other—Experience says it must be and Love says let it be." But Anina's death was different. Now she felt, as she wrote to Eliza Sadler, "if I was not obliged to live in these dear ones [her other children] I should unconsciously die in her."

Despite such personal blows, Elizabeth successfully guided the Sisters of Charity to new accomplishments. The school, the order's original mission, increased in size and quality. In 1813, its enrollment stood at fifty and it had become a self-sustaining enterprise. As with other schools at the time, most of its students were the daughters of wealthy families who could afford to pay tuition, though the population always included some orphans and poor girls.

The heart of the curriculum continued to be the teaching of "piety and sound morals," but after four years the academic program was, for its time, ambitious. Elizabeth herself taught history and religious instruction, the latter consisting chiefly of catechism and Rosary. In the first year, more money was spent on catechisms, spellers, and grammars than on any other texts, but as the enrollment swelled, the curriculum added reading, geography, arithmetic, music, needlework, and languages: French, Spanish, and Italian. These were areas that upper-class young ladies were typically expected to master. The girls' comportment was closely supervised by the sisters; those in charge of discipline were called "Angels," and students weren't allowed to go anywhere unaccompanied by at least one supervisory Angel. Even when the girls went walking, one sister always led them and another brought up the rear. Despite—or because of—the strict discipline, the school was a serene place. Parents occasionally sent daughters who had gotten into trouble at a school that was less isolated or strict; others thought the peaceful rural atmosphere was a good environment.

Elizabeth, who always thought of herself as a mother—of her own children, of her nuns, and of her students—wrote often to former students, and they corresponded with her. It's impossible to know with certainty whether the surviving letters are representative, but these lines from Juliana White, written at Advent in 1815, very likely echo the feelings of many St. Joseph's alumnae: "Could I but spend this happy time with you again it would be a happiness that your Julian [as she referred to herself in letters] has not experienced since I last spent it at St. Joseph's." To the boys at St. Mary's, she was equally attentive. Many boys' parents preferred to consult with her about their sons than with the priests who ran the boys' school. Yet despite her kindly disposition, she could be strict. She admonished students who didn't follow the rules, and if they remained obdurate, she dismissed them. Once, however, when the unsuitable student was the sister of John Hickey, a priest at St. Mary's, she wrote the letter expelling the girl, Eleanor Hickey, but couldn't bear to send it. So she asked John Hickey to deliver the bad news. "I never had a heavier heart for a child that left us than for Ellen," she wrote.

From 1814 onward, the Sisters of Charity began to establish satellites away from Emmitsburg. Their first mission was in Philadelphia, where several nuns moved to run an orphanage. In 1817, the order founded a second orphanage in New York, the city Elizabeth had left just ten years earlier in search of a more hospitable environment for her work. The next year, 1818, they took over an existing free school for Catholic children in Philadelphia, and by 1822 they had opened free and pay schools in New York City as well.

One reason for the order's outward expansion was the increased need for education and care for orphaned, abandoned, and neglected children in American cities. By the late twentieth century, the Sisters of Charity would have more than 11,000 members in the United States, whose work encompassed education, health care, and social work. In 1818 there were internal reasons to establish outposts in other places as well. Emmitsburg was overflowing with students and sisters. Enrollment at St. Joseph's had reached one hundred, and so many women were applying to join the Sisters of Charity that "we are obliged to refuse continually for want of room." It was about this time that Elizabeth, whose health was starting to fail, wrote to Eliza Sadler characterizing herself as "an old woman to whom the nearly 100 souls in our house look for their daily solace of a mother's smile, incapacitated by my *want of capacity to manage and bustle* from taking any other part, but to try and keep off the evil spirits which always would steal in such a multitude, and turn everything to the account of peace and order."

With her children, this passionately devoted mother was less fortunate. Her daughter Bec injured her hip in a fall in 1812 and never recovered. Although she was treated by Dr. Philip Syng Physick, a Philadelphia specialist in hip-joint diseases, in 1815 she developed a tumor and grew increasingly crippled. In her last weeks, she suffered constant pain that abated only when she sat up in a chair, which she did all night. Later, when Bec could no longer even sit, Elizabeth cradled her and, as she wrote to Kit, "We wet each other pretty often with tears." After Bec died in early 1816, Elizabeth wrote to William, her older son, "It would be too selfish of us to have wished her inexpressible sufferings prolonged and her secure bliss deferred for our longer possession . . . though in her I have lost the little friend of my heart." Bec was fourteen.

Neither William, born in 1796, nor Richard, two years younger, showed any interest in the religious life their mother had chosen or in their father's mercantile profession. Near the end of the War of 1812, William decided that he wanted to join the navy, and Elizabeth used her connections to secure a naval commission for him. Before it came through, however, the war ended, and in 1815 he was persuaded to go to Italy, where the Filicchis had offered to teach him their business. William spent two years with the Filicchis' company, but eventually left, more determined than ever to go to sea. Despite their many differences, the emotional ties between mother and son were strong, and they exchanged many letters. When she wrote to William, Elizabeth strove to shore up his shaky religious practice, as in this letter from 1815: "[A]s you know my stroke of death wd. be to know that you have quitted that path of virtue which alone can reunite us for ever. Separation, everything else I can bear—but that never. Your mother's heart must break if that blow falls on it."

In 1817, William announced that he had no stomach for commerce and came home bearing a letter from Antonio Filicchi, who wrote that the young man had shown no interest in trade and was so uncommunicative that Antonio hadn't been able to get to know him. Elizabeth secured a place in the navy for her son, under Commander Bainbridge, an old friend of her late husband. While William was in Boston, where Bainbridge's ship, the *Independence,* was docked, she wrote him incessantly (by then Elizabeth was in constant pain, and at night, when she could not sleep, she wrote) and kept a map of Boston harbor on her table in order to feel closer to him.

William, impatient to get to sea, transferred to a second ship, the *Macedonian,* bound for the Pacific for two years. He wrote often to his mother, and with affection, but he constantly asked her for money and she was blind to his machinations. Before the ship set sail, she told him not to come to say good-bye, because, she said, she couldn't bear to take leave of him. It may be, however, that she did not want him to see how sick she already was. As it happened, however, the ship was damaged in a storm off the Virginia coast and put in at Norfolk for repairs. William seized the opportunity to visit her in Emmitsburg for what would be the last time. Afterward, she wrote that she had had a "happy moment with my soul's William."

Richard, the younger son, was even more disquieting. He lacked motivation and performed indifferently during an apprenticeship with Luke Tiernan, a family friend and Baltimore businessman, in 1816. The following year, in December 1817, he went to Italy to work for the Filicchis. Although he stayed for two and a half years, Antonio wrote afterward that Richard had no aptitude for business and no desire to learn. Nevertheless, when Richard wanted to return to the United States in July 1820, Antonio, unfailingly generous and loyal, gave him money for his passage and to pay his debts. He also suggested that the navy might suit Richard, as it seemed to appeal to William. Even before Richard reached home, he wrote from Norfolk to say that he had borrowed money there, and Elizabeth had to ask Robert Goodloe Harper, a friend in Baltimore, to bail her son out. After visiting his mother briefly in Emmitsburg in December 1820, Richard apparently became a merchant seaman (the documents are vague) and died at sea in 1823.

Kit, the one daughter who enjoyed a long life (she lived from 1800 to 1891), expressed a desire for a worldlier existence than her sisters had. Elizabeth, who fretted about her children but never refused their wishes, sent Kit off on an extended visit to her friend Julia Scott in Philadelphia in spring 1818 armed with a little red book in which she had composed advice for dealing with all sorts of social situations. The book reveals Elizabeth as a woman of her age, proper, pious, and—on occasion—permissive. She writes, for example:

Gossip: You can never be bound, my love, to speak on any occasion, or on any subject, unless you are sure of doing good by speaking.

Dress: Be sure that simplicity should be your only rule.

Theatre: The best and wisest men who ever lived have thought the theatre a place of danger for young and old. Why should you or I put our conduct and opinion in opposition to theirs.

Dancing: I don't know much of the style of the present day, but I cannot remember the least of indecency or pride in dress, or the smallest familiarity or impropriety in dancing, which in truth, if you consider it as a good exercise and (if you must be in company) preferable to private chit chat.

Elizabeth almost certainly knew that she had little reason to worry that her daughter would behave recklessly or immorally. Once, when she was away from Emmitsburg, Kit wrote that she planned to postpone going to confession until she got home in order to have the chance to examine her conscience with her mother's help. "I have things I ought to talk first to you about," she explained. Later, Kit also became a nun, as a Sister of Mercy.

Elizabeth Seton frankly admitted that her devotion to her own children represented a "first claim which must ever remain inviolate." But she displayed a selfless concern for the young, the poor, and the needy as uncompromising as her attachment to her family, and that example inspired countless others, within the American Sisters of Charity and outside it. At St. Joseph's and elsewhere, the order led the way toward establishing parochial schools for the poor as well as the rich of both sexes. It is fitting that the woman who recognized the importance of service to others while our country was still in its infancy became the first native-born American canonized as a saint in the Catholic Church in 1975.

Elizabeth Seton died in 1821 of tuberculosis, the disease that took the lives of so many of her loved ones.

# Mary Baker Eddy

MARY BAKER EDDY, who founded the Church of Christ, Scientist, was born in 1821, in Bow, New Hampshire. Her parents, Mark and Abigail Baker, were Congregationalists, and she became a member of the church when she was seventeen. Through her family's frequent church attendance, prayer, Bible reading, and study and discussion of theology, Mary learned about religion, although she had very little formal education. She was often sick as a child and went to school irregularly, although her family was reasonably well-to-do and encouraged their six children to study. She suffered from unpredictable tantrums and fevers and may have had a congenital spinal problem. One brother, Albert, who graduated from Dartmouth and became Franklin Pierce's law partner, tutored her at home in Latin, Greek, and Hebrew during school vacations, but her later writings give no indication that she knew ancient languages. By the time she was twelve, however, she was writing poetry and did so for the rest of her life.

The Bakers moved to Sanbornton Bridge in 1836, where Mary attended school and married George Washington Glover in 1843. The couple moved to the South, where Glover died of yellow fever within six months, and Mary, pregnant, returned to her parents in Sanbornton Bridge. Her son, George Washington Glover II, remained with her until 1851; a local couple, Mahala and Russell Cheney, took a major role in his raising. When the Cheneys moved to Minnesota in 1851, George went with them and didn't see his mother again until 1879. Mary lived in her parents' house until she married Daniel Patterson in 1853. For nine years, from 1843 to the end of 1851, she suffered from extreme pain and hypersensitivity and began taking morphine (she depended on its pain-killing powers for the rest of her life) and sometimes submitted to hypnosis to relieve her symptoms. Her mother's death, in 1849, and her father's remarriage a year later were other sources of emotional trauma.

After her first husband died, Mary began to publish articles and poems in local papers. She earned some money from her writing, but she was really supported by her relatives, even after her marriage to Dr. Patterson, an itinerant dentist. Throughout the 1840s and 1850s, her symptoms—and her use of morphine—persisted. On her wedding day, she had to be carried downstairs, although when Dr. Patterson was away she tended to improve, so there was evidently a psychosomatic component to her illness. That may help to explain her search for cures that involved mesmerism, spiritualism, and homeopathy, popular practices at the time. While trying a water cure in 1862, Mary heard about Dr. Phineas P. Quimby, a mesmeric healer, and decided to consult him in Portland, Maine. She couldn't walk when she arrived, but almost immediately after meeting Quimby, she recovered enough to walk the 182 steps to the top of the tower at city hall. She stayed in Portland for several weeks, read Quimby's work, wrote an article about him, and continued to consult him until his death four years later.

Quimby was in fact not a physician, but the son of a blacksmith who became a mesmerist after seeing one perform. His original method involved an assistant, whom he would hypnotize; in a trance, the assistant would make diagnoses and prescribe cures. Later, Quimby practiced direct mental healing and started to develop a "science of health." He might have coined the phrase "Christian science," though he almost certainly did not develop the idea to the extent that Mary did later. He did believe, however, that disease resulted from "false belief" and that curing disease was also a mental operation. His ideas included two further concepts that Mary later adapted: that mental telepathy was possible (he believed that patients could be treated from a distance) and that the healer took on the sickness of the patient, a belief that Mary eventually abandoned.

Mary later denounced Quimby as a "primitive mesmerist," but for several years she was a devoted follower. She wrote about him, consulted him by letter and in person, and spread the word of his healing powers. A month after Quimby died, she fell on the ice, suffering back pain and probably injuring her spine. Later, she claimed that the doctor who examined her had said that she was dying (the doctor denied it), but that after reading the account of Jesus' healing of a paralyzed man in Matthew 9, she rose, healed, "on the third day." After this experience, Mary traveled for nine years lecturing and writing about Quimby's theories and their relationship to the Bible. She lived as a lodger or a guest in many different homes, often with people who shared her interest in spiritual healing. Over time, she came to believe that healing was purely spiritual and involved no physical component. In 1875, she set up the Christian Science Publishing Company, with money from two of her students, and published the first edition of *Science and Health,* a book she would revise fifty times before she died. In the same year, she bought a house in Lynn, Massachusetts, called it the Christian Scientists' Home, taught classes in the parlor, and rented the other rooms to her students.

For more than fifteen years after *Science and Health* appeared, Mary continued to work in relative obscurity. Some of her former students competed with her on the lecture circuit (public lecturing and healing were popular in late-nineteenth-century America, long before the age of mass communications), and there were occasional lawsuits charging the theft of ideas by one or another of them. The experience may have been Mary's source for what she called Malicious Animal Magnetism, or M.A.M. (today we would say bad vibes), which she included in the second edition of *Science and Health* in 1878. According to this theory, one person's mind could send negative telepathic signals that harmed the mind of another person. By the time the third, two-volume edition was published in 1881, M.A.M. had expanded into an entire chapter on "demonology."

Despite the turmoil, this was also Mary's most creative period, during which she enunciated her ideas about healing, formulated the theological concepts on which they rested, and created an organization to spread those ideas. Her idea that the only reality was spiritual, that matter was illusory, solved the problem of the existence of evil in a world created by God. Since the material world was an illusion, it had not been divinely created, and God was not responsible for it. People suffered physically because they believed their senses instead of being conscious of spiritual reality. She believed that right thinking meant release from suffering and from sin.

The outlines of the new movement emerged in the latter part of the 1870s, when the Christian Science Association was established (1876) and the Church of Christ, Scientist was chartered (1879). The number of converts increased during the 1880s, but the movement continued to be marked by factionalism and acrimony. Mary continually chose students as her protégés, only to banish them later on. This was the source of in-fighting and disorder within the organization as Mary searched for ways to encourage the spread of Christian Science while preserving her con-trol over it. Some of these relationships even took on a tragicomic as-pect, as happened when Mary legally adopted Ebenezer Foster and made him her spokesperson, only to expel him from the church and from her household in 1897. Her third marriage, to Asa Gilbert Eddy, in 1877 was a stable one. He was a mild-mannered former sewing-machine salesman, but unfortunately, he only lived another five years, until 1882.

In the early 1890s, after having dismantled the institution for three years, Mary finally worked out a way of organizing her church to satisfy her desire for control and to avoid the personal conflicts with individual followers that had led to schisms in the past. The church's authority was to be centered at the First Church of Christ, Scientist in Boston. Other churches were mere branches, although they were permitted to operate autonomously and to refer to themselves as, for example, First Church of Christ, Scientist but not *The* First Church of Christ, Scientist. A five-person board of directors was constituted to run the church, guided by the *Manual of the Mother Church* (first published in 1895), but the board did not replace Mary as head of the church. She took the title of pastor emeritus and dictated that henceforth the "pastor" would be *Science and Health with Key to the Scriptures,* supplemented by the Bible.

By this means, individual preachers could no longer introduce ideas of their own that might contradict or alter the essential teachings of Christian Science. In fact, nothing about Christian Science could be published without authorization, and regional Committees on Publica-tion refuted all criticisms of the sect that appeared. The church did not hesitate to use its powers of excommunication as a means of control.

Augusta Stetson, whom one scholar called "perhaps the most capable person ever won to Christian Science," was probably banned because her success as a preacher in New York City was perceived as a threat to the authority of the central organization. The formal charges, however, were that she practiced "malicious mesmerism" and was about to be deified by her followers.

Under the new regime, the church stabilized, internal dissension abated, and the movement gained a large following. Its success brought it increasingly into the public eye, and it received its share of critical attention. Mark Twain satirized the doctrine and its founder in magazine articles and a book, *Christian Science* (1907). The strongest condemnation came in a series by George Milmine that appeared in *McClure's Magazine* in 1907–8. But the church continued to grow. One of the reasons for creating the *Christian Science Monitor* newspaper in 1908 may have been to respond to early attacks, but the paper expanded, is published Monday through Friday, and has become highly respected and widely read. Today its news articles and opinion pieces are quoted throughout mainstream media on a variety of topics, especially foreign affairs. It is viewed as secular and fair. The *Monitor* is also one of the oldest continuously operating newspapers in America.

Mary Baker Eddy made a number of claims about the doctrine she presented in *Science and Health with Key to the Scriptures:* that it was of divine origin, that she and the church she founded were the sole authoritative interpreters of its meaning, and that her ideas represented the second coming. Many scholars and theologians disagree, but they acknowledge that she reclaimed the role that faith has to play in healing, a role that in the second half of the nineteenth century was increasingly being supplanted by science. She was also the only American woman to have founded an important, enduring religious movement. As one believer wrote in 1889, "We are witnessing the transfer of the gospel from male to female trust."

Mary died in 1910 at the age of eighty-nine, in Chestnut Hill, Massachusetts.

## *Mary Shindler*

ONE OF MY GREAT-GREAT-GRANDMOTHERS, Mary Shindler, was a published poet and composer of hymns whose beliefs and practice hewed closer to the great religious mainstream of nineteenth-century America than did those of Elizabeth Seton or Mary Baker Eddy. She moved to Texas in 1866 with her second husband, Robert Doyne Shindler, and their young son, Robert Jr. (Robert Jr. and Anna Mary Taylor Shindler are my great-grandparents). Forced to close the Ripley Female Institute, the girls' school Robert Shindler had founded in Ripley, Tennessee, in 1863, the Shindlers searched for a place to make a new start. It was several years before they arrived in Texas, where Robert, an Episcopal priest, taught in San Augustine before becoming rector of Christ Episcopal Church in Nacogdoches.

Mary Shindler, born in 1810 in Beaufort, South Carolina, was the second of eight children of the Reverend Benjamin Palmer and his wife, the former Mary Bunce. Only four of the children survived infancy— Mary, her two sisters, Sarah and Jane, and a brother, Keith. Benjamin Palmer believed in educating girls as well as boys. He started the first Sunday school in South Carolina and devoted considerable energy to improving church music, so it is not surprising that Mary's intellectual and artistic output eventually included a number of Christian hymns. Girls were rarely sent north to attend school at the time, but Mary spent one year in Elizabethtown, New Jersey, and later she and her younger sister, Jane, attended Dr. Herrick's school in New Haven, Connecticut.

Mary started writing poems, stories, and essays when she was still a child. As a young woman, she found a kindred spirit in Charles Dana, a writer and editor whose cousins included Charles Anderson Dana, editor of the *New York Tribune,* and Richard Henry Dana, author of *Two Years Before the Mast.* They married in 1835, and their son, Charles Morgan Dana (Charlie), was born in May 1837. Mary wrote this poem expressing her joy.

### THE MOTHER AND HER BABE

*A mother sat with eye upturned,*
*Within her heart love's pure fire burned,*
*For by her side, bright as the day,*
*A smiling little cherub lay;*
*It was her darling little son,*
*Her sweet first-born, her only one.*

*No ear had heard that mother speak,*
*Yet roll'd a tear-drop down her cheek;*
*But 'twas no tear-drop of distress,*
*It was a tear of thankfulness;*
*And, while she seem'd to Heaven praying,*
*These were the words her heart was saying:*

*"Father! Thou'st given me a blessing,*
*Daily my babe to be caressing!*
*Must not my heart each hour grow purer,*
*My hope of Heaven each moment surer,*
*When Innocence, and Love, and Joy*
*Smile on me through my darling boy?*

*"Oh, I have often had the feeling,*
*When by my sleeping infant kneeling,*
*An angel had to me been given,*
*I had the company of Heaven!*
*In this dark, stormy world 'tis rare,*
*To breathe so pure an atmosphere!*

*"I gaze in his confiding eyes,*
*And lo! Sweet tears in mine arise;*
*I kiss his rosy, velvet cheek,*
*And burn with thoughts I cannot speak;*
*My grateful heart overflows with joy,*
*That God has given me such a boy!*

*"And what if others cannot see*
*Beauties that ever shine on me?*
*What if my baby's sparkling eye*
*Should not attract the passer-by?*
*Or if his voice, so soft and clear,*
*Should fall unheeded on the ear?*

*"What if the sordid, worldly crowd,*
*The old, the young, the gay, the proud,*
*Who view my boy with glazes cold,*
*Gaze with delight on gems and gold?*
*'Tis well; my boy was given to me,*
*Not to the world's proud devotees."*

*Thus mused the mother, while the boy*
*Lay with his smile of tranquil joy;*
*At length he sigh'd; she, fearing then,*
*Her pensive look had given him pain,*
*Upraised him from his cradle rest,*
*And clasp'd him to her throbbing breast.*

Five days after experiencing the pure joy of her son's birth, Mary suffered the first of a series of tragedies that were to mark her life. Her sister Jane, her closest sibling and dearest friend, died of tuberculosis. Mary's response, as she expressed it in the poem "My Sister," was to take comfort from her faith and the presence of her family:

*I should not call it sad. It was not sad!*
*When morning came, they told me life had fled;*

*I saw my father's brow with paleness clad,*
*I saw my mother raise her aching head,*
*And they both told me that our Jane was dead—*
*But that she was in Heaven! Then all drew near,*
*And while they knelt around, my father pray'd;*
*He held my thin pale hand—and, o, that prayer!*
*His solemn deep toned voice e'en now I seem to hear!*


Less than a year later, however, her brother, Keith, a physician, died in Alabama. Mary's parents, who had been living with Keith, decided to return to South Carolina. At the same time, Mary and Charles briefly considered moving to Texas, but settled instead in Bloomington, Iowa, which they liked so well they called it the place of their dreams. With tragic irony, the entire family was stricken with cholera almost immediately after they arrived; Charles and Charlie died of the disease within two days of each other, the baby on August 20 and Charles on August 22.

Mary, who moved back to her parents' home in South Carolina, found solace and purpose in writing. She published her first book, a collection of religious poems titled *The Southern Harp,* in 1841; it sold 20,000 copies. A more personal collection, *The Parted Family and Other Poems,* soon followed, in the same year. Among the influential editors who encouraged Mary's literary ambitions were Sarah Josepha Hale of *Godey's Ladies' Book* and Caroline Gilman of *Rosebud,* who published some of her poems.

Mary's poetry was extremely well received, and the flood of her writing continued. She published *The Northern Harp* in 1842, in which she reflected on her past, as she did in "The Days of My Childhood":


*I love to remember the days of my childhood,*
*Those days when my heart was a stranger to pain;*
*When I roved with delight through the vine-tangled wild-wood,*
*Ere sorrow had bound me so fast with its chain.*
*The bright morning sun every moment grew whiter,*
*My light youthful heart every moment grew lighter,*
*As gaily I frolick'd, a stranger to pain. . . .*

In 1843, *Charles Morton, or The Young Patriot* appeared, and two
more collections, *The Young Sailor* and *Forecastle Tom, or, The Lands-
man Turned Sailor,* within a year. An unusual book, *Letters, Addresses to
Relatives and Friends,* was published in 1845. As the title suggests, these
were actual letters that Mary had written on various subjects. In one of
them, she sets forth for her parents her reasons for having left the Congregational Church in which they had raised her and embraced Unitarian theology. Writing with a tenderness that is sometimes surprising in
view of the close reasoning of her argument, Mary explained to her parents how her reading of the Gospel of John, among other texts, had persuaded her to abandon the doctrine of the Trinity, "after long and
earnest deliberation, much diligent study of the Holy Scriptures, and
fervent prayer to God for the assistance of his spirit." Nevertheless, she
continued to consider Jesus her "Saviour, and the Saviour of the world,"
and she wrote of his divine commission "to lead us to God, and to save
our souls." Toward the end of her letter, she took pains to reassure her
parents that she remained their devoted daughter and a true Christian.
"Mourn not over me, my beloved Parents, as over one lost to you forever. If you think me in error, rest assured it is not a fatal one."

The Rev. Palmer's reply to Mary has not been preserved, but parents
and daughter remained close. When Mary met Robert Doyne Shindler,
an Episcopal priest, in Charleston in 1846, she had apparently resigned
herself to living out her life as a widow and a Unitarian. But the schol-
arly, intellectually adventurous priest won her over, theologically and ro-
mantically, and they married in May 1848. The Shindlers settled in
Upper Marlborough, Maryland, a suburb of Washington, D.C., where
he assisted at church services but was not able to secure a church of his
own. In 1851, they moved to Shelbyville, Kentucky, after Robert was appointed professor of ancient languages at Shelby College. Their only
child, Robert Jr., was born in 1852, but by then Robert Sr., plagued by
moodiness and what many perceived as arrogance, was already at odds
with the Shelby administration. He left his professorship, and Mary
tried to earn money from her writing. Late in the 1850s, the Shindlers
started the Ripley Female Institute. The economic hard times brought
on by the Civil War forced its closure after three years.

Throughout the war and afterward work was scarce and even paper was in short supply. Mary continued to write, but she was unable to publish her books, and her poetry began to reflect even more prominently the themes of struggle and survival. She persevered, however, writing, looking for opportunities for herself and her husband, and keeping up their son Bobby's education. While Rev. Shindler was in Louisiana, a friend of theirs, Bishop Gregg, suggested that he go to Texas, where there was a job in San Augustine, teaching school. He did, but left San Augustine for Nacogdoches in 1868 to serve as rector of Christ Episcopal Church there. His problems persisted, however; he stopped performing his ministerial duties, which in any case carried no salary (ministers were expected to do other work), and sank into depression. In August 1874, he committed suicide.

Mary remained in Nacogdoches and continued to write and compose hymns. Following a common practice of the period, she sometimes set her compositions to music by renowned composers such as Mozart and Rossini, as well as by English and Italian composers who are now largely forgotten. Her secular work increasingly advocated an active role for women in various public spheres, especially literature and the arts.

Mary's son, called Bobby, became a Nacogdoches businessman, and married Anna Mary Taylor (my great-grandmother). Today Mary's hymns continue to be sung, and her poems have been included in anthologies of nineteenth-century American verse. A few of her best-loved compositions are "I'm a Pilgrim and a Stranger" (sometimes called "The Pilgrim's Song"), "O Sing to Me of Heaven," "Passing Under the Rod," and "Flee as a Bird."

Both her sacred and her secular writings invariably attest to a love of nature and a sense of life's fragility. Her hymns and their musical settings typically combine elements of melodrama and literary polish. As in "I'm a Pilgrim and a Stranger," she often envisions eternal life as a realm where nature is familiar, unchanging, and comforting. After a life of trials and disappointments, the promise is enticing:

> *I'm a pilgrim, and I'm a stranger,*
> *I can tarry, I can tarry but a night;*
> *Do not detain me, for I am going*
> *To where the fountains are ever flowing.*

Refrain: *I'm a pilgrim, and I'm a stranger;*
            *I can tarry, I can tarry but a night.*

*There the glory is ever shining;*
*Oh, my longing heart, my longing heart is there;*
*Here in this country so dark and dreary,*
*I long have wandered forlorn and weary.*

Refrain

*There's the city to which I journey;*
*My Redeemer, my Redeemer is its Light;*
*There is no sorrow nor any sighing,*
*Nor any tears there, nor any dying.*

Refrain

"Flee as a Bird," based on the Eleventh Psalm, echoes the same themes and perhaps even intensifies the hope of finding refuge from what Mary described in the first hymn as an unfamiliar and "dreary" country. In addition to its appearance in the collection *The Northern Harp,* this popular hymn was sold in large numbers as sheet music throughout the second half of the nineteenth century. In New Orleans, the melody of "Flee as a Bird" (identified simply as a "Spanish Melody" and described as sharing the characteristics of folk music) became the tune traditionally played at funerals as the hearse made its way from the church to the cemetery:

*Flee as a bird to your mountain, thou who art weary of sin;*
*Go to the clear flowing fountain where you may wash and be*
     *clean.*
*Haste, then, th'avenger is near thee; call, and the Savior will*
     *hear thee;*
*He on His bosom will bear thee; O thou who art weary of sin,*
*O thou who art weary of sin.*

*He will protect thee forever, wipe every falling tear;*
*He will forsake thee, O never, sheltered so tenderly there.*
*Haste, then, the hours are flying, spend not the moments in*
  *sighing,*
*Cease from your sorrow and crying: The Savior will wipe every*
  *tear,*
*The Savior will wipe every tear.*

Mary died in Nacogdoches in 1883, age seventy-three. "Flee as a Bird" may not have been played en route to the cemetery, but one of her hymns was undoubtedly sung at her funeral service in Christ Episcopal Church.

## Women of Today

ELIZABETH SETON was the first native-born American to be canonized as a saint in the Catholic Church. Mary Baker Eddy is the only American woman to found a major religious denomination. Mary Shindler was a well-published poet whose poetry has a strong religious influence. Some of her religious hymns were in hymnbooks widely used throughout the United States in the nineteenth century.

A century later, a woman attained the highest office in a major religious denomination. Marj Carpenter was elected moderator of the 2.8-million-member Presbyterian Church, U.S.A., in 1995.

### MARJ CARPENTER

MARJ CARPENTER served as moderator of the Presbyterian Church, U.S.A., from 1995 to 1996. A journalist by profession, she was president of the National Federation of Press Women in 1992–93. After losing her brother and sister, both of whom died tragically early in Marj's life, she came to believe that hers should be a life lived with purpose. Marj has traveled to over 115 countries throughout the world, visiting more than 5,500 congregations and missionary fields where the Presbyterian Church is active. Her message has been to focus the church on its mission, to perform good works that benefit others.

## IMPORTANT TRAIT FOR SUCCESS

MARJ CARPENTER: Believing that even when things go wrong, there's a reason for it, and absolute trust that everything's going to be all right. I've had some tough times in my life, and in the end everything turned out all right, and I firmly believed that all the way through it.

## BIGGEST OBSTACLE

MC: I lost my husband early and I had to raise my children and work. I worked on newspapers for a long time and then started working for the national Presbyterian Church as their main newsperson. My biggest obstacle sometimes was being a woman. I was the first— I've been a lot of firsts—but I was the first woman news director of a major denomination. Since then, they've had several women with great success. I know the Greek Orthodox have George Stephanopoulos's mother now as their news director, and I think sometimes it was just flat hard being a mother and a woman and trying to achieve.

## BEST PREPARATION FOR ROUGH-AND-TUMBLE OF LIFE

MC: Working on small newspapers where I covered wrecks and fires and murder scenes and politics. I got where I could just handle anything. By the time I worked for the national church, they would get all upset over someone who was upset in the church, and I'd just say, "Oh, that's nothing."

## BEST NEGOTIATING STRATEGY

MC: So many negotiators are inclined to just make speeches. They start saying the same things over and over. Listen, and let the other side talk a little more than you do. And the other thing I've learned is not to fight in every ditch. Pick your ditches to negotiate in. If you're constantly negotiating, it's just all you do—some things, just let go. If it isn't going to be extremely important, let that one go.

## HELPFUL CHILDHOOD MEMORY

MC: My mother was very strong, and she and my dad ran a business, but she really ran it, and I lost a brother and sister—there were three of us, and I ended up an only child. I felt like I had to achieve. I was the only one left. They'd had so much bad luck. My sister was killed by a horse; my brother died of kidney failure.

KBH: And how old was your brother when he died?

MC: Thirteen.

KBH: Oh, no. And your sister was?

MC: Four. She ran out behind a horse and tried to shoo it out of the yard—like she'd seen grown-ups do, and it kicked her and her head hit a rock. So I just felt like I had to achieve, but I had a couple of teachers along the way that were really outstanding. One of them was in high school, a journalism teacher, and one of them was in junior high, a history teacher that I particularly remember encouraging me.

## BEST ADVICE

MC: Oh, I remember that. A man named Dick Slack was a longtime state legislator in Texas when I was covering for the *Pecos Independent Newspaper* the Billie Sol Estes scandal. It was horrible, the Estes battle, and someone had set the paper on fire and somebody had thrown a brick through my bedroom window and somebody put a snake in my car. I went to him one day crying and he said, "Marj, the only way you can get through the forest is to walk through the trees." I've never forgotten that. And a lot of times I tell myself, you have to walk through the trees—just go on, you've got to walk through the trees.

I've tried to tell kids—I've worked with young people in churches—that they need God, they need something to hold on to; you're going to have some rotten times in your life. But at that point, they don't really think they're going to have any rotten times in their life.

# CHAPTER THREE

# EDUCATION FOR EVERYONE

ANY FACTORS HAVE CONTRIBUTED to the success of the U.S. democracy: the balance of powers—so carefully struck in our Constitution among the executive, legislative, and judicial branches of government; the rule of law that attempts to assure the equality of every individual in the courts; the separation of church and state; the Bill of Rights protecting individual liberties; and our system of free enterprise. Underlying all of these is the commitment to quality public education.

Our Founding Fathers showed this commitment in many ways. Benjamin Franklin formed a junta in Philadelphia, which later turned into a philosophical society. It was an organization of men who met periodically to share information from their own fields of expertise, reading, or experience to which the others may not have had access. Books were not widely available, so they sought to broaden their horizons through sharing what information they could obtain with their friends.

Thomas Jefferson was a leading proponent of public education, knowing that democracy could be safeguarded only by an educated electorate. As he wrote to James Madison in 1787, "Educate and inform the whole mass of the people. Enable them to see that it is their interest to preserve peace and order, and they will preserve them. And it requires no very high degree of education to convince them of this. They are the only sure reliance for the preservation of our liberty."

In my home state, the founding fathers of the Republic of Texas dedicated the public lands to a permanent university fund that would be held in trust, the proceeds going to support the University of Texas and Texas A&M University. When Texas became a state in 1845, it retained its public lands, rather than giving them to the United States. This became significant when oil was discovered under part of this land and has resulted in solid endowments of its two large university systems. The University of Texas is the second most highly endowed university in America, after Harvard. To support elementary and secondary education in the state, 25 percent of the gasoline tax is dedicated to the Public School Fund.

In the early years of the United States, however, public schools were established slowly. The Founding Fathers believed in the importance of universal education, but at first neither the federal government nor the states provided funding for schools, and the education of girls was almost totally neglected.

Even though the settlers had left Europe, where education was mainly reserved for the wealthy—mostly wealthy boys—it was many years after the Constitution was ratified before free public schools were established. Most often, it was sons who benefited from serious schooling, not daughters, whose education often didn't go far beyond reading, basic arithmetic, and the domestic arts. It was customary for boys to attend classes only during the winter, when there was no farmwork to be done; girls, if they attended school at all, often did so during the summer, when the boys were otherwise occupied, although they were gradually allowed into the winter sessions as well.

Girls who did attend all-female schools were typically instructed by women who were less qualified than the male schoolmasters—hardly surprising, given the fact that no American college was open to women until well into the nineteenth century and few people believed there was much value in educating them. By the late eighteenth century, young women from good families were expected to be able to read (not only the Bible), write letters, and play some role in the early education of their own children. Wealthy daughters sometimes attended boarding schools, where modest musical training, French, painting, and decorative arts were added to the rudimentary studies of their less affluent sisters. In other words, rich girls learned to entertain their future husbands and children, while the less well off prepared to look after theirs.

# *Emma Willard*

WHAT CHANGED AMERICAN thinking where the education of girls and young women was concerned were the efforts of a few visionary, determined women. Emma Hart Willard, born in Berlin, Connecticut, in 1787, was the first of them. Descended from early Massachusetts settlers who left the safety of Boston and Cambridge to farm the fertile Connecticut Valley, Emma traced her ancestry back to Stephen Hart, who is credited with discovering the site of what is now Hartford. The region's isolation brought with it the dangers of the frontier. When Emma's great-grandfather John Hart was eleven, his entire family was massacred by hostile Indians while he was away from home. Despite the dangers, this wilderness was also far enough from Boston and New York City to be free of those cities' powerful influence.

An only son, Emma's father, Samuel Hart, abandoned his own plans for higher education after his father died when Samuel was only thirteen. He took over the management of the family farm, but he never lost his thirst for knowledge and read widely in English literature, history, philosophy, and theology. He also followed political developments in the colonies with keen interest, shared his neighbors' enthusiasm for independence, and distinguished himself as a soldier in the Revolutionary War.

Widowed when his first wife, Rebecca Norton, died after bearing seven children, Samuel Hart married Lydia Hinsdale, with whom he had ten more children. Emma, second from the youngest, arrived when her father was fifty years old, and he evidently doted on her and encouraged her intellectual precocity. The entire family took books seriously, and evenings were often spent reading one of the volumes in the Harts' own small collection, one of the children's schoolbooks, or something borrowed from a friend or the local lending library. By the time she was twelve, Emma had begun to study geometry on her own—an unusual project for a girl in 1800. According to the conventional wisdom, women's minds were incapable of absorbing the intricacies of mathematics, and those who tried were at risk of running afoul of divine or natural laws.

Emma attended the local school, in Worthington, Connecticut, summer and winter, until she was fifteen. During the winter session, the teachers were likely to be university graduates—lawyers or doctors—men drawn by a sense of civic duty and, in many cases, the need to supplement their incomes. In the summers, the men farmed and women took over in the classroom. Throughout the year, the local clergy exercised considerable influence over the schools, although they didn't do the teaching themselves. Because Samuel Hart had rejected the authority of the Puritan leaders and joined the more liberal Congregational Church, Emma and her siblings were somewhat ostracized.

Rather than feeling persecuted, discrimination helped Emma gain an independent perspective on conventional schooling—which neither challenged her nor inspired her to revere her instructors. Years later, she wrote: "None of my teachers understood me so as to awaken my powers or gain much influence over me." Her earliest intellectual mentor was her father: "fifty years my senior—he had descended of a long lived race by slow generations from the early Pilgrims, and I have known no man who more retained their gravity and simplicity of manner. When I was fourteen, he often called me from household duties by my mother's side, to enjoy with him some passage of an author which pleased him, or to read over to me some essay which he had amused himself in writing."

When Emma was fifteen, a new academy opened in Worthington, and after some hesitation, Emma joined her older sister Nancy at the school. In order to catch up, Emma had to study on her own and submit to oral examinations by the principal, Dr. Thomas Miner, a Yale graduate. She studied hard and distinguished herself. Trained by her father to experience learning as a form of intellectual companionship, she developed a playful student-teacher relationship with Dr. Miner. Whenever he criticized her in class, she would work a reply into her required daily composition. Emma was the only student to pass all of her compositions, and she seems to have managed to amuse her instructor while taking considerable inspiration from him. "Thus my mind was stimulated, and my progress rapid," she wrote. "For two successive years, 1802–03, I enjoyed the advantages of Dr. Miner's school, and I believe that no better instruction was given to girls in any school, at that time, in our country."

Only seventeen when she completed her studies in Dr. Miner's academy, Emma turned to teaching herself when a family friend suggested that she take the position of schoolmistress at a local primary school. "Our school was soon the admiration of the neighborhood," she wrote, as word spread of how much the children were learning and—in a sign of things to come—her success in adding new, more challenging subjects to the traditional curriculum.

Between school terms—as a woman, Emma was initially restricted to teaching only in the summer—she studied in Hartford. When she returned to Berlin, she was asked to succeed Dr. Miner at the very school where she had been the star student, an appointment she described as an "uncommon honor [uncommon at that time for a female]." At nineteen, she had already overcome one of the prejudices about the proper role of women in education.

In 1809, Emma married Dr. John Willard, a physician who had traded in his medical practice for a career in politics and business. Willard was twenty-eight years older than Emma, had been widowed twice, and the eldest of his four children was as old as his young wife. They had begun to court after he took her side in a local controversy over her role at the Middlebury Female Academy, in Middlebury, Vermont. Their son, John Hart Willard, was born in 1810.

As it turned out, Emma didn't forget about education when she stopped teaching. On the contrary, the years between 1810 and 1813 were among the most important in making her aware of how unequal and inadequate educational opportunities for women were. In her early twenties, when her son was an infant, Emma lived across the street from the Middlebury College campus. One of her husband's nephews—also named John Willard—was a student at Middlebury and lived with the Willards. As a woman, Emma wasn't allowed to attend classes at the college, but she borrowed her nephew's texts and began to do the course work on her own.

Her "shadow" education at Middlebury was a bit of fortuitous timing. Among her husband's business ventures was the Vermont State Bank, of which he was a director. When the bank was robbed in 1812, the directors fell under suspicion. They were exonerated, but they bore financial responsibility for the depositors' losses, and John Willard's days as a rising entrepreneur and political player ended abruptly. By 1814, Emma had started a school in the Willard house. As she explained, "My leading motive was to relieve my husband from financial difficulties. I had also the further motive of keeping a better school than those about me." Economic need was undoubtedly a factor, but I suspect that Emma's desire to make profound changes in the way American girls were educated loomed large in her decision.

At the helm of her own school at last, Emma rapidly added "higher subjects"—mathematics, history, and foreign languages—to the curriculum. The students took to the new materials immediately, but there was one problem. Parents were unwilling to pay as much tuition to educate their daughters as they paid for their sons' educations, so the school couldn't hire competent teachers for the college-level courses. Emma tried to get around the problem by requesting permission for her students to attend some of the lectures at Middlebury as auditors. She also asked permission to be a member of the audience at the boys' oral examinations, since these were open to the public—but only a male public. The college rejected both requests on the grounds that the presence of women in classes or at the examinations would violate decorum.

Forced to rely almost entirely on her own resources, she studied the new subjects, developed her own methods, and taught them herself. She was proud enough of what her students learned, however, and confident enough of the level of achievement to which she had brought them that she invited the public—including the Middlebury College faculty—to attend the girls' oral examinations. She wanted, she said, to "bring to the notice of the public the fact that the female mind could comprehend collegiate studies."

Now that Emma Willard had demonstrated—to her own satisfaction and that of many others—that women's minds were capable of mastering the same subjects men studied, and that educated women wouldn't renounce their domestic, supportive roles and attempt to compete with men in traditionally masculine spheres, she was determined to put her methods to work on a larger scale. That meant a larger school, and she believed that to found such a school required public support. She began to reach out to men and women who might help her to rally the Vermont state legislature to her cause. In 1815, a year after her first triumphs in Middlebury, she lobbied the governor's wife in a letter that tactfully, but explicitly, drew attention to what she had achieved and why it mattered: "[W]hen I compare what I have done with my ideas of perfection, I have much cause to be humbled; but when I compare my labors with what are generally done in schools of a similar kind, I feel some cause to be satisfied with my own." She went on to dismiss the prejudices against educating women and to stress the crucial roles women play in influencing the values of their children: "When we consider that the character of the next generation will be formed by the mothers of this, how important does it become that their reason should be strengthened to overcome their insignificant vanities and prejudices, otherwise the minds of their sons, as well as of their daughters, will be tinctured by them!"

I have often thought that Emma Willard's argument should sway even the most male-dominated societies. But in 2004, nearly two hundred years after Emma's first efforts to change people's ideas about girls' education in America, many countries in the world still do not allow education of girls and thereby fail to take advantage of half the potential talent of their populations. Where girls are not permitted equal schooling, women are not allowed the same rights as men. Too often they are treated as second-class citizens and even abused. In most cases, they are in countries shut off from the modern world. Opening communication systems is one way to help women in these closed societies learn what is possible. Women like Emma Hart Willard will emerge to champion the cause of education—for all children—as a way to improve the quality of life for all.

Our women senators have united to speak out in many forums and on the Senate floor about the plight of women in Afghanistan, Iraq, and other countries where women are suppressed. We have passed laws to assure that all U.S. aid benefits girls and women as well as men in the newly formed governments in Afghanistan and Iraq, so that the girls who were not allowed education or health care under the Taliban and Saddam Hussein regimes can catch up and have a chance to improve their lives.

Emma set to work on what became known as *A Plan for Improving Female Education,* while at the same time looking for a community that would welcome and help promote and support the new school with its new philosophy. At first, even the name was a problem, since Emma didn't want to adopt the term college, in order to avoid the suggestion that women were competing with men in the sphere of education, although she knew perfectly well that was precisely what her students were doing. When she heard the phrase "seminaries of learning" in a lecture, she thought, " 'I will call it a Female Seminary.' That word, while it is as high as the highest, is also as low as the lowest, and will not create a jealousy that we mean to intrude upon the province of men."

Emma initially believed that she would be able to establish her school in Vermont, but the state legislature failed to throw its support behind the idea, and no individual community was willing to provide sufficient backing. She then considered Waterford, New York, because a number of her Middlebury students were Waterford natives, and the governor of New York, De Witt Clinton, was an enthusiastic advocate of state support for education and past president of the Free School Society in New York City. When Emma sent him a copy of her plan, he wrote to her, "I shall be gratified to see this work in print, and still more pleased to see you at the head of the proposed institution, enlightening it by your talents, guiding it by your experience, and practically illustrating its merits and its blessings."

Governor Clinton mentioned Emma Willard's *A Plan for Improving Female Education* in a speech to the New York legislature, though without mentioning her as the author, and he urged passage of a bill to improve women's education. When the bill came up for discussion, Emma went to Albany to lobby for it and even read her plan before a large public audience—a daring act in 1818, when ladies did not make public speeches. The legislature did pass a bill granting a charter to the "Waterford Academy for Young Ladies," but it failed to approve the $5,000 endowment that Emma had been hoping for. Instead, the school received modest financial support from the state's "literary fund" (actually an education subsidy).

Believing that the legislature would, over time, add its financial support to the formal encouragement the charter represented, the Willards moved to Waterford in 1819, and Emma prepared to open her school as the Waterford Female Academy. Meanwhile, she printed her plan in pamphlet form, at her own expense, and sent copies of *An Address to the Public; Particularly to the Members of the Legislature of New-York, Proposing a Plan for Improving Female Education* to many prominent people, including President James Monroe, John Adams, and Thomas Jefferson. The plan was widely read in the United States and Europe and earned the nickname "the Magna Carta of the rights of woman in matters of education."

Emma insisted that women's schools, as she conceived them, would be "as different from those appropriated to the other sex, as the female character and duties are from the male." She also argued that better education of women not only would benefit those who received it but would in fact have a civilizing effect on society: "if the female character be raised, it must inevitably raise that of the other sex: and thus does the plan proposed, offer, as the object of legislative bounty, to elevate the whole character of the community."

In place of the ill-conceived, ill-equipped schools that were the rule in girls' education, Emma offered what she called a "Sketch of a Female Seminary," consisting of a large building with living quarters for the students, classrooms, and a science laboratory, and a library, music room, and art gallery. She included "domestic instruction" as one of the four components of the curriculum, by means of which students would prepare to become good wives and mothers and avoid becoming estranged from their "domestic duties" as a result of spending so much time in the study of their academic subjects.

When I was a high school student in the late fifties, homemaking was still a required course: one semester of sewing, one of cooking. Though this was not my best course—honestly—it has made me very handy. My staff has caught me at my desk in my Senate office sewing on a button or fixing a hem. Most modern girls are not getting this practical skill, and that's not altogether a good thing. However, my home economics teacher still tells the story of my dropping a whole cherry pie on the floor and making popovers that came out of the oven as flat as pancakes. This is a lost skill I do not miss!

Another of Emma Willard's goals was to raise the level of primary education throughout the country by training her students to become schoolteachers. Not only did she believe that women were "better suited by nature than men to teach children," but she argued that making it possible for women to become teachers would free men for "services the state wants in many other ways." Finally, she suggested that since women were not the sole support of their families, they would be able to teach for lower salaries than men would accept. She was trying to persuade the all-male legislatures and electorates in New York and elsewhere to see the practical value of taking the unprecedented step of funding female education with public money. To attract much-needed support and not scare it off, she bent over backward not to appear too strident.

Despite her emphasis on the economic and political advantages of adopting her plan, she gained only isolated support for her ideas from politicians and the public. Nonetheless, Emma had given voice, shape, and coherence to a conviction that was beginning to take hold in the minds of American girls and women: that they had the ability, the desire, and the right to an education on a par with that offered to boys and men. Her words were quoted and reprinted throughout the nineteenth century, and as late as 1893, Thomas Wentworth Higginson wrote in *Harper's Bazaar,* "When in 1819, Mrs. Willard published her address to the public, particularly to the members of the Legislature of New York, introducing a plan for improved female education and establishing her school under State patronage at Waterford, she laid the foundation upon which every woman's college may now be said to rest."

Emma's methods in Waterford included a careful introduction of new, more challenging fields of study to the curriculum. For example, she considered mathematics the cornerstone of the Waterford program—she referred to geometry as "the ploughshare of the mind." Later, she added trigonometry, conic sections, and natural science (then called natural philosophy). She introduced atlases, globes, and map-making methods to the teaching of geography, believing that students learned more when their senses were more fully engaged; and she thought the available texts were so deficient and dull that she set out to write her own. When Professor William Channing Woodbridge, a well-known geographer, heard about her project, he asked her to collaborate with him on a new geography textbook. *A System of Universal Geography on the Principles of Comparison and Classification,* first published in 1822, was widely adopted, becoming the first of her many successful teaching texts.

There was no denying the immediate educational success of the Waterford Female Academy, though skepticism persisted. When a student, Mary Cramer, distinguished herself in geometry, some of those who had witnessed the public examination insisted that she must have memorized the answers because women lacked the intelligence to understand mathematics. Not surprisingly, then, the legislature rejected a second request to grant public money to the school, despite an eloquent appeal from Governor Clinton.

Disillusioned by what she characterized as "the malice of open enemies, the advice of false friends, and the neglect of others," Emma wrote, "I do not regret bringing [the request for public funds] before the Legislature, because in no other way could it have come so fairly before the public. But when the people shall become convinced of the justice and expediency of placing both sexes more nearly on an equality, with respect to privilege of education, then Legislators will find it in their interest to make the proper provision."

The people of New York State may not have been in a hurry to be convinced, but some of the influential people in one upstate New York city were. In 1821, the lease on Emma's school building in Waterford, New York, was coming up for renewal, and the legislature rebuffed the academy's third request for funds. Leading citizens of Troy, a thriving industrial center on the Hudson River that boasted nail and soap factories, tanneries, ceramics plants, and paper and cotton mills, were eager to add education and the arts to their commercial community. They persuaded their city council to pledge funds to purchase the former Moulton's Coffee House, a large three-story building across the street from the courthouse. They promised to raise additional money to renovate the building to Emma's specifications, and appointed a board of trustees.

The people of Troy and Emma Willard immediately hit it off. When she said, "I want you to make me a building which will suit my trade," they complied, covering the wooden exterior with brick and reconfiguring the floor plan to suit her. She explained that she didn't require a luxurious building—"I expect the life of the school will be on the inside, and not on the out."

In September 1821, ninety students arrived for the opening of classes in the new Troy Female Seminary building, twenty-nine girls from Troy itself and the others from as far away as Georgia. Emma Willard, now thirty-four, had founded a seminary on her educational principles, though without the state support that she had always insisted was essential. In a further irony, the lease for the property was in Dr. Willard's name, since as a married woman, Emma could not enter into a contract on her own. Legalities aside, John Willard put himself at the service of his wife's endeavor, serving as the school's business manager and physician.

By 1824, the school's enrollment was nearly a hundred and fifty. Most of the teachers were former students who were familiar with Emma's methodology, and all of them were women. In fact, teacher training was one of Emma's preoccupations from the beginning. A student whose family could not afford the Troy Seminary fees could defer paying tuition if she agreed to go into teaching after graduation. Later, when she could repay the tuition from her teacher's salary, that money went into a special fund to permit current students to defer their tuitions. Not all the students were later able to reimburse the school, but Emma managed Troy Seminary so efficiently that the school was never in danger of insolvency. In this informal way, she very likely became the first woman to provide academic scholarships and student loans to girls and young women.

Later in her life, she wrote: "I continued to educate and send forth teachers, until 200 had gone from the Troy Seminary before one was educated in any public normal school in the United States [the first normal school opened in 1838, in Massachusetts]. Thus early was my system of female education carried to every part of the country, and the school which, in 1814, was begun in Middlebury is fairly entitled to the honor of being the first normal school in the United States."

Despite fears that educated women would prefer to challenge traditional male authority, at home and in the public sphere, Emma actually found that the chief obstacle to turning out more teachers was that education made the young women *more* marriageable, not less. One Englishman who visited Troy told Emma, "Madam, you are making a grand experiment here; we have nothing to compare with it on our side of the water, but I fear you are educating girls too highly, and that they will not be willing to marry." She insisted that the opposite was the case: "The young men sought them so resolutely for wives that I could not keep them for teachers."

Almira Hart Lincoln, Emma's sister, joined the school's faculty after she was widowed in 1824. She eventually taught botany, chemistry, and geology. Almira became even better known as a writer than Emma and, like her sister, wrote her first book—a botany text—because she found fault with the existing textbooks. *Lincoln's Botany* remained for years the standard American school and college text for the subject and was translated into a number of foreign languages. Almira's presence was especially important to Emma the following year, when Dr. Willard got sick. During his final illness, Almira took over much of the day-to-day administration of Troy Female Seminary so her sister was able to nurse her husband. He died in 1825.

Emma continued her own writing as well, with particular focus on history. *History of the United States, or Republic of America,* which she would update and revise several times, first appeared in 1828. A survey of American history from the colonial period to 1826, it garnered praise from the likes of the Marquis de Lafayette, who admired her treatment of the War of Independence, and Daniel Webster, who wrote to her: "I keep it near me as a book of reference, accurate in facts and dates."

In 1830, Emma needed a change of scene and routine. She left the running of her school to Almira and took off on a tour of France and the British Isles. The trip was in effect a working vacation for Emma, who visited French and English schools and wrote a series of letters to the students at Troy. These were later published as *Journal and Letters from France and Great Britain* (1832).

Emma was shocked by what she considered the decadence of the art she saw in France, and her reactions reveal an uncharacteristically prudish side in a woman who would soon introduce the study of physiology to the curriculum of the Troy Female Seminary. After seeing the statues in the Tuileries Garden near the Louvre, her letter to the students declared: "No—my dear girls, I shall not take you to examine those statues. If your mothers were here, I would leave you sitting on these shaded benches, and conduct them through the walks, and they would return, and bid you depart for our own America; where the eye of modesty is not publicly affronted; and where virgin delicacy can walk abroad without a blush."

The French themselves made a more positive impression on the American visitor. When she met Lafayette, she wrote: "Lafayette, more than any other man of the present day, is making history for others to write, and for posterity to read."

When Emma returned to Troy in 1832, the school was even stronger than it had been when she left on her trip. The student body had grown to more than three hundred, faculty size had increased along with the students, and the school's finances were in excellent shape. Emma continued her curricular innovations. She was undeterred by the outcry that greeted her introduction of the physiology course and defended her ambitious vision with this comment: "If fine, genuine learning has ever been said to give polish to a man; why then should it not bestow added charms on a woman?" The charming woman, if she was a graduate of Troy Female Seminary, was likely to be more than a match for most young men, having mastered a curriculum that ran the gamut from algebra to zoology, with courses in astronomy, Bible, botany, chemistry, composition, dancing, drawing, elocution, French, geography, geology, geometry, German, gymnastics, history, Italian, Latin, literature, logic, philosophy, rhetoric, singing, Spanish, theology, trigonometry—and physiology, of course—along the way.

No other girls' school in America offered anything comparable at the time, but the 1830s proved to be a watershed decade for women's education. In 1833, Oberlin College opened its doors—to men and women, without regard to race—the first coeducational college in the country, and the first explicitly to renounce racial discrimination as well. Two years later, the *American Ladies Magazine* featured the Troy Female Seminary in its December issue. The article pointed out that though the United States had seventy-six men's colleges, it lacked even a single *women's* college. "Men of America," the writer asked, "shall this neglect of your daughters be perpetual?"

The vision of a school to train teachers was finally realized not in New York but in Massachusetts, in 1838, the same year that Emma made a disastrous marriage to Christopher Yates, a physician who schemed to get money from her to support his gambling habit and who tried to wrest control of her property from her. In January 1839, three months after their wedding in Troy, the couple moved to Boston, but by June, Emma had imposed a separation agreement on Yates and moved to her sister Mary Lee's house in Berlin, Connecticut. By a fortunate coincidence, she made contact with the education reformer Henry Barnard, who asked her to speak about schools in Kensington, Connecticut. Her talk was such a success that she was elected the town's superintendent of the common schools.

The unexpected opportunity to bring about improvements in the common schools helped Emma recover from her most troubling personal crisis since Dr. Willard's death in 1825. Almost overnight, Emma had secured the laboratory she had been seeking to test her ideas about primary education and the training of teachers. She and Barnard outlined what was essential for the schools in terms of physical plant, textbooks, and curriculum, and Emma got busy devising a training program for students who wished to become teachers. She also insisted that the local women get involved in the schools, helped them to form the Female Common School Association—a forerunner of the PTA—and lectured them about what they could do to improve their schools. Kensington quickly became a model for common schools everywhere.

Emma Willard's collaboration with Barnard had far-reaching effects. As publisher of the *Connecticut Common School Journal,* Barnard had a platform from which to broadcast his ideas, and contacts with other leading educational innovators, such as Horace Mann. Thanks to their collective efforts, Massachusetts established the country's first normal school, and though it would be another decade before Connecticut followed suit, the common schools there improved markedly, nourished on the diet of teacher training and curricular improvement that Emma prescribed.

Throughout the decade and after, Emma never retreated from her conviction that the spheres of men and women were different and that women should concentrate on the education of children, including religious, moral, and intellectual instruction, and the higher education of women. Business, war, and politics should be left to men. At the same time, she was convinced that the proper role of women was every bit as crucial as that of men because, in her view, civilizations had risen and fallen on the strength of just those values of which women were the guardians.

Her 1837 volume, *A System of Universal History, in Perspective: Accompanied by an Atlas, Exhibiting Chronology in a Picture of Nations, and Progressive Geography in a Series of Maps,* made this point explicitly: that virtue makes nations strong and vice weakens and destroys them. She believed that democracy as a political system was being tested in the United States; if it succeeded, it might spread to other countries, but if the American experiment failed, democracy was doomed. Since national virtue or lack of it could tip the scales in either direction, and women bore a large measure of the responsibility for communicating and inculcating values, the importance of their roles as wives, mothers, and teachers could not be overstated.

To Emma's thinking, the certainty that it was up to women to embody and transmit the essential values of a culture made their education all the more important. Every time the Troy Female Seminary set another precedent—as when Mary Hastings, head of the school's science department, became the first woman to include laboratory experiments as a component of her courses, or Emma herself published a book on a new subject—the status of American women was enhanced. At the same time, her own reputation rose with each new title. Her graphic presentation of world history—a time line in chart form called *Historic Guide to the Temple of Time*—received a gold medal at the World's Fair in London in 1851. At about the same time, the final volume of her sweeping historical survey of the United States, *Last Leaves of American History,* was published. Incorporating westward expansion and the annexation of Texas and California into the narrative, the book also emphasized Emma's belief that American prosperity and survival depended on adherence to the very values she had identified in earlier writings.

Emma's position as the undisputed leader in the struggle to make education a universal right earned her the respect of all American women. Elizabeth Cady Stanton, one of the founders of the women's suffrage movement in the United States, was a student at Troy Female Seminary in the early 1830s. Many years later, she recalled Emma's return from Europe in 1832: "I well remember her arrival, and the joy with which she was greeted by teachers and pupils. She was a splendid looking woman, then in her prime, and fully realized my idea of a queen. I doubt whether any royal personage in the old world could have received her worshipers with more grace and dignity than did this far-famed daughter of the Republic. She was one of the remarkable women of that period, and did a great educational work for her sex."

Emma Willard's efforts not only improved the education of girls, but through her focus on teacher training and her work on common-school education, she advanced the cause of primary and secondary education for everyone—boys and girls, rich and poor. She knew that the "experiment" in democracy had to succeed, and an educated population was an essential precondition for success. When the Republic of Texas was established, its founders followed the American lead with respect to education. The principles of public education for all supported with public money were developed and spread through Emma Willard's efforts. Texas's early leaders committed to these principles by creating public trust funds for both secondary and higher education.

## *Women of Today*

EMMA WILLARD devoted her life to educating and pushing for the education of girls in early America.

Almost a century later, Lynne Cheney is leading the effort to preserve and teach history to all schoolchildren in America, believing that knowledge of history shapes our culture and values.

Ruth Simmons's love of learning propelled her to become the first African American woman to head a seven-sisters college, as well as an Ivy League school.

Rosalyn Yalow, by being creative and determined, became the first American-born woman to win the Nobel Prize. She developed the measurement called RIA (radioimmunoassay). It makes it possible for scientists to use radiotropic tracers to measure the concentration of biologic substances in blood. She invented the technique in 1959 to measure the amount of insulin in a diabetic person.

### LYNNE CHENEY

"WHEN YOU READ about our country's founding, you understand that freedom isn't inevitable," Lynne Cheney says. "You realize how precious our liberty is and how well worth defending." As chairman of the National Endowment for the Humanities from 1986 to 1993, and currently as a scholar at the American Enterprise Institute, she has emphasized the importance of transmitting the story of our country to upcoming generations.

Dr. Cheney has authored or coauthored seven books, including *Kings of the Hill,* a history of the House of Representatives that she wrote with her husband, Vice President Dick Cheney. Her most recent books, *America: A Patriotic Primer* and *A Is for Abigail: An Almanac of Amazing American Women,* bring the great ideas, events, and personalities of the American past to the nation's children. Using proceeds from these bestselling books, Dr. Cheney has established the James Madison Book Award, an annual prize of $10,000 that recognizes outstanding historical writing for children and young people.

A summa cum laude graduate of Colorado College, Lynne Cheney holds a master of arts from the University of Colorado and a Ph.D. from the University of Wisconsin. She served on the Commission on the Bicentennial of the Constitution and on the education team of presidential candidate George W. Bush.

## IMPORTANT TRAIT FOR SUCCESS

LYNNE CHENEY: Stick-to-it-iveness. If you want to succeed, you can't be deterred from your goals. In the world of journalism and writing—as in so many other fields—you get told no so many times. You just can't take it for an answer.

## BIGGEST OBSTACLE

LC: I got a doctorate in English literature at a time when there was a glut of Ph.D.s. Not being able to get a teaching job was a pretty big obstacle, one I chose to go around by finding another use for the skills I'd cultivated. I went into writing and quickly discovered that the only thing harder than getting a job teaching English was getting people to publish your work. But I kept after it. I think it's worth observing that women in my generation generally didn't have mentors. We didn't even know they were a good idea. And so we often didn't have anyone familiar with the challenges we were facing who could give us advice and guidance as we tried to deal with the obstacles we came up against.

## BEST PREPARATION FOR ROUGH-AND-TUMBLE OF LIFE

LC: I have often thought that for today's women it's athletics. Women in my generation didn't really have athletics, so for me [she laughs] it was baton twirling. You know, it sounds so silly to talk about that, but it was good physical exercise. It taught you to keep going when you were tired; it taught you not to quit when you made a mistake or pulled a muscle. It inspired me to be competitive. It rewarded me for practicing. And I practiced four or five hours a day. Today's women derive so many benefits from competitive athletics, but maybe we got a few from baton twirling. I think cheerleading was probably like that, too.

KBH: Did you compete?

LC: Oh, yes. I was state champion for several years. To retrieve my dignity here, I think I should point out that Justice Ruth Bader Ginsburg was a baton twirler, too.

## BEST NEGOTIATING STRATEGY

LC: To know everything that's important to your side of the case and to know everything that's important to the other person's side of the case. When you're thoroughly prepared, you know where the other side might be willing to give, what the grounds for a good compromise might be. Being well prepared is the key not just in negotiations but to a lot of life.

## HELPFUL CHILDHOOD MEMORY

LC: I don't think it was purposeful, but my parents deployed a very effective strategy with me, playing good cop and bad cop, with my mother being totally encouraging and supportive and my father holding up the world's highest expectations. If I came in second in a spelling bee, my mother would hug me and tell me I was wonderful, and my father would say, "Second? Second? Is that the best you can do?" So I would feel good about myself—and I would do better.

# RUTH SIMMONS

RUTH SIMMONS WAS BORN in a sharecropper's shack in Grapeland, Texas, one of twelve children. Her family's faith in her, the encouragement of key secondary-school teachers in Houston, and her belief in herself took her to Dillard University in New Orleans, where she earned a B.A. in 1967, and to Harvard, where she received a Ph.D. in 1973 in romance languages and literatures, for a study of francophone writers of Africa and the Caribbean. As vice provost of Princeton University in the 1980s, she wrote what became known as "The Simmons Report," a study of race relations at the university, which became a model for improvement of black-white interaction on campuses. Princeton president Harold Shapiro characterized her as someone who "doesn't lose her perspective, doesn't lose her capacity to listen, and . . . doesn't forget her principles." In 1995, Dr. Simmons became the first African American woman to lead an A-list college or university, Smith College, and six years later left for Brown University, where she became the first African American president of an Ivy League institution.

## IMPORTANT TRAIT FOR SUCCESS

RUTH SIMMONS: As a very young person, I had a commitment to learning. I was a voracious consumer of every type of learning, from literature to science to math. I found that once I got interested, I gained more energy from what I was learning; the accumulated knowledge made me feel more self-confident, especially coming from my background where my parents didn't have an education. Also, I grew up in an environment in which there were lots of questions about whether or not African Americans had the requisite intelligence to perform challenging tasks. I gained confidence and was willing to take some risks because of the education I was acquiring.

BIGGEST OBSTACLE

RS: Complicated social structures make it difficult to move in a straight line toward success. Everybody experiences this. Two steps forward, one step back. It was like that for many different reasons, some of them personal. For example, I became a mother early in my career and I had to learn how to deal with marriage and, later, parenting and yet continue to grow professionally, not sacrificing my career interests.

As a young wife, I made choices to follow my husband's career, so I had a very circuitous route to success.

I wish somebody had told me when I was a very young person that it doesn't matter how you go about it. That you can take the time for your children, reinvigorate your career after your children have gotten to be a certain age, and focus intensively on your work when your personal life allows. I would have felt a lot more comfortable coming along if I had understood that I wasn't doing anything different or unusual, and that success for women, or for any one individual, doesn't have to look like the success that other people have. It can be very different. It can be particular to you.

When I was coming along, I didn't have mentors who reassured me that the circuitous route was perfectly normal and acceptable. So I always felt that I was doing things that were a bit odd and offbeat.

Now, as I look around and I talk to others who have come through the same kind of experience, I recognize that, in fact, that's the way many women, in particular, achieved professional goals. In addition, you do learn from those detours, and sometimes it's the detours that make you more successful.

BEST PREPARATION FOR ROUGH-AND-TUMBLE OF LIFE

RS: First of all, being one of twelve children is a rough-and-tumble world. Being a part of a large family certainly helped me immensely, because you learn to be resilient when you're dealing with that many different personalities as you grow up. As a college president, I'm managing a variety of different human resource issues all the time. I'm working with young people who have vastly different concepts of what life is all about. Being able to understand that variety definitely comes from my childhood and the fact that it was something that we had to work out daily in our family.

In addition to that, I would say being a part of a large family, one learns conflict resolution; one learns patience. I like to think that I'm the patient person calming things down when everything is flying around at a high rate of speed and general hysteria ensues. That comes from the kind of environment I grew up in as a child. I think most of the time leaders are expected to retain their perspective and to be the anchor when the community is torn, when something tragic happens, when people are anxious.

I also think that mediation skills that leaders require today are extremely important. In my time as a university president, there have been many instances in which I've had to mediate among very passionate extreme positions, and I think the skill in doing that comes from many of the values and experiences that I had as a child. My studies later on reinforced those things, but in the end I have to say that it all started with my family circumstances.

BEST NEGOTIATING STRATEGY

RS: Usually with opposing sides, neither is willing to admit that there is value in a differing position. When I'm in such a difficult stalemate, I try to assume the part of the individuals in the dispute, giving voice to what they're trying to advance but in a form that allows others to see the reasonableness of their position, if that exists. If you can identify that, you can really bring people together much more quickly.

Most individuals who are involved in conflict want to win. They may represent people who are not present in the negotiations. They need to be able to go back to their supporters with a sense that they have accomplished something on their behalf. There are powerful motives for not conceding, and so, coming out of a negotiation, you want people to feel they have gotten something out of it. That they've been able to achieve something for the people that they represent and that their particular role on the issue is respected.

BEST ADVICE

RS: When I think of all the times in my life when I wanted to give up on something . . . in the end I remembered that at any given moment, circumstances that appear to be overwhelming can in a day's time or two days' time or a week's time or a year's time prove inconsequential. Holding on and working your way through a situation is probably the best advice I was given. No matter how difficult the challenge, if you're patient and you apply your intelligence and skill through it, you come out okay most of the time.

## ROSALYN YALOW

A BRILLIANT PHYSICS STUDENT at New York City's Hunter College, Rosalyn Sussman took a job as secretary to a Columbia Medical School biochemist after graduation because she thought that no good graduate program in physics would grant financial support to a woman. When the University of Illinois did offer her a teaching assistantship in physics, she started graduate studies in September 1941 as the only woman on the faculty of the university's College of Engineering (and the first since 1917). She married a fellow graduate student, Aaron Yalow, in 1943, completed her Ph.D. in nuclear physics in 1945, and returned to New York City to teach at Hunter College and do research, first at International Telephone and Telegraph (ITT) and, starting in 1947, at the Bronx Veterans Administration Hospital.

In 1950, Yalow and Dr. Solomon Berson began a series of joint research studies that culminated in their discovery of the radioimmunoassay (RIA) measurement technique in 1959. In her words, "RIA is now used to measure hundreds of substances of biologic interest in thousands of laboratories" all over the world. In 1977, Yalow was awarded the Nobel Prize for Physiology or Medicine. Berson had died in 1972, and in the Solomon A. Berson Research Laboratory that was named in his memory, Yalow trained many of today's leading researchers in clinical and investigative medicine. Among her many awards in addition to the Nobel Prize, Yalow has received the Albert Lasker Basic Medical Research Award. When the Bronx VA Hospital became affiliated with the Mount Sinai School of Medicine, she was named a Distinguished Service Professor there.

## IMPORTANT TRAIT FOR SUCCESS

ROSALYN YALOW: Perhaps the earliest memories I have are of being a stubborn, determined child. Through the years, my mother has told me that it was fortunate that I chose to do acceptable things, for if I had chosen otherwise no one could have deflected me from my path.

## BIGGEST OBSTACLE

RY: Since the work for which I later received the Nobel Prize contradicted what we then thought was known science, there was initial resistance to the idea of insulin antibody.

## BEST PREPARATION FOR ROUGH-AND-TUMBLE OF LIFE

RY: I received a great deal of support from some of my college professors. And I would not have been able to achieve what I did without the support and assistance of my husband, as well as the teamwork with Dr. Solomon Berson, with whom I collaborated from early in my investigative career until his death.

## BEST NEGOTIATING STRATEGY

RY: Be right, and be prepared to defend what's right.

## INSPIRATION

RY: Reading the biography of Madame Marie Curie by her daughter, which should be a must on the reading list of every young, aspiring female scientist.

## BEST ADVICE

RY: You can be whatever you decide to be.

# CHAPTER FOUR

# SAVING LIVES

IN MY EXPERIENCE in the Senate, foreign travels, and at home, one of the most extraordinary organizations I have observed is the Red Cross. Though the ICRC (its formal title is the International Committee of the Red Cross) didn't start in our country, it is associated with America, a symbol of our caring hearts and generosity of spirit. The Red Cross has evolved into an organization that responds to emergencies— war, natural catastrophes, epidemics—all over the world. It is a trusted neutral party that can examine prisoners of war and report to the world on their treatment and well-being.

I visited refugee camps in Macedonia in 1999. Ethnic Albanians had fled Kosovo to avoid ethnic cleansing—thousands of men, women, and children pouring into Macedonia, a tiny country with few resources. Almost as soon as the refugees began arriving, Catholic Charities and the Red Cross were on the scene, setting up tents and providing food for these poor displaced people. Many countries contributed to this humanitarian effort, as the United States and its allies tried to arrange a peace in Bosnia and Kosovo so that the region's Muslims could live in safety. (One note that made an impression on me: Israel was a major contributor to this refugee camp. They provided a tent with games and entertainment to keep the children occupied. I watched Muslim children singing songs as Israeli volunteers cared for them.)

I have visited towns ripped apart by tornadoes, floods, and hurricanes. Whenever disaster strikes, the Red Cross is there. As a neutral humanitarian organization, it can go anywhere—on the battlefield or off—to treat the wounded and injured and help people with basic survival needs when their homes are destroyed. Because it commands such credibility, the Red Cross has been chosen to monitor the condition of prisoners of war as mandated by the Third Geneva Convention of 1929. What organization examined Saddam Hussein after his capture and reported on his condition to the world? The Red Cross. It has bridged many a gap—assuring communication even between belligerents—because it is trusted by all sides.

This status is the result of its leadership in crises since the late nineteenth century. Its vision and mission were shared and furthered by Clara Barton, the founder of the American Red Cross.

## Clara Barton

IN TERMS OF CASUALTIES to U.S. citizens, the American Civil War was by far the costliest in our entire history: between 1861 and 1865 more than 600,000 soldiers on both sides of the conflict died in battle or from wounds suffered during the fighting. In just one battle, Antietam, in western Maryland on September 17, 1862, more than 23,000 Union and Confederate soldiers lost their lives, in what has come to be known as "the bloodiest day in American history."

The war had been anticipated for months before Fort Sumter was fired on in April 1861, but preparations for the fighting, for the defense of cities, and for care of the wounded were woefully inadequate. On

April 19, members of the Sixth Massachusetts Regiment were on a train headed for Washington, D.C., when they were attacked by a prosecessionist crowd in Baltimore. Three soldiers died, and when the train reached Washington, Clara Barton and her sister, Sally Vassall, pro-Union Massachusetts natives, were in the throng that came out to meet them. Since Washington was an overwhelmingly southern city, many more were jeering than cheering. Reacting to the crowd's hostility, Clara, then a clerk-copyist in the Patent Office, decided to do whatever she could to help and comfort the wounded and unnerved soldiers. There was no hospital, so Clara brought the worst cases to Sally Vassall's house. Makeshift arrangements were made to shelter the other troops, billeting them wherever space could be found, including the Capitol building. The next day, Clara returned to the Senate chamber to distribute food and other necessities to the troops. Then, locating the soldiers of the Sixth Massachusetts, some forty of whom had been her students when she was teaching school, she did her best to raise their spirits. She had one copy of the *Worcester Spy* with her, so she climbed into the president's chair and read them news of the war from their local paper.

Almost overnight, Washington was transformed from a sleepy southern town to a city of soldiers, with 75,000 troops camped out in the capital and surrounding areas. Not everyone liked the change, but it exhilarated Clara. To her father, at home in North Oxford, Massachusetts, she wrote: "I don't know how long it has been since my ear has been free from the roll of a drum, it is the music I sleep by, and I love it." She and Sally found the camps disease-ridden, the food terrible, and the soldiers poorly clothed, so they started bringing them homemade food and sewing kits. When word got around that Clara Barton was distributing packages to Union troops in Washington, soldiers' families and relief societies throughout the North sent food, clothing, and other supplies to Clara, for her to deliver to their sons and husbands or wherever it was needed. Within weeks, Clara had collected so many boxes and barrels that she was forced to move to larger quarters, where she stored them behind a partition—living "a kind of tent life," according to her friend Fanny Childs.

Constant rumors circulated that the Confederate army was planning to attack the capital, but Clara resolved not to flee unless the Union

troops retreated from the city. She wrote to her brother Stephen in
North Oxford, "I will remain here while anyone remains and do whatever comes to my hand. I may be compelled to face danger, but never
*fear* it, and while our soldiers can stand and *fight,* I can stand and feed
and nurse them." Clara, then thirty-nine, had never witnessed war's devastation and held romantic ideas of what battle was like. But in her letter
she expressed the credo that guided her throughout the war years and
thereafter—to bring care and comfort to the victims of man-made and
natural disasters. This credo would inspire her to devote more than ten
years to the cause of founding the American Red Cross, and the rest of
her life to establishing it as the essential American relief organization, in
war and peace.

The woman who earned the sobriquet "Angel of the Battlefield"
was an unlikely candidate for her larger-than-life role. The youngest of
five children, Clarissa Harlowe Barton was born on Christmas Day,
1821, in North Oxford, Massachusetts, to Stephen and Sarah Barton.
Ten years younger than Sally and born more than seventeen years after
her eldest sibling, Dorothea, Clara also had two brothers, Stephen and
David. Clara, never more than five feet tall and inclined to plumpness,
was an insecure child, but she was precocious and quick-witted and rapidly became the darling of her family, with a sense of entitlement that
may have been fed as much by her mother's impetuous, strong-willed
personality as by her father's good-heartedness. Sarah Stone was ten
years younger than Stephen Barton—and four months pregnant when
they married in 1804. Clara recalled that her mother "must have been
born believing in the full right of woman to all privileges and positions
which nature and justice accorded her. . . . When as a young woman I
heard the subject discussed it seemed simply ridiculous that any sensible
rational person should question it."

A milling and farming town on the French River, North Oxford was
originally settled by Huguenots. Clara's ancestors—the Barton, Stone,
and Learned families—moved there in the early eighteenth century, becoming farmers and sawmill operators. Samuel Barton, the original
family member in the area, moved to North Oxford from Salem, Massachusetts, after coming to the defense of one of the accused women in the
notorious witchcraft trials. Liberal in politics and religion, the Bartons

were active community leaders, although they were neither pious nor wealthy. Clara could not recall that her father had ever attended the local Universalist church, but he had helped to build it and was one of its officers. He was also a charitable man, who supported the local poor and endowed a building where indigent families were cared for.

The gifted Barton children continued the family tradition of service to the community. Dorothea—called Dolly—Sally, and Clara all took up teaching, and Stephen and his younger brother, David, took over the family mills and joined the ranks of North Oxford's leading businessmen. Stephen, following in his father's footsteps, concerned himself with the poor. After his marriage, he took a number of poor children into his own household, and he continued to play an active role in the local schools, as well as holding elective office and supporting improvements to the roads and other amenities.

Clara, the youngest Barton, benefited from her mature, accomplished siblings. Later in life she recalled that David taught her to ride, something she did skillfully throughout her life, and Stephen tutored her in arithmetic: "Multiplication, division, subtraction, halfs, quarters, and wholes, soon ceased to be a mystery, and no toy equaled my little slate." But she was also sometimes terrified by baffling events like her sister Dolly's mental breakdown and her mother's violent fits of temper, as when Sarah Barton took apart the cast-iron stove her husband had given her and threw the pieces into the pond because she preferred her fireplace oven. When, at the age of eighty-five, Clara wrote *The Story of My Childhood,* she claimed that "in the early years of my life, I remember nothing but fear."

Although Clara was bright, curious, and well liked, her extremely self-effacing nature worried family members, especially her mother. When the celebrated phrenologist L. N. Fowler lectured in North Oxford, Sarah Barton asked him to examine her youngest daughter. Through much of the nineteenth century, it was believed that individual character and personality could be understood by studying the shape of the skull. Whatever scientific merits phrenology possessed, Fowler's observations about Clara were prescient: "She will never assert herself for herself," he told the Bartons; "she will suffer wrong first, but for others she will be fearless." With respect to what Clara might do in the world, his advice was less remarkable: as soon as she was old enough, he said, she should become a teacher. "She has all the qualities of a teacher." There were, in any case, very few other vocations open to an educated young woman in the 1830s—for women without education, only factory work or domestic service—but Clara took Fowler's insights to heart. Looking back on her career many years later, she wrote: "Know thyself has taught me in any great crisis to put myself under my own feet; bury enmity, cast ambition to the winds, ignore complaint, despise retaliation, and stand erect in the consciousness of those higher qualities that made for the good of human kind, even though we may not clearly see the way."

Clara did teach school for ten years, and by all contemporary accounts was a great success in the classroom. It wasn't easy in those days for a woman to command her students' respect; female teachers were still viewed as less desirable than men, to be hired only if no qualified male teacher was available. This was still the case even after schools began to abandon the practice of having men teach in the winter and women in the summer when the men and older boys were busy with farmwork. A female teacher was seen as someone not to be taken seriously, much as mischievous students of a later era would bedevil their substitute teachers. Still a teenager herself and shorter than many of her students, Clara found that disruptive older boys at first challenged her authority, but not long after she started teaching at the local common (public) school, her gift for bold gestures paid off. Confronting a potential troublemaker, an unruly boy, she used tactics that would be condemned today but were acceptable in a nineteenth-century classroom. First, she tripped the boy with her riding crop, then spanked him with it until he apologized—to her and to his classmates.

After that dramatic performance, there were no more discipline problems in Miss Barton's classroom. In fact, she became an extremely popular teacher and was besieged with offers to teach in other towns. One of those early offers was less than flattering, because the school board proposed paying her a lower salary than a man would have received. Her response made clear where she stood on the question of the value of a woman's work versus that of a man: "I may sometimes be willing to teach for nothing, but if paid at all, I shall never do a man's work for less than a man's pay."

Throughout the 1840s, Clara taught at schools in North Oxford and the neighboring towns of Charlton and Millbury. The period was one of economic expansion for the area, and as new mills opened and hired more workers, the existing local schools were no longer adequate. In 1844, Clara conceived a plan to create a new system of district schools adequate to the needs of the larger population. At first, there was strong resistance—the citizenry objected that district schools would be expensive, the school buildings would be too far from where many students lived, and they would saddle the town with the cost of educating the children of the poor factory workers. With her brother Stephen's help, she managed to overcome the opposition.

The redistricting plan was Clara's, but when the proposal was put before a town meeting the following spring, the speech that she had written had to be read by a local mill owner, since women had neither voice nor vote in local politics. As Clara put it at the time, "I was nobody." After the plan was voted in, Clara worked with the redistricting board to plan the new schools. Then she focused on a second innovation to make education more accessible to the millworkers' children by putting a school inside one of the mills. In this one-room school, Clara taught seventy pupils, ranging in age from four to twenty-four. Somehow, she inspired them to tackle an ambitious curriculum that went far beyond basic numeracy and literacy to include algebra and bookkeeping, chemistry and natural science, ancient history, philosophy, and literature. To encourage students to work on literacy, she introduced dramatic readings. These quickly became immensely popular—not only with the students, but with the workers, who came to listen to the "concert readings" in large numbers.

Suddenly, in 1850, Clara decided to return to school herself. Just past twenty-nine, she left Massachusetts for the first time to attend the Clinton Liberal Institute, a Universalist school with 150 students in Clinton, New York. Clinton was coeducational, and Clara made a number of lifelong friends during her year there, including several men.

Older than her schoolmates by ten years or more, and secretive about her past, Clara stood apart from them. Frugal and determined to pay for her year at Clinton from her meager savings, she made an eccentric impression by eating just two meals a day and always wearing one of the two nearly identical green dresses that made up her wardrobe. Some came to believe that the color green had special meaning for her. Clara—reminiscing in a letter she wrote years later to Abby Barker, one of her closest Clinton friends—imagined another student describing the two of them as "Abby Barker and the strange girl in the green gown."

Clara was so intent on learning as much as possible at Clinton that she continually asked permission to overload her schedule with additional courses. One day, she recalled, Louise Barker, the principal, laughingly said to her, "Miss Barton, we have a few studies left; you had better take what there are, and we will say nothing about it." Barker, who must have known more of the details of Clara's life than others did, encouraged Samuel Ramsay, a mathematics instructor at Clinton, to take her horseback riding from time to time in order to get her away from her books. The young instructor and his mature student became close friends, and according to some biographers, Ramsay even proposed marriage.

Clara treasured her experiences—educational and social—at the Clinton Liberal Institute. The news from home, however, was less satisfying. In May 1851, Clara learned that her brother Stephen had been accused of "having a part in" the robbing of a bank in New York State, not far from Clinton. Although Stephen was never convicted, he and his brother, David, acquired reputations as sharp, aggressive businessmen. Suspicion lingered that he might have played a role in the robbery, and the Barton creditors started demanding to be repaid. Stephen never completely recovered from the damage to his reputation. In 1856, he moved to North Carolina, ostensibly for health reasons.

Two months after his indictment, Stephen was the bearer of even sadder news. "Our excellent mother is no more," he wrote in a letter to his sister. Clara had known that Sarah Barton was gravely ill, but the shock of her mother's death precipitated one of the fits of despondency that occasionally afflicted her at times of bereavement or when she had no clear sense of purpose or direction. In July 1851, Clara was afflicted by both of these at once. By the time Stephen's letter arrived, their mother had already been buried, and Clara had no one with whom she could share her grief. She was nearing the end of what had been an extraordinarily enriching year of study, but she was no closer to having a vocation than she had been before coming to Clinton. She did not want to resume her life as a teacher in a small-town common school.

Charles and Mary Norton had been two of Clara's closest friends at Clinton. Mary, a serious sixteen-year-old, looked up to the older Clara with a feeling approaching reverence. Charlie Norton, twenty-one and more ebullient, was one of Clara's admirers at the school. Back home in Hightstown, New Jersey, they wrote to invite Clara to visit them, and after two weeks the Nortons insisted that she stay. Knowing nothing of Clara's years of teaching experience, Richard Norton (father of Mary and Charles) asked her whether she would be interested in teaching at the school in neighboring Cedarville. She accepted and rapidly set about to transform a backward schoolroom, where the students had never progressed beyond spelling and rudimentary arithmetic, into "a tale of wonder," as one of the locals called it. Clara added subjects like geography, American history, and science, and within a month, students from other districts were coming to Cedarville.

Past thirty, Clara was at the time literally surrounded by suitors—from Charlie Norton and his older brothers to Edgar Ely, a bookish Hightstown lawyer—but apparently she was interested only in Joshua Ely, a farmer who lived near Philadelphia. Almost nothing is known about Ely or how Clara met him, but they carried on their relationship, chiefly by letter, from late summer or early fall of 1851 until March 1852. When Ely's letters stopped coming, Clara at first worried that he'd gotten sick, and in mid-April she went to confront him in person. On April 20, she recorded this bitter, melancholy entry in her diary: "Have kept no journal for a month or more had nothing to note as I had done nothing but some things have transpired in the time which are registered where they will never be effaced in my lifetime."

Without saying a word to anyone, she began to make plans to leave Hightstown, confiding to her diary: "I shall survive it all and go on working at some trifling unsatisfactory thing, and half paid at that." On May 25, the Nortons drove her to the train station, and said good-bye to her as if she were leaving on a brief vacation and would soon return. "I knew," she wrote, "that I would not." Then she boarded the train, but traveled only ten miles, to Bordentown, New Jersey.

Why Bordentown? Clara herself claimed not to be sure. Whatever her reasons, she revived her idea of establishing free schools in New Jersey, where they had never taken root as they had in Massachusetts. She convinced Peter Suydam, editor of the local paper and a school board member, to propose setting up a free school in Bordentown, to be promoted by the school board and housed in a building maintained with public funds. In return, she agreed to teach—without salary—for one year.

The board approved the experiment, renovations were started on an old one-room schoolhouse, the *Bordentown Register* published announcements, and notices of the opening of school in early July were posted all over town. A half-dozen boys turned up on the first day, and Clara, as she had done in Hightstown, played the charmer, telling stories about distant places and punctuating her tales by pointing to continents, oceans, and countries on the maps hung around the classroom. In the afternoon, she picked up where she had left off. "In that three hours until four o'clock, we traveled the world over" without ever opening a book, and when it was time to leave, Clara casually mentioned that she would return the next morning. When she arrived, twenty boys were waiting at the schoolhouse entrance, and by the end of the second week there were fifty-five. When word spread of how much students were learning and that there was no unruliness, girls started attending classes as well.

In short order, Bordentown's experiment with free public education was a success. At Clara's urging, the school board added a second classroom for fall 1852 and hired Fanny Childs, Clara's friend from North Oxford, to teach the lower grades. The two teachers were offered yearly salaries of $250, and a few months later the citizens of Bordentown voted to build a new school, at a cost of $4,000, to accommodate all six hundred of its school-age children. This buoyed Clara's spirits. "I have learned to think I have as good a right to live as any body and I will in spite of them," she told Fanny.

Success of this magnitude turned out to have a hidden cost for Clara, however, because of her sex. Before the much-expanded school opened in the fall of 1853, Clara discovered that a new head—a man— had been hired at $600 a year, while she and the other teachers were designated "female assistants." The new head, J. Kirby Burnham, was less qualified and experienced than Clara, but the all-male school board had decided that a woman couldn't manage a large school and faculty. Despite criticisms of Burnham's autocratic manner by most of the teaching staff, the board held firm, and Clara reacted as she frequently did when outmaneuvered. Her spirit broke, she lost her voice, and her health failed. In February 1854, convinced that the situation at the school was irreparable, she and Fanny Childs resigned their teaching posts and left Bordentown. Three months later Burnham was dismissed, but by then Clara and Fanny were living in Washington, D.C., where Clara had found work as a clerk-copyist in the Patent Office.

Clara owed this job to the intervention of Alexander DeWitt, U.S. congressman from her family's district in Massachusetts, and the liberal views of Charles Mason, commissioner of patents. Still, her situation, like that of the other female clerks, was uncomfortable. As women, they were required to work in separate quarters from the men, and still they were resented—especially Clara, who helped Mason uncover cases of fraud committed by some of the clerks. From Mason's perspective, she was an ideal employee: industrious—she copied over one thousand pages per month into a huge ledger—and loyal. But she was a woman and she was outspoken. In the 1856 presidential election, she supported John C. Frémont, the antislavery candidate (she couldn't vote, of course, but she could campaign), and at the same time, her congressional patron, Alexander DeWitt, lost his seat. After Charles Mason resigned as commissioner of patents, Clara was let go in mid-1857 and had to return to North Oxford with no prospects for the future.

This time, she remained in Massachusetts for more than two years, unable to find work and unsure of just what sort of work she should be doing. She no longer wanted to teach—"I have outgrown that, or that me," she wrote. Her frustration finally spilled out in a letter to her nephew Bernard Vassall in early 1860: "Were you in my place you would feel [resentment at being discriminated against as a woman] too, and wish and pine and fret in your cage as I do, and if the very gentlemen who *have* the *power* could only know for one twenty-four hours all that oppresses and gnaws at my peace, they could offer me something to do in accordance with my old habits and capabilities before I am a day older. But they will never know and I shall always be oppressed no doubt. . . . I should be 'perfectly happy' today if someone would tell me that my desk and salary were waiting for me—that once more I had something to do that *was* something."

Before the end of the year, Clara had her old job back at the Patent Office. What happened isn't clear; she vaguely referred to the machinations of "personal friends." The appointment, however, was designated as temporary, and Clara immediately set about to give it more permanency. Among the Massachusetts congressional delegation, she decided that Senator Henry Wilson was her most likely protector and arranged to meet him. Clara's cousin Elvira Stone, who knew the senator, wrote to him about her kinswoman, and shortly after the inauguration in March, Clara visited Wilson at the Capitol. They struck up an immediate friendship, and Wilson would be an important ally of Clara Barton for many years.

Clara wanted her job to be made permanent, to give her some security and also increase her income. She was paid 8¢ per word, so she was earning between $35 and $60 a month. She had good reason for optimism. The new commissioner of patents, D. P. Holloway, was said to like having women workers in the office, and Wilson had apparently responded to a negative comment about women by saying he believed "that it was the design of the Almighty that women should *exist,* or he never would have created them, although it is a scanty chance we give them."

Clara's spirits soared as soon as she felt secure in her job, and she started thinking—as she'd done throughout her life, whenever her own situation was on a firm footing—more about the welfare of friends, family, and even people she barely knew than about herself. First, she expressed the hope that it might now be easier for other women to get similar jobs—"I had just as lief they made an experiment of me as not, you know it does not hurt me to pioneer." One friend who knew her during this period commented on how naturally she tried to help everyone who approached her: "orphan children, deserted wives, destitute women, sick or unsuccessful relatives, men who had failed in business— all who were in want, or in trouble, and could claim the slightest acquaintance came to her for aid and were never repulsed." One of Clara's first beneficiaries was her cousin Elvira Stone, the postmistress of North Oxford, Massachusetts. When the new federal administration took office in March, there were efforts to replace Elvira with a male political appointee. Clara helped put an end to the talk by telling Wilson and Charles Summer, the other Massachusetts senator, that Elvira had done nothing wrong, "except that she is guilty of being a woman."

Clara's carefree Washington "honeymoon" was, of course, short-lived. Civil War fighting began in earnest on July 21, 1861, when the Army of the Potomac attacked Confederate troops in Manassas, Virginia, and was badly defeated. As the wounded soldiers returned to Washington, Clara immediately perceived how ill-prepared the army's medical services were, and how crucial the supplies that she had been collecting would be. Hospitals were hastily set up all over the city—there was even one in the Patent Office, where Clara worked—and Clara quickly gave out all the food and clothing, soap and bandages she had stockpiled over several months. To replenish her stores, she wrote to friends and relief groups, and had newspapers publish notices soliciting contributions (one, in the *Worcester Spy,* read "The cause is holy; do not neglect an opportunity to aid it").

When it came to supplying the soldiers' wants, Clara proved remarkably indulgent. An officer told her that what the troops most needed was tobacco, so Clara overcame her personal objections to tobacco use. As she wrote to Elvira Stone, "It is needless to say that I trust soon to be a good judge of the product as it has become an article of commerce with me. You would smile at the sight of the half yard slabs of plug lying this moment on my table waiting for Dr. Sidney's Basket of Whiskey to arrive to accompany it to Kalorama."

There were plenty of people ready to volunteer in Washington hospitals, but Clara realized that it made more sense to minister to the wounded as close to the battlefield as possible. Her inspiration actually came from the example of Almira Fales, her ex-landlady, who, operating completely on her own, managed to get onto the ships transporting the wounded back from the battle zones, or even to the front lines, to nurse and comfort the soldiers. In the early months of the war, however, Clara was still working at the Patent Office and had to remain in the city. (Later, she paid a substitute to take over her clerical duties.)

In February 1862, however, Clara returned to Massachusetts. Her father was dying. It was Stephen Barton's stories of serving in the North-west Territories under General "Mad Anthony" Wayne that had planted the first seeds of Clara's fascination with war. Now she told him of her desire to aid soldiers on the battlefield. Stephen Barton gave his daughter his blessing and his gold Masonic medal to wear as an amulet against harm, telling her to "seek and comfort the afflicted everywhere."

Captain Barton died on March 21. Clara stayed in Massachusetts long enough to put his estate in order and then started looking for a way to step up her war work. She wrote to Governor John Andrew, hoping to be attached to the Sixth Massachusetts Regiment. Andrew responded politely and promised to write a letter of recommendation, but the commander of the Massachusetts volunteers, General Ethan Allen Hitchcock, turned her request down, writing blandly: "I do not think at the present time Miss Barton had better undertake to go to Burnside's division to act as nurse." Most men considered women on the battlefield nuisances, not nurses. In her case, members of the medical corps also resented her stinging criticisms of their lack of supplies and preparedness.

Back in Washington, Clara persisted in her quest to put the supplies that overflowed her warehouses to use close to the actual fighting. She finally found a man who agreed with her approach: Colonel Daniel Rucker of the Quartermaster's Corps. Waiting in the long line of people who gathered in Rucker's office to ask about back pay for soldiers, seek compensation for property the army had seized or damaged, or drop off food and clothing for their husbands or sons, Clara shocked the colonel when she tearfully blurted out, "I want to go to the front." Mistaking her for another distraught wife or mother, he explained that there would soon be renewed fighting, and it would be dangerous to wander around unprotected in the war zone. He quickly changed his tune, however, when Clara told him that she had three warehouses of food and medical supplies but no way of getting them to where they were most urgently needed. Rucker assigned six wagons and drivers to her and issued her a pass requesting everyone from the secretary of war on down to let her go pretty much wherever she wanted "with such stores as she may wish to take for the comfort of the sick and wounded."

Now that Clara had a means of transport, she began to distribute supplies to hospitals in Washington, to former slaves who had gravitated to the Union army bases, and to the large army encampment outside

Fredericksburg, Virginia. Her first convoy reached Fredericksburg on August 3, 1862. Then she returned to Washington for another six wagonloads of supplies, but before she could bring them back, news reached the capital that the Battle of Cedar Mountain had begun. Clara decided to try to reach the front lines, if possible, using the passes she had already obtained for herself and her handful of assistants. The existing passes were intended only for passage to the relatively peaceful army encampment, but Clara knew that it would be impossible to obtain new ones now that a battle was in progress. She requested additional supplies to be sent by rail and set off for Culpeper, Virginia. What she witnessed at Culpeper defied description, even though the fighting had ended four days before she arrived on August 13. All available medical supplies had been exhausted, so the new materials Clara brought were desperately needed. James Dunn, an army surgeon from Pennsylvania, wrote to his wife about Clara's fortuitous appearance: "I thought that night, if heaven ever sent out a homely angel, she must be one her assistance was so timely."

Clara didn't stop to eat or sleep for the next two days and nights. She and a handful of assistants gave clothing to the wounded, many of whom lay unattended and unsheltered in the summer heat; cooked food and doled it out; prepared bandages and assisted the surgeons; and corralled volunteers to clean the makeshift field hospitals and the patients. Clara visited as many of the improvised hospitals as she could, including one that housed wounded Confederate prisoners of war. More neglected than the Union casualties, they at first took Clara for a Virginia woman and were astonished when they discovered that their benefactress was a Massachusetts native.

As Civil War battles went, Cedar Mountain was relatively modest— about 1,400 Union casualties and 1,300 on the Confederate side—but seeing the effects of war up close for the first time taught Clara a number of sobering lessons. The supplies she had brought with her were applauded by doctors and soldiers alike, but they had done much less good than Clara believed they would. Furthermore, after just one battle, her warehouses stood empty, and now that she had seen what war was like, she could hardly expect many people to follow her example. Years later, in an address to a group of women, she described her experience at

Cedar Mountain as "such a course of labor as I hope you may be spared from ever participating in, unless you have sinews of steel and nerves of iron." Clara was given to exaggerating for dramatic effect (she later claimed to have gone five days and nights without sleep at Cedar Mountain, though in fact she slept for twenty-four hours straight after her two sleepless days), but she herself wasn't sure how best to continue the effort she had begun in this battle. Back in Washington, she wrote a series of letters that she probably hoped to have published; in them she tried to bring home to people far from the fighting the horror and tragedy of the war. She redoubled her efforts to solicit contributions of supplies, and she may have thought that her patriotic, emotional letters would convince people to make material sacrifices to match those the soldiers were making.

Before Clara's supporters had time to replenish her supplies, however, the second battle of Bull Run, on August 29–30, forced her to rush back into the field. From Colonel Rucker and the Sanitary Commission (a private relief agency whose purpose was to augment the army's own medical supplies), she received a freight-car load of materials. On the morning of September 1, she and her four helpers climbed into the boxcar with their goods for the eight-mile trip to Fairfax Station. There, the sight of thousands of wounded soldiers greeted her. They lay on the hills surrounding the depot, waiting for a surgeon or the train that would take them to a hospital in Washington. Clara described her crew as "a little band of almost empty handed workers, literally by ourselves in the wild woods of Virginia with 3000 suffering men crowded upon the few acres within our reach." First, Clara tried to feed as many of the wounded as possible. Many had not even had a drink of water for two days, and there were so few surgeons available that medical attention was slow to arrive. Nor was there much to eat, but Clara improvised a sort of porridge made of wine, water, crushed biscuits, and brown sugar.

Away from the cooking fire, Clara and her crew dispensed bandages, clothing, and comfort to as many as they could. Again, her resources were inadequate to the carnage of the battle, but Dr. Dunn, who was also at Fairfax Station, wrote home of the surge of confidence the surgeons, "with nothing but our instruments, not even a bottle of wine," felt when the train pulled into the depot and "the first person on the platform was Miss Barton again to supply us with bandages, brandy, wine, prepared soup, jellies, meals, and every article that could be thought of."

Clara Barton's bandages and brandy, however, were no match for the damage done by bullets and bayonets. The army's lack of well-organized hospitals—in the field or behind the lines—limited what could be done to save lives or restore the health of the wounded. There was no ambulance corps; rescue work was left to the troops and often had to wait until after the fighting subsided. What medical attention was available was compromised by everything from lack of doctors to unhygienic conditions to an almost total absence of drugs for treating infection or killing pain.

Clara realized that the odds were heavily stacked against those who struggled to save lives in the midst of these deadly battles, but her conviction that she was doing the right thing only increased as one battle followed the other. She regretted that she had hesitated for the first year of the war before finding a way to the front, and condemned "the folly or wickedness of remaining quietly at home. . . . I know I should *never leave a wounded* man there if I knew it, though I were taken prisoner forty times." In fact, she was often among the last to retreat from the advancing Confederate army.

During August and September 1861, Clara again distributed supplies, nursed the wounded, assisted in surgeries, cooked food, and fed and comforted the wounded at the field hospitals in Harpers Ferry and Antietam. At Antietam, she even removed a bullet from the face of a young soldier and was as proud of her surgical skill and courage as she was of the patient's stoicism. Among the injured she found another soldier who had been wounded in the chest but refused to allow the surgeons to help. When Clara approached, the soldier took her into her confidence, revealing that she was a woman named Mary Galloway. Clara somehow managed to dress her wound and also safeguard her secret, helped her find her lover, and learned, after the war, that the couple had named their first child Clara.

After contracting typhoid fever in the fall, Clara went back to Washington to recuperate. By December, she was back in the field in Fredericksburg, Virginia, and then was sent to Hilton Head, South Carolina, where Union forces were preparing to attack Charleston. There, where her brother David was assigned to the Quartermaster's Corps, she met Colonel John Elwell, a married officer from Ohio, with whom she developed a lifelong friendship.

In 1862, cracks began to appear in Clara's relationship with the army establishment. As long as there were no alternatives to her small, independent operation, it was often applauded and always appreciated. But with other nursing and supply options now available, officers who had chafed at her vocal criticisms of the army's inefficiency and her privileged access to powerful people and supplies began to react. She worked as she was accustomed to during the early stages of the South Carolina siege, but she was soon told that she would henceforth be doing her work at the hospital in Beaufort, far from the fighting.

Clara's unhappiness at being prevented from working at the front and other personal and professional setbacks had the effect on her that such frustrations often did: a deep, almost suicidal depression. One of Clara's mainstays in the field throughout the war, Rev. Welles, died; her job at the Patent Office was in jeopardy; she was distressed by her enforced separation from her brother and from Colonel Elwell (though by this time Elwell's wife had joined him in Hilton Head); and she felt threatened by Dorothea Dix's growing success in integrating the Department of Nursing with the army medical services. Clara's diary entry for April 19 reads, in part: "I can not raise my spirits. The old temptation to go from the world. I think it will come to that some day."

Clara's spirits improved after Ulysses Grant took over from George McLellan as general of the Army of the Potomac and the tide of the war turned in the Union's favor. Fortuitously, Grant's strategy—to put pressure on the Confederate army itself rather than focus on capturing key cities—revived the need for Clara's unique services, because high casualties inevitably accompanied the new military tactics. Other factors also made Clara's style of nursing essential, at least temporarily. After the battle at Spotsylvania Court House, for example, heavy rains created a sea of mud that immobilized the ambulance wagons when they attempted to transport wounded soldiers behind the lines. Back in nearby Fredericksburg, Clara enjoyed another victory over the Union army brass, albeit one that increased their resentment of her: When she learned that the officers had failed to order the quartering of wounded soldiers in the elegant private homes near the battlefield, on the grounds that the soldiers were too dirty, she complained to her friend Henry Wilson in Washington. The senator immediately threatened to send an investigating team to Fredericksburg if the War Department failed to improve medical care for the wounded, and the army issued the orders.

One of Clara's reports from the next major battle, at Cold Harbor, gives a graphic sense of her working style—an uninterrupted mix of catering, mothering, nursing, and social work. She was responsible for nursing at a field hospital under the command of General Benjamin Butler, a Massachusetts officer Clara knew through Henry Wilson. Dealing with crisis exhilarated her. On a day like many others, she wrote, "I have had a barrel of applesauce made today and given out every bit of it with my own hands. I have cooked ten dozen eggs, made cracker toast, corn starch blanc mange, milk punch, arrowroot, washed hands and faces, put ice on hot heads, mustard on cold feet, written six soldiers' letters home, stood beside three death beds . . . now at the hour of midnight I am too sleepy and stupid to write a totally readable scrap. It has been a long day, and mercury is at something over a hundred and no breeze."

In this brief passage, Clara's passion and energy are palpable, as is her willingness to do anything, however humble, that is useful and gives comfort. With Butler's protection, she was safe, and even managed to extricate her brother Stephen from a risk of prosecution for trading cotton for medicine in violation of the North's blockade of southern ports. Soon afterward, an ailing Stephen was brought north to their sister Sally Vassall's house in Washington, the war ended, and Butler was relieved of his command. Once again Clara's fortunes—and her spirits—fell. Stephen's death a few weeks later, followed by that of Clara's young nephew Irving Vassall (who suffered from chronic tuberculosis), only deepened her sense of personal crisis.

Clara's style of nursing, grounded in the emergencies that follow battle and associated in her mind with the effort to preserve the Union, could not easily be adapted to peacetime. Fortuitously, she hit upon the idea of creating a missing soldiers' bureau, and through Henry Wilson's intervention received a commission from President Lincoln. His brief note, written just a month before his assassination, read:

*To the friends of Missing Persons:*
    *Miss Clara Barton has kindly offered to search for missing prisoners of war. Please address her at Annapolis, giving her the name, regiment, and company of any missing prisoners.*

Clara's plan was to help reunite former prisoners of war with their families, or to ascertain the fates of those who had died. At the time she and her staff of perhaps a dozen volunteers set up the Office of Missing Men in Annapolis, she probably didn't realize that she had set herself an impossible task. Only about half the Union dead had been identified; as many as 200,000 lay in unmarked graves in cemeteries that dotted the landscape from Pennsylvania to Georgia. A small team, no matter how dedicated, could never hope to match more than a handful of the letters from relatives to the hundreds of thousands of veterans, living and dead.

The government funded the operations of the Office of Missing Men, but Clara never drew a salary as its director and—as she often did—she spent her own money to keep the office running. In a matter of months, inquiries to the office all but ceased to arrive, and Clara once more looked for a way to support herself and also keep the office open as a shoestring operation. Friends encouraged her to go on the lecture circuit with her Civil War stories—"Tell the world as you told me of the sufferings of our brave boys in blue," Frances Gage advised. In fact, Clara's window onto the war was unusual by any measure and unique among women. With talks titled "Work and Incidents of War," "How the Republic Was Saved, or War without the Tinsel," and "Scenes on the Battlefield," to name several, the lecture series was immensely popular and lucrative. She visited towns and cities throughout the East and Midwest, where she entertained admiring audiences who agreed with her pro-Union politics, even if they didn't always concur with her harsh criticisms of the army. Clara's gift for the dramatic phrase and gesture made her a success at the lectern. Her fame as "the American Florence Nightingale" attracted large crowds, and her popularity on the lecture circuit added to her celebrity status. After two years of touring, however, she collapsed. Late in 1868, just before an engagement in Portland, Maine, she lost her voice and returned to Washington to recover. She submitted her final report on the Office of Missing Men to Congress and ceased operations in the process, bringing the Civil War chapter of her life to its symbolic end.

To convalesce, she made a trip to Europe in 1869. There, she had her first encounter with the organization with which her name became inextricably linked and that she would employ to change the way Americans think about human suffering and the role of relief work. The existence of the International Committee of the Red Cross was itself the product of a series of accidents. Ten years before Clara made her trip to Europe, Jean Henri Dunant, a Swiss banker, happened to witness the Battle of Solferino, a bloody clash of the Italian Risorgimento (Italy's war of independence) that resulted in 40,000 casualties on the Italian and Austrian sides. Dunant's memoir of his experiences, *Un souvenir de Solferino,* deeply affected another Genevan, Gustave Moynier, who organized an international meeting in 1864, where the Geneva Convention for the Amelioration of the Condition of the Wounded and Sick Armies in the Field was endorsed by twelve nations. Charles S. F. Bowles of the U.S. Sanitary Commission attended the meeting as an observer, but the United States made no move to ratify the convention. By the time of Clara's trip, the number of signatory nations had risen to thirty-two.

Clara had never heard of the International Red Cross and knew nothing about the details of the convention, which established for the first time the neutrality of civilian volunteers performing medical work in battle zones and mandated humane treatment of wounded soldiers. The Geneva Conventions (substantially expanded between 1899 and 1977) continue to define standards of conduct for treatment of the wounded, prisoners of war, and civilians during wars. The familiar Red Cross symbol—a red cross on a white ground—was simply the Swiss flag with the color scheme reversed.

Louis Appia had been a doctor at a hospital near Solferino in 1859; he knew Clara's Civil War reputation and hoped that she would become the IRC's standard-bearer in the campaign to bring the United States into the fold. As soon as Clara read the materials about the IRC that Appia gave her, she was persuaded that the United States should ratify the convention. She returned to the United States in 1873, but she suffered a setback the following year when her sister Sally died, and she did not return to Washington until 1877. As soon as she did, as the IRC's sole American representative, she began the work of selling the Red Cross idea to President Rutherford B. Hayes and other powerful figures in the capital. Clara wrote a pamphlet, *The Red Cross of the Geneva Convention: What It Is,* which explained that the Red Cross was humanitarian, not political; that each national organization was independent and self-governing; that its centralized operations guaranteed its preparedness for emergencies and its neutrality in war; and that it was as well suited to providing relief in peacetime—in emergencies like plagues, fires, and floods—as in war.

President Hayes and the members of his cabinet evinced little interest in associating with the International Red Cross, so while Clara waited for the political climate to change, she made efforts to cultivate support elsewhere. One group she knew she could count on was the Grand Army of the Republic, the organization of Civil War veterans, whose members included Generals John Logan, Ben Butler, Phil Sheridan, and James Garfield (who succeeded Hayes as president in 1881). By the time she met with President Garfield after his inauguration in March 1881, she had also lined up the support of a number of important newspaper editors and reporters. The new president favored establishing an American Red Cross organization. James G. Blaine, secretary of state, assured Clara that the Geneva Convention was not in conflict with the Monroe Doctrine—"The Monroe doctrine was not made to ward off humanity," he told her—and offered to write to Gustave Moynier personally to assure him of American support. When Clara gently reminded him that the convention, as a treaty, required ratification by the Senate, he promised her that "if it needed the action of the Senate, that could be had."

In fact, by this time, there was little *political* opposition to the establishment of an American Red Cross. The lingering resistance was more personal. A rival relief group, the Women's National Relief Association, counted Hannah Shepard and Fanny Atwater, former devoted protégées of Clara Barton, among its leaders. Shepard and Atwater had broken with Clara out of exasperation with her autocratic style of management and her reluctance to delegate authority or share credit for accomplishments that depended upon collective effort. Shepard, a journalist, wrote articles criticizing Clara, promoting the WNRA (known as the Blue Anchor, after its symbol) as better organized and run, and suggesting that it could easily add the Red Cross emblem to its own. Unlike the Red Cross, which was short of funds, the Blue Anchor had the financial backing of a number of well-heeled benefactors, including the politically influential Mabel Boardman.

Clara protected her turf by starting a drive to found local Red Cross chapters, to give the new organization a physical existence to match its legal one. The first chapter was in Dansville, New York, where Clara had moved after Sally Vassall's death; others soon followed in Syracuse and Rochester. She also expanded her earlier Red Cross pamphlet, in order to make Americans more aware of what the organization stood for. What most helped to imprint the Red Cross in the minds of people around the country, however, were natural disasters, especially those that occurred within the nation's borders, where the Red Cross was able to demonstrate its capacity for delivering relief. Starting with a forest fire in Michigan in September 1881, the Red Cross became a visible presence in one emergency after another, and in its wake it left a trail of goodwill, grateful beneficiaries, new local chapters, and glowing newspaper reports.

The disasters were natural, but Clara shrewdly exploited the occasions to polish the image of her fledgling organization. In the Michigan fire, for example, where five hundred people lost their lives, Clara collected only modest gratuities of cash, clothing, bedding, and tools, but she sent Mark Bunnell, son of the editor of the Dansville newspaper, to distribute them. Bunnell was joined there by Julian Hubbell, a young man who had made a pilgrimage to Dansville just to meet Clara, attended medical school in Michigan at her suggestion, and then became the most indispensable field agent of the American Red Cross, directing the distribution of supplies and aid in every major relief effort. Although local Michigan groups made a much greater contribution to the recovery effort, the Red Cross garnered excellent publicity. The fire underscored the need for a single organization to take charge in emergencies of this sort—and Clara drove home her point that the Red Cross was the very model of that organization.

As had always been her habit, Clara had decided what the Red Cross ought to do in the Michigan fire without consulting or even informing the organization's board until after she had acted. To make amends, she wrote a letter of apology, but in truth she was unrepentant. The institutional structure required by an entity such as the Red Cross was becoming was anathema to Clara's nature. The very qualities that made her so fearless an innovator during the Civil War—willing, even eager, to take risks where others couldn't even see that it was possible to help—also made her incapable of the consultation and compromise that collective action demands.

Wherever the Red Cross went, its reputation grew. It served as one of the organizations—not always the only one—capable of delivering federal relief funds and materials in emergencies. The military began to view the Red Cross as a collaborator, not a competitor, in dealing with disasters; and the American public started to think of the Red Cross as *the* relief organization. For example, when the Mississippi River flooded in 1882, contributions to the Red Cross amounted to $8,000; two years later, the response to the Ohio Valley flood disaster reached $175,000. The 1884 floods were much more severe, but the difference was more a measure of the Red Cross's new stature than of the severity of the crisis. In both floods, the Red Cross used the rivers as its highways, chartering riverboats to reach out-of-the-way places long before the floodwaters subsided, which cut the time it took for people to put their homes and their lives back together again. All along the path the Red Cross traveled, new Red Cross chapters were founded—in Cincinnati, Louisville, St. Louis, New Orleans, Vicksburg, and Natchez. The embrace of the Red Cross in places like Louisiana and Mississippi was crucial to its growth into a truly national entity, because Clara Barton, who symbolized the American Red Cross, was still widely thought of in the South as nurse to the Union.

It was President Chester Alan Arthur who signed the Geneva Convention on March 1, 1882, after the Senate ratified it. President Garfield had died the previous September, assassinated by a frustrated jobseeker. Clara's persistence had been largely responsible for the public's shift from ignorance and indifference to enthusiastic endorsement. Just when she should have been focusing on developing the American Red Cross as an organization, however, she slipped off in the spring of 1883 to serve as superintendent of the Massachusetts women's prison in Sherburn. Her old friend and benefactor from the Civil War, Benjamin Butler, now the Massachusetts governor, talked her into taking the job—for just six months, Clara insisted—by promising to lobby President Arthur to grant federal funds to the American Red Cross.

When the Third International Conference of the Red Cross was held in Geneva in 1884, Clara hesitated to make the trip, out of concern about her health, but Secretary of State Frederick T. Frelinghuysen insisted that she was the only person who could represent the United States. In fact, Clara was the only *woman* officially representing any country at the conference, and she was also the first woman ever to serve as an American diplomatic representative. The meeting was a personal triumph for Clara; she was applauded everywhere she appeared, and doted on by her friends Moynier and Appia. It was also a political boon for the United States. The so-called American Amendment—which expanded the mandate of the Red Cross to include peacetime as well as military emergencies—was accepted.

Back home, natural disasters continued to test the ability of the Red Cross to respond quickly and appropriately. In the days before instant communication, it was sometimes difficult to gauge the severity of an emergency on the basis of early reports, or to monitor how effectively relief was being administered. Thus an outbreak of yellow fever in Florida turned into a public health and public relations disaster for Clara and the Red Cross when she was unable to oversee the operations herself—because of the risk of contagion—and her appointed representative botched the relief effort. Then in 1889, Clara and Julian Hubbell mistrusted initial casualty reports from the Johnstown flood, when the truth turned out to be much worse: 3,000 people—one-tenth of the population of the city—died when an earthwork dam collapsed and floodwaters thirty feet high poured through the narrow Conemaugh River valley. That the tragedy was in a sense man-made (the dam, built to create an artificial lake for the use of wealthy Pittsburgh businessmen wasn't strong enough to withstand heavy spring rains) only served to heighten the sense of loss. Clara's first impressions of Johnstown draw an indelible picture: "I cannot lose the memory of that first walk on the first day. The wading in the mud, the climbing over engines, cars, heaps of iron rollers, broken timbers, wrecks of houses, bent railroad tracks, tangled piles of iron wire, bands of workmen, squads of military—the getting around of bodies of dead animals and often people being borne away. The smoldering fires and the drizzling rain."

In the end, however, the Red Cross spent five months in Johnstown and helped more than 20,000 people rebuild their lives and their city. To shelter the large numbers of people whose houses had been destroyed, the Red Cross constructed three large frame buildings, using lumber donated by citizens in Illinois and Iowa. When Pennsylvania governor James Addams Beaver wrote a statement of gratitude to Clara, he mentioned that she—nearing seventy—was one of the first to come to Johnstown's aid. What made the greatest impression, however, was *how* she made her contribution: "She made her own organization for relief work in every form, disposing of the large resources under her control with such wisdom and tenderness that the charity of the RC had no sting, and its recipients are not Miss Barton's dependents, but her friends."

Clara's gift for seeing the individual lives in large-scale disasters was the other side of the coin of her much-criticized inability to delegate, to plan, and to organize. Several years later, when the Sea Islands on the coast of South Carolina were devastated by a hurricane, she was determined to help the residents recover, although the Red Cross lacked the necessary funds, and neither the federal nor the state legislature voted relief for the area. Clara had spent time on the islands during the Civil War, and she felt a strong personal bond with the residents, all former slaves and their descendants. With a mere $30,000 in contributions, she managed to cobble together a relief program, starting with food and clothing, and then brought in medical personnel and supplies to cure the cases of malaria and dysentery that spread throughout the region.

The argument over whether Clara was capable of directing the organization she had brought into existence would never be settled. Even after the federal government bestowed official recognition on the American Red Cross by enacting the law incorporating it in 1900, that gesture entailed legal responsibilities—such as reports on field activities and detailed accounting—that Clara found constricting. Nearly seventy-nine, she tendered her resignation as president—and was immediately re-elected anyway. To preserve her autonomy, she got rid of the board of control and replaced it with a less powerful board of directors. She objected to moving the national headquarters to New York City, closer to wealthy benefactors but away from her Washington home. And she tried to ignore the powerful—and rich—local chapters in Philadelphia and New York, whose wealthy members wanted a voice in the running of the Red Cross in return for their financial support.

Despite her advancing age, Clara was able to meet the challenge of a severe natural disaster more easily than she could the less familiar political infighting that was undermining her control of the growing organization. When Galveston, Texas, was struck by a hurricane and tidal wave in 1900, she rushed to its aid. In terms of destruction, this was the worst nonmilitary crisis the Red Cross had ever confronted. In fact, it is still today the gravest natural disaster ever recorded in the United States. The $120,000 the organization had for relief work was woefully inadequate. Clara recorded her first impressions of the city in *A Story of the Red Cross:* "The uncoffined dead of a fifth of a city [6,000 had died] lay there. The lifeless bodies festering in the glaring heat of a September sun told only too fatally what that meant to that portion of the city left alive. The streets were well-nigh impassable, the animals largely drowned, the working force of men diminished, dazed, and homeless. The men who had been the fathers of the city, its business and its wealth, looked on aghast at their overwhelmed possessions, ruined homes, and, worse than all, mourned their own dead."

Not only did Clara, nearing eighty, insist on going personally to Galveston, but city leaders later stated that her presence had inspired them to rebuild. One reason may have been that Clara could often make just the right gesture to restore the faith of disaster victims in their power to put their lives back together. In Galveston, the symbolic act of rebirth may have been the planting of one million strawberry plants that Clara had shipped to local farmers. Planting and harvesting the strawberry crop became a sign of Galveston's recovery.

Such triumphs were real, but they merely postponed the day of reckoning, when Clara would have to yield so that a more modern Red Cross could come into existence. Before facing the growing discontent with her leadership, she made one last grand tour as the first lady of disaster relief. At the Seventh International Red Cross Conference in St. Petersburg in 1902, the czar awarded her the Decoration of the Empire, for the aid the Red Cross provided during the Russian famine of 1892.

At home, Clara confronted accusations of financial mismanagement. The charges were dismissed, but the dissension that had brought the American Red Cross and its only begetter to this impasse meant the end of Clara's formal relationship with the organization that even today is more closely associated with her than with any other American, living or dead. Clara lived for another ten years, surrounded by family and friends, but isolated from the institution she had created.

## Women of Today

CLARA BARTON had a vision for the American Red Cross to save lives on the battlefield and in natural disasters. She fought hard for the organization to be preeminent in this endeavor. She succeeded and it has grown beyond even her expectations.

A century later, women are still breaking ground in the health-care field. Elizabeth Dole, now a U.S. senator, is only the second woman, after Clara Barton, to serve as president of the American Red Cross. She expanded it into a global presence.

Dr. Bernadine Healy also headed the American Red Cross and was the first woman to head the most important health-research agency in the United States, the National Institutes of Health.

Dr. Antonia Novello was the first woman, and first Hispanic American, to hold the position of surgeon general, the number one official on general health matters in the United States, and was in charge of the U.S. Public Health Service.

### ELIZABETH DOLE

ELIZABETH HANFORD DOLE was elected to the United States Senate from North Carolina in 2002, continuing a public-service career that has spanned nearly four decades. A native of Salisbury, North Carolina, Mrs. Dole received her undergraduate degree from Duke University and holds both a master's degree in education and government and a law degree from Harvard University.

After serving as deputy director of the White House Office of Consumer Affairs in the Nixon administration, Mrs. Dole was appointed as a member of the Federal Trade Commission, serving there from 1973–79. From 1981–83, she served in the Reagan administration as assistant to the president for public liaison. From 1983–87, she served as secretary of transportation, the first woman in history to hold that position. She joined the George H.W. Bush administration as secretary of labor from 1989–90. From 1991–98, Mrs. Dole served as president of the American Red Cross, the world's largest humanitarian organization. Mrs. Dole is married to former senator Bob Dole, who represented Kansas in Congress from 1960–96. Bob Dole served as the majority leader of the Senate, and was the Republican nominee for president in 1996.

## IMPORTANT TRAIT FOR SUCCESS

ELIZABETH DOLE: During my public-service career I have had the privilege of working with many remarkable and successful men and women. There are three traits that I have seen again and again in these individuals.

First, integrity. (There are a lot of things in life over which we have no control, however, integrity is one area over which each of us has 100 percent control.) If you are to succeed in Washington, D.C.—or in life—then your word must be your bond. The second, a passion for what you do. When it comes from the heart, you apply great energy to the tasks and that tends to drive you forward, opening new opportunities. The third trait is perseverance. Some issues clearly are going to require a marathon and not a sprint.

Let me give an example. As secretary of transportation, I determined that an expensive aberration should be ended: Uncle Sam should not operate a pair of airports, Washington National and Dulles International. Deficits, belt tightening, and limited federal funding were stalling much needed modernization. The gateway to the capital of the free world was embarrassingly shabby. Why not move them off the federal dole so that these airports could get revenue bonds?

My husband, then the Senate Republican leader, said it could not be done. Administrations of both parties, he told me in "pillow talk," had attempted eight times since 1949 to move National and Dulles airports out of the federal government, but the legislation had never come out of committee in either the House of Representatives or the Senate. The gauntlet, in my view, had been thrown down! Three years later, the legislation not only came out of committee but passed both houses of Congress and was signed into law by President Reagan. How? Through coalition-building: a coalition of airport users, CEOs of airlines, key congressmen and senators, the governor of Virginia, and the mayor of the District of Columbia. Together we persevered over three long years using persuasion, reason, and old-fashioned horse trading. P.S. Enjoy the beautiful new airport when you fly into D.C.!

BIGGEST OBSTACLE

ED: I began my career at a time when women in policy-making positions at the highest levels of government were very rare. Indeed, there were many times early in my career when I looked around the meeting table and realized that I was the only woman there. I recall in the early 1970s, while I was working in the White House Office of Consumer Affairs and hurrying to a downtown Washington, D.C., club for a meeting that the doorman stopped me at the entrance and told me I wasn't allowed in the club. I explained that my name was Elizabeth Hanford and I was there to meet some attorneys and businessmen who had flown in from Cleveland, Ohio, for the meeting. "I'm sorry, ma'am," the doorman said. "I don't care if you're *Queen* Elizabeth, you're still not coming in. Women are not permitted in this club."

Thankfully, Washington, D.C., and our society have come a long way since then, but we still have a way to go before we remove every last vestige of discrimination from the American workplace.

BEST PREPARATION FOR ROUGH-AND-TUMBLE OF LIFE

ED: I will never forget the time when President Reagan and I were sitting alone in a holding room prior to a speech he was to give. I said, "Mr. President, you have the weight of the world on your shoulders, yet you are always so kind and so gracious. How do you do it?" He sat back and said, "Well, Elizabeth, when I was governor of California, it seemed that each morning began with someone standing before my desk describing yet another disaster. I had the urge to look over my shoulder for someone I could pass the problem to. The feeling of stress became almost unbearable. One day I realized I was looking in the wrong direction. I looked up instead of back. I'm still looking up. I don't think I could face one more day in this office if I didn't know I could ask God's help and it would be given." I couldn't agree more. Life is not just a few years to spend on self-indulgence and career advancement. It's a privilege, a responsibility, a stewardship to be lived according to a much higher calling—God's calling. This alone gives true meaning to life.

## BEST NEGOTIATING STRATEGY

ED: First and foremost, you need to be *willing* to negotiate. There are some in Washington, D.C., who think that negotiating and looking for common ground is a sign of weakness. Nothing could be further from the truth. Before going into a negotiation, I always have my arguments lined up, but I am also very willing to listen patiently to the other side, and I am willing to work to find middle ground. If you define success as achieving 100 percent of what you want, then victories will be few and far between. As Ronald Reagan used to say, "Get 80 percent, if you can. You can always go back and get the other 20 percent later." More often than not, a good result comes only when everybody gives up a little something.

## BEST ADVICE

ED: Shortly before I became president of the American Red Cross, my mother reminded me that she had served as a Red Cross volunteer during World War II, and she recalled, "Nothing I ever did made me feel so important."

I share that story often with young people and urge them to search until they find something—whether it be in the workplace or in the home—that fills them with a sense of mission, where they can make a difference, a positive difference in the lives of others, causing them to say, "Nothing I ever did made me feel so important." I consider myself very fortunate to have found my mission field in the public-service arena.

## BERNADINE HEALY

BERNADINE HEALY succeeded Elizabeth Dole as president of the American Red Cross in 1999. In her administrative roles, Dr. Healy, a Harvard-trained cardiologist and former professor of medicine at Johns Hopkins Medical School, focused on policy and research issues affecting women and on reversing the unstated but widespread bias against women in medical research. For example, in the late 1980s, knowing that "coronary heart disease is also a woman's disease, not a man's disease in disguise," she initiated a successful and long-lasting nationwide campaign, Women and Heart Disease, which was the centerpiece of her term as president of the American Heart Association. As director of the NIH, she created the sixteen-year-long, $700 million Women's Health Initiative, often called the "mother of all clinical trials." The WHI was the largest clinical research study known to women at the time. With much still ahead, the WHI has already radically changed our approach to key women's health practices like hormone replacement therapy. After retiring from the Red Cross, Dr. Healy became a columnist and senior writer on health and medicine at *U.S. News & World Report.*

### IMPORTANT TRAIT FOR SUCCESS

BERNADINE HEALY: I think it is what I would call an intellectual fearlessness with regard to knowledge or ideas and new ways of doing things. I'm appropriately fearful of physical threats, but when it comes to the intellectual domain, I have a practical ability to assess situations freshly, listen carefully to critical thinking, and—the next important trait—the courage to take action if it is needed. These traits are important in one's personal and professional life. As for leading organizations, you always have to be imagining better ways of doing things, and unless you're intellectually fearless, you don't allow yourself to wander in those new and often threatening territories.

## BIGGEST OBSTACLE

BH: I think that if you're straightforward and are able to openly lay out what you believe and propose for others to understand, criticize, modify, or accept, it can work wonders in building trust and getting things done. But it can be an obstacle, too. It's sometimes threatening, especially if change is involved, and in the political world—despite its spoken allegiance to "transparency"—it can be folly. Surely environment matters. In academic circles such openness works well, particularly after one has tenure. In medicine it's essential. In a heavily entrenched or bureaucratic world, or in an environment that is highly charged with rigid ideology, or even skulduggery, such openness can be a huge obstacle to getting what you need to get done. Sometimes a little guile is good and I don't do guile very well.

## BEST PREPARATION FOR ROUGH-AND-TUMBLE OF LIFE

BH: My genes and my upbringing. But upbringing first: I grew up in Queens, New York, in a dream-driven Irish Catholic family that lived in the midst of a small and very kind Italian immigrant neighborhood. I was proud of our "block." We shared the belief that we were lucky to live there, to be in America, and for Thirty-ninth Street to be the springboard for almost anything we wanted to do or be. There, I gained a lot of grit and an appreciation of the fact that you don't win every time, but you stay in the game if you believe in it. You sometimes get a few scratches when you grow up on the concrete pavements of New York, but with the spiritual and emotional support that came from our tight-knit families, we learned a lot about hard work, courage, and faith in tomorrow. And I never for a moment forget where I came from.

## BEST NEGOTIATING STRATEGY

BH: Affirm, don't deny. In any negotiation, by definition, you're going to disagree, but if you are going to get anywhere, you have to rally around the positive. And hopefully that lays out a higher common ground that is beyond both parties. If you pile up enough you can affirm, it's easier to then come to agreement or even a nondestructive standstill on the negatives. In general, deny no more than you need to, and avoid the irreconcilable disagreements until you come to terms with the best of what you can both affirm.

### HELPFUL CHILDHOOD MEMORY

BH: Of honest parents who worked very hard. You achieve nothing without hard work, and without integrity, what you achieve has no value. The only way the fruits of your labor have meaning is if they are obtained the right way.

### BEST ADVICE

BH: You never get more than you dream for, so you better have big dreams both for yourself and for those that you are leading.

## ANTONIA NOVELLO

BEFORE HER APPOINTMENT as surgeon general, Dr. Novello, who graduated as a physician in her native Puerto Rico, trained at the University of Michigan and became clinical professor of pediatrics at Georgetown University Hospital. She later joined the U.S. Public Health Service and was assigned to the National Institutes of Health. She served in multiple capacities while at the National Institutes of Health, ultimately becoming the deputy director of the National Institute of Child Health and Human Development, where she chaired the first report from the Department of Health and Human Services that demonstrated the vital need to address the transmission of HIV/AIDS in children. As surgeon general, she brought greater professional focus to public health problems such as AIDS, women's health issues, domestic violence, underage drinking, and prevention, particularly in the area of immunization.

## IMPORTANT TRAIT FOR SUCCESS

ANTONIA NOVELLO: Perseverance—the ability to do the job despite obstacles in your path. It is important to always do your research to inform your decision-making. Once you have determined your long-term goals, build coalition and rally stakeholders around those goals to overcome any barriers you may face. I never lose sight of the fact that to effect change, I must motivate people to achieve a particular goal, but always with the most up-to-date information.

## BIGGEST OBSTACLE

AN: Learning to adapt to an English-speaking culture, I became part of the minority who spoke "with an accent." I found that because I spoke with an accent, people seemed to believe I had a hearing deficit, and spoke slower and/or louder when addressing me. Just because I have an accent, it does not mean I think with an accent.

## BEST NEGOTIATING STRATEGY

AN: I find that the best negotiation skill, particularly in the jobs I have served in, is to know your facts and always do your homework. Women, as a whole, are sometimes stereotyped as being emotional and letting emotions influence their decision-making. I always remove any emotion from the equation and deal solely with facts. Therefore, I use the element of surprise as my best negotiating strategy—knowing the pros and cons of an issue before I even enter the room.

## HELPFUL CHILDHOOD MEMORY

AN: My mother was the principal of the junior high school where I studied. Her words of advice to me during this time in my life resonate with me to this day: "Education is the key to success, it will allow you to succeed, but always remember, do not invent what you do not know." She said that people will respect you more for acknowledging what you do not know than for inventing facts out of fear of failure.

BEST ADVICE

AN: My mother always said: "Never forget your roots—your language, where you came from, your culture, or your values." In my career ascension, I have always tried to make sure that my core values guide my decision-making and never forget the cultural influences that led to the establishment of those values.

WHAT BEST DESCRIBES YOU

AN: I have been described as a combination of Margaret Thatcher, Mother Teresa, and Charo. Margaret Thatcher, because she said something to the effect that if you set out just to be liked, you will compromise on anything and everything and will accomplish nothing. An analogy has been drawn to Mother Teresa, as I have also been characterized as being kind but tough. Last, I have been compared to Charo, as it is said of her that she always enjoys life, looks younger than her age, and says the most amazing things, always with humor.

# CHAPTER FIVE

# THE VOICE OF
# HER PEOPLE

## *Sarah Winnemucca*

S ARAH WINNEMUCCA WAS BORN near Pyramid Lake in western
Nevada, probably in 1844. In her memoir, *Life Among the
Piutes,* written in 1883, she admitted that she didn't know the precise date. At the time, her people, the Northern Paiutes (*Paiute* is the
more common spelling, but Sarah preferred *Piute*), had yet to make their
first contact with whites and still lived by the seasons, not the calendar. A
loosely knit group of clans, extended families of perhaps two hundred
Paiutes roamed the Great Basin that spread from central Nevada to parts
of California, Oregon, Idaho, and Utah. Led by an ad hoc headman, a
band followed its food supply, rarely spending long periods with other
Paiute bands except during annual fishing or hunting festivals and the
pine-nut harvest. The absence of hierarchy suited the small Paiute bands
well. Their elders, following the lead of the headman, an expert hunter or
a shaman, easily reached consensus about most things, and there were

also general councils where everyone—including the women—could express their views. Furthermore, since the Paiutes were a peace-loving people in relation to other Indians and white settlers, they had little need of the security that larger numbers could provide.

Sarah's maternal grandfather, Captain Truckee, was the headman of his band, and he may even have been "the chief of the entire Piute nation," as Sarah later claimed. The Paiutes began naming chiefs only after the Americans demanded that every tribe or nation have a designated leader, and Truckee would certainly have been a likely candidate. She recalled that he had long looked forward to the arrival of the Americans, and when a group from California was nearing Humboldt Lake, in Nevada, he exclaimed, "My white brothers,—my long-looked for white brothers have come at last!" and went off to meet them. He didn't have much luck in this first encounter—the suspicious travelers made him keep his distance—but he persisted. Later, he guided people bound for California across the Sierras. Even before gold was discovered in California in 1849, so many whites used the Humboldt trail that went through the Paiutes' region that John C. Frémont nicknamed it "the emigrant road."

Frémont, an explorer, entrepreneur, and politician, conducted several expeditions in the West and led the Bear Flag Revolt that won California's independence from Mexico in 1846. He became one of California's first U.S. senators and was the Republican candidate for president in 1856. There is no record of when Frémont and Truckee first met, but the Paiute led a group of Indian guides in the California uprising. As a reward for his loyalty, Frémont gave Truckee a letter of introduction and safe passage that the illiterate chief called his "rag friend." Someone in Frémont's party apparently nicknamed him Truckee because he continually repeated the Paiute word for "all right," which to white ears sounded like *truckee*. Today, the Truckee River that flows from Lake Tahoe to Pyramid Lake bears the name of the first Paiute leader who sought to live in harmony with the white settlers.

Truckee never abandoned his dream of coexistence with his "white brothers." He persisted in his beliefs even as settlers claimed more and more of the fertile land and scarce resources—water, vegetation, and wildlife—the Indians relied on for subsistence; when a fishing party that included one of his sons was shot at by settlers when the Paiutes came to fish in the Humboldt River; and even when an outbreak of typhus—against which Native Americans had no resistance or immunity—claimed the lives of many in their band. Some suspected that the whites had poisoned the water, but Sarah wrote that Truckee realized disease was to blame and urged his people, "[D]on't let your hearts work against your white fathers; if you do, you will not get along. You see they are already here in our land; here they are all along the river, and we must let our brothers live with us."

Truckee's passion for learning how to get along in the white man's world was the reason Sarah and her sister Elma spent some time living in the household of Major William Ormsby, an adventurous speculator who settled in Genoa, Nevada, in 1857, and who actively pursued good relations with the Paiutes. Sarah characterized the Winnemucca girls as playmates for the Ormsbys' daughter Lizzie, and Mrs. Ormsby taught them to speak, read, and perhaps even write English along with Lizzie. Shortly after Truckee's death in 1860, when Sarah was about sixteen, she and Elma spent a few weeks at a convent school in San Jose, California. Truckee had asked a friend named Snyder, known as "the white Winnemucca," to take the girls to school in California. They probably never formally enrolled and were quickly forced to leave, most likely because of complaints from some of the other students' parents. Always sensitive about her image in white eyes, Sarah later claimed to have been "convent educated," though in fact she was largely self-taught. It's not clear exactly how long Sarah remained in California, but while there she not only gained greater mastery of English but added Spanish to her growing repertoire of languages.

Sarah's father, Winnemucca (Truckee's son-in-law), was less sanguine about the prospects of accommodation with the whites. A shaman, like many Paiute headmen, he had a vision of whites gunning down Paiutes. He opposed war but preferred to avoid contact with the settlers. Both sides considered him the de facto chief of the Paiutes, however, and his diplomatic skills were often called upon. For a time, it appeared that efforts to live side by side might succeed, as when Winnemucca and the settlers at Honey Lake brokered a treaty stipulating that each community would rely on the other's system of justice to redress wrongs: the Indians would mete out justice for any crimes they committed against settlers, and the settlers would punish any of their members who wronged the Indians.

Despite such local—and temporary—successes, the Indians' traditional way of life was impossible to sustain. Frederick Dodge, the first Indian agent whose exclusive responsibility was the area of Nevada where Winnemucca's and other Paiute bands were centered (then part of the Utah Territory), foresaw that the Indians and settlers were on a collision course. As the "emigrants" enlarged their towns, farms, and ranches, they usurped the grazing lands of the game the Indians subsisted on; but if the Indians poached on the hunting grounds of other tribes, they risked war with their traditional neighbors. In other words, Dodge concluded, "[t]hey must either steal or starve." When the winter was severe, many Indians starved. Sarah later blamed the settlers for not sharing their supplies with the Indians, the Paiute custom being always to share with those in need. "During the winter my people helped them," she wrote. "They gave them such as they had to eat. They did not hold out their hands and say: 'You can't have anything to eat unless you pay me.' No,—no such word was used by us savages at that time."

By the spring of 1860, the sentiment for war was growing even among the normally peace-loving Northern Paiutes. Deteriorating relations with the settlers, distrust fed by crimes on both sides, and the shrinking of their hunting range disheartened them. During the spring fishing run at Pyramid Lake, Sarah's cousin Numaga (also known as Young Winnemucca) tried unsuccessfully to convince the others that war would be suicidal. He warned that the whites were like the stars in the sky and the sands of the riverbeds, too numerous to defeat, as well as too well armed. If the Paiutes kept the peace, there was hope of preserving their way of life and remaining in the region.

But events overtook them. The Williams brothers, who operated a trading post, kidnapped two young Paiute girls and hid them in a cellar under their barn. An Indian discovered where the girls were being held and returned with other men, including relatives of the girls. The outraged Indians killed the Williams brothers and three other white men at the trading post and set fire to the buildings. Many settlers acknowledged that whites bore a significant share of responsibility for what had happened, but others, led by William Ormsby, previously one of the Winnemuccas' and the Paiutes' firmest allies, were determined to punish the Indians.

A brief series of skirmishes, which became known as the Pyramid Lake War, followed. The battles themselves caused the Paiutes little harm—they used their superior knowledge of the geography and terrain to outmaneuver the small volunteer force—but even victory proved costlier to the Paiutes than to the whites. The large number of white casualties—about two-thirds of the initial force of a hundred or so—shocked the settlers because it was unprecedented. Among the casualties was the Winnemuccas' friend, Ormsby, who was shot while Sarah's brother Natches Overton was attempting to save his life. Later, a larger, better-trained force commanded by Colonel Jack Hays pursued the Paiutes, who retreated into the Black Rock Desert. Sarah's cousin Numaga had led the warriors in the Pyramid Lake War, but this was to be the Winnemuccas' last military involvement. Not even after the Mud Lake massacre in 1865—where Sarah's mother, Tuboitony, and twenty-eight other Paiutes died when a company of army volunteers, drawn from the settler population, fired on a camp of old people, women, and children—did the family consider violence. "This almost killed my poor papa," Sarah wrote. "Yet my people kept peaceful."

In the mid-1860s, most Paiutes, including Sarah and most of her family, began to submit to the policy of the Department of Indian Affairs to resettle the Indian population on reservations. Winnemucca himself never fully acquiesced to the system, however. He and a small band of followers preferred to endure the hardships in the mountains of Nevada and eastern Oregon. From time to time he would agree to move onto the reservation, only to leave again. At Pyramid Lake and elsewhere, Sarah witnessed the corruption and cruelty of the Indian agents toward their charges. As a result, she became both a creature of the reservation system and one of its harshest and most outspoken critics. As an interpreter in discussions between government officials and the Paiutes (as well as other tribes, especially the Shoshones), she became an invaluable mediator between the white and Indian cultures. She and her brother Lee helped persuade the Paiutes to move from Camp Smith, which the army planned to close, to nearby Camp McDermit, where in 1869 she began working as an interpreter. The position must have been difficult for Sarah, who could be intemperate, but at McDermit she evidently had the full support of the camp commander. At his urging, she wrote to Nevada's superintendent for Indian affairs, Major Henry Douglas, to complain about the abuse and neglect of Indians on the state's reservations.

Douglas, a Civil War veteran appointed by President Grant to oversee Nevada's Indians, was sympathetic. He sent Sarah's letter on to Washington; as a result, it was reprinted in some newspapers, in *Harper's Magazine,* and in Helen Hunt Jackson's *A Century of Dishonor* (1881), making Sarah's name known to a wider public. At Pyramid Lake, Sarah charged, the Indian agents sought their own profit, not the Indians' benefit. They failed to distribute food rations and didn't teach the Indians how to become self-sufficient through farming. As a result, she wrote, "[i]f we had stayed there, it would be only to starve." Despite the fact that the best lands were now generally off-limits to the Indians, she asserted that "it is much preferable to live in the mountains and drag out an existence in our native manner" than to submit to the agents' cruelty on the reservations.

In writing her letter, Sarah was taking on the role her father had rejected: representative of the Paiute nation to the white world. At McDermit, she also enjoyed good relations with the army, and she proposed that in the short term, the Indians be put under the army's supervision, since then they would be treated fairly, given food and shelter, and protected from confrontations with settlers. A more permanent solution, in Sarah's view, would be to allow the Indians to settle where they had traditionally lived, educate them, and prohibit settlers from seizing the Indians' land.

What Sarah did not know in 1870 was that the army was already losing the battle for control of the unsettled, undeveloped lands of the American West to the Interior Department, which increasingly held the keys to the Indians' future. Sarah considered it impossible to reach an accommodation with the agents and continued to rail at their corruption. In 1873, she told the *Nevada State Journal* that the agents preserved their positions by preventing Indians from becoming self-sufficient and lined their own pockets with rental fees from cattlemen who grazed their livestock on reservation lands. "Should my people raise their own provisions his [the agent's] place would be worth but little."

The following year, a confrontation that involved Sarah's brother Natches illustrated the agents' hostility toward the reservation Indians. The Paiutes at the Walker River reservation were told by their agent, C. W. Ingalls, that blankets would be distributed to them at the Pyramid Lake reservation, more than fifty miles away. At Pyramid Lake, however, Agent Calvin Bateman sent them back to Walker River empty-handed. Natches demanded to know why the Indians were being "shuttle-cocked" by the agents without receiving anything. Bateman accused him of inciting the Paiutes at Pyramid Lake to abandon the reservation and had him arrested by Captain Henry Wagner, commander of Camp McDermit (Wagner was probably responsible for Sarah's later losing her position as interpreter at the camp), and imprisoned at Alcatraz. Fortunately, General John M. Schofield, commander of the Pacific Division and familiar with the Winnemuccas, questioned Natches, recognized immediately that the charge against him was groundless, and ordered his release.

Sarah, Natches, and Winnemucca petitioned Schofield to keep Camp McDermit open. Without the soldiers' protection, they told him, the settlers would prevent the Paiutes from hunting, and the Indians would be forced to steal from the settlers. Looking ahead, they also wanted help in obtaining the materials and training they needed to learn to farm. Schofield sympathized with them but referred them to the Indian agents (who had for years withheld aid earmarked for the Indians) and Nevada senator John P. Jones, a mining millionaire who gave Sarah a twenty-dollar gold piece at the end of their visit but did nothing. At McDermit, Captain Wagner answered that "it was not within the province of the military to provide for the Indians, but only to protect white men and good Indians and to punish the bad." He suggested that they go to the reservations, where he said large sums had been allotted to feed and clothe them.

Much had changed for the Paiutes in the five years since Henry Douglas had circulated Sarah's letter. Douglas had supported the policy of placing the Indians on reservations, but he believed that doing so was a means of protecting their ways of life as well as allowing them to inte-

grate more fully into white culture. Shortly before being informed that
his authority over the Indian agents had been transferred to the American Baptist Home Mission Society, he had planned to open schools on
the Pyramid Lake and Walker River reservations and to appoint Sarah as
the teacher at Pyramid Lake. "[T]he good elementary English education
she has received, and her knowledge of Indian language and character,
would make her invaluable as an instructress," he wrote.

The local press and the settlers tended to agree with the Paiutes that
it was desirable to keep Camp McDermit open, since the military guaranteed the peace and provided a market for local produce and other
goods. But on other matters they supported President Grant's "peace
policy" of confining the Indians on reservations, converting them to
Christianity, and pressuring them to abandon hunting and gathering in
favor of farming. Sarah opposed the government's policy of assimilation,
especially as filtered through the missionary agents, whose control of the
reservations grew continually tighter; she believed it was possible to educate Indian children while also preserving their traditional languages
and ways of life. Before the decade ended, however, she herself apparently converted to Methodism (perhaps more out of convenience than
conviction) and interpreted Yakima reservation agent James Wilbur's
sermons for the Paiutes there. How effective the missionary efforts were
is unclear. Sarah, who possessed the Paiute gift for oratory, was dismis-
sive: "I know something about sermons myself and can preach a better
sermon than any of them."

The Malheur reservation had been created in 1872 to gather up "all
the roving and straggling bands in Eastern and Southeastern Oregon,
which can be induced to settle there." A hilly expanse of 1,778,560 acres
irrigated by three branches of the Malheur River, but with only 12,000
arable acres, it had been called "destitute" in a government report. A
short distance from Winnemucca's habitat in the Steens Mountain
region, Malheur enjoyed a rare commodity for a short time in the
mid-1870s: an honest agent who had the best interests of the Native
Americans at heart. The son of a Methodist missionary, Samuel Parrish
referred ironically to his own lack of missionary zeal when he introduced
himself to the Indians at Malheur: "I am a bad man; but I will try to do

my duty, and teach you all how to work, so you can do for yourselves by and by."

Parrish offered Sarah the interpreter's job when her cousin Jerry Long left the post to seek medical help in San Francisco. He promised a salary of $40 a month and a room. Sarah hesitated because of her previous problems with agents, but her brother Lee convinced her that Parrish was a man of his word. She saw Parrish at one of his first meetings, when he pledged to teach the Paiutes to grow potatoes, turnips, watermelon, barley, and oats and to irrigate their crops with water from the river. He also proposed training six of the young men as blacksmiths and carpenters and promised to build a school for the children. He said that whatever they grew would be theirs—a break with the general practice of treating reservation Indians as sharecroppers, claiming a large percentage of the harvest for the agents, and charging exorbitant prices for supplies. "The reservation is yours," Parrish told them. "The government has given it to you and your children."

Only Oytes, a maverick Paiute headman who followed the Dreamer religion (called the "Messiah Craze" by whites, it predicted the eventual expulsion of the whites by a leader from the East who would restore all dead Indians to life), refused to work as Parrish proposed. All the other chiefs responded enthusiastically to Parrish's proposal, and nearly everyone at Malheur—including most of Oytes's own band—"went to work," in Sarah's words, "with a good heart" the next morning. Eventually, even Oytes agreed to join the collective effort. Despite a new federal law that denied rations to anyone who did not work, Parrish exempted old men from field labor, reasoning that it would be too arduous. Most of the Indians were totally unfamiliar with farmwork, but they made rapid progress. Within six weeks, the irrigation ditch was ten feet wide and over two miles long. Parrish reported to Washington that "the Indians show such willingness to work that even those who have no tools will go into the ditch and throw out dirt with their hands."

Pleased with how the work had progressed and determined to prove that with proper treatment and training the Indians could learn to be self-sufficient, Parrish praised them lavishly: "All my people say that you won't work; but I will show that you can work as well as anybody, and if you go on as we have started, maybe the Big Father at Washington will now give us a mill to grind our corn. Do all you can, and I know [the] government will help you. I will do all I can while I am with you. I am going to have a schoolhouse put up right away, so that your children can go to school, and, after you have cut your hay, you can go out hunting a little while and get some buckskins; I know you will like that."

By the end of 1875, between seven and eight hundred Paiutes had settled at Malheur. Not only was the schoolhouse under construction, but blacksmithing and carpentry shops as well, and the Paiutes had planted 120 acres of crops. Parrish's generosity and scrupulous fairness buoyed their spirits. He paid them well for their work, purchased grain from them at a fair price, and insisted that any work the Paiutes did for him or his employees—from cutting wood to running errands—be paid for. Before they went off to hunt, he distributed flour, gunpowder, and lead, and reminded them that when they returned, the potatoes would be ready for digging.

Under Parrish's tutelage, the Paiutes labored through the winter, digging a second irrigation ditch and completing the schoolhouse. When the school was ready, Annie Parrish, the agent's sister-in-law, became the teacher; Sarah was her assistant but was paid an equal salary. Jerry Long, back from California but nearly blind, resumed his position as interpreter. The Paiute children loved the school, took to calling their teacher "our white lily mother" (Paiute girls were traditionally named for flowers; Sarah's name, for example, was Thocmetony, meaning Shell Flower). Sarah wrote, "They learned very fast and were glad to come to school. Oh, I cannot tell or express how happy we were!"

Sensitive to official skepticism about spending money to educate Indians, Parrish took pains to justify the costs of the building and the teachers' salaries. He wrote to Indian Commissioner E. P. Smith that the "industrial branch" he had added—where boys would learn farming skills and the women and girls would sew all their clothing under Annie's and Sarah's supervision—would pay for itself. "I think that enough can be saved to the government from material thus saved to almost pay the salaries of the teachers."

General Oliver O. Howard, appointed commander of the Department of the Columbia (Alaska, Washington, Oregon, and part of Idaho) in 1874, visited Malheur at about this time. Born in 1830 into a prosperous Maine farming family and educated at Bowdoin College and West Point, Howard was considering a career as a minister when the Civil War intervened. He lost his right arm in 1862, but he quickly returned to the front and saw action in many of the war's major battles and campaigns. As a general, Howard was not considered brilliant, but what he lacked as a military tactician, he made up for in diligence and humaneness. After the war, he headed the Freedman's Bureau and helped found Howard University, which was named for him, in 1867. He treated everyone with respect, even his adversaries. Because of his devoutness, he was sometimes called "the praying general" and criticized by some of his military colleagues. Even General William T. Sherman, who appointed Howard to command the Army of the Tennessee in 1865, is supposed to have said, "Well, that Christian-soldier business is all right in its place, but he needn't put on airs when we are among ourselves."

At Malheur, Howard liked what he saw. In one of his memoirs, he wrote of meeting Sarah and recalled that she spoke English perfectly and carried herself with dignity. Samuel Parrish impressed him, too, despite the agent's lax attitude to Christian piety. Howard's telegram to the adjutant general stated his enthusiastic judgment succinctly: "Think it very important that present Agent be continued. Indians whites and army officers commend Parrish for successful management of remote and difficult agency. Please inform Commissioner of Indian Affairs."

Howard almost certainly included praise of Parrish and his accomplishments at Malheur in an effort to reverse the decision to dismiss him as agent. Settlers had complained to Oregon's senators after Parrish slightly extended the reservation's borders to include some rich farming land, two hot springs used by the Paiutes, and land farmed by Egan, born a Cayuse but now headman of one of the Paiute bands. William V. Rinehart had been selected to replace Parrish, whether because the settlers' complaints had reached Washington or because Parrish had no interest in converting the Indians—or both—is not clear.

Sarah had already told the Malheur Paiutes about Parrish's dismissal, so when the agent addressed them at the schoolhouse toward the end of May, they were dejected and angry. Parrish assured them, "I am sorry to leave you, because I know I can make a good home for you," but he said that Rinehart was a decent man who might do even more for them. Meanwhile, before the new agent arrived on the first of July, he suggested, they should get their spring planting in.

Egan and Oytes, the leading figures among the Paiutes at Malheur, spoke out against Parrish's removal. Egan naively wondered whether anyone at the reservation might have complained about Parrish: "You all know that white men make a mountain out of little things, and some of them may have heard something and told it on him." Oytes, whose initial resistance had vanished, said simply, "We will not let our father go. . . . We will all stand by him. He has taught us how to work, and that's what we want, and the white lily is teaching our children how to talk with the paper, which I like very much. I want some of the young men to go and tell our father Winnemucca to come here as soon as he can. I know he will think as I do."

Winnemucca prevailed upon Parrish as the others had done, but the agent assured him that there was no reversing the decision. "I would like to stay, but your Big Father in Washington says that I must go." He explained that even the army could do nothing to change the decision of the Bureau of Indian Affairs, but the next day Winnemucca, Sarah, Egan, and Oytes rode the fifty miles to Camp Harney, where Sarah informed Major John Green that her father had something to discuss. Green told Sarah to return the next morning, but before she left he made sure that the Paiutes had accommodations for the night.

Winnemucca compared the Malheur reservation with Pyramid Lake, where the settlers had taken the good farming and grazing land and the agents gave nothing to the reservation Indians, who were thereafter forced to subsist on whatever fish they managed to catch. Because conditions at Malheur were so much better, he said, many Pyramid Lake Paiutes were planning to move up there. Of Parrish he said, "He gives us everything we want. He and his men are all friendly. They are teaching us how to work, and our children are learning to read, just like your children. What more do we want? There can be no better man than he, and why send him away?"

Major Green promised to write to Washington on the Paiutes' behalf, and he also sent a letter to the assistant adjutant general of the Department of the Columbia. Besides the Indians' reasons for wanting

Parrish to remain, he added Winnemucca's statement that had someone like Parrish been the Paiutes' Indian agent in 1860, the Paiutes would not have gone to war. He concluded, "It seems to me strange to remove an agent who is doing so much for the Indians and one whom they are so unwilling to lose."

Rinehart moved into Malheur on June 28. He was greeted by Parrish, who did his best to impress on the new agent how much the Indians had accomplished, showed him the planted fields and gardens, identified the band or family that had planted each one, explained his routine for distributing supplies and rations, and assured Rinehart that the Indians were honest and hardworking. Then he left, and Rinehart immediately set about undoing the good his predecessor had accomplished. When Sarah got a glimpse of the new schoolteacher, blacksmith, and farmer, who arrived with their families, she thought them "the poorest-looking white people I ever saw." But Rinehart gave them clothing Parrish had ordered for the Indians, and "[i]n a few days they were all well clothed, men, women, and children."

To the Indians, Rinehart was less generous, telling them that the land was the government's, not theirs, and that the crops they raised belonged not to them but to the government. If they agreed to work, however, he would pay every worker a dollar a day. When Egan complained that Rinehart was contradicting what Parrish had told them, Rinehart retorted, "I don't care whether any of you stay or not. You can all go away if you do not like the way I do."

The Paiutes stuck it out through the fall 1876 harvest, despite Rinehart's constant shortchanging of them on their wages and his mistreatment of their children. They hoped the harvest would be sufficient to get them through the winter. The bulk of the wheat had been planted in the fields Parrish had assigned to Egan and Oytes, but when they asked for their share of the grain, Rinehart replied, "Nothing here is yours. It is all the government's."

"Did the government tell you to come here and drive us off this reservation?" Egan asked.

Did the Big Father say, go and kill us all off, so you can have our land? Did he tell you to pull our children's ears off, and put handcuffs on them, and carry a pistol to shoot us with? . . . Is the government mightier than our Spirit-Father, or is he our Spirit-Father? Oh, what have we done that he is to take all from us that he has given us? His white children have come and have taken all our mountains, and all our valleys, and all our rivers; and now, because he has given us this little place without our asking him for it, he sent you here to tell us to go away. . . . I have had only two dollars, which I gave you for a pair of pants, and my son-in-law gave you the same for his. That is all the money the government is going to get out of me; and tomorrow I am going to tell the soldiers what you are doing and see if it is all right.

Few at Malheur were as outspoken as Egan, but discontent was widespread. Sarah had not encouraged the hostility, and in any case she did not need to. She had complained about Rinehart to the officers at Camp Harney, however, and she may have petitioned Washington for Rinehart's removal, although no such letter has ever been found. The agent held her responsible for the resistance, fired her as interpreter, and banished her from the reservation. To justify his actions, he wrote to General Howard that "[m]ost of the real trouble and all the reported or imaginary threats of the Indians are believed to have originated with this unfaithful employee."

At the same time as conditions were deteriorating for the Northern Paiutes, neighboring tribes were suffering similar fates, and for similar causes: as settlers arrived in growing numbers, the Indians' hunting-and-gathering subsistence was threatened, and they were forced onto reservations that failed to supply their needs or help them learn to become self-sufficient. One such tribe was the Bannocks, who spoke the Paiute language but had never been allies. Belligerent and one of the earliest tribes to adopt the use of horses, the Bannocks subsisted on camas roots, which they dug over a large area of Idaho, and buffalo meat, which they hunted. They were scornful of the rabbit-hunting, peaceable Paiutes, regarded all whites as their enemies, and cultivated a reputation for savagery. Common privations impelled some Paiute bands to join forces with the Bannocks in the 1878 uprising known as the Bannock War.

Historians disagree about what precipitated the war; it may have been Bannock chief Big Horn's fury at General Howard's unwillingness to turn a blind eye to the murders of some Nez Percé herders who had encroached on Bannock territory, or the whites' execution of the Indian Tambiago, who had avenged the rape of a Bannock girl by killing a white man suspected of the crime. But there were deep, systemic causes about which everyone agrees: The Indians were slowly being starved into extinction. They were not receiving rations, but their food sources were threatened. For example, farmers' hogs ate the Bannocks' camas roots, despite the Fort Bridger Treaty expressly protecting the Indians' food-gathering areas.

Winnemucca remained dead set against war to the end—on practical grounds, in addition to his principled objections. He wanted the Bannock chiefs to visit San Francisco, to see for themselves that war was futile, that the Indians would be outgunned by the army, but by the time he and Natches arrived for a parley, the other chiefs had passed the point of no return. At Malheur, a group of Bannocks and Paiutes asked Sarah—who had disobeyed the order to stay off the reservation in order to attend the meeting—to help them appeal to the officers at Camp Harney or even to go to Washington to seek relief from their desperate situation. Their immediate complaint was that their horses and guns had been taken from them. When she asked why they didn't get the reservation's interpreter, her cousin Jerry Long, to represent them, they insisted, "You are the only one who is always ready to talk for us. We know our sister can write on paper to our good father in Washington if she will."

Sarah left Malheur in early June. She planned to board an eastbound train in Elko, Nevada, but en route, she passed many abandoned houses. It was several days before a passing traveler told her that "the greatest Indian war that was ever known" had broken out. She sought refuge at a nearby ranch, where she got her first news of the fighting from an Indian scout known as Paiute Joe. He had been guiding a group of army volunteers that fled when they crossed paths with a Bannock raiding party. Paiute Joe perceived that his best chances of escaping alive lay in killing the raiders' leader. He did not realize until later that the warrior he shot was Buffalo Horn, the Bannock leader of the uprising. The news of Buffalo Horn's death took some days to reach the other Bannocks, but it was a key event in the brief war. The rebel confederation—which by then included Paiutes, Shoshones, Umatillas, Cayuses, and others—never successfully regrouped after it was known that they had lost their chief, and some tribes that had been leaning toward joining the coalition opted not to.

Sarah offered her services as guide and scout to Captain Reuben Bernard of the army, risky work because the troops had no intelligence about where the Bannock warriors were. The hostile Indians had cut the telegraph wires wherever they went. Information was exchanged via dispatches carried by Indian riders on horseback. Sarah's first mission was to get back to Malheur or Camp Harney to learn the Bannocks' whereabouts. Sarah volunteered for the dangerous mission when two other Paiute scouts, afraid of running into Bannocks, refused. Shamed by Sarah's fearlessness, the other scouts relented and decided to accompany her.

Captain Bernard also ordered Sarah to try to persuade the Paiutes who had joined forces with the Bannocks to come over to the army's side. In return, he promised, they would be fed and protected. The three scouts rode off, carrying a letter of transit from the captain, which read: "To all good citizens of the country—Sarah Winnemucca, with two of her people, goes with a dispatch to her father. If her horses should give out, help her all you can and oblige." They soon overtook a group of volunteers, asleep. Sarah taunted them, "Is this the way you all find the hostiles? We could have killed every one of you if we had been they." The volunteers gave them fresh horses, and the Paiutes continued toward the Bannocks' encampment. Along the way, they passed a spot where the Bannocks had stopped to mourn for Buffalo Horn—by breaking beads, cutting their hair, and tearing their clothes—and then renewed their energies by dancing around the scalps of several of their white victims.

After a day's hard riding, Sarah and her companions found the Bannock encampment, well concealed in the mountains near the Oregon border. Six miles from the camp, she met her brother Lee, who explained that their family's bands were being held virtual prisoners by the hostile tribes, which included the Paiutes led by Egan and Oytes. He warned her not to enter the camp. The war faction's suspicion of the

Winnemuccas was extreme, especially after Sarah's brother Natches had escaped a few days earlier with three white men, in an effort to save them from a certain death. "They will surely kill you," Lee told her, "for they have said that they will kill every one that comes with messages from the white people, for Indians who come with messages are no friends of ours."

Sarah planned to dress in Bannock style and wear war paint, in order to blend in with the encamped Indians, but Lee insisted that Oytes, now the leader of the uprising, would be sure to recognize her. Sarah was undeterred: "I must go to my father, for I have come with a message from General O. O. Howard, I must save my father and his people if I lose my life in trying to do it, and my father's too. That is all right. I have come for you all. Now let us go."

Sarah never wavered in her commitment to peaceful coexistence between Indians and whites, notwithstanding the many injustices that had been done. But as she gazed down at the Bannock encampment, she felt proud of the show of strength made by her dispossessed and humiliated compatriots: "Oh, such a sight my eyes met! It was a beautiful sight. About three hundred and twenty-seven lodges, and about four hundred and fifty warriors were down Little Valley catching horses, and some more were killing beef. The place looked as if it was all alive with hostile Bannocks." Then, reminding herself of her mission, she and the other two Paiute scouts slipped undetected into the camp.

Inside Winnemucca's lodge, Sarah lost no time. "I have come to save you if you will do as I wish you to and be quiet about it," she told the band. "Whisper it among yourselves. Get ready for to-night, for there is no time to lose, for the soldiers are close by. I have come from them with this word: 'Leave the hostile Bannocks and come to the troops. You shall be properly fed by the troops.'" Almost immediately, the women left the camp as if to search for firewood, and Lee went to round up horses. The men followed Sarah as she retraced the route she'd followed to enter the encampment, and the band regrouped at Juniper Lake, ate, and set off on foot and horseback toward a rendezvous at Summit Springs. When Lee returned to help rescue the blind Jerry Long, who was being held a "close prisoner," the Paiutes' escape was discovered, and the Bannocks set out in pursuit. Someone reported that Oytes had ordered his warriors, "Go quickly, bring Sarah's head and her father's too. I will show Sarah who I am."

Most of Winnemucca's band turned back to help their comrades escape, while Sarah and Mattie, Lee's wife, pressed on to reach the army. When she reported that she had covered over 220 miles in two and a half days, many did not believe her, but General Howard knew that she was telling the truth. He sent a contingent of volunteers to meet Winnemucca's band and bring them back to the army camp. He also immediately retained Sarah and Mattie as guides and interpreters. Sarah wasn't surprised that the soldiers, few of whom could match the Indians' stamina, were skeptical of her story. In her memoirs, she proudly described her mission as "the hardest work I ever did for the government in all my life—the whole round trip, from 10 o'clock June 13 up to June 15, arriving back at 5:30 P.M., having been in the saddle night and day; distance about two hundred and twenty-three miles. Yes, I went for the government when the officers could not get an Indian man or a white man to go for love or money. I, only an Indian woman, went and saved my father and his people."

General Howard went after the Bannocks with a relatively light force, but carrying their heavy equipment over rocky, often mountainous terrain hampered their progress. An old Bannock woman, who turned out to be Buffalo Horn's aunt, and who may have been abandoned because she could not keep up with the retreating Bannocks, told them the enemy had gone north to recruit the Umatillas and perhaps even Chief Moses across the Columbia River. Howard ordered gunboat patrols on the Columbia to prevent the Bannocks from crossing and continued his pursuit. Despite the fact that the Indian warriors traveled with their families (Sarah estimated that 1,500 people had camped at one spot they passed), the army had trouble catching up with them. Recalling the chase nearly thirty years later, Howard compared it to an antelope hunt, where the quarry's "quick ears and native fleetness" allowed it to escape. "Unlike the hunter, my object in pursuing these Indians was not to kill, but—like my dear father chasing bees—to hive."

Sarah impressed the officers with her skills as a guide and interpreter and with her dignity. Captain Mason, whose letters to his wife form an invaluable eyewitness account of the war and of frontier life, wrote of her: "Sarah is a remarkable woman—a full-blooded Piute Indian, yet well educated, speaks the best of English, and can read and write as well as anybody. . . . She is very much more a lady in her manner and address than many white women I know. . . . It would interest you to see [Sarah and Mattie] go anywhere with a dash few men could excel." General Howard, who had taught at West Point with the father of Edward Bartlett, a dissolute army officer to whom Sarah was briefly married, wrote—without naming names—about their marriage, mentioning that he knew both of them personally and judged Sarah "far superior."

The tide of the war took a decisive turn in July, when the Umatillas offered their services to the army—a rarity in the Bannock War, even for tribes that had aided the army in earlier conflicts. Umapine, a Cayuse chief who had joined the Umatillas, lured Egan to a meeting on the pretext of discussing an Indian alliance, killed him and the warriors in his entourage, and captured a number of Paiute women and children. To prove to the army that Egan was dead, Umapine brought his severed head and left arm. Howard wrote of Umapine: "In war he displayed profound treachery and positive enjoyment of murder. Even his mates shuddered at his brutality. After committing atrociously wicked acts he would strut with pride and boast of his brutal prowess."

With the uprising's outcome certain, Sarah was eager for the Indians to surrender, in order to win some measure of protection from the settlers. General Howard, too, counseled surrender and sent Sarah to appeal to them to return to their reservations. Her declaration read: "Tell them I, their mother, say come back to their homes again. I will stand by them and see that they are not sent away to the Indian territory." All told, twenty-seven men and seventy-two women and children surrendered, but whether they had in fact been rebels is far from certain. One cavalry search led by Colonel James Forsyth tracked an Indian whose distress signal they had spied in the mountains. It took three days to find the man, and when he arrived, Sarah recognized him. "He was one of the best Indian men Mr. Parrish [the beloved agent at Malheur] had to work for him."

The threat to the Indians' safety was real enough. Settlers sometimes berated soldiers for not killing prisoners, despite the prohibition against such inhumane treatment. The regular army could be relied on to go by the book, but the undisciplined volunteers were often less fastidious. Even after hostilities had ceased, Sarah herself was sometimes in jeopardy from the volunteers, as happened when she and Mattie got separated from the lieutenant during a search mission. Three volunteers approached, and one of them said, "Come, boys, here are the girls, and the lieutenant is not with them." Sarah and Mattie, better horsemen than nearly all the soldiers and more familiar with the terrain, managed to escape on horseback.

In general, where there had been fighting, the settlers desired revenge and didn't distinguish between hostile and friendly Indians. An editorial in the *Idaho Statesman* was representative: "It is idle to talk about mercy to such vile wretches, or to think of treating them when caught and forced to surrender as ordinary prisoners of war, and worse than idle to indulge any idea of another effort to bring them within the pale of civilization." The soldiers of the regular army showed a better understanding of the state of things and expressed sympathy for the Indians. Mason, a thoughtful man with firsthand knowledge of the war, the settlers, and the qualities of people like the Winnemuccas, wrote: "I am so disgusted with the vile, low people on the frontier—I have no heart to fight for them."

Among Indians, feelings were just as polarized. Some Indians mistrusted anyone who had sided with the whites; for example, some tribes, like the Shoshones, considered Sarah an informer for the army and refused to talk to her. In fact, throughout the twentieth century some Indians continued to believe that Sarah was to blame for the Indian casualties in the Bannock uprising.

Finding herself close to Camp McDermit, Sarah visited Winnemucca. When she told the Paiutes how Umapine had lured Egan to his death, some of them wanted to take revenge. Natches persuaded them that it was more important to save the lives of the women and children still held captive by the Umatillas. He proposed publicly condemning Umapine and his accomplices before Colonel Forsyth and then trying to secure the captives' release.

Before Natches and Sarah left camp at the head of the Paiute delegation, Winnemucca seized the opportunity to praise his daughter's exploits and to chastise the young men who had failed to support the army in the Bannock War.

> Where is one among you who can get up and say, "I have been in battle and have seen soldiers and my people fight and fall." Oh! for shame! for shame to you, young men, who ought to have come with this news to me! I am much pained because my dear daughter has come with the fearful things which have happened in the war. Oh, yes! my child's name is so far beyond yours; none of you can ever come up to hers. Her name is everywhere and every one praises her. Oh! how thankful I feel that it is my own child that has saved so many lives, not only mine, but a great many, both whites and her own people. Now hereafter we will look on her as our chieftain, for none of us are worthy of being chief but her, and all I can say to you is to send her to the wars and you stay and do women's work, and talk as women do.

Winnemucca's intention was not to unseat Natches as headman, but to praise Sarah's courage. Natches was certainly a much better diplomat than Sarah, and his temperate intelligence was crucial to the Indians at this juncture, as the quandary over how to deal with Umapine demonstrates. In this instance, the delegation had to settle for condemning him in absentia, since Umapine had gone into hiding and did not face his accusers. Forsyth assured them that Howard would take measures against the murderers. As it turned out, however, nothing was done to Umapine—he was considered too valuable as a scout. Nor is it clear whether Oytes, who eventually surrendered and was tried, was punished. He had expressed contempt for the proceedings, taking refuge in the rhetoric of the Dreamer religion: "Do what you will with my body," he said, "because I will return and show you a much greater battle."

With the war at an end, the Paiutes hoped to remain in their historic region and not have to return to the reservation—certainly not Malheur, where Rinehart continued as agent and they were assured of mistreatment. Mystifyingly, the Office of Indian Affairs decreed that all the Paiutes were to be relocated to the Yakima reservation, 350 miles north in Washington State. The reason may have been the planned closing of McDermit, or General Howard's insistence on punishing Indians for every misdemeanor, even if it was just abandoning Malheur. To avoid moving to a distant, inhospitable place, some Indians wandered away from Camp Harney, but all who remained were forced to trek north in winter, poorly clothed and ill equipped. At Yakima, they were at the mercy of James H. Wilbur, a stern missionary who later wrote that as he saw the "people committed to my charge" moving "from a state of degraded barbarism to comparative civilization, from the gross blackness of heathen corruption, to the glorious light and liberty of the Gospel of the Son of God, I can realize that from month to month, and from year to year, solid progress and improvement is being made."

It may have been at Yakima that Sarah finally converted to Methodism. She certainly translated Wilbur's sermons into Paiute and assisted at the conversions of others. She also taught in the reservation school, where she found the education, at least, better than it had been since the Parrishes left Malheur. Overall conditions for the Paiutes, however, were desperate. The Yakimas stole from them, and they struggled to subsist on poor wages and with inadequate allotments of clothing.

Sarah wasn't compelled to live at Yakima; she apparently accompanied her people out of a sense of solidarity. As their hopelessness grew, she decided to take her campaign public and turned to the lecture stage again, as she had briefly done in 1864 in Nevada and California. The first programs had been more of an entertainment, with Sarah playing a supporting role to Chief Winnemucca. This time she sang Paiute chants with other family members—Natches Overton, Jerry Long, and Charlie Thacker—and interpreted Natches's short speeches, but the focus was on her own words. Speaking without notes, she narrated tales drawn from Paiute history, her own reminiscences, and her exploits during the Bannock War, and she excoriated the whites for their unjust treatment of the Indians. Her San Francisco lectures, in November and December 1879, were almost certainly the first large-scale public-relations effort by an American Indian woman.

Sarah next visited Washington, accompanied by her father, Natches, and other family members, to petition Interior Secretary Carl Schurz to allow the Paiutes at Yakima to return to the Malheur reservation. Schurz had a mixed record with respect to Indian rights, but the Winnemuccas were optimistic because a year earlier he had allowed the Bannocks to return to the Fort Hall reservation. Schurz gave Sarah an order authorizing the Paiutes to return to Malheur, where they would receive land in severalty, grants of land to individuals rather than the tribe as a whole. Further, Paiutes would not be compelled to live on the reservation; those who had settled among the whites, for example, could continue to live where they pleased.

Sarah had thought about lecturing while in the East, but Schurz dissuaded her, arguing that since the government had paid for her travel, it would be unethical for her to pursue a moneymaking activity. She returned directly to Yakima, where Wilbur tried to bribe her not to reveal Schurz's order to the Paiutes, and the Indians accused her of selling them out. After she explained the order, however, they agreed unanimously to return to Malheur—even Oytes, whom the others forgave for his past betrayals in the excitement of returning to their traditional region, even to a reservation.

Wilbur tried to delay their departure by insisting that he needed more explicit orders from Washington, whether because he wanted the benefits of having them in his charge or to prevent their return to Malheur, where settlers had already seized much of the land. The instructions never came. Perhaps Schurz changed his mind after seeing accusations against Sarah written by Rinehart, the Malheur agent, or perhaps he had never intended to follow through on his "Paiute Magna Carta." He had written, though, "it gave me the most heartfelt pleasure to comply with all their requests," so his real intentions are an open question. Sarah blamed Wilbur for the delays. "You are starving my people here, and you are selling the clothes which were sent to them; and it is my money in your pocket; that is why you want to keep us here, not because you love us. I say, Mr. Wilbur, everybody in Yakima City knows what you are doing, and hell is full of just such Christians as you are."

Whatever was responsible, Malheur reservation was closed and the land given to settlers. The action revived suspicions that Rinehart's role had all along been to drive the Indians away from Malheur, as Egan had charged several years earlier. In the West, however, only one person of any authority at that time was interested in evicting the white squatters from Malheur to allow the Paiutes to return: General McDowell, now the Pacific Division commander.

The army exercised great power in keeping the peace, but McDowell had little influence over the reservations, whose administration was now firmly in the hands of the Department of the Interior. In general, the soldiers treated the Indians kindly, while the Indian agents exploited them. Sarah, like her father (who wore the military coat that General Crook had given him until the end of his life) and grandfather, believed that the Indians were better off when the army ministered to them. "Have not the Indians good reasons to like soldiers?" she wrote. "There were no Custers among the officers in Nevada. If the Indians were protected, as they call it, instead of the whites, there would be no Indian wars. Is there not good reason for wishing the army to have care of the Indians, instead of the Indian Commissioner and his men? The army has no temptation to make money out of them, and the Indians understand law and discipline as the army has them; but there is no law with agents. The few good ones cannot do good enough to make it worth while to keep up that system. A good agent is sure to lose his place very soon, there are so many bad ones longing for it."

There were other, better options for the Paiutes than Yakima and Malheur, and the Winnemuccas tirelessly lobbied for them. When President Rutherford Hayes and Lucy Hayes visited the California State Fair in 1880, Winnemucca and Natches managed to speak to them, and Sarah followed up when the Hayeses spent a day at Fort Vancouver, near Yakima. "I will see about it," the president politely replied to Sarah, but, she wrote, "Nothing was ever done that I ever heard of." Many Paiutes already lived outside the reservation, but the Winnemuccas also wanted to improve conditions at existing reservations, like Pyramid Lake, and open others, such as Duck Valley, a Shoshone reservation since 1877, to their people.

Sarah encouraged the Paiutes at Yakima to resist all efforts to bind them to that reservation by refusing to farm, accept grants of land, or build houses. Wilbur acknowledged that Sarah was succeeding, and at the same time, Paiutes were starting to escape. He was wearying of trying to keep them and wrote that it "would be an inexpressible relief to me" to get rid of the Paiutes. He said he was merely waiting for Washington's instructions about letting them go. Whether or not this was posturing on the agent's part is uncertain. When he fell ill, Robert Milroy, a wounded Civil War veteran and former superintendent of Indian affairs, replaced him. Milroy, interested neither in exploiting the Indians nor in converting them, sympathized with the Paiutes' plight, proposed that they be allowed to return to their traditional region, and turned a blind eye as they quietly departed. By the end of 1884, the last Paiute had left the Oregon reservation.

At the end of her San Francisco lecture series in 1879, Sarah had met a group of Bostonians, who suggested that she lecture in their city. They promised, "You will meet a better class of people to aid you." In the spring of 1883, after a brief series of talks in Ogden, Utah, she headed east. On this trip, Sarah was accompanied by Lewis Hopkins, whom she had recently married. The two of them had most likely met during the Bannock War, in which Hopkins had served as a soldier. Unlike her first husband, Edward Bartlett, Hopkins was not from a distinguished military family, but like Bartlett, he exploited Sarah terribly. Among other things, he stole money from her—including funds intended to benefit the Indians—to pay gambling debts, and yet she doted on him until he died of tuberculosis in the late 1880s.

# *Elizabeth Palmer Peabody*

IN BOSTON, SARAH SPENT most of her time as the guest of Elizabeth Palmer Peabody, a personage at the center of Massachusetts philosophical inquiry and reform efforts from the 1830s onward, and her sister, Mary Mann, the recently widowed second wife of the educator Horace Mann. Through Elizabeth's assiduous efforts, Sarah spoke in the homes of a number of New England's leading thinkers and artists, including Ralph Waldo Emerson and John Greenleaf Whittier, and met congressmen and other members of Boston's elite. With an introduction from Elizabeth, Sarah wrote to Senator Henry Dawes, author of an important bill that addressed Indian rights, to propose that the power to distribute land in severalty be conferred on the Indian chiefs, not the interior secretary, and that the tribes be able to choose their own agents. Dawes was impressed by Sarah's letter, but he didn't change his bill. They did meet in Massachusetts, however, and he had her speak to the Subcommittee on Indian Affairs, which he chaired. Her testimony helped remove the threat of punishment of Paiutes who had left Yakima without authorization. Senator Dawes also encouraged Peabody to schedule as many lectures for Sarah as possible, in order to increase public—and thereby congressional—support for the Indian cause.

Elizabeth shared Sarah's conviction that her people had been unjustly treated, embraced the belief that the Indians should preserve their language and culture, prized Sarah's gifts as a talker (a friend called Elizabeth "the narrative Miss Peabody"), and supported her efforts to educate young Indian children. As soon as they had met in 1883, Elizabeth and Mary espoused Sarah's causes as their own. Elizabeth wrote, for example, that "to scatter the Indians among our population—instead of keeping them together—would be like scattering the members of a private family." Besides finding lecture venues for Sarah, Elizabeth traveled with her to engagements as far away as Philadelphia. She solicited support from potential donors and politicians and pressured newspaper editors to give good reviews to "the Paiute Princess." Even after Sarah's credibility was undermined by the Lewis Hopkins scandal, when he gambled away money that was intended to benefit the Paiutes, Elizabeth stood by her.

Both sisters also urged Sarah to write her memoirs, which she did at the Peabodys' house over several months in 1883. *Life Among the Piutes: Their Wrongs and Claims* was edited by Mary Mann and published by Peabody cousin George Putnam. Mary wrote, "I was always considered fanatical about Indians, but I have a wholly new conception of them now, and we civilized people may well stand abashed before their purity of life and their truthfulness." The first book written by an Indian woman, Sarah's work is part memoir, part polemic, and part ethnographic record of the Paiute way of life. Mary believed that "[i]t is of the first importance to hear what only an Indian and an Indian woman can tell," and was chagrined by skeptics who claimed that Sarah could not have written the book herself. Mary was amused by Sarah's written English, but she affirmed that Sarah was the author of her memoir. "I don't think the English language ever got such a treatment before," she wrote. "I have to recur to her sometimes to know what a word is, as spelling is an unknown quantity to her. . . . She often takes syllables off of words & adds them or rather prefixes them to other words, but the story is heart-breaking, and told with a simplicity & an eloquence that cannot be described."

Between the spring of 1883 and the summer of 1884, Sarah gave more than three hundred lectures throughout New England, as well as in New York, Pennsylvania, Baltimore, and Washington. An October 1883 lecture in Philadelphia was representative: a large crowd (in this case, 1,500) gathered early; her husband, Lewis Hopkins, opened the program by narrating Sarah's personal history; then Sarah, dressed in beaded deerskin, talked about how the corrupt agents mistreated the Indians, blamed the wars waged against the whites on the Indians' desperation, and proposed putting the army in charge of Indian affairs.

According to Elizabeth, "She never repeated or contradicted herself once, though it was obvious that except in the choice of some particular subject to be made her theme, she took no previous thought as to what she should say, but trusted that the right words would be given her by the 'Spirit Father,' whose special messenger she believed herself to be, and impressed her audiences to believe that she was." With her talent for extemporizing, Sarah would often tailor her speeches to her audience: For example, proposing to a feminist audience that women would make better Indian agents than men, and stressing virtues of Paiute culture—their enlightened child-rearing, considerate courtship customs, and respect for the elderly—that appealed to women.

Elizabeth, who was nearly eighty years old when she met Sarah, had taken up the twin causes of Indian rights and the creation of schools for

Indian children with the zeal that was characteristic throughout her
long, active life. Educated at home by her father, a former teacher at
Phillips Andover Academy, and her mother, who founded a school in
Salem, Massachusetts, whose philosophy was to give all children an education appropriate for geniuses, Elizabeth mastered ten languages and
developed interests that ranged through philosophy, theology, history,
literature, and early childhood education. She was one of only two
women invited to become charter members of the Transcendentalist
Club in Boston in 1837 (Margaret Fuller was the other), and she collaborated with important figures such as the Unitarian minister and
philosopher William Ellery Channing and Bronson Alcott, with whom
she opened a school in Boston and whom she made famous by publishing her journal, *Record of a School,* in 1835.

After Elizabeth's defense of Alcott's controversial theological ideas
short-circuited her own career as a teacher, she returned to Boston four
years later to open a bookshop, which one of her biographers has called
"one of the most important and influential bookstores in American history." Besides being an outlet for foreign and domestic books and peri-
odicals, it also became the Transcendentalists' gathering place in Boston.
There Margaret Fuller first discussed her ideas, and plans for the *Dial*
magazine and Brook Farm, the utopian experiment, were formulated.
Elizabeth, who published the magazine from 1842 on, as well as books
by Channing, Nathaniel Hawthorne (her sister Sophia was Hawthorne's
wife), and *Aesthetic Papers* (1849), in which Thoreau's essay "Civil Disobedience" first appeared, was also the first woman publisher in Boston,
and she may well have been the first in the United States.

After Elizabeth closed her bookstore in 1850, her interests increasingly coalesced around children's education. From Margarethe Schurz,
the wife of Carl Schurz, who visited Boston with her young daughter,
Agathe, in 1859, she learned about the theory and practice of Friedrich
Froebel, who had conceived of the kindergarten as a learning environment based on "organized play and interaction with nature," where
children's activities would be perfectly matched to their stages of mental
and physical maturation. Elizabeth observed that Agathe seemed "a
miracle,—so child-like and unconscious, and yet so wise and able, attracting and ruling the children [of their hosts], who seem nothing short

of enchanted." When she praised the child, Margarethe Schurz replied, "No miracle, but only brought up in a kindergarten," and launched into a description of Froebel's theories. Within a year, Elizabeth had studied Froebel's work and opened the first kindergarten in Boston, with thirty students. She founded a magazine, *Kindergarten Messenger,* to spread knowledge about what the kindergarten was, encouraged public schools to add them when they could afford to, and pressured philanthropists to underwrite them in neighborhoods where the public schools lacked the funds.

By the time Sarah returned to Pyramid Lake in 1884, Hiram Price, commissioner of Indian affairs, had written to Mary Mann that he was "ready to cooperate with all her definite plans for education." Sarah herself had almost no formal schooling, but she had proved herself an inspired teacher again and again—at Malheur, Yakima, and Fort Vancouver, as well as, in another sense, on the lecture circuit. Despite Price's assurances, however, Nevada's chief Indian agent, William D. C. Gibson, preferred to perpetuate the practice of giving reservation jobs to political appointees and refused to hire Sarah. Elizabeth persuaded her to open her own school on a shoestring, as she herself had done in Boston, and assured Sarah that she would send whatever money came in from sales of her memoirs. On the 160-acre ranch that Natches purchased from railroad magnate Leland Stanford in 1885, Sarah opened the Peabody Indian School. The curriculum was unusual; it replaced the assimilationist approach with a bilingual program that combined literacy, general education, and the preservation of traditional Indian culture. The last was Sarah's strongest selling point. By the end of the first year, twenty-four students had enrolled, and other parents were thinking about transferring their children from the reservation's government school to the Peabody School. The parents also applauded Sarah's insistence that children continue to live in their own communities and not be sent to boarding schools far from their homes, a practice that was gaining support among the assimilationists.

Elizabeth sent lesson plans for reading and arithmetic, and praised Sarah's approach as "a spontaneous movement, made by the Indian himself, *from himself,* in full consciousness of free agency, for the education that is to civilize him," instead of white "spiritual, moral, and intellectual" superiors imposing their civilization on the Indians. Rather than learning minimal English—frequently Christian hymns—by rote while remaining illiterate, Sarah's Paiute students learned to speak English as she translated their Paiute speech, and then they learned to *read and write* in English. The children were so excited that they could write that they soon covered the fences of the Lovelock ranch with English-language graffiti. Sarah described what she viewed as a critical pedagogic process thus: "The most necessary thing for the success of an Indian school is a good interpreter, one that can and will do. . . . I attribute the success of my school not to my being a scholar and a good teacher but because I am my own Interpreter, and my heart is in my work."

Funds were always short. Now in her eighties, Elizabeth exploited her acquaintance with Grover Cleveland's sister, Rose, to meet with the president, and made a futile attempt to secure funds for Sarah's school from the commissioner of Indian affairs. She even published a short work, *The Piutes,* praising Sarah's bilingual pedagogy, her emphasis on combining Anglo and Indian cultures, and her opposition to sending young children to boarding schools far from their families. Elizabeth finally succeeded in raising $1,400 in private donations—half of it her own money—so that Sarah could build a permanent schoolhouse before winter arrived. Fund-raising was difficult because many donors preferred to support the missionary and boarding schools, and others feared that Lewis Hopkins might embezzle any new gifts as he had done in the past. Some also believed the slander leveled against Sarah by enemies like Rinehart and the Indian Rights Association, that she sought personal profit and fomented insurrection against the whites.

Despite seemingly insuperable difficulties, the Peabody School thrived, and word of its successes spread. Sarah managed to feed, clothe, and teach her students in 1886, to the delight of western journalists. One wrote, in *Alta California,* "We believe that the Indian Department should found an Indian school in Nevada and put Sarah at the head of it. The cost would be small compared to the value of the experiment, and surely it would command the support of all right-thinking people." Alice Chapin, an Indian teacher and friend of Elizabeth's, visited the school, the commissioner of Indian affairs having promised Sarah's benefactor that if Alice's report was favorable, government funds would be forthcoming. Alice wrote that the students, between the ages of six and sixteen, were "decidedly superior to white children of the same age" and "so interested and zealous to learn that they were perfectly obedient."

Sarah was ill when Alice visited—probably suffering from malaria, which she may have contracted at Yakima, as well as rheumatism and neuralgia—but she managed to teach, and Alice nursed her as well as she could. Even some of the neighboring ranchers, who had earlier refused to share water rights with Natches, praised the school. Another visitor, Louisa Marzen, after observing the students reading and writing, wrote to Elizabeth: "It is needless to say, Miss Peabody, that we were spellbound at the disclosure. Nothing but the most assiduous labor could have accomplished this work. But most amazedly did I rudely stare (and most of our party were guilty of the same sin) when these seemingly ragged and untutored beings began singing *gospel* hymns with precise melody, accurate time, and distinct pronunciation."

Many parents even wanted Sarah to build housing for the children, so they could live at the school when the adults left to work as agricultural migrants. Otherwise, they feared, the children might be sent to boarding schools. But despite the Peabody Indian School's demonstrated success, the boarding schools continued to gain favor. Their problems—which included fatal illnesses from diseases to which the Indian children had no resistance, and children's attempts to run away, which sometimes ended in death—failed to change the policy. Sarah tried to prevent Paiute children from being shipped to a boarding school in Colorado against their parents' wishes, but children were sometimes simply abducted, and many disappeared after being sent away.

Chronically short of money, the Peabody School eventually foundered. "I could not feed on love, so could not renew the school; and I was perfectly discouraged and worn out," wrote Sarah, whose health was also deteriorating. Elizabeth refused to lose faith in her protégée and searched for the means to keep the school going. "Sarah Winnemucca is one of those characters that make eras in history—like Isabella of Spain & Elizabeth of England—and a greater than they—and it seems to me that all my own life has been a special preparation to enable me to understand and help her," she wrote. Late in 1886, Elizabeth reported to Sarah that two hundred copies of *Life Among the Piutes* had turned up and she would be sending the proceeds from their sale. Sarah immediately reopened the school with twenty-one students. Elizabeth even raised sufficient funds to house twelve boarding students and published two more pamphlets, *Sarah Winnemucca's Practical Solution of the Indian Problem* (1886) and *Second Report of the Model School of Sarah Winnemucca, 1886–87* (1887).

By January 1887, the Peabody School had an enrollment of forty-five, and its aging Massachusetts benefactor, exhausted, was persuaded to rest from her labors. Paiute parents had applied for places for four hundred children, and Sarah, hoping to raise money to enlarge her school tenfold, wanted to apply for funding for an industrial training school—a concept in favor with the government and private associations—to be built on 40 acres of Natches's property. It may be that a planned lobbying trip to Washington—which she seems never to have made—had to be scuttled after Lewis Hopkins, recently returned, stole the money Natches had received from his harvest of wheat, oats, and barley.

Sarah didn't close her school immediately, but from this point on, it declined. Within two years, enrollment had fallen to fifteen or sixteen students, and in the summer of 1889, it closed its doors permanently. Eighteen years would pass before the federal government opened a school for Paiute children, and another twenty before Indian children were permitted—in 1927—to share classrooms with their white neighbors. Her disgraced husband gone, exhausted and in deteriorating health, Sarah went to live with her sister Elma Smith, at Henry's Lake near the Montana-Idaho border, where she died, of unknown causes, on October 16, 1891, between forty-seven and fifty years of age.

General Oliver O. Howard had known Sarah primarily as a guide, scout, and interpreter, and only later did he become familiar with her other roles: teacher, lecturer, and writer. In *My Life and Personal Experiences Among Our Hostile Indians,* he summed up Sarah Winnemucca's achievements in these words: "She did our government great service, and if I could tell you a tenth part of all she willingly did to help the white settlers and her own people to live peaceably together I am sure you would think, as I do, that the name of Toc-me-to-ne should have a place beside the name of Pocahontas in the history of our country." Nearly the entire twentieth century would pass before the people of Nevada recognized the truth in Howard's judgment and took the first step toward recognizing her achievements by naming an elementary school in Reno in her honor.

Each of our fifty states is allowed to have two statues placed in the U.S. Capitol. The statues are selected by state legislatures and represent notable people from their state's history. Nevada was one of two states that have had only one. In 2001, the Nevada legislature unanimously designated Sarah Winnemucca as that state's second representative in the Statuary Hall collection of the U.S. Capitol. She is one of only eight women to be so honored.

# CHAPTER SIX

# A Woman's Art

ONE OF THE TOUGHEST political positions I have taken in my Senate career is to support the National Endowment for the Arts (NEA). After the 1994 election, Republicans took the majority of the House and Senate, with a promise to balance the federal budget. I supported this goal.

In order to keep the commitment, every federal agency and program was scrutinized, and there was a strong movement to eliminate the NEA. The agency was very controversial, and among my constituents there were very strong views opposing it. It had made some ridiculous grants to groups that should never have received taxpayer dollars. Some of the works supported weren't fine art at all, and some were even pornographic in content. So it was the sentiment of a substantial number of members of Congress to save money and send a message. However, there was a slim majority, including myself, who believed we could shape up the agency without abandoning the arts in America. I felt the message should not be, America is a disposable society in which everything is for now, nothing of permanent quality.

Arts help define a culture; they are as important in depicting the life and times of a nation as the written word of history. Most other civilized countries in the world subsidize arts more heavily than we do in this country. To eliminate support for fine arts and performing arts would not only stunt their growth but curtail access to the arts as well.

The NEA subsidizes major performing arts companies like the Metropolitan Opera in New York, the National Symphony Orchestra in

Washington, and the New York City Ballet. But it also gives grants to art museums in small towns and helps performing companies travel to less populated areas.

One of my memories from elementary school was of a symphony orchestra that visited Galveston, Texas, fifteen miles from my hometown of La Marque, population 15,000. Most of the school piled into a bus to hear our first symphony, a major experience for us. Houston, a thirty-five-mile trip for us, also provided cultural opportunities for the entire Gulf Coast. The NEA helps regional performing arts companies and museums throughout the United States. Because my parents made the effort to expose me to these wonderful experiences, I had a modicum of knowledge about some of the arts. Ballet was my love. I took ballet for fifteen years, starting when I was five. I performed with the Houston Youth Symphony Ballet when I was in high school and was able to study under the well-known teachers Emma Mae Horn and Patsy Swayze. These performances gave me many skills and a knowledge of ballet that has enriched my life.

All this was possible because I had caring parents and lived near communities that supported the arts. With these opportunities making such a difference in my life, I decided to take a leading role in supporting a commitment to the arts in our country. There should be a basic standard for use of taxpayer dollars that doesn't offend people, but good old-fashioned common sense can be used. If our nation doesn't make the effort to help up-and-coming talent and give the general population, especially children, access to the best arts, the loss to our culture will be unacceptable.

My appreciation for ballet, symphony, opera, theater, and museums made a chapter on women contributors in this important field essential. The performing arts and fine arts were among the first to be acceptable careers for women. But the earliest women in this field had to overcome the prejudice against women having careers at all!

# Mary Cassatt

L OOKING AT Mary Cassatt's life from the outside, it is tempting to view it as one of uninterrupted privilege. Born in 1844 into a wealthy, distinguished Pennsylvania family, she was spared the economic and political upheavals that threatened most Americans' lives throughout the nineteenth century. She even appears to have escaped the need to justify her role as a woman. She studied what she wanted, lived where and as she wanted, and never married. As a single woman, she didn't have to steal time from her domestic duties in order to paint, nor did she worry about having to find "a room of her own" in which to work.

This overview, while correct as far as it goes, ignores one crucial factor: When Mary Cassatt decided in 1863 to study painting in Europe, she was doing something that only a handful of Americans of either sex had attempted before her. When she met the leading continental artists, notably Edgar Degas and other Impressionists, cast her lot with them, settled in France, and gradually emerged as the preeminent female American artist of her time, she broke entirely new ground. Young American women from well-to-do families often followed the English custom of visiting France, Germany, Greece, or Italy to view masterpieces of art and architecture at first hand, but they rarely stayed to become artists. Before the 1920s, expatriate American artists were few and far between. James McNeill Whistler led the way in 1855, and John Singer Sargent was actually born in Europe. Mary Cassatt, a decade after Whistler, was the first woman to gain an international reputation as a major artist.

Mary Cassatt started out with a number of advantages, material and cultural. She was descended from old French Huguenot, English, Irish, and Scottish families who settled in central and western Pennsylvania during the second half of the eighteenth century. One of her maternal grandfathers was the first director of the Bank of Pittsburgh. Her mother, Katherine Kelso Johnston, attended primary school in the home of an American woman who had grown up in France, and this may have been where the seeds of Mary's interests were planted. Katherine Johnston was orphaned when she was sixteen, but the income from her father's investments left her well provided for as a young woman. Mary's father, Robert Cassat (he added a second *t* later), made his own way financially. His father had made speculative investments in land that failed to show a profit before he died, but the son turned out to have a gift for business. He was at various times head of an investment partnership, a cotton manufacturer, and a commission and forwarding agent (what today would be called a commodities trader), who purchased raw materials that originated in the West and resold them to eastern merchants and manufacturers. Although some of the more staid members of the Cassatts' social circle had reservations about Robert's appetite for business, by the time he was forty-five he was wealthy enough to live purely off his investments.

When Mary, the fourth of the Cassatts' six children, was born in 1844, Robert was already thinking about retiring. For several years he was involved in politics in Allegheny City, now part of Pittsburgh but then richer than its neighbor because it was an important transshipping point. He served as a city selectman and mayor. In 1848, he moved east, first to Lancaster, Pennsylvania, and the next year to Philadelphia. Then the entire family spent four years in Europe, mostly in France and Germany, and the Cassatt children attended local schools. The principal purpose of the extended stay on the continent was to give the children a better education than they could get at home and to take the "grand tour" that Robert and Katherine had missed out on when they were young. Mary's eldest brother, Alexander (Aleck), who later became president of the Pennsylvania Railroad, studied at the famous technical university in Darmstadt, Germany. By the time they returned to the United States in 1855, after the death of thirteen-year-old Robbie, all the Cassatt children were fluent in French and German.

For several years the Cassatts shuttled back and forth between Philadelphia and suburban West Chester, where Robert's widowed sister, Mary Gardner, lived with her six children. In 1858, however, they bought a house in Philadelphia, probably to permit Mary and her younger brother, Joseph Gardner (known as "Gard"), to attend schools in the city. In any case, Mary, who had decided to be an artist when she was fifteen, was taking courses at the Pennsylvania Academy of Fine Arts by 1860. She most likely continued studying languages—adding a third, Italian—but otherwise concentrated entirely on the art school curriculum. The academy counted twenty-one women among its one hundred students during Mary's three years (1859–61), and it also exhibited American and European works by contemporary artists, including women. Curiously, years later Mary told her French biographer that she had never attended art school, although it is unlikely she would have forgotten the experience: one of her classmates at the academy was Thomas Eakins (1844–1916), generally regarded as among the greatest American painters of the nineteenth century.

Mary would probably have left for Europe before 1865 had it not been for the Civil War. Little is known about what anyone in the Cassatt family thought about the war itself, but the Cassatts benefited from it economically. During the 1850s, Robert's investments had suffered, leaving him still comfortable but no longer wealthy. The economic boom brought on by the war inspired him to found Cassatt & Company, a Philadelphia investment firm, through which he managed to recoup his fortune. Mary's brother Aleck grew rich in his own right through his association with the Pennsylvania Railroad, another company that prospered thanks to the war. Robert vociferously opposed Mary's decision to return to Europe to study art. Most likely he wanted his children to remain close to home, but he may also have believed there was something disreputable about being an artist—especially if one was a woman. According to one of Mary's early biographers, her father told her, "I would almost rather see you dead." Robert may also have thought that at twenty-one, it was time for Mary to marry. She never did, and neither, as it happens, did her sister, Lydia.

Shortly before Christmas, 1865, Mary arrived in Paris. Her mother traveled with her, probably to reassure Robert, and stayed about six months. Nor was Mary the only member of her Philadelphia Academy class who intended to continue studying in Europe. Her closest friend from Philadelphia, Eliza Haldeman, was planning to come, and so were several others, including Eakins; but Mary was the first to arrive. Other Americans from other parts of the country were already in Paris. One of them was Elizabeth Gardner, from Exeter, New Hampshire. She had never attended art school but had been in Paris since 1864 and studied with a number of French painters. Gardner was later recognized in France as an American painter of merit, but she painted in a more traditional, academic style than Mary, and her work has not stood the test of time. Like Cassatt, who was seven years younger, Gardner spent her life in France and eventually married Adolphe-William Bouguereau, a French academic painter.

Jean-Léon Gérôme, the most renowned of the academic painters at the time, agreed to take Mary on as a private student. This was an indication of her promise, since Gérôme pretty much had his pick of students (later in 1866 he also accepted Eakins). Besides private lessons, she also attended group classes and joined the throngs of painters copying the works in the Louvre. Alongside the art students at the museum, whose goal was to learn the techniques of the great artists, were professional copyists, who reproduced famous paintings for sale to tourists, sometimes making replicas of masterpieces to order. The sale of reproductions was one way for a struggling artist to earn money, and even Mary sold some copies to the tourist trade.

In 1867, Mary and her friend Eliza Haldeman decided to leave Paris for Écouen, thirty miles north of the capital, to study with the genre painter Paul Constant Soyer. They became part of the sizable artists' colony in the town and also succeeded in having paintings accepted in the prestigious Paris Salon. Although Mary and many of the other aspiring painters were ambivalent about the neoclassicism mandated by the Salon (they preferred the work of Gustave Courbet and Édouard

Manet, or even Gérôme, who represented a more adventurous off-shoot of neoclassicism), they recognized that the exhibition was a convenient stepping-stone to a career as a painter. She and Eliza returned to Paris for the Salon, and afterward Mary hurried back to Villier-le-Bel, near Écouen, to study with Manet's teacher, Thomas Couture. Couture's style embraced sensuality and spontaneity, qualities that Mary preferred to the restraint and, in her view, artificiality of the academics.

Eliza Haldeman returned home in December 1868. A year later, Mary's mother, Katherine, returned to France and accompanied her to Rome, after which the two of them sailed to Philadelphia. She may have gone to "rescue" Mary, who seems to have lost her sense of direction after Eliza's departure. Or it may be that after four years Mary had absorbed as much of French painting as she could and was ready to leave. Whether she looked forward to coming home or not, once back in the United States she felt out of place. Seeing her American artist friends again—Thomas Eakins, Eliza Haldeman, and others—was a pleasure, as was reuniting with her family, but she also recognized that after nearly five years on her own in Europe, she had changed too much to settle in again. One good indication of how uncomfortable she felt was the discomfort she caused in others. Lois Buchanan, whom Aleck married about a year before Mary's return, was a lightning rod for Mary's disapproval. A niece of former president James Buchanan and the darling of her own large family, Lois apparently bore some resentment toward several members of the Cassatt family, but toward Mary she felt particular bitterness. Ten years after their first meeting, she still could not contain her feelings. Writing to her older sister, Harriet, Lois said, "The truth is I cannot abide Mary & never will—I can't tell why but there is something to me so utterly obnoxious about that girl. I have never heard her criticize any human being in any but the most disagreeable way. She is too self important, & I can't put up with it."

Mary seems to have been oblivious to Lois's antipathy. In fact, she agreed to spend the summer of 1871 with the rest of her family near Altoona, where her brother and sister-in-law lived. Lois was expecting her second child, and Mary was content to set up a studio in Hollidaysburg, where her parents had rented a house, and painted nearly everyone who would agree to model for her. At the same time, her letters reveal that she was desperate to get back to Europe. From her academy colleagues Eakins and Will Sartain, she had heard about Spain, which she had never visited, and although she spoke no Spanish, she fixated on the country as her destination—almost her destiny. To Emily Sartain, Will's older sister, herself an artist, she wrote: "I really feel as if it was intended I should be a Spaniard & quite a mistake that I was born in America."

Her parents refused to underwrite another stay in Europe or even the cost of setting up as an artist in the United States, whether because they felt they could not afford to or, quite possibly, because Robert Cassatt continued to object to Mary's choice of career. In another letter to Emily, she expressed her frustration. She had yet to sell a single painting, and she was convinced that she would never be able to support herself by painting "unless I choose to set up to work & manufacture pictures by the aid of photographs." She had stopped painting entirely, "nor ever will again until I see some prospect of getting back to Europe." With no immediate likelihood of doing so, she thought about going out west to find a job, but she revealed no hints of where or what sort of work she might do. Instead, armed with two of her paintings, she went as far west as Pittsburgh, where the Catholic bishop commissioned her to make two copies of paintings by Correggio for the Pittsburgh Cathedral. The commission would cover her costs for about six months in Europe, so she continued to Chicago, hoping to get additional commissions or find buyers for the two paintings. She had no luck in that city, where, incredibly, her paintings were destroyed in the Chicago fire, on October 8.

Barely a month later, Mary and Emily Sartain were en route to Parma, Italy, where the Correggios she planned to copy were on display. They were welcomed by the director and faculty of the Parma Academy, who gave them studio space at the school, and endeared themselves to other members of Parma's artistic and intellectual circles. Instead of immediately getting to work on the Correggio copies, Mary started a painting using live models that she planned to submit to the Paris Salon in 1872. It was probably *Two Women Throwing Flowers During Carnival,* which was accepted for the Salon and was also purchased—the first work she had ever sold. From Italy, she finally made her longed-for pilgrimage to Spain, albeit without Emily, who had already gone on to Paris to study paintings. The art Mary discovered in Madrid was equal to the fantasies of Spain she had concocted in her letters to Emily. In particular, she was overwhelmed by the works of Velázquez, Murillo, Titian, and Rubens. A few weeks later, in Seville, she took in another group of Murillos and settled into a studio to paint a series of portraits of bullfighters, dancers, and other costumed figures, which comprise the earliest group of Mary's works to have survived.

Mary's spirits soared during her first months in Italy and Spain and remained high thanks to the sale of her painting and a visit from her mother. In 1874, she realized that to make her reputation as an artist, she had to be in Paris and moved into an apartment in the Montmartre district. Her older sister, Lydia, joined her there and served as Mary's companion, chaperone, and frequent subject until her early death in 1882. To earn her living, Mary followed the lead of other American painters in the city and set up as a portrait painter for American tourists who wanted artistic mementos of their visits. As a calling card, she executed two portraits—one of Lydia and the other of a young girl—that she also submitted for the 1875 Salon. When the study of Lydia was rejected (though the second painting was accepted), Mary blamed Évariste Luminais, Emily Sartain's teacher, and Emily herself. Emily had become extremely close to her teacher, who was miffed when Mary's slighting comments about his work got back to him. As Emily wrote in a letter to her father, "Miss C. is a tremendous talker & very selfish. . . . I shall never become intimate with her again, no matter how she receives my letter" (she'd written to Mary to explain why Luminais had taken offense).

Mary and Emily never patched up their relationship. Other Americans, however, like the young art student Louisine Elder, who met Mary at around the same time, were almost worshipful. "Miss Cassatt was the most intelligent woman I had ever met," she wrote, "and I cherished every word she uttered, and remembered almost every remark she made." Louisa May Alcott, the author of *Little Women,* used her sister May's enthusiastic letters about Mary Cassatt as the basis for an American artist in Paris in her unfinished novel, *Diana and Persis.*

The Salon jury that chose the paintings to be included in the all-important annual exhibitions was far from objective. Few, if any, works were seriously considered that were not by students, friends, or acquaintances of the powerful artists who represented the establishment. That Mary's paintings were accepted even after her criticisms of the academic style and a number of its practitioners became widely known is a tribute to her talent. By 1877, however, the rupture between her and the academy was irreparable.

Fortunately, in that same year, Edgar Degas approached her about showing her work with the group of painters known as the Independents or Impressionists (the term by which history now remembers them). Then rebels against the establishment who later supplanted the academics at the forefront of European painting, the group included, besides Degas, Gustave Caillebotte, Paul Cézanne, Claude Monet, Berthe Morisot (the only woman, until Cassatt joined them), Camille Pissarro, Pierre-Auguste Renoir, Alfred Sisley, and Édouard Manet. Manet didn't exhibit his paintings in the Impressionist shows, but he was considered one of the group.

Mary felt at home among the Impressionists almost immediately, despite being the sole American. She admired their combativeness, identified with their radical aesthetic program, and accepted her role within the group whose guiding lights were Degas and Caillebotte. She took inspiration from their innovative approaches to subject matter, composition, and color, even though her own work was less sensual and bold than, say, Degas's, with its subtle references to prostitution. Degas, in particular, encouraged Mary, dispensing advice during frequent visits to her studio, helping her to find models, and nudging her away from formal studio portraits and toward more natural compositions. One of her earliest successes in the Impressionist style is *Little Girl in a Blue Armchair* (1878), now in the National Gallery of Art in Washington.

Eighteen seventy-seven turned out to be a watershed year for Mary, personally and artistically. At the same time as she was exploring new directions in painting, her parents decided to move to Paris. Robert and Katherine Cassatt settled into an apartment with their two unmarried daughters, first in the fashionable neighborhood near the Arc de Triomphe and then closer to Mary's studio in Montmartre. Paris was a less expensive city for retirement than Philadelphia, but Mary's parents also signaled their acceptance of her choice of the artist's life by joining her in

Europe. After years spent apart, the Cassatts had to reacclimate themselves to living as a family, and it took time for Robert and Katherine to get used to living abroad, away from their friends, their sons, and their grandchildren. After about a year, however, Mary's gradually emerging celebrity began to absorb them.

The Impressionists opted not to exhibit their work in Paris in 1878, in order not to compete with the World's Fair that was taking place at the same time. One of Mary's paintings was displayed in the American Pavilion's art gallery, but the jury infuriated her by rejecting *Little Girl in a Blue Armchair*. Other American artists shared her low opinion of the jury's judgments. Elizabeth Gardner had two paintings accepted in the exhibition, but she complained that the jury preferred the lesser painting and had stuck her *Ruth and Naomi* where it could not be appreciated, "over a door. It was unjust and I wish the man who did it was hung in its place."

The World's Fair attracted large crowds, but Mary was already looking ahead to the Impressionist show of 1879. In a room in an Avenue de l'Opéra apartment that the group had converted to a temporary gallery, eleven of her paintings, pastels, and gouaches were displayed for a month. Some of the reviews were glowing—"There isn't a painting, nor a pastel, by Mlle. Mary Cassatt that is not an exquisite symphony of color," began one—while others scoffed at the perceived ineptness of Degas, Monet, and the other rebels against the academy.

Mary was gratified by the praise of her paintings and relieved that critics and collectors were starting to buy her work. After 1879, she was able to pay the costs of maintaining a studio out of her earnings as an artist. She intensified her ties to the Impressionists by joining Degas and others in founding an avant-garde art journal and followed Degas's lead by taking up printmaking, especially etching. Prints made from drawings she did at home and at the theater—which she attended regularly—constitute a sort of visual diary of the Cassatts' family and social life. To learn printmaking techniques, Mary worked in Degas's studio and printed her work on the press there. The two artists spent a great deal of time together—at museums and galleries, at the theater, and at dinner at the Cassatts' or Degas's apartment. They were rarely alone, but it is possible that Mary began to expect more from her relationship to

the brilliant, charismatic forty-five-year-old Degas than mere professional and aesthetic comradeship. Then Degas suddenly abandoned the
printmaking project and the plans to publish *Le jour et la nuit* (*Day and
Night,* the journal he had envisioned) and distanced himself from Mary
as well. It was a pattern he repeated often throughout his life, capri-
ciously and cruelly dropping friends and projects without warning. In
this case, the connection remained a warm one, but after Degas's incon-
siderate behavior, Mary was more guarded in their relations.

Alexander Cassatt brought his family for an extended visit to France
in the summer of 1880, and thereafter he and his brother, Gardner, visited their parents and sisters in alternate years. The Cassatts rented a
summer house in Marly-le-Roi, near Paris, and Mary took advantage of
the presence of her American relatives to draw and paint her nieces and
nephews and her brother. For the most part, Lois, Alexander's wife,
kept her distance. She grew to like her in-laws and visited the Cassatts at
their country house, but she spent more of her time in Paris, where Lydia
helped her shop for stylish clothing. Mary's overpowering personality
was one of the reasons Lois avoided Marly-le-Roi, but she admitted that
"the children seem to prefer her to all the others, strange to say," and
complained that her younger son, Robert, had even started painting
under his aunt's influence.

The summer and fall produced a rich harvest of paintings of family
members that would be part of the 1881 Impressionist exhibition. Lydia
continued to be Mary's favorite model; she was the subject of three of
Mary's eleven paintings in the show. Much to the artist's delight, she had
offers to buy all her paintings from that year's exhibition, and even had to
reclaim one painting—*Katherine Cassatt Reading to Her Grandchildren*—
from the buyer because her parents wanted to keep the work at home.
She also became a shrewd collector of the other Impressionists, and occasionally purchased works to resell at a profit. At the same time, Paul
Durand-Ruel, the first dealer to recognize the importance of the Impressionists, began to show and sell her paintings.

Almost as soon as Mary felt that she was on a secure footing as an
artist, her equanimity was undone by a series of personal and professional crises. Lydia, whose health had always been fragile, declined during the summer of 1880. It wasn't clear what Lydia suffered from,

though some of her doctors believed that she had Bright's disease, a kidney disorder. The therapeutic measures in use at the time—morphine, arsenic, the blood of freshly slaughtered animals—were ineffectual. Lydia and her mother, who suffered from a heart condition, sought relief in the warmth of the south of France. Mrs. Cassatt rallied, but Lydia died in Paris in November 1882. Just before Lydia's death, Gardner, the youngest Cassatt sibling, was hit with severe financial losses at Cassatt & Company, the family investment firm.

The distress in Mary's family was paralleled by dissension among the Impressionists. Some major artists—Monet, Renoir, and Sisley—had elected not to participate in the annual exhibition, and others objected to Degas's choice of his friends Jean-Louis Forain, Jean-François Raffaelli, and Federico Zandomeneghi to replace them, on the grounds that their work was not good enough. An offended Degas decided to boycott the 1882 show and apparently talked Mary into withdrawing as well. Bereft of her chief artistic outlet within six months of the death of her dear sister and companion, Mary stopped painting. She began to reach out to family and friends much more than she had done in the past—even to her sister-in-law Lois, who arrived in Paris with her family in December 1882. Alexander, now quite wealthy, had resigned from the Pennsylvania Railroad in October and brought his wife and children to Europe for an extended visit. Lois found that the grief-stricken Cassatts were especially kind, and she found herself drawn even to Mary, who, she wrote, "seems to be most anxious to be friendly and proposes something for us to do together every day."

Lydia's death and the collapse of the annual Impressionist exhibition may also have impelled Mary to seek social and personal ties among a wider circle than formerly. She forged closer friendships with other members of the Impressionist group: Berthe Morisot and her husband, Eugene Manet (Édouard's brother), who had moved to a house outside Paris; Degas; Pissarro; and Renoir. She cultivated connections with writers like Stéphane Mallarmé, politicians like Georges Clemenceau, and Paul and Marguerite Bérard, wealthy collectors. She also renewed contacts with distant relatives of the Cassatts, some when they visited France and others by letter. Another friend who came back into Mary's circle around the time of Lydia's death was Louisine Elder. Louisine never became an artist, but under Mary's tutelage she collected paintings by the Impressionists and some of their contemporaries. Later, after Louisine married Harry Havemeyer, head of the American Sugar Refining Company, Mary helped the couple amass one of America's most important art collections.

Over the next several years, Mary gained full acceptance in the artistic and intellectual circles in Paris that were ordinarily accessible only to the French. Unlike other Americans, she did not condescend to the Europeans, and her art continued to be shaped by French influences. At the same time, her ties to her family also deepened, partly because after Lydia's death Mary became even more responsible for her aging parents' care, but also because maturity had somewhat softened Mary's acerbic edge. The Cassatts moved into a larger apartment in 1886, one that would be Mary's Paris home for the rest of her life, and welcomed her brothers and their families on their frequent visits. Lois, the sister-in-law most uneasy with Mary, wrote of her in 1888, "She is the kindest soul in the world."

The Alexander Cassatts spent an entire year in Europe between 1887 and 1888. Aleck continued to have a number of business interests, but he devoted most of his time to his family and raising Thoroughbred racehorses on his farm, Chesterbrook, in Pennsylvania. During this period, Mary painted portraits of both her brother and sister-in-law. Aleck had modeled for his sister in the past, but either Lois had never consented to do so, or Mary had never offered to paint her, before this visit. Mary frequently did portraits of her relatives, and in 1888, with a painting of her brother Gardner's wife, Jennie, and their infant son, also named Gardner, she embarked on a subject that quickly became one of her signature themes: mother and child. There has been much speculation about the attraction the subject held for Mary, who never had children, but in fact it is not known why she found the mother-and-child subject so appealing. What is certain is that Mary loved children and fascinated them, and a number of Mary's best-known and most admired pictures, paintings and prints, both are of mothers and their infants— for example, one from 1889 of Hélène de Septeuil holding her child.

Mary's interest in printmaking revived during the late 1880s, and her series of drypoint engravings were an instant success when her dealer,

Durand-Ruel, showed them in 1890. She continued to make print series and soon combined techniques of etching and aquatint with the original drypoint, as in *The Letter* of 1890–91, a copy of which is in the National Gallery in Washington. Even the death of her father in December 1891, at the age of eighty-five, did not derail her artistic progress for long. Jennie Cassatt had arrived in Paris with her son Gardner shortly before Robert Cassatt's death; she helped Mary find a villa in Cap d'Antibes, on the Riviera, where they and the newly widowed Katherine spent the winter, to recover their spirits and shelter from the cold Paris weather.

When Mary returned to Paris in the spring, she was greeted with an unusual offer from Bertha Honoré Palmer and Sarah Hallowell, two friends and art lovers from Chicago who were commissioning murals for the Woman's Building at the 1893 World's Columbian Exposition in their city. Two paintings would be installed in the curved twelve- by fifty-eight-foot spaces below the roof. Mary Fairchild MacMonnies had agreed to paint one, to be titled *Primitive Woman;* Mary was invited to execute the mural devoted to *Modern Woman.*

Cassatt had never done a mural, and at first she thought it was antithetical to her art, but, as she wrote to Louisine Havemeyer, "gradually I began to think it would be great fun to do something I had never done before." She conceived of a colorful, vibrant work, showing "young women plucking the fruits of knowledge or science" in the large central panel and other young women "pursuing fame," playing music, and dancing in the smaller left and right panels. Hallowell, Palmer, and others, who were the first to see the painting when it arrived in Chicago in early 1893, were impressed. But when the painting was installed high on the wall of the Woman's Building's Hall of Honor, the effect was less successful. Cassatt's pictorial approach to painting proved inappropriate to a work that had to be seen from such a great distance. The figures were too small, and the colors, which she had intentionally rendered bright and lively, failed to lend a sufficient decorative effect. Degas had in fact anticipated the problem; as he later wrote, a mural "is an ornament that should be made with a view to its place in an ensemble, it requires the collaboration of architect and painter." And since that wasn't possible in this case, he had tried to steer Mary away from accepting the commission. After sending her mural to the exposition, she apparently lost all interest in it. When the fair ended in October 1893, both murals were apparently put into storage and vanished without a trace. They survive only in studies and contemporary photographs.

Accepting the mural commission, however, may have given Mary a sense of liberation that she had not felt before. In the summer of 1893, she again began to paint portraits of people outside her immediate family, on commission. She resumed a practice she had adopted years before, which was to make a second version of each portrait to show or sell, in addition to the portrait for the sitter or sitter's family. She also had her first solo exhibition, at the Durand-Ruel gallery in Paris, in the fall of 1893. It consisted of nearly a hundred works covering the fifteen years from 1878, when she first associated herself with the Impressionists, to 1893: paintings, pastels, and prints. The critical and commercial success of the show was capped by a request for one of her paintings from the Luxembourg Museum, which housed France's official selection of works of art by living artists. Mary, whose work was known in her native country only by a small number of collectors, was already a successful artist in France. Now she had been accorded the nation's official recognition. As she wrote to Hallowell at the time, "After all give me France—women do not have to fight for recognition here, if they do serious work."

If 1893 ended triumphantly, the next year began on a more sobering note. Katherine Cassatt, Mary's mother, who was seventy-eight, grew frail, forcing Mary to contemplate losing the last of the three people closest to her. In hopes of restoring her mother's health, Mary rented a villa on the Cap d'Antibes in early 1894 as she and Katherine had done after Robert Cassatt's death. Both women enjoyed the seacoast vistas, although Mary suffered terribly from seasickness and avoided even short boat rides whenever possible. *The Boating Party,* her major painting of this period, was almost certainly posed on dry land, using a boat on the property as a prop. In general, the Cassatts passed a quiet winter. Mary dealt with business matters, absorbed her disappointment when the Luxembourg's negotiations for her painting fell through (the museum finally acquired a work three years later), and, sight unseen, bought a mansion in the village of Mesnil-Théribus, almost next door to Bachivillers, where the family had spent the previous three summers in a house that her landlord had decided to occupy himself.

The next year continued in this up-and-down fashion. Renovations on the new house—Beaufresnes, the first Mary had ever owned—exasperated her to the point where she considered selling it, and Katherine was caught in an influenza epidemic. Mary's friend Berthe Morisot died five days after coming down with the deadly flu. Mary herself stayed healthy and succeeded in nursing her mother back to health, while also managing to complete several pastels and arranging for her first New York exhibition, at Durand-Ruel's Fifth Avenue galleries.

The New York show was smaller—only sixty-four works, mostly borrowed from American collections—and less enthusiastically received than Mary's show in Paris had been. She knew that American tastes lagged far behind the French, so she was not surprised, and sales were brisk, mostly to wealthy Americans eager to add a Cassatt or two to their collections. Thus Mary returned to Beaufresnes for the summer of 1895 in good spirits, concerned about her mother's health but full of plans for work and buoyed by visits from friends. Among other things, she intended to increase her output of prints, in order to make it possible for American art lovers of limited means to own her work. "I should like to feel that amateurs in America could have an example of my work, a print or etching for a few dollars," she wrote. In France, the availability of inexpensive artworks was helping to spread interest in art more widely, and Mary wanted to encourage a similar democratization in the United States.

The Cassatts were still at Beaufresnes when Katherine died on October 21. Fortunately for Mary, her close friend Louisine Havemeyer was with her throughout Katherine's last weeks. Extremely fond of her friend's mother, Louisine kept Katherine company in her final illness and wrote glowingly about her after her death. She believed that it was from their mother that Mary and Aleck had inherited their respective talents, and in her memoirs, published after Mary's death, she wrote: "Mrs. Cassatt had the most alert mind I ever met. She was a fine linguist, an admirable housekeeper, remarkably well read, was interested in everything, and spoke with more conviction, and possibly more charm than Miss Cassatt." Louisine also knew that the loss nearly undermined Mary's own will to live, but at last Mary wrote, "[N]ow I know I must," and got back to work as quickly as possible.

One reason Mary found painting therapeutic was that it gave her the chance to spend time with the people she felt closest to: her sister-in-law Jennie; her nieces and nephews, especially little Gard and her namesake, Ellen Mary; and Louisine and her daughters, who also visited often. To a degree, the ebb and flow of Mary's personal and familial relationships can be tracked by means of a careful inventory of her paintings at the various stages of her life. In the mid-1890s, for example, she seems not to have seen much of Aleck and his family, although they were often in France. When she returned to the United States in 1898—to see her family, to attend a second show of her work in New York, and to consult about potential portrait commissions—she stayed with Gardner and his family, though on this visit she also saw a good deal of the Alexander Cassatts.

There is irony, then, in the fact that probably no small part of her American success is due to her brother Aleck's stature as an industrialist. Less well known today than men whose philanthropies have made their names familiar, Aleck was an eminent captain of industry at the turn of the twentieth century. He was called back as president of the Pennsylvania Railroad in 1900, thoroughly reorganized the system, and built the railroad's first New York City terminal, allowing it to compete successfully with the Vanderbilts' New York Central. Until Aleck died in 1906, wealthy patrons who bought art were sometimes as interested in getting close to him by patronizing Mary as they were in collecting the work of the most accomplished American woman artist of her time. Still, the belated acknowledgment of her painting—as when the Pennsylvania Academy of Fine Arts awarded a prize to *The Caress* in 1904—was on her own artistic merits.

The critics took notice of her, however, on both sides of the Atlantic, and acknowledged her as a major—or, sometimes, minor—painter, and *minor* only in relation to Degas or Renoir, whose stars shone brighter than those of their contemporaries. Cassatt also helped many of her friends and acquaintances to assemble major collections of old master and Impressionist paintings. Although she herself ceased to be a member of any art movement after the early 1880s, she had a discerning eye for quality in her contemporaries' work and that of their predecessors. For the Postimpressionists and later artists, she had little patience and years later complained to her friend Sarah Sears at an exhibition of the work of Henri Matisse, "I have never seen in my life so many dreadful paintings in one place; I have never seen so many dreadful people gathered together and I want to be taken home at once." But it was her taste that guided Louisine and Harry Havemeyer in selecting the Impressionist and old master paintings, including El Greco, that later formed an important part of the Metropolitan Museum's collection, as well as those of other major museums.

Mary rarely bought any of the older paintings for herself, partly for financial reasons and also because they affected her so strongly that she feared they might prevent her from painting. After seeing Domenichino's work in Italy, she exclaimed, "It upsets me terribly to see all this art. . . . It will be months before I can settle down to work again." It was through the influence of her own work, and of her ideas about other artists, on collectors, art lovers, and aspiring artists that she made her lasting mark. Young painters often sought her out and were received with varying degrees of civility. One young woman from Toledo, Ohio, made her way to Mary's summer home in Beaufresnes with a bouquet of flowers for her idol. After being shown into the room where the white-haired artist sat, she was greeted with "How do you do? So, you're an American? I don't like Americans. I've been in France too long. But sit down, you've come a long way to see me and we'll talk."

Mary tended to distrust most art and writing that was more modern than she was. In the current writers—especially Henry James and Edith Wharton—she had no interest at all. Urged to read *The House of Mirth,* she found it an imitation of Paul Bourget, a French novelist "I cannot endure. I would rather go back and read Miss Austen's novels over again for the 100th time." Perhaps her isolation from the people who were finding new directions for art was the reason she was unsympathetic to it, or perhaps, as she herself remarked, she had sold her soul to her dealers, who wanted more of the same to please the limited sensibilities of their clients. The one modern movement she supported enthusiastically was political rather than aesthetic: women's suffrage. When Louisine Havemeyer proposed a show of works by Degas, Cassatt, and—at Cassatt's suggestion—old master paintings to benefit women's suffrage in 1915, Cassatt enthusiastically agreed. In fact, she broke with some members of her family who opposed ratification of the Nineteenth Amendment.

In Mary's later years, her isolation increased, mostly because of the effects of diabetes on her vision and general health. She outlived her siblings (Gard, the last survivor, died in 1911) and many of the artists who had been crucial to her development. Despite the volatility of her friendship with the unpredictable Degas, and his increasing debilities, his death in 1917 saddened her. Feisty to the last, she told Louisine that because her sight was failing she would henceforth read nothing but Milton: "When one can read but little, one must read the best." She had at least four cataract operations, but she never recovered enough sight to permit her to do much work or reading, though her mind remained vigorous until shortly before she died, on June 14, 1926, in Beaufresnes, surrounded by her gardens but otherwise alone except for Mathilde Valet, her loyal maid of many years. Mathilde wrote to Louisine Havemeyer: "I'm sure although she had many friends, nobody in the world loved her as Madame [i.e., Louisine] and I have loved her, and she knew it well."

## Marian Anderson

MARY CASSATT had to struggle for recognition as an artist despite the privileges of wealth and class. Marian Anderson would struggle to be recognized as a singer without either advantage. Her voice was legendary. Recordings of her do not do justice to her talent, but critics and music lovers agree with Arturo Toscanini's assessment. After the great conductor heard her sing at the Salzburg Festival in 1935, he told her, "Yours is a voice such as one hears only once in a hundred years."

Born in 1897, in Philadelphia, Pennsylvania, where her parents had moved from Virginia, Marian was descended from freed slaves. In Lynchburg, Marian's mother, Annie, had been a schoolteacher, but in Philadelphia she stayed home to raise her three daughters, while John Anderson sold coal and ice at the Reading Terminal Market and earned extra money selling liquor, although he was a devout Christian who never drank. When she was six, Marian began singing in the choir of the Union Baptist Church. The remarkable quality and range of her voice (nearly three octaves) were apparent early on, and she quickly graduated from the children's choir to the adults'. Thanks to her vocal range, she could sing any part and sometimes filled in when other choir members were absent. Handbills announcing her performances with the choir read "Come and hear the baby contralto, ten years old."

Reflecting on her early life, Marian Anderson wrote, "We lived in the kind of atmosphere where the family and home happened to be our whole world." For the young Marian, then, her community was focused on family, neighborhood, and church. In the last decade of the nineteenth century, when Marian was born, her South Philadelphia neighborhood was a heterogeneous mix of African Americans and Irish, Italian, and Jewish immigrants. When she was about ten, her father suffered a head injury at work and died not long afterward. Annie moved her three children into her mother-in-law's house; to support her family, she took in laundry and cleaned houses and stores in Philadelphia.

Despite the poverty that encompassed most of Philadelphia's African-American community, members of several local churches pitched in to help pay for Marian's voice training. Her local celebrity received an occasional boost when a well-known singer performed at the church and took note of the talented youngster. Roland Hayes, a celebrated tenor whose concerts included classical selections and black spirituals, would call Marian to the stage to perform with him. As a result, the Philadelphia Choral Society supplemented the money members of her church choir collected for her singing lessons by staging benefit recitals. Her first voice teacher, Mary Saunders Patterson, took Marian on as her protégée at no charge, and even gave her a dress to wear at an early recital.

Marian's prodigious talent was noticed outside the black community as well. The white principal of her high school, the South Philadelphia High School for Girls, encouraged her to transfer from the commercial course to an academic program that included more music classes. Ironically, perhaps, poverty was less of an obstacle to the young Marian's studies than racial prejudice. The Philadelphia primary school Marian had attended was integrated, so although she was used to a world separated along racial lines, she did not immediately realize that this separation governed education as well. As a result, she attempted to enroll at a local music school and was surprised to discover that it was closed to her. No first-rate music school in Philadelphia would accept an African-American student. Marian continued to study with the best black teachers available, but since they themselves had relatively little training in classical technique, her efforts to master the vocal techniques required for opera and lieder were frustrated.

Marian worked to help pay for her voice lessons, which she continued with her family's encouragement. A common scenario in poor families, especially those where the chief breadwinner had died or was incapacitated, was to send the eldest child to work to help support the others, but Annie Anderson never considered doing that. "My mother always encouraged me to do anything I wanted," Marian told an interviewer many years later. And of course, what she wanted to do was sing. Eventually, thanks to the efforts of the Philadelphia Choral Society and other benefactors, she was able to study with two well-known voice coaches, Agnes Reifsnyder and Giuseppe Boghetti.

Within the black community, Marian's reputation flowered. At the National Baptist Convention in 1919, held in Atlantic City, New Jersey, she was the featured vocalist. She also competed successfully in local competitions, appearing, among others, with the Philadelphia Philharmonic Society. By 1925, when Marian was twenty-eight years old, Boghetti had decided that his student was ready to appear before more musically cosmopolitan audiences. He had her enter a vocal competition in New York City; first prize was a concert appearance with the New York Philharmonic Orchestra. She won against three hundred other contestants, appeared with the Philharmonic at New York's Lewisohn Stadium, and was signed to a management contract by Edward Judson.

Popular and critical reaction to Marian's outdoor concert with the New York Philharmonic was enthusiastic, but the public and the critics were cool to the solo concert she gave at Town Hall. She herself recognized that she needed training and experience to develop her voice and to impart greater depth of feeling and expression to her interpretations. Thanks to a grant from the Rosenwald Fund, Marian went to Europe in 1930, where she studied and worked with a number of teachers and accompanists. Just as important, she learned German, essential to rendering the works of the art-song repertoire with the same authority she brought to spirituals. For several years, she spent more time in Europe than in the United States, but that changed when the influential impresario Sol Hurok heard her sing and signed her to perform at Town Hall in 1935. This time the reception was different, as the *New York Times* review asserted in its lead sentence: "Let it be said at the outset: Marian Anderson has returned to her native land one of the great singers of our time."

Thanks to the glowing reception her singing received, Marian also began recording for RCA. Her singing continued to retain elements of too much emotional restraint, but the power of her vocal instrument overcame that limitation. She was an immediate critical and popular success, and by 1938 her annual earnings approached a quarter of a million dollars. The fact that her dramatic range continued to be somewhat limited may be the result of the fact that segregation forced her to work primarily as a concert performer, since she could not be a member of the cast of a staged opera.

Despite being a victim of racial discrimination, Marian was no social activist. Hurok, looking for a way to extend Marian's geographic reach, wanted to book her into southern venues, and Constitution Hall in Washington, D.C., was a logical choice. The Daughters of the American Revolution, which owned the auditorium, refused to allow a black person to perform there, even after First Lady Eleanor Roosevelt registered her protest by resigning from the organization.

The outdoor concert that was held instead was the brainchild of Hurok, who saw the public-relations potential of having Marian perform before a huge audience, and Interior Secretary Harold Ickes, who hoped that allowing blacks to attend a major performance would encourage African-American voters to switch their allegiance from the party of Lincoln to the Democrats. The political results cannot be measured, but the open-air concert—attended by 75,000 people, including Supreme Court justices and senators—transformed Marian overnight into a musical and social icon. The program was as varied as the audience. It included "America," Schubert's "Ave Maria," and the spirituals "Gospel Train," "Trampin'," and "My Soul Is Anchored in the Lord."

Unfortunately, her voice was not holding up as well as her image. A grueling concert schedule—ninety to one hundred performances a year—was taking its toll, and she wisely cut it back to protect her delicate instrument. In 1955, Marian was finally able to make her Metropolitan Opera debut, as Ulrica in Verdi's *Un Ballo in Maschera,* becoming, at the age of fifty-eight, the first African American to sing with the renowned company. What audiences heard (in the concert hall and on recordings) in that performance and in the handful of other roles she performed at the Met was an extraordinary singer, although no longer the once-in-a-century voice that Toscanini had witnessed. But through her combination of gift and grit, she had turned a once unbridgeable gulf into a manageable distance.

Marian Anderson the singer, of course, cannot easily be separated from Marian Anderson the symbol. She believed that being a great singer was the best way to help the cause of racial equality: "It is my honest belief that to contribute to the betterment of something, one can do it best in the medium through which one expresses one's self most easily." And of course the almost insuperable obstacles to her musical training resulted from just one cause: the color of her skin. Had she been able to study with trained teachers and attend a conservatory together with her contemporaries—many of whom were blessed with lesser natural gifts—she would not have had to wait until she was nearly sixty years old to step onto the stage of a major opera company for the first time. Ten years later, she had retired from professional singing, after a long career, too much of which had been spent in the shadows.

Long before her Met debut, Marian had enjoyed recognition from many quarters. Beginning with the Spingarn Medal in 1939, she received innumerable honors. With her Philadelphia Award of 1941, she created a scholarship fund, the Marian Anderson Scholarship Fund, to make annual grants to aspiring singers. In 1958, the State Department appointed her a special delegate to the United Nations. When she received the Presidential Medal of Freedom in 1963, the other musical awardees included Rudolf Serkin and Pablo Casals. Her eightieth birthday was celebrated at Carnegie Hall in 1977 with performances by Leontyne Price, Shirley Verrett, and others whose paths to the Metropolitan Opera were smoothed by Marian's trailblazing efforts. Among other awards presented at the gala was the United Nations Peace Prize, in recognition of her work at the UN, with First Lady Rosalynn Carter's description of her "untiring and unselfish devotion to the promotion of the arts" in the United States over more than fifty years. Five years later, Shirley Verrett saluted her at another Carnegie Hall tribute, this time along with Grace Bumbry. In 1984, she had to be helped out of her wheelchair at New York's City Hall to accept the first Eleanor Roosevelt Human Rights Award, but she thanked her audience in a strong voice and wept as the crowd sang "He's Got the Whole World in His Hands," one of her signature spirituals. A National Arts Medal followed in 1986. The Marian Anderson Award, an endowed prize given annually to help outstanding singers advance their careers, was perhaps the most fitting tribute, since its purpose was to provide support to vocal artists based solely on their talent and promise.

Marian Anderson made it possible for younger singers of color—Leontyne Price, Jessye Norman, Shirley Verrett, Grace Bumbry, and Kathleen Battle, to name just a few—to take for granted that they could sing at the Met if they were good enough, as Marian Anderson had done. Martina Arroyo, who made her Metropolitan debut in 1961, summed up Marian's iconic importance in these words: "She has been a legend all my life. When I didn't know what opera singing was, I knew her name."

# *Latina Performers*

L ATINA PERFORMERS GRAPPLED with obstacles similar to those with which African-American singers and actors contended. In the early years of Hollywood, before the advent of sound and even later, actresses like Dolores Del Rio (1904–83) and Lupe Velez (1908–44) became stars by playing a range of exotic "foreigners" whose mysterious beauty they embodied in film after film. Their characters might be Russian peasants, American Indians, French aristocrats, or even Mexicans or Spaniards. Velez, born in San Luis de Potosi in 1908, appeared in a few Hal Roach comedies before she was twenty, and was not above overplaying her accent for comic effect. "Sometimes I sound just like Donald Duke," she once quipped. For the most part, however, her role was that of "Latina spitfire." She actually starred in a popular series of films in the early 1940s with titles like *Mexican Spitfire at Sea* (1942) and *Mexican Spitfire's Blessed Event* (1943). Del Rio, the daughter of a banker and distant cousin of Mexican president Francisco Madero, refused to be typecast as a hot-blooded temptress, but her accent limited her to foreign roles. In 1942, she returned to Mexico and thereafter acted in more Mexican than American productions. *María Candelaria,* released in Mexico in 1943 (and in the United States as *Portrait of Maria*), was awarded the Grand Prix at the 1946 Cannes Film Festival, the first year that event was held after it was interrupted by World War II in 1940.

Velez, Del Rio, and other early Latina stars paved the way for younger performers like Rita Hayworth, who in the late 1930s made the transition from Margarita Cansino, minor Latina starlet, to Rita Hayworth, American movie star and favorite pinup girl of World War II GIs. Born in New York City in 1918 to Eduardo Cansino, a Spanish dancer, and Volga Haworth, a Ziegfeld showgirl from an English acting family, Margarita began her career as her father's partner in the Dancing Cansinos. Discovered by a studio executive while dancing in a club in Agua Caliente, Mexico, she had small roles—often as a dancer, always as an ethnic character—in a series of films without attracting much notice. Only after her husband, Edward Judson, whom she married at eighteen, took over as her manager, changed her stage name to a variation on her mother's surname, and had her lighten her dark hair did Rita Hayworth become a star in Howard Hawks's *Only Angels Have Wings* (1939), playing Cary Grant's unfaithful wife.

Nearly another generation would pass before a Latina actress succeeded in breaking out of the limiting stereotype without having to camouflage her identity. Even then, it would be a struggle. Rita Moreno, born in Puerto Rico in 1931, started life as Rosa Dolores Alverio. Her parents divorced, and she and her mother settled in New York City in 1937. Bitten by the theater bug early on, young Rosa studied dancing with Rita Hayworth's uncle, Paco Cansino, and started performing in children's theater. Although she adopted several stage names—first, Rosita Cosio, then Rosita Moreno (her stepfather's surname), and finally Rita Moreno—her goal was to create an alluring Latina persona, not to conceal her roots.

Like her predecessors, for a number of years Rita was unable to secure roles outside the confining mold of "Latina spitfire." For a while, in fact, the press regularly referred to her as "Rita the Cheetah." Even after she won an Academy Award as best supporting actress for her portrayal of Anita in *West Side Story* (she had refused Jerome Robbins's invitation to audition for the role of Maria in the 1957 stage production), she had difficulty finding challenging film roles that didn't typecast her as an exotic temptress. Rather than settling for whatever movie parts were offered, she looked elsewhere—to the British and American stage, and to television. As a result, she continued to grow as an actress and became the first person to win all four of the most coveted U.S. performance awards. Besides her 1962 Oscar, she won a Grammy for her singing on the Electric Company album for children in 1972, a Tony for *The Ritz,* on Broadway in 1975, and the first of two Emmy awards for *The Muppet Show* in 1977. In June 2004, Rita received the Presidential Medal of Freedom in recognition of her contributions to the performing arts.

# Selena Quintanilla

ONE OF THE FIRST Latina singers to garner popular appeal was Vikki Carr, born in 1942 in El Paso, Texas. She began to bridge the gap from Spanish music to popular—winning Grammys in 1985 and 1992. But the breakthrough for a Latina singer who bridged American and Tejano cultures was Selena in the late twentieth century. Selena Quintanilla Perez might have seen Rita Moreno's award-winning TV performance on *The Muppet Show* in 1977, unless the six-year-old and her brothers were busy singing at their father's restaurant. Abraham Quintanilla had hoped for a musical career of his own, and he pushed his talented children—Selena, in particular—to succeed. He taught songs in his native language to his daughter, who did not then speak Spanish. In 1982, after the Quintanilla family moved from southeast Texas to Corpus Christi, Selena y Los Dinos started performing in clubs in and around the city. The band included Selena's sister, Suzette, and her brother, Abe; a few years later, Chris Perez, whom she married in 1992, became the bass player. It was in this region, not far from the Texas-Mexico border, that Selena discovered Tejano music, and soon the group's focus shifted from country music to Tejano, a heterogeneous style that borrows elements from diverse sources including Mexican ballads, rock, R&B, polka, country, hip-hop, and techno.

Selena y Los Dinos recorded their first album (for a regional Tejano label) in 1983; four years later she was named Best Female Vocalist for the first time and in 1988 was also recognized as Performer of the Year at the annual Tejano Music Awards. Still in her teens, the young singer was acclaimed the Queen of Tejano Music, a distinction that she retained even after her early death. In 1989, EMI-Latin executive José Behar signed the group to a recording contract after seeing Selena perform at the Tejano Awards in San Antonio. Their third album for EMI, *Entre a Mi Mundo* (1992), was the first by a Tejana artist to sell more than 300,000 copies. Music lovers and reviewers, noting that Selena's range embraced *ranchera* rock, ballads, and numerous styles in between, began to expect her to cross over to a larger musical audience. The band's appeal continued to broaden as well, and in 1993 and 1994 it won Grammy Awards in the Latin Music category in addition to Tejano honors. Selena, already the most successful Tejana singer in history, drew a crowd of over 60,000 to her February 1995 concert at the Houston Astrodome.

As Selena's appeal broadened, she retained her core Spanish-language base of fans. Her new recording label, SBK Records, decided to release a bilingual Spanish/English album, instead of the all-English disc they had originally planned. Her fans' loyalty and her staying power owed as much to her ability to connect to her audience as to her musical talent. During her concerts, she often talked to her audience, encouraging them to dance and to sing along, and even holding the microphone out to the audience when it was time to sing the chorus of a familiar song. She occasionally performed free for local groups or during radio interviews, willingly participated in charity fund-raising events, and often patiently signed autographs following concerts until long after the other performers had gone.

Her fans, then, appreciated more than her ability to interpret a number of musical genres—Tejano, romance, cumbia, tropical, pop, rap, and salsa—for bilingual Latino fans, Spanish-only speakers, and Anglo music lovers who didn't know a word of Spanish. Just as she herself had rediscovered her Latin musical culture without turning her back on the American dream, her public yearned to bridge the two worlds as well. They also admired her onstage sensuality and the skintight outfits that earned her the nickname "the Tex-Mex Madonna." At the same time, she projected a wholesome "girl next door" aura. In fact, Selena and her husband lived next door to her parents in their working-class Corpus Christi neighborhood, and she spoke often of her desire for a large family. Many of her fans lived that paradox as well, and they took strength from her public endorsement of a lifestyle that commingles sexiness and solid family values. Similarly, they applauded her involvement in helping to solve problems that plagued their communities by lending her prestige to campaigns to discourage drug and alcohol abuse, address the problem of AIDS, and protect battered women.

Selena was poised on the doorstep of a success that would have bridged her two cultures—Tejano and American—when she was shot, on March 31, 1995, by the former manager of the two clothing boutiques she owned. She died ten hours later in a Corpus Christi hospital. *Dreaming of You* was still in production at the time of her death; as soon as it was released, the album reached number one on the national *Billboard* Top 200. Her bold first step in bringing Tejano music to a larger musical public earned her a unique place in American music history.

## Women of Today

WOMEN HAVE MADE enormous contributions to the arts and entertainment for the entire life of our country. In the nineteenth and early twentieth centuries, they overcame the prejudice against women having careers and broke through racial barriers. Beverly Sills overcame personal tragedy to become one of the most acclaimed opera stars of the later twentieth century, and after her singing career ended, she turned her energy to assuring access to the arts by all sectors of society.

### BEVERLY SILLS

BEVERLY SILLS has been a dominant presence in American opera since the early 1950s. Born in Brooklyn, New York, in 1929, she joined the New York City Opera in 1955, the same year that Marian Anderson sang her first role at the Metropolitan Opera. Over a span of thirty years, Sills sang more than seventy roles with City Opera, the Metropolitan Opera, La Scala in Milan, and many more of the world's major opera companies. Except for the period between 1961 and 1964, when she retired in order to care for her hearing-impaired daughter and mentally retarded newborn son, Sills regularly sang in as many as a hundred performances a year and recorded a total of eighteen full-length operas. From 1980 to 1990, she was the general director of the New York City Opera; she served as chairwoman of Lincoln Center for the Performing Arts from 1994 to 2000; and in 2002 she accepted the position of chairwoman of the Metropolitan Opera. She actively supports charities and research efforts devoted to finding cures for birth defects. Among her many awards and honors, she has received the Presidential Medal of Freedom.

## IMPORTANT TRAIT FOR SUCCESS

BEVERLY SILLS: I have a passion for opera and really loved what I did for a living. It's a highly disciplined art form and you can't fool the audience. They know what they want and like.

## BEST NEGOTIATING STRATEGY

BS: During my career in the corporate world and running the New York City Opera for ten years, and as chairman of the Lincoln Center for the Performing Arts for eight years, and in my present job as chairman of the Metropolitan Opera, the only negotiating strategy is to do everything with a sense of humor.

## HELPFUL CHILDHOOD MEMORY

BS: My mother told me I could do and be anything I wanted if I was willing to work hard for it. She was right.

## BEST ADVICE

BS: Dream big.

# CHAPTER SEVEN

# CONQUERING THE SKIES

## *Amelia Earhart*

A MELIA EARHART TOOK her first flying lesson in California
about 1920, but she had caught the flying bug at the tail end of
World War I. As a twenty-year-old Red Cross volunteer at a
Canadian military hospital, she met members of the Royal Flying Corps
and heard them talk about their exploits. In 1920, she was living in California with her parents, hoping to help them save their shaky marriage,
when she met Neta Snook, a pioneer woman pilot. Within a year Amelia
was flying solo; and in 1922 she scraped together enough money to buy
a Kinner Canary, the plane she flew to set her first record: 14,000 feet, an
altitude record for women. Before long, she was participating in air
shows and stunt-flying exhibitions all over Southern California.

Amelia and her mother moved to Medford, Massachusetts, in 1924,
following her parents' divorce. Her sister, Muriel, was teaching in Medford; to support herself, Amelia taught English to immigrants and was a

social worker in a settlement house in Boston. She continued to fly, often as a demonstration pilot for Bill Kinner, the manufacturer of her plane.

The year after Charles Lindbergh made the first solo flight across the Atlantic, Amelia (who had flown solo before Lindbergh ever climbed into a cockpit) stumbled onto the chance to become the first woman to cross the ocean by air. Amy Phipps Guest, a wealthy American, bought a three-engine Fokker from Arctic explorer and aviator Richard E. Byrd, intending to claim the distinction herself. Guest was an experienced pilot, but her family objected to the risky venture, so she asked some friends, including the publisher George Palmer Putnam, to help find an American woman to replace her. Putnam, who had already published books by Byrd and Lindbergh, chose Amelia as much for her looks as for her aeronautical skills, intending to make a celebrity out of the first woman to fly across the Atlantic. She was a tall, attractive, effortlessly charming woman, whose daring would appeal to young people while her modesty and respectability (she neither smoked nor drank) would attract older, more conservative people.

In fact, Amelia probably needn't have known much about flying, much less be a crack stunt pilot, to set the precedent as first woman to cross from North America to Europe in a plane. The three-person crew that took off from Trepassey Bay, Newfoundland, on June 17, 1928, included a pilot and a mechanic, both men. Her job was merely to keep the flight log, but it was Amelia whose name became a household word overnight and who earned the sobriquet "First Lady of the Air." When the plane landed in Wales the next day, having missed Ireland in overcast skies, it was the female member of the crew who received nearly all the attention. Furthermore, it was Amelia who wrote *20 Hrs. 40 Min.,* the bestseller about the flight, and was appointed aviation editor of *Cosmopolitan,* who lectured all over the country and performed a string of flights that were intended to attract publicity as well as advance the cause of flying.

Concurrently, Amelia continued to focus on being a serious pilot. She competed in long-distance air races against the best female fliers from around the world. There were experienced women pilots at the time—only thirty or so American—and they quickly formed a close-knit group. In 1929, Amelia was one of the founding members of the Ninety-

Nines, an international association of women pilots, and she served as its first president (1929–33). The Ninety-Nines took its name from the number of licensed women pilots who became charter members of the group. They included three women who were Amelia's serious competitors for the distinction of being the first woman to cross the Atlantic solo: two Americans, Elinor Smith and Ruth Nichols, and the German stunt flier Thea Rasche.

For several years, no woman was able to accomplish the feat. Ruth Nichols crashed her Lockheed Vega while attempting to land in St. John, New Brunswick, on a refueling stop in 1931. The following year Amelia decided to make an attempt, also in a Vega, a plane that pilots liked for its speed but that was difficult to handle. On the evening of May 20, 1932, coincidentally the anniversary of the start of Lindbergh's historic 1927 flight, Amelia took off from Harbor Grace, Newfoundland. She flew effortlessly for the first four hours, at a cruising altitude of 12,000 feet. Then she ran into an electrical storm, and her altimeter stopped functioning, so she had to try to estimate her altitude in the dark sky. She tried to climb above the storm, but as the plane gained altitude, ice formed on the wings and caused the plane to spin when she attempted to descend again. By the time she regained control of the Vega, the plane was so close to the water that she could see the whitecaps through the darkness.

Having flown through the storm and survived the spin, Amelia wasn't sure whether the plane was still on course. At her low altitude, the plane was unable to fly on instruments, so she climbed high enough to use them but made sure to keep low enough to prevent the wings from icing up again. Unsure of the latitude, she was at least flying east again, but she noticed a number of potentially disastrous problems on the plane. Exhaust flames were shooting out through a crack in the manifold, and a fuel leak that was dripping gasoline into the cabin had also disabled the fuel gauge, so she wasn't sure how much fuel she had left. At dawn, she abandoned hope of reaching Paris, Lindy's destination, but could see that she was near the Irish coast. She couldn't find an airfield, so she set the plane down in a field where cows were grazing. She climbed out of the cockpit and asked the cowherd, "Where am I?" "In Londonderry," he replied. Her flying time of fifteen hours and eighteen minutes was the fastest by any pilot—man or woman over the distance. She washed up at a nearby farmhouse, caught a ride into the city of Londonderry to phone Putnam, and then rushed back to the farm to arrange a guard to protect her plane from souvenir hunters. As soon as word of her feat got out, she was mobbed in the evening by the locals but next morning by reporters, photographers, and the curious, for whom she answered questions, smiled, and signed autographs. By the evening of May 21 she was in London, where she was the guest, first, of Andrew Mellon, the American ambassador, and then of Nancy, Lady Astor, an American married to Waldorf Astor who became the first woman elected to the House of Commons.

Amelia married Putnam, the publisher who had launched her career as a celebrity and who capitalized on her fame by putting her name on luggage and women's clothing and publishing several more of her books. What she called "the zoo part" of her career was the price she paid for being able to pursue her passion wherever it led her. And her string of authentic flying achievements grew as rapidly as her fame: among others, first person to fly solo from Hawaii to the U.S. mainland, first nonstop flight from Mexico City to Newark, New Jersey, both in 1935. Purdue University invited her to be special adviser in aeronautics and career counselor to the school's female students, purchased a Lockheed Electra for her, and set up a research fund in aeronautics. Amelia called the plane her "Flying Laboratory" because so much scientific equipment was installed on the aircraft. The Electra had a top speed of over 200 miles per hour, and it was roomy enough so that the extra gear and gas tanks required for long-distance flights posed no problem. She had been dreaming of attempting something that no pilot had yet done, circumnavigating the globe at the equator, its widest point, and now she had a plane that could do it. The scientific experiments she would conduct—into how human beings and machines would stand up to long periods at high altitudes and under extreme atmospheric conditions, whether men and women react differently to air travel, at what point pilot fatigue would set in—were legitimate, but the real motive for the flight was that Amelia wanted to do it. Her role as aviation icon comfortably absorbed into her persona, she also planned to report on the airports where her plane would land around the world, thereby promoting plane travel.

The circumference of the Earth at the equator is just under 24,902 miles, but the route as Amelia planned it would actually cover some 29,000 miles. Because of the airfields' locations, the flight path would continually cross and recross the equator. Starting in Oakland, California, Amelia planned to fly west to Honolulu, Howland Island, New Guinea, Australia, Africa, and Brazil and finally back to her starting point. The Electra was damaged while taking off in Hawaii, however, and had to be shipped back to California for repairs. The revised flight plan had the plane starting from Miami, Florida, on June 1, in an easterly direction. Amelia also abandoned her original plan to fly solo for the final legs of the voyage, since traversing the Pacific would be the chanciest portion of the voyage. Her crew consisted of just one person, Fred Noonan, former chief navigator and navigation instructor for Pan American Airways until a drinking problem cost him his job. Because she and Noonan were unfamiliar with Morse code, she jettisoned a heavy marine frequency radio that used Morse code for communications and removed the antenna required for the Western Electric telephone-radio that was the plane's chief device for signaling its position.

The Electra took off from Miami on schedule, and for the first month everything went smoothly. Their itinerary took Amelia and Noonan to Natal, Brazil, where Air France flights took off to South Atlantic destinations. Their first stop in Africa was to be Dakar, Senegal, starting point for a beeline across Africa to the Gulf of Aden and Saudi Arabia. The flight to Karachi, Pakistan, was considerably longer than anticipated because the Sultan of Muscat denied their request to fly over his sultanate, but they took the thirteen-hour-plus trip of nearly 2,000 miles to Karachi in stride. In a letter to his wife, Noonan praised Amelia's endurance under difficult conditions, and he was right: she slept very little and remained at the controls for long periods and over long distances.

Noonan's navigational prowess never failed them, not even when the available maps were inaccurate, as the African maps proved to be. As long as she followed his directions, they stayed on course. Sometimes, however, she ignored them, as when she flew north instead of south in

Senegal and missed Dakar by 163 miles. She was quick to take the blame
for her lapses, however, and all indications are that the two of them got
along well until they reached India. On the phone from Calcutta, Amelia
told Putnam that she was having "personnel trouble," although she insisted that she could keep flying. Friends who were present in Putnam's
hotel suite and overheard the conversation surmised that Noonan had
started drinking again. She insisted that she was handling the problems,
and the pair pushed on.

In Calcutta, they encountered monsoons, and the heavy rains im-
peded their progress until they reached Rangoon, in Burma. In order to
get off the ground in Calcutta, they decided to fly with less gasoline than
planned, and got only as far as Akyab, Burma, a distance of a little over
300 miles. They had to abort their first attempt to fly out of Akyab after
two hours; the heavy rains forced them back to the airport. The next day
they made it only halfway to Bangkok before deciding to touch down at
Rangoon instead. From then on, the weather improved, and they covered the 1,200 miles to Singapore easily. In fact, on the flight from Rangoon to Singapore, Amelia won a $25 bet from a KLM pilot who had
taken off at the same time by beating the Dutch plane to the Malay island.

At Bandung, Indonesia, their next stop, the KLM mechanics made
repairs and adjusted some of the Electra's instruments, which were similar to those on the DC-3s that KLM flew. By this point, the plane had
logged 135 hours in the air and covered over 20,000 miles. Two days
later, however, the plane flew only as far as the Javan port of Surabaya
before turning back to Bandung for further repairs to "long-distance flying instruments" that Amelia did not identify more specifically. Because
they waited nearly a week before taking off again from Bandung, there
has been speculation about the reasons for the long delay, but all the indications are that neither she nor Noonan was suffering from any physical or mental ailment.

Two hops and two days later, on June 28, they landed in Port Darwin, Australia, where they replaced a blown fuse in the direction-finder
receiver and tested it. On their 1,200-mile flight to Lae, New Guinea,
the next day, the Electra maintained radio contact with Darwin for the
first 200 miles. Everything seemed to be in order for the longest, most

arduous leg of the voyage: 2,556 miles to Howland Island. Less than two miles long and a half-mile wide, the island, smaller than New York's Central Park, sits just above the equator in the Pacific vastness. The USS *Ontario* waited at the midpoint between Lae and Howland to provide communications and navigational assistance if necessary, and the navy and coast guard were at the island itself to help bring the Electra in on one of Howland's three runways.

The plane was carrying 1,100 gallons of fuel, more than enough to allow it to reach its destination even if it encountered stiff headwinds. Despite the difficulties of calculating longitude—east-west position—everyone was confident that Noonan's navigation would locate the tiny dot of land, or at least get close enough so that radio communications from the coast guard cutter *Itasca,* or the black smoke signal it was emitting, could guide the Electra to a safe landing. The first signs that there might be trouble came when the *Itasca*'s radiomen had difficulty "reading" some of Amelia's messages (sent fifteen minutes before and after the hour) and realized that she was not receiving their information about weather and the plane's position (sent on the hour and half hour). Seventeen hours into the flight, she radioed that the plane was about 200 miles from Howland, and fifteen minutes later she promised to send another message when they were within 100 miles. For the next three hours, the *Itasca* received a series of messages from Amelia: "We must be on you but cannot see you. Gas is running low. . . . We are flying at altitude 1000 feet." "We are circling but cannot see island cannot hear you. . . ." She and Noonan were not receiving the *Itasca*'s messages, however, until one arrived nineteen and a half hours into the flight, and she replied, "Earhart calling *Itasca* we received your signals but unable to get minimum please take bearings on us and answer on 3105 kilocycles." The *Itasca* could not make contact with the plane. The next message they received—"We are on the line of position 157 dash 337 will repeat this message on 6210 kilocycles. We are now running north and south"—was the last. If Noonan's calculations of longitude were correct, the plane was a long way from Howland, whose longitude is 176 dash 37. They had not spotted the island, nor had they seen the *Itasca*'s black smoke plume, which apparently dissipated without rising. Amelia Earhart was never heard from again.

The *Itasca*'s officers assumed that the Electra had gone down north-west of Howland, reasoning that clouds in that direction might have impaired visibility. Amelia had also made no mention of Baker Island, thirty miles southeast of Howland, which they should have seen. A PBY seaplane (a patrol/bomber seaplane manufactured by the Consolidated Aircraft Corporation) that took off from Honolulu was forced to turn back after storms made refueling impossible, so for four days only the *Itasca* was available to search for the plane. The Electra's empty fuel tanks would keep the plane afloat in water, and the plane also carried an inflatable raft and emergency supplies. These facts served to keep hope alive that Amelia and Noonan had survived. The cutter covered 4,500 miles and monitored radio transmissions, on the off chance that the Electra's radio might still be functioning. Between July 6 and 16, Ameri-can planes and a British minesweeper searched dozens of tiny islands and a 150,000-square-mile circle based on the maximum distance the Electra's available fuel might have carried it. The Frontiers of Flight Mu-seum, which recently moved to a marvelous new home at Dallas's Love Field, has documents related to Amelia Earhart, the WASP, and many other pioneering figures and phenomena in the history of American avi-ation. One of the most fascinating items in the museum's archives is "Confidential Search Plan" of July 8, 1936, that describes the areas one of the search groups was responsible for. I have examined that docu-ment, the summary of searches carried out by twenty-one of the planes from the aircraft carrier USS *Lexington,* and a commemoration of all sixty-five planes and three ships that participated in the agonizing search. I have rarely had a stronger sensation of connection to Amelia's courageous quest and the brave effort to locate her than I did as I held those yellowing sheets of paper. Of course, none of the search missions sighted any sign of the plane, the lifeboat, survivors, or bodies. The mys-tery of Amelia's disappearance has yet to be solved.

# Jacqueline Cochran

A MONG THE MILLIONS who mourned Amelia's death, only a relative handful were friends and fellow aviators. One who was both was Jackie Cochran. The two probably met in 1935, when they competed in the Bendix cross-country race, at the time the most prestigious flying competition in the country. Women had been barred from the Bendix two years earlier after a woman pilot crashed and died in another event, but Amelia badgered Vincent Bendix and Clifford Henderson, the organizers and sponsors, to reopen the competition to all qualified fliers. Cochran, who had begun flying in 1932, quickly followed Amelia's lead. She washed out of the race that first year, while Amelia finished fifth overall and was the woman's winner. In 1938, Cochran led all fliers, male and female, to win the Bendix.

Born in Florida in 1906 or 1910, Jackie was brought up by foster parents. She had no memory of her biological parents, who were most likely Ira Pittman, a mill hand, and his wife, Mary. In adulthood, Jackie picked her surname out of a phone book because she liked the sound of it. She had left school after third grade and was on her own by age fourteen. Jackie worked in a cotton mill and a beauty shop, among other jobs; and in 1929 she was a partner in a beauty parlor in Pensacola, Florida. Two years later she was living in New York City and working at Antoine's, a beauty salon with a branch in Miami Beach. A number of her wealthier clients spent the winters in Florida, and Jackie sometimes followed them there. Impressed by her drive and intelligence, some of the women whose hair she styled invited her to dinner parties, where one evening in 1932 she met Floyd Odlum, founder of the Atlas Corporation.

According to one version of the story, Jackie told Odlum that she was thinking of becoming a traveling rep for a cosmetics company, and he suggested that she learn to fly in order to cover a larger territory. Another account has a friend offering to take her up in a plane, but however she got into the air, she was hooked instantly. She also discovered that she was a natural-born pilot, and in short order she had earned her commercial pilot's license and bought her first plane. By 1934, she was racing competitively, and in 1936 she married Odlum, who helped her to start her own business, Jacqueline Cochran Cosmetics, which she built into a successful concern while continuing to race. An intense competitor, she set more records over a quarter century than any other pilot—in excess of two hundred for speed and distance.

Immediately after the German invasion of Poland in 1939, Jackie wrote to her acquaintance Eleanor Roosevelt, suggesting that the country start training women pilots to fly noncombat assignments so that when the United States entered the war it would be prepared. The idea went nowhere until 1941, when General Hap Arnold, chief of the Army Air Force, suggested that Jackie recruit a group of American women to ferry planes for the Air Transport Auxiliary (ATA), the British counterpart to the program that she was proposing for America. In the process, Arnold reasoned, she would see how the British dealt with the problems of integrating women into an all-male air force. As an ATA flight captain, she led the group of two dozen women fliers she had recruited.

In May 1940, Nancy Harkness Love wrote to Colonel Robert Olds, chief of the Army Air Corps Ferrying Command, to suggest pretty much the same thing that Jackie Cochran had urged on the First Lady and would soon be proposing to Hap Arnold. The response Nancy received was similar to Jackie's: interesting idea, maybe too radical for the army, and for the moment, the men are handling the workload. Except for the fact that the two women were both passionate pilots married to aviation entrepreneurs (Robert Love later founded Allegheny Airlines), they couldn't have been more different. Nancy Harkness was a daughter of a wealthy Michigan family with roots in Boston. Graduate of a New England boarding school, she dropped out of Vassar College in the middle of her junior year, either because her family's financial reversals in the Depression made it impossible for her to continue or because her fascination with flying won out over French history. After some adolescent high jinks, she entered only two races. Instead, she developed a methodical, conservative flying style perfectly suited to the role she would later have as head of a ferrying operation, where pilots must quickly learn to fly unfamiliar aircraft.

In 1942, the Air Corps Ferrying Command was renamed the Air Transport Command and placed under a new chief, Brigadier General Harold George. With the United States now at war in Europe and the Pacific, George needed ferrying pilots and was ready to consider even women to fly his planes. Eleanor Roosevelt, in her popular "My Day" column, declared on September 1 that "women pilots are a weapon waiting to be used," and ten days later, the Women's Auxiliary Ferrying Squadron (WAFS) was established. The squadron leader was to be Nancy Love. Hap Arnold, recuperating from a heart attack, didn't know about the WAFS announcement and in fact had called Jackie Cochran back from England in midsummer to put her in charge of an air force training program for women pilots. Jackie returned on September 12; three days later, the Women's Flying Training Detachment (WFTD) was created, with Jacqueline Cochran as its director. The WFTD (pronounced "Woofted") would train pilots to fly military planes following military protocols. When the women completed their training, they would begin ferrying planes as WAFS. To shield the air force from negative publicity, the program was to be kept secret, so the first training class—designated 43-W-1—took to telling the curious that they were "a women's basketball team."

By mid-1943, the training program was no longer a secret. It had expanded into its own quarters at Avenger Field in Sweetwater, Texas, and sent hundreds of pilots on to ferrying duty. As the numbers and types of planes increased, the demand for WFTD graduates increased along with them. Jackie Cochran, alert to opportunities to raise the profile of her detachment, was eager to take on new assignments, like target-towing for antiaircraft gunners, radio-control flying of drone aircraft, cargo flights, administrative flights, testing of new aircraft, and even simulated strafing flights that required pilots to dive at high speeds from 10,000 feet toward the antiaircraft batteries. To reflect their expanded role, Jackie and Arnold agreed to rechristen the group the Women's Airforce Service Pilots (WASP). She would have the title director of women pilots and be based at the Pentagon. Nancy Love was named WASP executive in the Ferrying Division, reporting directly to the head of domestic flying. Indirectly, Love was also a subordinate of Jackie's, but their relations had always been frosty and they had little direct contact with each other.

At the same time as the WAFS and WFTD were experiencing their growing pains and emerging as the WASP, the other military services also added women's branches and debated whether and how fully to grant them military status. The Women's Army Auxiliary Corps (WAAC) was renamed the Women's Army Corps (WAC) on July 1, 1943, and fully militarized under its director, Oveta Culp Hobby. The navy created the WAVES (Women Accepted for Voluntary Emergency Services), with Wellesley College president Mildred McAfee as director. The Coast Guard organized the SPARs ("Semper Paratus" was the Coast Guard motto), under Dorothy Stratton. And even the Marines, after losing a large number of men at Guadalcanal, saw the wisdom of having noncombatant women and appointed Ruth Streeter to direct the Marine Corps Women's Reserve (MCWR).

Jackie was ambivalent about the militarization issue. She was aware of the advantages to the women—prestige, permanent status, insurance, and death benefits—but she was loath to risk wrapping her program in the red tape that came with being part of the army. Just as important, she didn't want to serve under Colonel Hobby, someone with a will and personality as strong as her own and with whom she didn't see eye to eye. She convinced Arnold, who already favored the separation of the air force from the army, that the WASP should either become part of the air force or retain its civilian status.

By January 1944, the WACs and the WAVES had already been granted full military status, and Arnold decided that the WASP's moment had arrived as well. Thinking the change was a mere administrative formality, he applied to the air force, only to be told that the provision of the War Powers Act that made it possible to commission temporary officers in wartime applied only to men. To do the same for women, a separate act of Congress was required. To this end, Representative John Costello of California submitted House Bill 4219. The bill was greeted with powerful resistance both inside and outside the halls of Congress. Arnold—and perhaps Jackie, too—had miscalculated. Flight training had peaked by the end of 1943; the military's pressing need was for infantry to fight the anticipated land war in Europe. Of the 14,000 civilian flight instructors and trainees who were losing their jobs and their draft deferments, about one-third were being absorbed into the air force, but there wasn't room for everyone. Besides, many of these civilians could not meet the more rigorous standards of the military.

From Arnold's perspective, it made sense to retain the services of WASP pilots, who were better trained, more qualified, and more highly motivated than the male civilian pilots who were clamoring for admission to the air force. These women were the cream of the crop—barely 1,800 of them had been admitted to WASP training out of more than 25,000 applicants—and they had proved their value over two years of demanding service. The training course for women was as rigorous as the men's, but a higher percentage of women graduated in both 1943 and 1944. He was not willing to jettison them in favor of men who had failed to qualify for the air force, and he would not lower the bar in order to let more of the male applicants in. The House Committee on Military Affairs supported the bill militarizing the WASP, and so did President Roosevelt, whose secretary of war, Henry Stimson, wrote a letter endorsing General Arnold's position.

Spearheading the opposition was Georgia congressman Robert J. Ramspeck, chairman of the House Civil Service Committee. Since the WASPs were technically civil service employees, they fell within the committee's purview. A committee investigation concluded that the WASP was a waste of money, that the War Department had exceeded its authority in creating it, and therefore the program should be disbanded. The press, which had earlier praised the women pilots, now shifted its position. Except for a few newspapers in New York and Boston, the condemnation was nearly universal. *Time* editorialized, "The need to recruit teen-aged schoolgirls, stenographers, clerks, beauticians, housewives, and factory workers to pilot the military planes of this government is as startling as it is invalid."

The bill was defeated, 188 to 169, on June 21, 1944. Even after the vote, *Washington Post* columnist Drew Pearson continued sniping at the WASP. On August 6, he wrote, "Magnetic Miss Cochran has even persuaded the Air Force's smiling commander to make several secret trips to Capitol Hill to lobby for continuation of her pets, the WASPs. After Congress refused to let WASPs into the army, Arnold and Cochran adopted a backdoor strategy. . . . The WASPs, like the WACs, claim they were recruited to release men for active service. Now they say the WASPs are just 'replacing men, period.' "

The Civil Service Committee and its allies had scuttled HR 4219, but they didn't have the authority to scuttle the WASP. Training continued, and WASP who had earned their wings continued flying. In September 1944, when test pilot Ann Baumgartner took off from Wright Field in Dayton, Ohio, in a YP-59A Aircomet, she became the first American woman to fly a jet and had already flown every fighter and bomber in the air force arsenal between 1943 and 1944. On December 7, the eighteenth WASP class completed training at Avenger Field. A total of 1,074 women had made it into this elite sorority; over 900 of them were still on active duty; 38 had lost their lives. All in all, the WASP had flown every one of the more than seventy planes the air force operated during World War II, logging over 60 million miles in the air.

Hap Arnold had already called the WASP "the best women pilots in the world," and in his final graduation address he said, "It is on the record that women can fly as well as men." Both the graduates and the more than one hundred WASPs who attended the ceremonies knew that, but still it made them proud to hear it from the chief of the air force. The day was suffused with an air of sadness, however, because in early October every WASP had also received a letter from the general telling them that "the war situation has changed and the time has come when your volunteered services are no longer needed." The WASP program would end on December 20, just two weeks after the ceremony where Arnold had sung its praises. The war continued, of course, for another nine months, but for many of the WASPs who were unceremoniously dropped back into civilian status, the shift was disorienting. When a reporter asked Nancy Love what she was going to do, she replied simply, "I have no plans. I want to get away and think about what all has happened to me . . . and to us."

Jackie Cochran didn't want to get away; she'd grown used to the excitement at the center of the storm. First she wangled an assignment from *Liberty* magazine to write a series of articles about Asia in the aftermath of the war, but Jackie was a talker rather than a writer and never filed a single story. She managed to use her connections to get on military flights to the Far East and back, became the first American woman in Japan after the surrender, met with Mao Tse-tung and Madame Chiang Kai-shek, had an audience with Pope Pius XII at the Vatican, and sat in on a few sessions of the Nuremberg Trials. When she returned, she insisted that General Arnold, not President Truman, present her Distinguished Service Medal. She was the first woman honored with a DSM, and as usual she got her way.

Arnold retired in 1946, but he continued to speak out on the importance of making the air force an autonomous branch of the military. Jackie, back to running her cosmetics business full-time, suggested that she become a spokesperson for the cause. She was already logging about 90,000 miles a year in business travel, flying a surplus P-51 Mustang, and she would bring the air force story to the public and the press. The air force got its independence in July 1947. In the effort, Arnold also had an ally in Chief of Staff General George C. Marshall, but Jackie's campaign had contributed to the victory as well.

The WASPs, for their part, continued to be largely forgotten; they had no official status, and they were not entitled to veterans' benefits. In 1949, the first signs of change appeared when the air force offered former WASP members commissions. There was a hitch, however: none of the former WASP pilots would be allowed to become air force pilots. Nevertheless, 115 signed on, and 25 women made the air force their career. Thirty years later, service in the WASP was classified as military service for the purpose of computing veterans' benefits, and in 1980 members began to receive honorable discharges.

Jackie took another life-altering step in 1947 when she introduced herself to Chuck Yeager, not long after he became the first person to fly faster than the speed of sound. Before long, Yeager, most likely the world's best-known pilot, and his wife, Glennis, were close friends of

Jackie and Floyd Odlum, who now lived on a ranch in Indio, California, about 120 miles from Edwards Air Force Base. As jet-propelled flight took over the skies—and the headlines—Jackie decided that the records she had set flying propeller planes belonged to the past. One of her WASP pilots, Ann Baumgartner, had been the first woman to fly a jet plane; she wanted to be the first of her sex to break the sound barrier.

First, she would need a plane, an F-86 Sabre. But the air force owned them all, and there were rules against allowing civilians to fly them. Jackie was on a first-name basis with just about everyone at the top of the air force hierarchy, from chairman of the Joint Chiefs of Staff Curtis LeMay to Edwards flight testing director General Fred Ascani, and somehow she got permission to use Edwards, but not to fly the planes. Fortuitously, Canadair, a Canadian company, had started making a version of the F-86. Floyd Odlum bought one for Jackie, thus adding credence to talk that she held as many flying records as she did because she was married to a man who built airplanes. But she also got Yeager to agree to be her flight instructor, and that was something that wasn't for sale. On May 18, 1953, with Yeager following her in a second F-86, Jackie went into a steep dive at 40,000 feet, in order to use gravitational force to boost the plane's speed to 652 miles per hour, and flew into the record books yet another time, breaking the sound barrier.

As long as her health permitted, Jackie kept flying and setting new records. Northrop hired her in 1961 as a pilot in hopes of getting publicity for its T-38, which it was planning to modify into the F-5 fighter. She set new women's speed and altitude records of 842 miles per hour and 56,071 feet, and in 1964 she became the first woman to fly at twice the speed of sound. She had heart and circulatory ailments that gradually worsened, however, and after Floyd Odlum died in 1976, her spirits and health continued to decline. She died at home in Indio, California, on August 7, 1980.

# Women of Today

WILBUR AND ORVILLE WRIGHT flew the first few hundred feet in a crude handmade propeller airplane on December 17, 1903, in Kitty Hawk, North Carolina. Less than thirty years later, in 1932, Amelia Earhart became the first woman to fly solo across the Atlantic Ocean. Twenty-one years after Amelia Earhart's historic flight, Jackie Cochran became the first woman to break the sound barrier on May 18, 1953.

Fast-forward to June 18, 1983, and Dr. Sally Ride became the first female astronaut selected for a mission into outer space.

## SALLY RIDE

BORN IN LOS ANGELES, CALIFORNIA, in 1951, Sally Ride was a nationally ranked junior tennis player and briefly considered a career as a professional tennis player. At Stanford University, she was a double major (physics and English) as an undergraduate and then received M.S. and Ph.D. degrees in physics from Stanford in 1975 and 1978. Sally was one of only six women accepted as a candidate for the astronaut corps as she was finishing her doctoral studies. In 1983, she became the first woman in space and in 1984 made a second mission, both on *Challenger.*

Sally ended mission training in 1986, in order to join the presidential commission on the space shuttle *Challenger* accident. After the commission produced its report, she became special assistant to the administrator for long-range and strategic planning at NASA. In 1989, concerned about the scarcity of women in the sciences, she joined the University of California, San Diego, as a professor of physics. She is also director of the California Space Institute, a research institute at the University of California, and has written or cowritten five science books for children.

## IMPORTANT TRAIT FOR SUCCESS

SALLY RIDE: I think it's the ability to work with other people. That's been critical to me both in my career as a physicist, interestingly enough, because I chose to collaborate with several others, but maybe more important, in my career as an astronaut. You can't be an astronaut if you can't work with other people.

KBH: That's so interesting. Gosh, I would have thought you would say perseverance.

SR: (Laughter) Perseverance might be a close second.

## BIGGEST OBSTACLE

SR: I think the biggest obstacle was having to overcome the perceptions of other people that a career as an astronaut was not for women.

KBH: When you were chosen, had they already made the decision that they were going to have a woman?

SR: They had already made the decision that they were going to bring women into the astronaut corps, and they had already made the decision that they were going to fly women on the space shuttle, but that decision, even though it was made a couple of years before I got there, was made by administrators in Washington and people high up the chain. But that didn't mean that it was entirely accepted by everyone at the Johnson Space Center. They were all very, very, very supportive, but also just a little skeptical.

KBH: (Laughter) Been there.

SR: Yeah, I have a feeling you can relate to that.

## BEST PREPARATION FOR ROUGH-AND-TUMBLE OF LIFE

SR: Here the word *perseverance* might be the right one. You have to be fairly dedicated and willing to work hard to get a Ph.D. And I had trained myself to buckle down and work to learn what I had to learn. That was absolutely critical, I think, in being able to prepare myself for being an astronaut, because to overcome those perceptions of other people, I felt that I had to be at least as well prepared as everyone else, maybe a little bit better prepared. So I had to work hard to make sure I knew everything that I needed to know.

## BEST NEGOTIATING STRATEGY

SR: I had not had much negotiating experience before I got into the astronaut corps. But now, issues are coming up all the time, and people, of course, have different points of view. The strategy that I found most effective is to just try to remain engaged, be well informed going into the negotiation, and be equitable in the negotiation. Really try to keep things on a professional but friendly level and try to keep any animosity that can easily develop in a negotiation out of it completely.

## HELPFUL CHILDHOOD MEMORY

SR: You know, it's funny. It was actually an issue in school and—I don't even remember what it was, but I got discouraged by something in school. I came home and my father basically said, "Well, you've just got to reach for the stars." That's ridiculous to think about that right now—

KHB: It is.
SR: —but it, in fact, happened.
KBH: (Laughter) He didn't intend for you to take that literally, but you did.
SR: I don't think he knew what he was getting us all into. (Laughter) But that does actually serve as a source of inspiration to me when I come up against something and just have to take a deep breath and say, "Okay, keep going."

## BEST ADVICE

SR: Treat other people the way that you want to be treated.

# CHAPTER EIGHT

# PUBLIC LIVES,
# PUBLIC SERVICE

## *Margaret Chase Smith*

I N 1897, THE YEAR Margaret Chase Smith was born, Skowhegan, Maine, was embarking on its quarter-century heyday as an important manufacturing town. Numerous mills along the Kennebec River produced oilcloth, shoes, wood products, wool, and other textiles. In 1910, Skowhegan had more factories than any other town in Maine, but by the time the Depression arrived, its boom had faded.

Margaret's parents didn't share in the boom. Her mother's family was French-Canadian and had emigrated from Quebec in the mid-1800s. To shield his family from anti-French-Canadian and anti-Catholic prejudice, Lambert Morin changed his name to John L. Murray. Her father's ancestors were of English stock. They arrived in Fairfield, close to Skowhegan, in 1771. After serving in the Civil War, her paternal grandfather, John Wesley Chase, became a Methodist minister, but he died of pneumonia at forty, leaving his widow, Margaret Nolan Chase, with four children and a mound of debt. Her son George failed to make his fortune out West, returned to Maine, married Caroline (Carrie) Morin Murray, and had a daughter, Margaret Madeline, and three sons. They moved in with Caroline's father, John Murray, and lived with their four surviving children (including two more daughters, born in 1909 and 1912) in the small house he had built, under circumstances that were often strained. George's modest earnings from his barbershop were often reduced or eliminated because he suffered from migraines and depended on alcohol to ease the pain, and the fact that he was a Methodist and his father-in-law a Roman Catholic may have added another source of friction. Carrie worked hard to maintain harmony in the household and also to make ends meet, waitressing, clerking in the five-and-dime, stitching shoes at the local shoe factory, taking in laundry, and even selling milk from the family cow—with young Margaret as her delivery girl. As the eldest child, Margaret also helped with her younger siblings and worked—for as little as 5¢ an hour—to add to the family income. "We were poor, I guess," she said many years later, and poverty made her determined. At twelve, she went to work at the local five-and-dime and bought herself a life insurance policy, with her parents as beneficiaries, so that if she were to die they wouldn't suffer from the loss of her income.

Despite saddling herself with responsibilities, Margaret found time to play on the first Skowhegan High School girls' basketball team and was captain in her senior year, 1915–16, when Skowhegan won the state championship. She also had an active social life and even managed—with a $60 loan from her grandfather—to make the senior class trip to Washington, D.C. The students visited with George Otis Smith and his wife, Grace Coburn Smith. Smith was then head of the United States Geological Service, and his wife was related to one of Margaret's classmates. Maine congressman John Peters also introduced the seniors to President Wilson.

Margaret had planned to study physical education in college, but just before her high school graduation, she took a job as a clerk in the tax assessor's office, a position arranged by Clyde Smith, a local businessman and town selectman. Closer in age to Carrie than to Margaret, Clyde Smith courted Margaret with equal parts propriety and persistence, and he also tried to guide her future career choices. He encouraged her to attend business college rather than study education, and when he failed to change her mind, convinced her to teach, which she did in the one-room schoolhouse in Pitts, a few miles outside Skowhegan. After six months, she returned home. At first, she worked at the phone company, but two years later she was offered a job at the local weekly, the *Independent-Reporter*, where she did reporting as well as business jobs. In Skowhegan, she also joined the first of a series of women's clubs: the Daughters of the American Revolution, the Skowhegan Sorosis, and the Maine Federation of Business and Professional Women's Clubs (BPW), the state branch of a national organization dedicated to "the absolute elimination of the sex of the person in occupation, opportunity, or remuneration." In 1925, she was elected president of the Maine BPW, and she later characterized it as her training ground in political leadership and success.

All through the 1920s, Clyde Smith was a constant presence in Margaret's life. He had divorced his first wife, Edna, daughter of Smith's political mentor Ed P. Page, in 1914, and acquired a reputation as an incorrigible ladies' man, but had not remarried. In 1925, Smith and Margaret were briefly engaged but canceled their wedding plans, without, however, breaking off their relationship. In 1927, Emma Dot Partridge, executive secretary of the national BPW, teased them in her speech to the Maine BPW convention, which Margaret attended as president and Smith as a speaker: "Not long ago, one of the neighbors of the place where [Clyde] frequents heard this conversation. 'Well, Senator [Smith was a Maine state senator],' as the window was thrown up with a bang, 'I don't object to your sitting up half the night with Margaret—I don't object to your talking for two hours on the front doorsteps, but for the sake of the household, take your elbow off the bell-push.' "

By 1930, Margaret was a Maine Republican Party state committeewoman, at the urging of her then boss, Willard H. Cummings. Cummings was a mill owner and campaign manager for Wallace White, candidate for the Republican nomination to the U.S. Senate. White's primary opponent was former governor Ralph Owen Brewster, who had Clyde Smith's support, while White's supporters included Blin Page, Smith's ex-brother-in-law and now his political adversary.

Brewster won the election, but the Brewster-White rivalry somehow didn't prevent Clyde and Margaret from getting engaged for the second time and marrying on May 14, 1930. After moving into Clyde Smith's house, a thirty-room mansion built in the 1880s, Margaret wrote, "We are still enjoying ourselves attempting to make our entire life together one long honeymoon." Her experience would turn out differently. Smith, she later observed, "loved the ladies and they loved him." He declared his love for her in a series of letters written while on a business trip in 1931, but his devotion apparently did not last. To one correspondent, Margaret wrote in 1980, "[A]s great a man as Clyde was, he was not as devoted to me as you seem to think. . . . It was not a great love, not that kind. It was more a business relationship."

With the advent of the Depression, Clyde Smith's business and political fortunes both suffered. By 1932, he had lost his positions as chairman of the State Highway Commission, state senator, and town selectman. Margaret, meanwhile, continued to be active in the BPW and as Republican state committeewoman. Her connections to women's groups represented a potential political advantage for her husband. He reentered elective politics in 1936 as a candidate for governor, running against Blin Page. Margaret assisted her husband's campaign, traveling the state with him, and sometimes they appeared together, despite the awkwardness created by Page's attacks on Smith for his philandering. Much of the time, while he politicked she worked on a portable typewriter in the car. The *Lewiston Evening Journal* called her "one of the cleverest women political workers in Maine."

When Maine secretary of state Lewis Barrows entered the governor's race, Clyde withdrew to run for a U.S. congressional seat instead, ostensibly to spare the party a divisive contest between two Skowhegan adversaries, but really because party leaders offered to support him for Congress but not for the governorship. He narrowly won the primary but easily defeated the Democratic opponent in the general election and took Margaret with him to Washington, where she handled his schedule, research, and correspondence, helped write his speeches, and dealt with voters, visitors, reporters, and bureaucrats. She was recognized as that rare congressional wife, who actually did political and administrative work for the congressman, and she characterized their relationship as "a sort of partnership."

Officially, Ronald Patten, Clyde Smith's longtime law partner, was Congressman Smith's secretary, but Margaret did the real work. Smith took to referring to Patten as his "other" secretary. Thus Margaret was busy in Washington, but she was missing the connection to women's groups that she'd enjoyed in Maine. Then she discovered the Congressional Club, whose members were the wives of congressmen, cabinet members, and Supreme Court judges. The club offered a way for women to learn their way around "social" Washington. It had its own protocols, as did all things in political Washington. For example, new congressional wives (or others) would call on other women by leaving their *cartes de visite*, but they didn't expect to be received. Officially, no one was "at home" when a caller left her card—though Mrs. Hamilton Fish surprised Margaret by inviting her in for tea. Margaret felt uncomfortable in sophisticated circles, thinking of herself as more of a rural, working-class person (although she was DAR on her father's side). She was shown the ropes by Dorothy Foss Brewster, the wife of longtime Smith political associate Robert Owen Brewster, who was now a member of Maine's congressional delegation. In the Congressional Club, she got to be on good terms with representatives' wives and became club treasurer. She felt it smoothed the way when she was later elected to Congress: "The men in the House were so nice to me because their wives probably told them to be."

Working for Clyde, she learned how the Congress worked. Even as a congressional wife, she began to stake out political positions of her own that differed from her husband's. As his health began to fail (he had a heart attack in 1938), she started doing more of the politicking in Maine while he stayed behind in Washington. Speaking to women's groups, she voiced her support for equal rights and her opposition to protective measures for women (which Smith supported), and she favored spending on military preparedness, which Smith, a categorical isolationist, opposed.

On October 27, 1938, Navy Day, she made a speech to the Kennebec County Women's Republican Club, entitled "The Experiences of a Congressman's Wife in Washington." Margaret started out with a brief description of the capital's social protocols. Then she turned to the widening war in Europe (the Munich pact ceding the Sudetenland to

Germany had been signed a month earlier) and argued that the United States must prepare for war. "Development of our navy means self-preservation. Money spent in this direction, although from the viewpoint of many is expensive, maybe extravagant, is at all times an insurance . . . [and] the best insurance for peace is preparation for war." Maine was a shipbuilding state, so there were political advantages to her position, but she believed in what she was saying. Her husband had been elected while opposing all military buildup and voicing suspicion of profit-seeking defense contractors.

Congressman Smith kept working in Washington, but in December he was diagnosed with tertiary syphilis; that disease had probably aggravated his heart condition and was now widespread. He may not have told Margaret of his condition, and he certainly kept working instead of following the doctors' advice to rest as much as possible. He continued to assume the posture of a candidate for governor in 1940 (his announced ambition was to cap his political career with the governor's mansion), and even after bowing out of that race on the pretext that a more qualified candidate had entered the race (four other Republicans declared), he continued to look forward to reelection to Congress in 1940 and attacked the rumors that he was sick. "My activities in Congress bespeak good health."

Margaret apparently didn't realize how sick Smith was when he sent her to the 1940 Maine Republican Convention in his place: "He always seemed to find some illness to stop him from doing what he didn't want to do." But a day after arriving in Maine, when she and her parents stopped for the night in Boston en route back to Washington, there was a message from the state police at their rooming house: her husband was ill and she should hurry home. She took a taxi to New York City in order to get a train to Washington. For a couple of days, Clyde seemed to improve. Concerned about his congressional seat, however, he got her to file as a candidate in her own name, and wrote a press release endorsing her if he should be unable to serve: "I know of no one else who has the full knowledge of my ideas and plans or is as well qualified as she is, to carry on these ideas and my unfinished work for my district."

Clyde Smith died late that night, April 8, 1940. Margaret had almost no time for recovery—or even grief—before making good on her pledge to run for her late husband's congressional seat. In the special election for Clyde's unexpired term, she faced only nominal opposition in the primary, and the Democratic candidate graciously conceded the election. Nine months later, however, she faced tough contests in both the primary and general elections. With the country on the brink of war, Margaret lost no time in highlighting her efforts to strengthen the nation's defenses and win Maine its share of the lucrative defense contracts. She proved herself a formidable campaigner, and she and her army of volunteer supporters effectively neutralized doubts about whether it was prudent to trust a woman with issues like military readiness. Margaret outpolled all four of her primary opponents and then won an easy victory in the general election.

Winning acceptance in the House proved a trickier business than winning the trust of Maine's voters. Margaret struggled to obtain appointments to the committees concerned with defense and labor, the issues that interested her and concerned her constituents. She quickly won favor with Mainers and the press by voting for the Lend Lease Act (which permitted the United States to supply armaments to Britain and other friendly countries without having to receive cash payments—President Roosevelt said, "[W]hat I am trying to do is eliminate the dollar sign and to repeal the Neutrality Act.") As one of just seven women in the House, she made a point of doing nothing to suggest that she expected special treatment because of her sex. She did form close friendships with some of her female colleagues, especially Frances Bolton, an Ohio Republican, but the women members took pains not to appear to form a bloc. They were convinced that doing so would make the wrong impression in Washington and at home, where they wanted men and women to believe that they represented all their constituents, just as male congressmen did.

This is still, today, the thinking of women in the Senate. There are fourteen of us. We come together on some issues, but we are not a caucus and never pressure one another on votes. We recognize that our states and philosophies are different. When all the women of the Senate do join on an issue, as we did to assure that U.S. aid to Afghanistan would help girls catch up on the education they were denied under the Taliban, or to set a standard for the quality of mammograms, we always win. Despite the press's tendency to treat women legislators as novelties and report about what they wore rather than their committee and legislative work, Margaret managed to convince the voters that she was an effective presence on Capitol Hill.

Following her convincing reelection as Maine's congressional representative from the Second District in November 1942, Margaret redoubled her efforts to be appointed to the House Committee on Naval Affairs, where she would be able to contribute directly to the war effort and push her agenda of military preparedness. Her 1938 Navy Day speech had made a strong impression on powerful Naval Affairs chairman Carl Vinson, a Georgia Democrat first elected to the House before World War I, who admired the way Margaret comported herself. Margaret's appointment—like Connecticut representative Clare Boothe Luce's to Military Affairs—was probably also given a boost by the perception in Washington that it made political sense for the service committees to acknowledge the contributions American women were making to the country's defense.

As one of only seven women in the House of Representatives in 1943, Margaret was part of a highly visible group. She used her new committee post to project a persona that was equal parts lady and no-nonsense politician. She dressed the part, appearing in conservative suit, hat, gloves, and heels no matter what the place or the weather, at a time when many congressmen still wore wrinkled suits and made ample use of the House chamber's ubiquitous spittoons. She insisted on following congressional protocols where seniority was concerned and refused all deference to her sex, but made herself an expert on military matters who was an uncompromising advocate of a strong national defense. At the same time, she brought a woman's perspective to her work from her very first days on Naval Affairs, when she was appointed to a subcommittee charged with investigating the impact of vice—in this case, chiefly prostitution and venereal disease—on armed services personnel in "Congested Areas," the port cities of Norfolk, San Diego, San Francisco, Portland, and Newport. Stung by criticism from Surgeon General Thomas Parren and stymied by the failure of legislative and policing efforts to bring the problem under control, Margaret and her colleagues had a firsthand look at life in towns and cities struggling to cope with populations grown to several times their prewar size as soldiers, sailors, civilian defense employees, service workers, and people without jobs or even places to sleep flooded into the ports.

Congress had passed a law that made prostitution near a military installation a federal crime. As a result, streetwalkers and brothels decentralized, which made them harder to find but did nothing to drive them out of business. Housing was woefully lacking for the people crowding into the cities, so conditions of health and hygiene deteriorated in general, and this in turn exacerbated the spread of sexually transmitted diseases. As the committee members listened to testimony, they quickly realized that prostitutes were often not "professionals," thus relatively easy to identify, round up, and put out of commission. They were as likely to be waitresses or workers in other low-paid jobs trying to earn extra money, or even transients—some of them as young as thirteen—who had gravitated to the excitement and anonymity of the wartime boomtowns.

On her own, Margaret talked to girls and young women in a Norfolk jail. In one case, ninety-one were sleeping on mattresses on the floors of cells built to house just twenty-five people. She discovered that it was enough for a woman just to be alone on the street to come under suspicion of soliciting for prostitution. Some of the women told her that they had come to Norfolk hoping to find their boyfriends or brothers, a difficult challenge when there might be eighty thousand uniformed men in town on any given night, many of them sleeping in hotel lobbies and public parks rather than in barracks or on board ship. Women who were simply out for a walk—not streetwalkers—were arrested; the sweeps often failed to draw a distinction. Margaret perceived that women without jobs—and without the skills for doing them—sometimes gravitated to prostitution as their one means of earning a living. Besides condemning the conditions of the jails and the indiscriminate methods of policing, she also criticized the absence of efforts to provide job training for unskilled girls and young women *before* they were arrested. Most of the time, they languished in jail until they were sentenced or, if they were uninfected, released. "I can't think of anything less effective than sending them home at random," Margaret stated at a committee hearing.

There were other dimensions to the problems in the congested areas that Margaret helped bring to the subcommittee's attention. Among civilians working in war industries, some difficulties affected men and women equally: housing shortages, long workdays that began before stores and restaurants opened and ended after they had closed, inadequate health care. As a woman, however, Margaret took particular note of what working wives and mothers had to cope with. In general, women shopped, cooked, kept house, and took care of their husbands and children, even when they worked as long hours as their husbands. Despite a growing demand for women to replace men who were leaving jobs for military service, nothing was done to create the part-time jobs, flexible hours, and child care that mothers needed to be able to work and take care of their children. Rather than making child care more widely available, one congressman proposed cutting the funding in half, and another charged that the need for child care existed only because women went out drinking after work instead of returning home to their children. Margaret's maiden speech on the House floor helped turn back the effort to cut funding, but she wasn't able to get it increased. "We found many women waiting in line for medical care, for themselves and their children. We found them waiting hours after work to get their groceries and other necessities. We found children roaming the streets and some even locked in automobiles, not only because their war-working parents were absent from home but also because of the lack of child-care facilities and schools. This is an emergency. . . . [W]e can economize, but not when it comes to the care of our children."

As early as 1943, Margaret tried to leverage the gains that women were making because of the exigencies of the war—equal pay, greater acceptance in the workplace and public sphere, a military presence as WAC, WAVES, and SPAR—by campaigning for an equal rights amendment. In one form or another, an ERA had been under discussion since 1923, but Margaret was the first woman to speak in favor of it in the House. She shrewdly couched her support in evolutionary terms. Alluding to the Nineteenth Amendment, introduced in Congress in 1919, she said, "Women gained the vote as free citizens of the United States in the last war period. It is fitting that the principle of equal rights should be recognized in this war period." Massachusetts congresswoman Edith Nourse Rogers cosponsored the bill, along with forty-two male congressmen.

The struggle to pass the ERA was complicated by the fact that not all women wanted to sweep aside legislation that discriminated on the basis of sex. Working-class women and groups that supported women's labor, in particular, wanted to preserve existing protective legislation. In Margaret's view, any legislation that gave preferences to one group at another's expense was harmful in the long run. She favored a completely gender-blind society. In 1943, this was an idea far ahead of its time. Although the bill narrowly carried the Senate, in the House it failed even to come up for a vote.

On other fronts, Margaret and like-minded allies like Edith Rogers achieved incremental success during the period between America's entry into World War II and the beginning of the Cold War. Rogers, who had been a Red Cross nurse during World War I, introduced the bill in 1941 that would create the Women's Army Auxiliary Corps (WAAC). In Margaret's view, the WAAC was to become a part of the regular army, except that women would be noncombatants. Despite the need for women to perform work that would free servicemen for combat duties, the demonstrated superiority of women in doing work that involved manual dexterity and repetitious motions, the desire of many women to pull their weight as citizens in wartime, and the advantages of placing the women's activities under military control, most members of Congress opposed the legislation on the grounds that it would be too expensive and would undermine American womanhood.

Only after war was declared did Congress bow to necessity and the insistence of General George C. Marshall, the army chief of staff. A little more than a year later, the WAAC was reorganized into the Women's Army Corps (WAC) and integrated somewhat more closely into the army itself. The WAVES, Marine Corps Women's Reserve, and SPARs followed a similar trajectory, helped along by the WAC's pioneering experience. Even at the end of the war, however, it was always stipulated that the women were auxiliaries, that they were allowed to perform only specified work, for the purpose of freeing men for combat. Their numbers were limited, their leadership could not rise above the rank of colonel or captain, and their service would be terminated no later than six months after the war ended.

Throughout the war, especially when she toured the Pacific with other members of the Naval Affairs Committee, Margaret discovered what we would now call a Catch-22. Because officers were required to release a permanent soldier (or sailor or marine) for each *temporary* woman they took on, they were reluctant to accept the women. To change the situation, Margaret understood, would require permanent status for women in the military. She proposed that Congress consider the matter for all women in the military after the war had ended, and more urgently focused on the predicament of army and navy nurses, who were working under horrific conditions and, again, without permanent status. If a nurse got sick, she was simply relieved of duty.

In 1943, when Margaret talked to nurses serving in the Pacific, female nurses and other servicewomen were already stationed everywhere the army and navy were active, in Europe, North Africa, and the Pacific theater. Still, Congress—especially the Senate—refused to endorse the principle of regular status for women, despite the fact that Admiral Chester Nimitz had appealed for 5,000 WAVES so that he could send men into combat. The chairman of the Senate Naval Affairs Committee told Mildred McAfee, the WAVES' director, "The Navy, to my mind, is a male organization."

Once the war ended, political resistance to women in the military solidified, although the need for them led some politicians and military officers to propose that women be allowed to serve in a permanent reserve status. That didn't make sense to Margaret, who said, with characteristic directness, "The Navy either needs these women or they do not." If they did, their situation should be regularized. Ironically, when the matter came up again in 1947, it was the military—Dwight D. Eisenhower, general of the army, and Fleet Admiral Nimitz, as well as the heads of the women's branches, WAC Colonel Mary Hallaren, WAVES Captain Joy Hancock, and Marine Colonel J. W. Knighton—who argued fervently in favor of permanence for women. In their view, women had become essential to an efficient military, and it was crucial to have trained women in place in the event of a sudden emergency. Eisenhower recognized that women were better at clerical work, among other things, than men were, and they were cheaper. There was no reason to expect them to give up secure civilian jobs in order to serve in the military without the security and retirement benefits that men enjoyed.

When the arguments in favor of regular military status for women failed to persuade Margaret's male congressional colleagues, she maneuvered to scuttle the Women's Armed Services Integration Act on the grounds that no law was better than one that discriminated against women. To draw attention to the shortcomings of the bill, she proposed renaming it the Armed Services *Reserve* Act and insisted on a House floor debate instead of one conducted behind closed committee doors. Then she asked Secretary of Defense James Forrestal to look into the politicking that had resulted in stripping away the provisions granting women regular status. After Forrestal wrote to express his full support for the stronger Senate bill, regular status for women was restored during the joint Senate-House conference, and the Women's Armed Services Integration Act became law on July 12, 1948.

By the time President Truman signed this groundbreaking piece of legislation, Margaret had already set her sights on another target: a seat in the U.S. Senate. Frustrated, perhaps, by party conservatives who obstructed her efforts to win appointment to the high-profile Appropriations Committee, she declared that she would be a candidate for the Senate seat that Wallace White was vacating. There was a Maine tradition that the senior member of the House delegation replaced a retiring senator. Margaret intended to follow tradition, even if she would be setting a precedent as the first woman to do so. Well liked and respected beyond the borders of Maine's Second Congressional District, she nevertheless faced formidable obstacles. Her opponents in the primary would be the sitting governor, Horace Hildreth, and his predecessor, Sumner Sewell, who had already built statewide political organizations and fund-raising networks. Margaret, in contrast, took pride in her bare-bones organization and her frugality; in her House campaigns, she typically spent about $2,000. When I talked to one of Maine's present senators, Olympia Snowe, about Margaret, she recalled the description of the 1948 race by later party activists. It was a David vs. Goliath battle; the governor and former governor were considered Titans. Margaret was not only breaking the gender barrier, she was doing it against opponents with big money and big organizations. In the beginning, she was not favored to win.

Margaret, however, had assets that the skeptics overlooked. From her first days in Congress, she encouraged Mainers from other constituencies to contact her office with issues or questions if their own representatives were not helping them. She made a point of answering all mail to her office the day it arrived, a practice she had picked up from her husband, and she followed up to make sure that citizens' issues were addressed. Whenever she visited overseas military installations, during the war and afterward, she looked up the men and women from Maine, and when she got home, would call their families to let them know how their sons and daughters were doing. As a result, the people of Maine knew Margaret, they liked her, and they trusted her.

The press liked her, too, notably the Gannett chain, which published five newspapers in the state, owned two radio stations, and was the source of the news that appeared in most of Maine's weeklies. Her greatest asset was probably William Chesley Lewis, Jr., the Oklahoma-born attorney whose first contact with Margaret was as legislative assistant to the House Naval Affairs Committee. In 1946, Lewis, an officer in the Naval Reserve during World War II, switched to the Air Reserve to work with his father, a colonel, to lobby to make the air force an independent branch of the unified armed services. As a congresswoman, Margaret helped the Lewises' efforts, and Bill Lewis began to assist her with legislative work and hearings. He supported her decision to run for the Senate (he may have been the first person to tell her that she could win), and he managed her campaign.

Before she started campaigning in earnest, Margaret toured Europe and the Middle East in the fall of 1947. She returned a champion of the Marshall Plan for European recovery combined with a strong defense posture. "[W]e must back up our Marshall Plan dollars with arms," she declared. "The surest way to prevent war is to be ready to go to war." She had been planning to turn her international trip to political advantage on the campaign trail, but her plans changed when the most devastating fire in Maine history destroyed forests, farms, houses, and businesses from the mountains on the western border to the Atlantic Ocean. After surveying the damage, Margaret hurried back to Washington to lobby for federal aid to the state, as well as for Europe, whose political unrest and need she compared to Maine's in the wake of the fire. In fact, her response to the catastrophe may have aided her campaign as much as campaigning could have, since President Truman rewarded her efforts with federal assistance, while Governor Hildreth hesitated over whether to use state funds to help pay for rebuilding.

Margaret understood that running for the Senate would be much more difficult than her House campaigns had been, and much more expensive. Clifford Carver, a powerful figure in shipping and state politics, signed on as finance manager of her campaign, but she continued to highlight the grassroots nature of her support in her campaigning style. Her volunteers fanned out across the state to collect far more signatures than she needed to be assured a spot on the primary ballot, and a postcard was sent to each person who signed, inviting him or her to volunteer to work in Margaret's campaign. Other cards were targeted to specific interest groups, detailing how Margaret's voting record was geared to benefit them and asking for their support in return. She herself traveled indefatigably around the state, meeting people as she had always done as a congresswoman. Her opponents—who now included a minor candidate, Albion Beverage, a minister—ridiculed her as someone whose only virtue was that she always answered her mail, but Margaret capitalized on her image as accessible and concerned about the people of Maine.

Nearly two-thirds of Maine's registered voters were women, and Sewell and Hildreth worried that many of them might prefer Margaret. They drafted their wives to make public statements that women wouldn't make good senators, but Margaret turned the issue on its head by comparing government to housekeeping: "Women administer the home. They set the rules, enforce them, mete out justice for violations. Thus, like Congress, they legislate; like the Executive, they administer; like the courts, they interpret the rules. It is an ideal experience for politics." Shrewd campaigner that she was, Margaret balanced her opposition to preferential treatment based on sex with awareness of how others viewed her. Many of the journalists who followed her campaign were women, and one of them marveled at the possibility that if Margaret, who was characterized as "modest, hard-working, just plain Margaret Smith," was elected to the Senate, it wouldn't be long before there would be as many women as men in Congress. *(Fifty-six years later, there are only fourteen women in the U.S. Senate.)* True to her principles, Margaret declared, "I am proud to be a woman, but I want it distinctly understood that I am not soliciting support because I am a woman. I solicit your support wholly on the basis of my record of eight years in Congress."

My own personal experience has been similar to Margaret's. I have always run for public office on my qualifications and the issues I believe are most important to all constituents. I don't focus on gender, nor do most successful women candidates. However, I also believe a legislative body should include people from diverse backgrounds so that the diversity of life experience is brought to the table in the decision-making process.

For example, when I was a single working woman in the seventies, I started an individual retirement account (IRA). I married in 1978 and learned that while a working person who was single could set aside $2,000 to earn tax-free retirement savings, a married woman who didn't work outside the home could only set aside $250. I was incredulous. My view was that all women need retirement security, and a woman who works in the home raising her family may be the most vulnerable if she loses her husband through death or divorce. In addition, a woman who goes in and out of the workforce to respond to her family priorities would lose the opportunity to build the tax-free account that would add to her own and her family's retirement security.

I vowed to do something about it if I ever could. After I was elected to the U.S. Senate, one of the first pieces of legislation I introduced was the homemaker IRA. I teamed with Senator Barbara Mikulski (D-MD) to pass the bill. Today, whether a woman works inside or outside the home, she can set aside the same amount. If a person sets aside the maximum ($3,000 in 2004, with an added $500 after age fifty and increases in future years) for forty years, the resulting nest egg could build to a million dollars. As you can see, this added option for women can make a huge difference to the financial stability of the individual or a family. The reason Barbara Mikulski and I knew this change was a critical one was that we had brought our personal experience to the Senate. Men were not against this issue; they just hadn't thought about it. Therefore, it had never been addressed.

\*     \*     \*

Margaret's record in 1948 reflected, as it always did, her independent
thinking rather than a desire to curry favor with her party or Maine's
electorate. On many issues, like defense, most of Maine's citizens agreed
with Margaret, but on others they were divided. When she voted for the
Taft-Hartley Law, which put some constraints on the right to strike, because she believed that the legislation benefited the public, she ran afoul
of the state's organized labor groups. Still, labor leaders conceded, her
record was better than that of the rest of Maine's congressional delegation. As the June primary date approached and Margaret's position as
front-runner appeared unassailable, the opposition resorted to anony-
mous attacks on her character and her voting record. She was accused of
having affairs with a number of men and blamed for the failure of her
husband's first marriage, although Clyde Smith was divorced from Edna
Page in 1914, two years before he met Margaret. Her legislative record
was attacked in a long, also unsigned, mailing that insinuated that she
was no Republican, but a Communist sympathizer and a tool of organized labor. She gave the attacks short shrift, defending her record in detail and sending postcards that bore the slogan "Fight Money Politics
and Smears." The negative attacks affronted Maine voters' sense of fairness, and even some Democrats cast write-in votes for Margaret in their
own party's Senate primary. On the Republican side, she outpolled all
three of her opponents combined and then breezed past her Democratic
rival in the general election, a result that the Democratic candidate compared to "the Dutch taking Holland."

She may have been one of the first female candidates to have mud slung
at her, but she was certainly not the last. Women have never been exempted from the hardball politics that have been an unfortunate feature
of American democracy throughout our history. Rumors of affairs are a
common tactic directed against women, especially single women. In
Margaret's case, the voters had the good sense to see the smears for what
they were. In general, I think that voters judged women more skeptically
on issues in the early days of women's entry into elective politics, but

they have treated women and men the same when smear tactics were introduced into campaigns. Recently, I have seen a trend that gives me hope that perhaps mudslinging causes a backlash against the slinger. Political differences are fair game—but people should not have their families embarrassed or their reputations ruined just because they offer themselves for public office. There is a clear line between relevance and bad taste.

To appreciate the convincing quality of Margaret's victory, it must be seen against the backdrop of the election of 1948. The Republicans had been expected to win the White House and retain control of Congress, but Harry Truman pulled a surprising upset victory in an election that also resulted in Democratic majorities in the House and Senate. The Republicans suffered a net loss of nine Senate seats in 1948, but Margaret became the first woman of any party to be elected to both houses of Congress, and she was now the only woman in the U.S. Senate.

The excitement surrounding Margaret's election to the Senate echoed around the country. Hundreds of prominent women converged on the capital for her swearing-in, and the woman from Skowhegan acknowledged that she now bore the "responsibility of being senator-at-large for America's women." And that was how the country saw her. In *Adam's Rib,* a 1949 film starring Katharine Hepburn as an attorney named Amanda Bonner, audiences saw a framed photograph of Margaret Chase Smith, the country's most prominent professional woman, on her desk. At the same time, May Craig, a reporter for the *Portland Press Herald,* reminded her readers in Maine that the press was still paying more attention to what Margaret was wearing than to what she was saying.

Attracting a wide national audience was no problem. Margaret had already been writing a weekly syndicated column, "Washington and You," a mix of political commentary and commonsense advice, for several years. Once in the Senate, she went to a daily column, joining Eleanor Roosevelt, who had been writing "My Day" since 1935, in sharing reflections from the nation's capital. Getting the attention of her Senate colleagues, however, was more difficult. As the only woman, she was uncomfortable in the Senate's "men's club" atmosphere, where displays of courtesy by male colleagues were as likely to mask condescension as to express respect. She tended to avoid informal socializing in political Washington, either because she didn't realize how essential it was to political success or because, as she told an interviewer, "a woman unescorted is conspicuously alone." She often declined invitations, even those that were more formal than social, because she preferred not to go alone.

The Inner Sanctum is a small room in the Capitol where senators can gather informally to eat meals any time the Senate is in session. There are only two large tables, and whoever comes in sits with anyone who happens to be there. No one brings guests—it is senators only—and business is rarely done. It is one of the few places senators just have a good time with one another. I once heard one of the oldest senators observe that in all the years Margaret was a member of the Senate, she never set foot in the Inner Sanctum. I thought to myself, No one thought to assure her she would be welcome. The same could be said for the Senate fitness facility. There has always been a small fitness facility for exercise in one of the Senate office buildings; it never was a great place, but until 2003, it definitely had a males-only atmosphere.

When I came to the Senate in 1993, I was interested in having a place to exercise and was assured that women could use the "gym." So I called to ask if I could see it. The person who answered the phone wanted to know exactly when I would be coming. So I went at the appointed time and found a sign on the door announcing that Senator Hutchison would be on the premises at that time. I took a two-minute tour, long enough to know it would be very disruptive for a woman to try to use it. There were seven women senators at that time. By 2003 it was clear that the trend was going upward, and the facility was upgraded to include a woman's locker room and exercise room. It is quite adequate now for our changing demographics, and because of the long hours we work and the scarcity of safe, convenient places for exercise, it is very welcome.

One person who might have filled the social (and emotional) void in Margaret's life was Bill Lewis, who had been her political aide de camp ever since they first met through the Congested Areas Subcommittee.

When she won her Senate seat, Lewis became her administrative assistant. Fourteen years her junior, Lewis had an apparently limitless devotion to Margaret that ended only with his death in 1982. Margaret eventually moved into an apartment in a house Lewis's family built in suburban Maryland, and she grew close to the extended Lewis family. But as one of Margaret's biographers put it, the passions of both of them "were reserved for politics."

Margaret herself was less sure, at least late in her long life. Lewis's death—apparently from cardiac arrest while he was alone in his summer house in Maine, next door to Margaret's—devastated her. She probably never admitted as much to him, but seven years after his death, she told an interviewer, "We loved each other, [but] I could not marry a younger man, and I could not marry and keep my job. I wish that I had made more time for love." By the time she made her declaration, she was more than ninety years old.

While the press speculated about whether Margaret might be headed for the vice presidency or even the presidency, and her Republican colleagues tried to exploit the political advantages of having the only woman in the Senate, she got down to the business of working her way up the committee ladder. Robert Taft, whom she agreed to support for head of the Senate Republican Policy Committee, called her the "Joan of Arc of the Republican Party," but she failed to secure appointment to the Armed Services Committee and had to settle for the Committee on Expenditures in the Executive Departments and the District of Columbia Committee. Senator Joseph McCarthy, the senior Republican on Expenditures, agreed to appoint her to the Permanent Investigations Subcommittee, where she soon quarreled with McCarthy and Karl Mundt, its other Republicans, about their reluctance to condemn the government corruption they had documented. But this disagreement was mild compared with the abyss that opened between them after McCarthy's notorious speech in February 1950, when he claimed to be privy to the names of hundreds of Communists working in the State Department.

At first, McCarthy's charges of Communist agents in government didn't seem far out of line with the widespread fears and suspicions of the early Cold War era. The conservative wing of the Republican Party supported him unequivocally, but moderates, Margaret among them, were skeptical. When she asked McCarthy for evidence to support his claims, what he showed her seemed to have nothing to do with his allegations. Then he called Judge Dorothy Kenyon of New York a member of "at least twenty-eight Communist front organizations," and Margaret was sure the accusation was the groundless fabrication of a publicity seeker. Despite McCarthy's recklessness, or perhaps because of it, no one challenged him—not the Democrats, whose ability to govern was being undermined by questions about their loyalty, nor moderate Republicans who agreed with Margaret—probably because they were afraid of being targeted themselves. As a freshman senator, she hesitated to speak up, but after realizing that no one else was going to answer McCarthy, she resolved to confront him. Her method would not be to answer smear with smear, however, but to rescue the Senate, which she called "the greatest deliberative body in the world," from being "debased to the level of a forum of hate and character assassination sheltered by the shield of congressional immunity."

Margaret had probably not yet spoken at length in the Senate, where, she said, "in those days, freshman senators were to be seen and not heard, like good children." She had certainly not made a major speech before June 1, 1950, when she asked Senator Irving Ives, of New York, the day's presiding officer, to recognize her. Ives was also one of six senators who had signed a statement she had prepared (the others were George Aiken, of Vermont; Robert Hendrickson, of New Jersey; Wayne Morse, of Oregon; Edward Thye, of Minnesota; and Charles Tobey, of New Hampshire). Not even they were prepared for her "Declaration of Conscience."

Her speech asserted that people should not be threatened because they exercise their fundamental rights to criticize, hold unpopular beliefs, protest, or think independently, nor was there anything wrong in knowing someone who did these things. Without mentioning names, she condemned those who abused their rights of free speech so egregiously that others were afraid to exercise theirs. In Margaret's view, the country's efforts to defend itself against the threat of Communism were wrongheaded: "Republicans and Democrats alike are playing directly into the Communist design of 'confuse, divide, and conquer.' . . . As an

American, I condemn a Republican 'Fascist' just as much I condemn a Democrat 'Communist.' I condemn a Democrat 'Fascist' just as much as I condemn a Republican 'Communist.' They are equally dangerous to you and me and to our country." The desire to guarantee political victory for one's party did not justify demagoguery.

The speech spared neither the Democrats nor the Republicans, but for the most part the response divided along party lines: liberals applauded and conservatives were dismayed. Official Washington, however, said almost nothing. McCarthy supposedly told friends that he would not respond because "I don't fight with women senators." Even a Senate subcommittee report that characterized McCarthy's tactics as "perhaps the most nefarious campaign of half-truths and untruths in the history of the republic" was dismissed as just another act of party politics. McCarthy continued his indiscriminate attacks as if nothing had happened, but he hadn't forgotten about Margaret's speech, and neither had the Republican power brokers in the Senate. After the 1950 elections, she was replaced on the Investigations Subcommittee by freshman senator Richard Nixon and transferred to the Rules and Administration Committee instead of being allowed to continue on the District of Columbia Committee. Not even the start of the Korean War succeeded in refocusing attentions on Capitol Hill. Margaret and McCarthy continued dueling, especially after she helped prepare another subcommittee report that found McCarthy had acted improperly in connection with the 1950 Senate campaign in Maryland. McCarthy argued that Margaret and Hendrickson, one of the signers of her Declaration of Conscience, should have disqualified themselves from investigating the Maryland election because they had already stated their opposition to him. Margaret refused to be cowed. Her reply was "I shall not permit intimidation to keep me from expressing my honest convictions."

Dwight Eisenhower's presidential victory in 1952 swept the Republicans back into the majority in the Senate. Margaret also became Maine's senior senator when Robert Owen Brewster was bested in the state Republican primary by then governor Frederick Payne. Her new eminence restored her to the Republican Policy Committee and gave her entrée to the two committees she had hankered after since her arrival in the upper house, Appropriations and Armed Services. As chairman of the Preparedness Subcommittee, she directed a major investigation—the first woman to do so—into the impact of supply shortages in Korea. To a man, the commanders in Korea—General MacArthur, Admiral James Van Fleet, and General Matthew Ridgway—made the same points: shortages of ammunition and other supplies hampered the military effort and cost American lives, and forcing the troops to wage a limited war made victory impossible.

Margaret was uncompromising in her belief that the nation must be prepared to make sacrifices at home if they were necessary to ensure its security. She drove the point home repeatedly in questioning and in the final subcommittee report, over the resistance of administration officials like Secretary of Defense Charles Wilson, who so often dodged her questions about whether cuts in defense spending would compromise national security that she finally demanded answers in writing "from someone capable of providing them." Firm, persistent, always prepared, she gradually earned the respect of the men on both sides of the table. Where her colleagues were cautious, she showed herself to be intrepid. "The men loved it when I went after Wilson," she said, "but they wouldn't do it themselves."

As if to prove her bona fides with respect to anti-Communism, Margaret proposed legislation making Communist Party membership and distribution of "Communist propaganda" federal crimes. Although there were already laws on the books covering pretty much the same ground, Margaret wanted to light a fire under the people at the State Department, who were not, in her view, zealous enough in counteracting the Communist threat. In one 1954 speech, she asked, "How close do the Reds have to get before we stand up to them?" At around this time, in fact, a CIA-assisted coup in Guatemala replaced a leftist government there, and another one returned the shah of Iran to power when his successor proposed nationalizing the country's oil industry. Margaret's focus was on traditional warfare, however, as in Korea. When it appeared that a negotiated solution to that war was out of reach, she wrote in one of her columns, "We have tried everything else—maybe the atomic bomb will bring the Red barbarians to their senses as it did the Japanese. I know that some will protest that the atomic bomb is an immoral weapon. I agree that it is. But so are all other man-killing weapons."

As if to see for herself what the world's attitudes to the United States were, Margaret planned to tour Europe and Asia, in two parts, after the fall 1954 election. In October she visited Western Europe and the Soviet Union, and in the spring of 1955 she went to countries in the Middle East and Asia, twenty-three countries in all. Between the two stints of travel, the Senate had scheduled hearings to decide whether to censure Senator McCarthy. Margaret did not want to miss them. Abroad, her intention was to meet people from all levels of society everywhere she went: rich and poor, working people and families, bureaucrats and politicians, villagers and city dwellers.

She didn't travel incognito. When Edward R. Murrow got wind of her plans, he proposed sending a camera crew along, and a number of her interviews were broadcast on *See It Now.* In addition, Margaret wrote her own reports for her syndicated column, sharing her impressions of the countries she visited, the leaders she met, and the way people abroad felt about the American people and its government. Although she admitted that her observations were necessarily limited by the shortness of time—she spent one week in the USSR and less in other countries—she reported confidently that the United States was winning the Cold War, that our allies were as resolutely anti-Communist as we were, and that we were right not to trust the Soviets, whose "leaders smile only with their faces—never with their hearts."

Margaret returned to Washington in time for the Senate's consideration of the recommended censure of Joseph McCarthy. The Wisconsin senator's friends tried to protect him from himself by urging him to make at least a mild show of contrition for his personal attacks on Senate colleagues. McCarthy, unrepentant to the last, declared, "I don't crawl." Instead, he self-destructed. He accused the investigating subcommittee of being a Communist Party tool, and after an acrimonious debate on the Senate floor, two-thirds of the membership voted to condemn his actions but stopped short of censuring them. A censure would have required that the Senate vote on expulsion. McCarthy remained in the Senate—no longer a threat, without friends or power—until his death in 1957.

In 1955, voters and politicians alike were starting to look forward to the coming elections—not for Margaret but for her party and President

Eisenhower—so she returned from the second phase of her twenty-three-nation tour to mend some political fences. She communicated her judgments of the political leaders she met to her Senate colleagues, to her constituents, and even to the president, who wanted to discuss foreign policy. From the vantage point of the twenty-first century, some of her assessments may appear naive—for example, her assertion that Francisco Franco "had been so erroneously pictured to the American public" and was "an able man, and a very good man in his place in Spain"—but they were thoroughly consistent with her conviction that the critical principle of America's global posture must be to present a solid front against the spread of Communism.

Eisenhower's visit to Skowhegan that summer bolstered Margaret's image in her home state and even inspired some talk of her as Ike's running mate if the "dump Nixon" movement gathered steam by convention time. But Nixon's star was ascendant again by mid-1956, and Margaret threw herself behind the effort to unseat Democratic governor Edmund Muskie (after 1958 her Senate colleague and rival). She drew criticism for urging Mainers to support the Republican challenger, William Trafton, Jr., as a "personal favor" to her. The ploy backfired; Muskie won reelection handily. Two days before the 1956 presidential election, she returned to the national stage by debating Eleanor Roosevelt on Eisenhower versus Adlai Stevenson on *Face the Nation.* Relations between the former First Lady and the Maine senator, never warm, were further cooled by their televised confrontation, but the exposure considerably increased Margaret's national recognition factor.

Always mindful of her constituents, who were more likely to worry about wages and farm subsidies than about the Cold War, Margaret spared no effort to make sure Maine shared in the benefits of the military policy she espoused. Her state's location made it a strategic place for air bases; building, maintaining, and servicing those bases provided much-needed jobs for Maine residents. She also made sure that Maine got its share of shipbuilding contracts, and she supported local industry and farm products by advocating trade and price policies that encouraged domestic self-sufficiency.

Margaret was unopposed in the 1960 Republican primary, but in the general election she was confronted with an unusual Democratic challenger: a woman. Lucia Cormier was an experienced state legislator whom Edmund Muskie had handpicked to run against his Senate rival. The contest attracted considerable attention from the national press because this was the first Senate election pitting two women against each other. The novelty, rather than the ideological differences between them, may have been the most striking thing about the contest. Cormier attacked Margaret for being out of touch with the people of Maine, but she admitted that she admired her personally, and leveled most of her criticisms at the opposing party, not her opponent. For her part, Margaret campaigned almost as if her opponent did not exist until just before the election, when she agreed to a single televised debate. Her strategy—suggested by Bill Lewis—was to deny Cormier the opportunity to become better known.

The strategy worked. Margaret was an icon in Maine, and as one voter told a reporter, "I'm a Democrat. I think Lucia is a smart gal and all that, but I haven't heard a single reason why we shouldn't send Margaret back to the Senate." Neither had most of Maine's voters. Margaret polled the largest popular tally in Maine electoral history and the highest vote in percentage terms of any Senate candidate that year, even as John F. Kennedy was defeating Richard Nixon for the presidency. When the Senate reconvened in January, she snubbed Edmund Muskie by refusing to walk down the aisle with him to be sworn in. It is Senate tradition for incumbent senators to escort the elected (or reelected) members from their states to the well of the chamber for the swearing-in ceremony. Instead of Muskie, Margaret asked Maurine Neuberger, the widow of Senator Richard Neuberger of Oregon, to serve as her escort. Maurine Neuberger had been elected to succeed her late husband, and Margaret explained afterward that she was marking the "historic occasion," the first time two women, elected to full terms, were serving at the same time in the U.S. Senate. Most observers suspected a less symbolic, more personal motive. Adding to the irony—and the insult to Muskie—was the fact that though Margaret had admired Richard Neuberger, she and Maurine were never personal or political allies. Their closest encounter may well have been that January morning in 1961 when they walked arm in arm to the well of the Senate.

When the Eighty-seventh Congress convened, however, Margaret had much more on her mind than her interparty rivalry with Muskie. Ever since the 1960 Republican National Convention, she and other leading Republicans had been contemplating what roles to play in the party's future. After Richard Nixon lost the presidential election to John F. Kennedy, the maneuvering increased. Moderate Republicans like Nelson Rockefeller courted her support, while conservatives—notably Barry Goldwater, who astonished observers by appearing in public with Muskie rather than Margaret—kept their distance. Rather than doing her part to anoint a man who would lead her party back to power, Margaret began acting as if she might be thinking about making her own run for the White House.

If she was going to pursue the presidency—or the vice presidency—1964 seemed to be the year to make her bid. Margaret would be sixty-seven that year; if she waited another four years she might seem too old to set a precedent as the first woman candidate of a major party for the top office. Whether or not higher office was on her mind, a change in Margaret's political style was visible during the Kennedy administration. She spoke out more often—and on more formal occasions—to criticize the president's policies, especially with respect to Cold War matters. She felt that by signaling clearly to the Soviet leader, Nikita Khrushchev, that the United States would not consider using nuclear weapons in the event of an all-out war, the United States was betraying weakness rather than strength. She criticized Kennedy for admitting that "we do not have the will to use that one power with which we can stop him. In short, we have the nuclear capability but not the nuclear credibility."

Margaret most likely had several reasons for being tough on Kennedy. She considered him a political opportunist; she resented his having failed to stand up to McCarthy, and even being absent from the Senate when the censure vote came up; and she passionately believed that he was putting the country at risk by not confronting the Soviets over Cuba, Berlin, and Southeast Asia. Whatever her motives, her words had effects on both sides of the Iron Curtain. Kennedy began taking a harder line in his statements of American positions, and Khrushchev called her a "bloodthirsty little woman." These acknowledgments that her messages had gotten through pleased—even emboldened—her. After observing that men had failed to bring peace to the world, she said, "I don't see how women could do any worse—and, of course, we will never know unless women are given a chance."

Was she testing the waters for an attempt of her own for national office? It's impossible to say. True to her style, Margaret dropped hints but kept her own counsel. In one speech, she made pointed reference to Hannibal Hamlin, a Maine native who had been vice president during Abraham Lincoln's first term, but said nothing about her own ambitions. When she was asked whether she might be Barry Goldwater's running mate in 1964, she said no, but she added that people had been writing to urge her to run for president ever since she had begun speaking about the need for firmness in the face of the Soviet threat. In the fall of 1963, she stopped short of calling herself a candidate but admitted she was thinking about entering a few primaries to give voters a "third choice" in addition to Rockefeller and Goldwater. Allies and supporters pressed her for a more definite answer, but she promised only to announce her intentions before the end of the year. History prevented her from keeping that promise. After the Kennedy assassination, she interrupted all her political activities and didn't return to the public stage until early the next year.

When Margaret did return to politics in early 1964, she continued to tantalize her audiences, talking about letters from people all over the country who wanted her to run for president, on the one hand, and the impossibility of waging a campaign without the support of powerful political machines and large financial contributions, on the other. Furthermore, she insisted that no woman could currently hope to be elected to the nation's highest office, though perhaps if a woman made the effort now, it might make things easier for women in the future. Clearly, Margaret was hedging her bets. Finally, comparing the 1964 presidential race with her first Senate contest, in 1948, when no one believed she could win either, she announced that she had decided to see how much support a candidate like herself could attract. She would enter the New Hampshire and Illinois primaries, as a test of whether it was possible to run for president on a shoestring, supported by volunteers, staying mainly on the job in Washington, and relying on her record rather than campaign rhetoric.

Although Margaret insisted that she was a candidate for the presidency and not angling for a vice-presidential nomination, it was never clear how seriously she took her effort. She began receiving unsolicited campaign contributions, most of them small, but hadn't decided whether to keep them or to solicit larger amounts (she eventually returned all the money). Barry Goldwater, whose relations with Margaret were now warmer than they had formerly been, offered her a ride to New Hampshire on his campaign plane, though he was probably also hoping that her presence on the ballot would help him by further fragmenting the moderate vote (Henry Cabot Lodge, who won, and Nelson Rockefeller were running). In the end, she finished a distant fifth, after Lodge, Goldwater, Rockefeller, and Nixon. Undeterred, she claimed that Lodge's one-third share of the votes would have gone to her had he not been running, and waited for Illinois, where she would face Goldeater in a head-to-head contest. There, Goldwater's winning margin was better than two-to-one, but Margaret was exuberant. She had campaigned her way—frugally and on her record—and in her view the outcome had demonstrated that a woman could be a viable presidential candidate.

Defying yet another tradition, Margaret the candidate insisted on attending the Republican Convention in San Francisco, where her friend George Aiken, senator from neighboring Vermont, placed her name in nomination for the presidency. In his speech, Aiken saluted Margaret's courage and integrity. She had no chance to win, of course, but she became the sentimental favorite at what one Goldwater supporter conceded was an otherwise "acrimonious convention." When Aiken's nomination speech ended, the band played "Everything's Comin' Up Roses" and all eyes in the Cow Palace turned to Margaret, holding one of her trademark flowers. There was even an effort to have one delegate from each state cast a vote for Margaret on the first ballot, in tribute to her trailblazing candidacy (since Goldwater was assured of the nomination). The initiative was rejected by the Goldwater people, but Margaret had the last word. She left the hall without releasing her delegates, so when the call came to make the Goldwater nomination unanimous, some in the Maine delegation hesitated to switch their votes. As a result, Margaret later quipped, she was second in the balloting for the 1964 presidential nomination.

In November 1964, Goldwater was routed in his contest against Lyndon Johnson, but Margaret's star seemed to shine brighter than ever. Her presidential candidacy had added one more accomplishment to her string of firsts; she was still Maine's revered senior senator, and she was easily reelected to her seat in 1966. Imperceptibly, however, some things had begun to shift. Johnson's overwhelming victory in Maine was merely part of a broad repudiation of Goldwater, but when Maine's Democrat-controlled legislature watered down a tribute to Margaret on the occasion of her twenty-five years in Congress, it was obvious that something was changing in the relationship between the state and its most illustrious public figure.

To Margaret, however, the world had not changed. She saw Vietnam as another chapter in a Cold War that had lasted as long as she had been in the Senate. When Johnson intensified the bombing of North Vietnam after Congress passed the Gulf of Tonkin Resolution in 1964, Margaret hoped only that the president had not waited too long to show the People's Republic of China (which she believed was propping up the North) that the United States was committed to halting the progress of Communism in Southeast Asia. At home, she deplored the increasingly militant style of civil rights protests, and she was convinced that the American antiwar movement was encouraged—and even guided—by our Communist enemies.

Her relations with the Democratic administration, especially Defense Secretary Robert McNamara, reached new lows during this period. Her differences with Johnson's military policies were part of the reason, but Margaret was also rankled by what were known as "early notices," whereby word of new programs—for example, federal contracts or plans to build a military base—was leaked to members of the party in power before the opposition learned about them. The tactic allowed those who had the news first to claim the political credit. Margaret, who had built her career on military policy and expenditures, believed that McNamara lacked respect for her and she was furious at his evasiveness. She complained to Johnson that "if the Secretary of Defense will be less than truthful to me on relatively small matters, how can I believe him on the really big matters?"

The big matter that irked her the most was McNamara's commitment to reducing the country's nuclear capability in an effort to improve relations with the Soviet Union. What the secretary saw as either good foreign policy or a necessary trade-off to pay for the war in Vietnam, Margaret saw as compromising military preparedness and naive trust in the good faith of implacable enemies. She favored full-scale war "to stop the Communists from conquering the world," in Vietnam or anywhere else. She preferred the calls for increased manpower and arms coming from the chiefs of staff and commanders to the statistically based analyses of McNamara, although he had helped plan the World War II bombing of Japan for General Curtis LeMay.

The war came home to Margaret after Nixon succeeded Johnson in 1969. She supported the new president's plans to bring American troops home by relying on South Vietnamese soldiers to wage the ground war while increasing the bombing of supply lines in Vietnam, Cambodia, and Laos. The Cambodia bombing of 1970 triggered protests all over the United States, including one by college students in Maine, who wrote to Margaret to demand that she come home to talk with her constituents. She did, and was disheartened by what she saw as largely ill-informed, ill-mannered protest for its own sake. In a second "Declaration of Conscience," she again claimed the moderate middle ground andcondemned both the anarchy of the left and the repression of the right. Her new declaration won praise from her political colleagues and from the press, and for a while it looked as if the old Margaret was coming back.

There were signs, however, that this recovery might be more difficult. She would be seventy-five by the time the 1972 election rolled around. Mentally, she was as vigorous as ever, but she had undergone surgery to replace both hips and was suffering from macular degeneration, which seriously affected her vision and for which there was no cure. Nevertheless, she was determined to run again, despite her medical problems and despite the fact that a wealthy Massachusetts businessman had established residence in Maine with the intention of challenging her in the 1972 primary. Robert Monks would be her first primary opponent since 1954, and he was so bent on unseating her that he simultaneously supported Democratic congressman William Hathaway, who had announced his plan to seek the Democratic senatorial nomination.

Monks's millions didn't intimidate Margaret, although he spent between $150,000 and $300,000, probably three to six times what she spent on all of her congressional campaigns combined. She didn't raise money for her campaigns, conspicuously avoiding the fund-raisers that are prevalent in politics now. She had generally paid whatever expenses she incurred from her own funds. She knew that Mainers distrusted displays of wealth and were suspicious of outsiders. She successfully neutralized her opponent's challenge with the motto "Monks, Millions, Massachusetts," and took two-thirds of the votes. Much more troubling to her reelection was the fact that Bill Lewis suffered a serious heart attack in December 1971. He recovered, and she resumed campaigning in February 1972. But Lewis was unable to play the energetic role that had been indispensable to her four previous Senate campaigns, and she was simply too worn out by the strenuous primary and Lewis's crisis to travel the state as she had in the past in order to demonstrate that she was as energetic a senator as she was an indelible icon. Instead, it was Hathaway who was everywhere, in person and in the media, where he spent the bulk of his $200,000 war chest. In addition, his views were more in tune with the times and the voters.

Defeat left Margaret crushed. In fact, it would be nearly five years before she had mellowed enough to return to Skowhegan and take her place as beloved elder stateswoman. Two years after that, construction began on the Margaret Chase Smith Library there, and in August 1982 the combination research library and museum opened, with a special atrium where she greeted visitors, posed for photographs, gave interviews, and answered her mail. Bill Lewis had helped plan every detail of the library, but he did not live to see it open. He died of another heart attack only a few weeks before it was dedicated. Margaret soldiered on until May 29, 1995, when she was ninety-seven. By that time even former adversaries like Edmund Muskie acknowledged her political integrity and strength of character.

Her friends, of course, had recognized what an extraordinary woman she was, years earlier. Frances Bolton, the congresswoman from Ohio who had served with Margaret, credited her with knowing how to read a colleague. "In minutes she could tell me what to watch out for, whether he could be trusted." When Margaret was nominated for the presidency in 1964, Bolton spoke for many of her friend's admirers when she commented, "After a bit, you know, you men are going to have a woman for president. It's just too bad you didn't take this one."

Because Margaret conducted herself so professionally and had such a reputation for integrity, she has left a lasting legacy. Maine's current senators, Olympia Snowe and Susan Collins, believe their quest for the Senate was made easier because Mainers thought it was a normal thing to have one woman senator—and seemed not to consider it any different if there were two. (Three states now have two women senators; California and Washington are the other two.) Incredibly, one of Susan Collins's opponents in 1996 was the same Robert Monks who had challenged Margaret in 1972. Senator Collins said to me, "When I look back at my life, a defining moment was the time that I spent with Margaret Chase Smith, and I was a high school senior here for the Senate Youth Program, ironically, and she spent nearly two hours with me." All of us meet with school groups, never knowing if one of the young people will be affected by the meeting and later pursue a political career. In this case, Margaret was an inspiration and role model for both of Maine's present senators, as well as for men who have been officeholders in Maine. Her independence and integrity have set examples for many who have followed her into the U.S. Senate.

Young people often ask me what they should do to get into politics. I always say, do something else first. Have a career in business or a profession so you learn about the real world, how laws will affect working people. I believe the best public officeholders are (1) those who don't need the job and will therefore be independent, and (2) those who have had other experiences, so they are not unduly swayed by political expediency.

Knowing the barriers I had to cross to win a seat in the state legislature in 1972, I can't imagine the hurdles in a race twenty-five years earlier for a much more high-profile office. So from my standpoint, Margaret Chase Smith was a legend. The year she started her first elected term in Congress, I was born. I didn't really know who she was until I became involved in politics myself. When I did hear about her, it was from Senator John Tower (R-TX), one of my biggest supporters and a great friend to my husband and me. He had served on the Armed Services Committee with her and said she was "one of us." He meant she was a strong supporter of national defense and could be counted on if things got tough.

He thought I had some of the same characteristics with my naturally conservative pro-defense background. Senator Tower encouraged me to run for office and always helped me by making appearances with me, especially when I ran for state treasurer in 1990. When many other state leaders didn't think I had a chance to win, Senator Tower was my strongest backer. His experience with Margaret Chase Smith was one of the reasons he thought I could be an effective leader.

There is no telling how many young people she has had an effect on: directly, as on her own state's senators, or indirectly, as on a senator from Texas.

## Women of Today

MARGARET CHASE SMITH was the first woman to be elected to both houses of Congress and the first to serve four terms in the United States Senate. While she was the first woman nominated for president at a major party convention, in 1964, it was twenty years later that Geraldine Ferraro became the first woman to win the nomination for vice president of a major party. In 1984, she was the Democratic nominee on the ticket with Walter Mondale.

Just three years before, in 1981, President Ronald Reagan appointed the first woman to the Supreme Court of the United States, Sandra Day O'Connor.

## GERALDINE FERRARO

GERALDINE FERRARO was born in Newburgh, New York, in 1935, to Italian immigrant parents. Her mother sacrificed to enable Geraldine to complete her education after her father died. She graduated from Marymount College and Fordham University Law School, and was an assistant district attorney for Queens County before being elected to Congress in 1978. Geraldine was the first woman to run for the vice presidency as a major-party candidate—as Walter Mondale's running mate in 1984. Two campaigns for the Democratic nomination for the U.S. Senate in New York were unsuccessful. From 1988–92, she was a fellow of the Institute of Politics, John F. Kennedy School of Government at Harvard University. She has been president of the International Institute for Women's Political Leadership and is a permanent member of the United Nations Commission on Human Rights. Geraldine has also been a major spokeswoman for blood cancer research and education efforts after being diagnosed with multiple myeloma. In her honor, the Geraldine Ferraro Education Fund was established at the National Institutes of Health.

IMPORTANT TRAIT FOR SUCCESS

GERALDINE FERRARO: I think the ability to work hard and, if something doesn't work, to learn from the mistake and move on. That's what's happened with my own life. It goes to the personal side from watching my mother, who moved on after becoming a widow with two kids to support. She was thirty-nine years old—God, I don't know how she did it. Then I watched her move on and do whatever was necessary to get the job of educating her children done. I'm exactly the same way. I'll do whatever is necessary to get the job done, whatever it is. And then if I do something that doesn't work, then I go to the next goal.

BIGGEST OBSTACLE

GF: I'm sixty-eight. The obstacles in my life have changed with time. An obstacle when I was a kid was being in a boarding school away from my mother because my father had died. I had no choice. It wasn't like the boarding schools or the prep schools of today. I was in a semicloistered convent. It was lonely, and I had to work hard. I wanted to go to college, but we didn't have the money for college, so I knew I had to get top marks in order to get scholarships. That was my obstacle then.

Money was always an obstacle when I was a kid. I taught when I went to law school at night, because I couldn't afford to go during the day. When I applied, they would say things like, "Gerry, are you serious, because you're taking a man's place," you know. That was thrown at me.

And then getting out of law school I was faced with the challenge of trying to find a job. I interviewed at five law firms. I was in the top ten percent of my class. I went down to Wall Street and went through job interviews—the last and most promising was at Dewey Ballantine. I went through four interviews and was called back for a fifth. I raced down after work; I was very excited in my hat and gloves; I can tell you the suit I was wearing, the hat I was wearing. I went down to Wall Street where Dewey Ballantine was at the time and parked my car—you know how narrow the streets are there, so I parked my car kind of half on the sidewalk because I was late, ran up to the meeting, and one of the seven partners spent forty-five minutes or so talking to me. Then after we finished, he said, "Miss Ferraro, you're wonderful, but we're not hiring any women this year." I was so annoyed, I said—here I am, a smart-ass kid, twenty-four years old—"You know, what you've told me for the last forty-five minutes about how wonderful I am; my mother tells me that every morning." Then I got up and walked out.

There were a lot of obstacles I met at that point in my career—it was a combination of gender, going to a Catholic law school, night sessions, being Italian American. I mean, I had all those things. So each thing was an obstacle that I had to get by. Here [in Congress], I don't think I had too many obstacles. Congress was very generous to me. Tip O'Neill was kind of like the shoehorn that eased my foot right into the shoe that was here. He could not have been more wonderful.

## BEST NEGOTIATING STRATEGY

GF: I think the most important thing is to listen to both sides. You're trying to be the person in the center. Listen to both sides and let both sides know you're not only genuinely interested in what they have to say, but that you'll give them respect for what they're saying and try to make an accommodation. That, I think, is the most important thing. It's to listen and make them believe that you're genuine.

I think this also works in negotiating legislation. Kay, I was never a person who insisted upon the whole. If I wanted something and I couldn't get it all, I would negotiate for half of it because I felt at least I would get something, and if I couldn't get it all the first time, I'd go back the next time. I'm very patient. I'd go back and back and back. I do that with my life. I really do. If you can't get it all, get one little piece.

KBH: A start.

GF: Yes, a start. That's what you have to be patient about. I think what happens with a lot of people who come to Congress today is that they want it all right away and they want it all from their view. I really think that's why you have such dissension right now in the House, because members are on such ideologically different paths. They just don't seem to want to give—some people consider that weakness. I consider finding solutions a strength.

## SANDRA DAY O'CONNOR

SANDRA DAY O'CONNOR was born in El Paso, Texas, in 1930, but spent much of her childhood on her parents' 128,000-acre Lazy-B Ranch in southeastern Arizona. During the school year, she lived with her grandmother in El Paso. After graduating from high school, she majored in economics at Stanford University. Sandra's intention was to apply her knowledge of economics to running the family ranch, but she decided to attend Stanford Law School after a legal dispute involving the ranch started her thinking about legal issues.

In 1952, Sandra graduated from law school after just two years, but was nevertheless third in her class and a member of the law review. Unable to find work in a law firm in California, she worked as a deputy county attorney in San Mateo County, and then was a civilian lawyer for the Quartermaster's Corps, while her husband, John Jay O'Connor, spent three years in Germany as a member of the Judge Advocate General Corps.

In Arizona, Sandra started her own small law firm. When her children were young, she stopped practicing and did volunteer work for, among other organizations, the Arizona State Hospital, the Arizona State Bar, the Salvation Army, and local schools. She returned to the law as an assistant state attorney general and then entered politics, becoming majority leader of the Arizona state senate. In 1974, she became a superior court judge, then a judge on the Arizona Court of Appeals. In 1981, she was unanimously confirmed to replace retiring Justice Potter Stewart on the U. S. Supreme Court.

## IMPORTANT TRAIT FOR SUCCESS

SANDRA DAY O'CONNOR: I'm blessed with having a lot of energy. I think I inherited it from my mother, but to be a working mother requires an enormous amount of energy to do your job and to manage to take care of the family and to go nonstop all the time with never any personal downtime. I can't remember a time in my life when I had time for myself, so perhaps that's a blessing.

Another attribute that perhaps has been helpful is a curiosity about things, how things work. I think a love of learning and finding out about things is useful.

Then third, probably, is liking people and enjoying talking to them, whoever they are, with whatever lifestyle or standard of living. I've always enjoyed talking to people. I think I got that, maybe, from my grandmother in Texas.

## BIGGEST OBSTACLE

SDO: I had a hard time getting a job as a lawyer after I got out of law school. I think I was very naive because I always assumed that of course I'd have a job; there'd be all kinds of offers; I'd done well in school, done well in law school. I always expected to have opportunities come my way.

KBH: What year did you graduate?
SDO: Nineteen fifty-two. Only about three percent of law school classes in the United States at that time were comprised of women, and today it's over fifty-two percent. So look at the

change that has come about. There were very few women going to law school, and I couldn't even get a job interview in a law firm in California. I had graduated from Stanford, had excellent grades, and law firms had notices all over our bulletin boards begging Stanford graduates to apply. They wouldn't even talk to me.

KBH: What did you do then?

SDO: I had met my husband, John, we got engaged, we married—he was a year behind me in law school, so we had a year when he would still be in school and one of us needed to work. So that was me. We liked to eat, and we needed a little income, and I was having trouble finding work. So I finally went to the county attorney of San Mateo County, California. It was not far from Stanford. He had once had a woman lawyer in his office. I thought if he had had one, maybe he could have another. We had a nice conversation. I told him I'd love to work in his office, and he said that I had a very fine record and he would enjoy having me, he was sure, but he had no vacancy and he also had no place to put me. His office space was in the old county courthouse. It was very small, and he had no vacant office. I said that if he was willing to do it, that I would be happy to work for him for nothing until he had a vacancy, and that if his secretary would permit me to do it, I would sit in her office. He had a very nice secretary. She was a wonderful woman, and she said she'd be happy to have me. So he took me on.

I hadn't been there long when he was appointed the county judge for San Mateo County. That created, of course, a vacancy, and the chief deputy, who was my supervisor, became the county attorney, and I acquired a bona fide job and office, so that was great. It all worked out. But I had to really struggle to get that job.

KBH: You know, I graduated in 1967, fifteen years later, and I went through the same thing. Not one major law firm in Houston hired women as regular attorneys. I had interviews, but none of them—

SDO: But at least you had interviews.

KBH: True. Fifteen years got us interviews! Finally, the city attorney offered me a job, but by then I had decided I was going to be-

come a television news reporter and do something different, and
that, of course, worked out great.

SDO: But it was the public law offices that first made options available for women lawyers. I spent much of my life in public service
as a result of it. That's how it started.

## BEST PREPARATION FOR ROUGH-AND-TUMBLE OF LIFE

SDO: Probably ranch life, where everybody had to carry their share
of the load, and you just had to make do. You couldn't look up anything in the Yellow Pages and call for help; you had to do it yourself.

## BEST NEGOTIATING STRATEGY

SDO: We don't negotiate solutions here [on the Court], but certainly
as a legislator you need to negotiate your way through some sticky
wickets, and I used to do that. Certainly as a lawyer you'd have to do
that. I think probably the most important thing there is to learn how
to listen to people with an open mind and then weigh things subjec-
tively and see what you can put together.

## HELPFUL CHILDHOOD MEMORY

SDO: It was being a part of the ranching family, helping with everything that was done, whether it was my father's work or my
mother's, and learning to do a job well if you took it on. My father
did not look kindly on sloppy work, and we had to learn if we were
going to do something, to do it well enough that it would meet with
his approval. We had to learn to solve things independently. If we
would be asked to go do something by ourselves, you never knew
what you were going to run into. There weren't any road maps or
road signs. So you learned early on to, I think, be responsible and be
somewhat independent.

## BEST ADVICE

SDO: All the things that one learns in a good family: be honest, be
hardworking, have a good sense of humor—all those things that any
child lucky enough to grow up with decent parents would learn.

# CHAPTER NINE

# RENAISSANCE WOMEN

O NE OF THE MOST INTERESTING American women of the twentieth century has had very little written about her. Oveta Culp Hobby did not write (or talk much) about herself and discouraged any biographies or articles about her by others. I knew her because she gave me the first break in my fledgling career.

When I graduated from the University of Texas Law School in 1967, there were 13 women in my class of 390. None of the major law firms in Texas hired women as associates in the partner track. Harriet Miers, who is now deputy chief of staff at the White House, also graduated in 1967, from Southern Methodist University Law School, and became a law clerk to Federal District Judge Sarah T. Hughes.

Finding a job as a lawyer in Houston, Texas, was a serious challenge for a woman. As I describe it: "I hit my first brick wall in life." I went to law firm after law firm—for months. My law school classmates were going right to work, while I was still looking. It was a tough time for me.

Finally, I decided to look for some other way to use my law degree. Driving to my apartment (shared with my college roommate, Mary Anderson, who was a wonderful friend during those challenging times, and is now Mary Anderson Abell, godmother to my son, Houston) one day after yet another discouraging interview, I made a snap decision. I dropped in cold, without an appointment, to KPRC-TV, the local NBC affiliate and Houston's number one station at the time. It was owned by the *Houston Post;* the chairman of the board of the *Post* was Oveta Culp Hobby (though I did not know it at the time).

I asked the receptionist if I could talk to someone about a job. She said, "What kind of job?" I said, "News reporter." She said, "Oh, you want to talk to the news director?" I said, "Yes, the news director," not knowing what the head of a newsroom was called.

To everyone's surprise, Ray Miller, who was known as one of the best local news directors in the country, came out to visit with a person who didn't have an appointment. We had a nice interview. He said, "We don't have an opening right now, but don't take another job until you talk to me." Subsequently, Ray told me that most news directors would never meet a drop-in, but he believes it can be very productive. He has told people he hired Tom Jarrell (later a network correspondent for ABC) and me from cold calls, a record he considered successful.

There were no women television news reporters in Houston at that time. Of course, I had no journalism experience or background. I was a government major in college. But Ray later told me he was intrigued because no one with a law degree had ever applied for a job at KPRC before. He went to the station manager, Jack Harris, and said he thought they should find a place for me. Jack Harris later told me he talked to Mrs. Hobby, who was enthusiastic about a young woman with a law degree working for the station. Jack said that having her television station put the first woman on broadcast news was right up her alley.

The station assigned me to a post in Austin during the legislative sessions, covering the legislature full-time. After being exposed to it, and being well known because I was on TV every night, in 1971 the Harris County Republican Party chairman, Nancy Palm, asked if I would consider running for the Texas House of Representatives myself in the election of 1972. I thought about it and decided to go for it.

About the same time, I interviewed Anne Armstrong, a Texan who had just won the cochairmanship of the National Republican Party. She asked me if I would go to Washington with her, to be her press secretary. I told her I wanted to run for the legislature, but asked if I could go to Washington temporarily to help set up her office and find her a press secretary. She said yes, so I left KPRC and worked for Anne for six months, learning politics from her before returning to Houston full-time in January 1972 to launch my campaign. I was elected and held that position until I resigned in 1976 to become vice chairman of the National Transportation Safety Board, appointed by President Gerald R. Ford.

So I had two of the most remarkable women I have ever known giving me that early boost, when there were still very few women in careers. They were on top—and they reached down to give a start to the next generation.

By giving me my first chance, Oveta Culp Hobby changed my career path dramatically. Had she not taken the bold step of putting Houston's first woman television news reporter on the air, I would probably be a partner in a Houston law firm today. I jokingly say that I would have been wealthier, for sure, but life would probably not have been nearly as interesting!

## Oveta Culp Hobby

IT IS NO EXAGGERATION to say that Oveta Culp Hobby got her start in public service at her mother's—and her father's—knee. Born on January 19, 1905, in Killeen, Texas, she was the second of Ike and Emma Culp's seven children. By the time she enrolled in the town's elementary school, she had begun helping her mother deliver baskets of food, clothes, and cash to needy people in the community. Her father, an attorney in Killeen, encouraged the young Oveta's curiosity about the things that most interested him: law, government affairs, and riding horses. After school, she got into the habit of stopping at Ike Culp's office on her way home, to listen while her father discussed his legal and legislative work and to read the books in his extensive library. By the time she was ten, the *Congressional Record* was part of Oveta's regular reading, and when Ike Culp served in the state legislature in 1919, Oveta accompanied him to Austin to attend the sessions as an observer, even though that meant missing school.

The time in Austin only served to broaden Oveta's intellectual range, and she graduated from Temple High School near the top of her class. Along the way, she won prizes in elocution (dramatic recitation) and was chagrined when her parents forbade her to join a touring troupe of entertainers. Instead, she entered Mary Hardin Baylor College for Women in Belton, Texas. She was active in the college dramatic society, but it was the law that continued to hold the greatest fascination for her. She attended the University of Texas Law School and, when barely twenty, was invited to become the parliamentarian of the Texas House of Representatives, a post she held for six years.

Throughout her time in Austin, Oveta was active in Democratic politics—secretary of the Democratic Club, National Convention planner (the 1928 Democratic Convention was held in Houston), and campaigner for Al Smith's presidential bid and Thomas T. Connally's successful contest for the U.S. Senate. After the national elections, she helped Walter Monteith win election as mayor of Houston, and he, in turn, asked Oveta to become assistant to the city attorney in his administration. She accepted, with the proviso that she return to Austin for the legislative session, so she could continue as parliamentarian there.

Austin had been Oveta's base throughout the late 1920s; besides her duties as parliamentarian, she'd codified Texas banking laws as clerk to the State Banking Commission and clerked for the House Judiciary Committee. But in 1930, after the Houston mayoral election and an unsuccessful campaign of her own for a seat in the state legislature, her focus shifted to Houston. While working in the city attorney's office, she renewed her acquaintance with an old family friend, William P. Hobby. The former governor of Texas—and still known to everyone as "Governor"—Hobby was now president of the *Houston Post-Dispatch*. He was also a widower (Willie Chapman Cooper Hobby had died in

1929), and in February 1931, twenty-six-year-old Oveta married the newspaper publisher, fifty-three, and formed the partnership that made an indelible impression on her future. Later in life she would say, "Everything that ever happened to me fell in my lap and nothing would have been possible without Governor."

In rapid succession, Oveta went from being book page editor to assistant editor to, in 1939, executive vice president of the paper. By then it had been renamed the *Houston Post,* after Governor Hobby bought it from his friend Jesse Jones, who had obtained it from former Texas governor Ross Sterling. The *Post* remained closely associated with both Governor Hobby and Oveta, despite several leaves of absence for Oveta, one precipitated by a horseback-riding accident in which she broke her leg and wrist, others by the births of her two children. Both children were born on her own birthday, January 19—William, Jr., in 1932 and Jessica in 1937. Even a more serious accident—in 1936, a small plane flying the Hobbys and others from Dallas to Houston caught fire and was forced to crash-land in a cotton field—failed to slow her down. Oveta and the others who were not badly hurt pulled the unconscious Governor Hobby and the pilot from the burning plane, borrowed a car, and drove into town, where they found an ambulance to take her husband to a Dallas hospital. It was only after they had arrived that the doctors realized that Oveta, too, had been a victim of the accident, and hospitalized her as well.

During her breaks from journalism, Oveta wrote *Mr. Chairman,* a widely consulted parliamentary manual, and returned for two more brief stints at the legislature in 1939 and 1941. At the same time, she threw her energies into local cultural organizations and community service. She joined the board of Houston's Museum of Fine Arts, helped to found the Houston Symphony Orchestra, and served as regional chairperson of the Mobilization for Human Needs, which had been created to address the economic deprivation that resulted from the Depression. When downtown Houston was flooded in 1935, she was the only woman on the committee set up to develop a flood-control plan, and she later chaired the Texas branch of the advisory group for women's participation in the 1939 World's Fair in New York.

Back at the *Post* after her daughter, Jessica, was born in 1937, Oveta, now an assistant editor, introduced a series of articles about "subjects of international significance" in their historical contexts, including pieces on the Ottoman Empire, the constitution of Turkey, the pact between England and Egypt, Afghanistan, and the Greek constitution. At about the same time, she served on the Texas State Committee for Human Security, an organization that solicited funds for blind and needy children. This experience inspired a series about community welfare—health, child welfare, leisure-time problems, the merging of social agencies— that revealed interests and expertise Oveta would later call on when she became the first secretary of health, education and welfare under President Eisenhower.

By 1941, as the United States edged closer to entering World War II, Oveta was often in Washington, D.C., to deal with the Federal Communications Commission, now that the Hobbys also owned the Houston radio station KPRC ("Kotton Port Rail Center"). Men were being drafted for military service—the first peacetime draft in American history—and as many as 10,000 letters a day were pouring into the capital from women who wanted to know what they could do to aid the war effort. General David Searles asked Oveta to direct a woman's initiative in support of the army, but she refused on the grounds that she could not be away from her family in Houston. Searles then proposed that she merely outline what such an organization would look like, but after she sent him the organizational chart he again asked her to serve as director. She refused a second time, but when Governor Hobby heard about the offer, he told her, "Any thoughtful person knows that we are in this war, and that every one of us is going to have to do whatever we are called on to do." She accepted the job.

At a salary of a dollar a year, Oveta moved to Washington, D.C., to head the Women's Interest Section, War Department Bureau of Public Relations, where her role was primarily informational. As she explained it, "For every one of the 1,500,000 men in the Army today, there are four or five women—mothers, wives, sisters, sweethearts—who are closely and personally interested. Mothers are more interested in their son's health than they are in army maneuvers. They want to know what their man or boy is doing in his recreational hours, what opportunities the men have for training and promotion, about the health of camps and the provisions made for religious life."

Her mandate changed with the country's declaration of war on December 8, 1941. Henry Stimson, secretary of war, and General George Marshall wanted to know which military jobs women could do with minimal training, and they requested a plan for forming a women's army.

Congress passed a law establishing a Women's Army Auxiliary Corps (WAAC). The author of the bill was Representative Edith Nourse Rogers (R-MA). General Marshall asked her whom she would recommend to lead the new WAAC, and Congresswoman Rogers suggested Oveta Culp Hobby.

General Marshall asked Oveta to submit a plan for the new corps, which she did, and to lead the organization, which she agreed to do. Oveta considered General Marshall a mentor as they worked together to craft the women's corps into a viable and essential part of the war effort.

The idea now was to free men for combat by having women do as much of the noncombatant work as possible. General Marshall identified the areas in which civilians could perform, and Oveta implemented the training and deployment of the new women's force. As Oveta explained in her speeches, "The gaps our women will fill are in those noncombatant jobs where women's hands and women's hearts fit naturally. WAACs will do the same type of work which women do in civilian life. They will bear the same relation to men of the Army that they bear to the men of the civilian organizations in which they work."

At first, the work of the director of the WAAC was essentially a one-person recruiting marathon. Racing from city to city, wearing the one WAAC uniform that had been made, Major (later Colonel) Hobby carried an electric fan and iron in her luggage so that each night she could wash, dry, and press her dress khakis before the next day's appearance. "I never did learn to salute properly or master the thirty-inch stride," she later said, but she proved herself a masterful speaker, persuading large numbers of women to take the unprecedented step of enlisting in a women's army. Along the way, she learned quite a bit about the subtle— and not so subtle—ways in which women were discriminated against. To house the women who had volunteered for the WAAC, she requested army engineers to draft plans for barracks, only to be told that since the WAAC wasn't the army, the engineers didn't work for them. To design an appealing uniform, Oveta called on clothing designers to donate designs, but the Quartermaster Corps objected to pleated skirts as a waste of material and the belt as without function.

The director's job involved a difficult balancing act between concerns that being in the army was unladylike and fears that women would be a corrupting influence on the male soldiers. One volunteer, Charity Adams, who later rose to lieutenant colonel, stressed the concerns of propriety when she said, "I made a conscientious effort to obtain every item on the list of suggested supplies for training camp except the slacks and shorts. I had never owned either, feeling that I was not the type to wear them." Still, many army commanders were so fearful of the effects of fraternization between soldiers and WAACs that they went to extraordinary lengths to limit contact—restricting the nights that women were allowed to go to the movies shown on army bases, or even fencing in the women's barracks. Given Oveta's status as an officer, she was personally invited to use the Army-Navy Club, but the invitation requested that she enter through the club's back door.

No issue was too important—or too insignificant—to become a bone of contention, not even medical care. The comptroller general claimed that WAAC doctors couldn't be paid because they weren't, strictly speaking, in military service, so Secretary Stimson had to ask Congress to pass special legislation authorizing salaries for them. Despite the fact that in the army even NCOs had a jeep at their personal disposal, when the director of the WAAC needed a car, she had to request one from the motor pool.

These discouragements aside, the WAACs were invaluable. The initial list of 54 army tasks that women might perform quickly mushroomed to 239, and in many of them—ranging from office work to folding parachutes—the women's aptitude, experience, and dexterity led them to outperform their male counterparts. The army came to recognize it, too; within two years, there were more than 600,000 requests for WAACs from around the world, though the strength of the women's army wasn't authorized to exceed 200,000. In 1942, their name was

changed to the Women's Army Corps, or WAC, and the corps was better integrated into the military services. Ultimately, WACs were posted
to Europe, the South Pacific, and the China-India-Burma theater. Everywhere they went, they served with distinction, despite the continuing discrimination against them. Sometimes the inequities were simply
insulting—as when WACs in the South Pacific were restricted to
barbed-wire compounds except when they were working, and had to be
accompanied by armed guards on their way to and from work. Others,
however, posed serious risks; for example, women were much more
likely than men to catch malaria, because they were not issued the sorts
of lightweight protective clothing the men were.

First Lady Eleanor Roosevelt supported the WACs and was impressed with their leaders. She asked Oveta to accompany her to England just before D-day. There, Oveta met with General Eisenhower, a
meeting that began a long friendship and resulted in Oveta's crucial support for him when he later ran for president.

In July 1945, with the war in Europe at an end and the Japanese
close to surrender, an exhausted Colonel Hobby resigned her commission and returned home with new perspectives on the importance of
equal opportunity for all Americans. The first woman to wear the uniform of a U.S. Army officer and recipient of the Distinguished Service
Medal, the nation's highest noncombat award, was again a private citizen, but one with an unusual profile. Director of KPRC and the new
KPRC-TV and executive vice president of the *Houston Post,* she also resumed her role in Houston's community affairs. Among other things,
when she cochaired the local Armed Forces Day celebration in the years
immediately after the war, she ruffled more than a few feathers when she
declared that "No celebration of Armed Forces Day will be held in
Houston which is not open to every one who has served in our armed
forces—regardless of race." Governor Hobby, who had intervened during the war to protect local Japanese Americans from discriminatory
treatment and the threat of internment, supported Oveta's stance, and
he later used his newspaper as a forum for discussion and support of the
1954 Supreme Court decision mandating the integration of public
schools.

Oveta's convictions about diversity were straightforward: "The rule of thumb is a simple one," she wrote. "Regard each man, each woman, as an individual, not as a Catholic, a Protestant, or a Jew; not as an Indian, American, or European. Like or dislike a person for his own intrinsic qualities—not because he belongs to a different race or subscribes to a different religion. Dignify man with individuality."

An enthusiastic proponent of the United Nations, Oveta covered Security Council meetings for the *Post* and later was a delegate to the UN Freedom of Information Conference. She declared her support of the UN as early as 1946, in a speech to the National Council of Jewish Women, where she stressed that it was imperative to implement the body with "an international bill of rights." At the same time, she expressed her suspicions about the USSR's intentions, in words that harked back to England's misguided attempt to appease Germany in 1939: "Shall we now insist that one of our former allies observe its agreement with Manchuria? Observe its agreement with Iran? Or shall we make a timid bid for peace in our time? . . . Does Russia think that we have not learned that small aggressions lead to larger ones?"

Her interest in politics never waned, and as the presidential elections of 1952 loomed, she decided to get involved. Her 1945 meeting with General Eisenhower, and her respect for him, impelled her to take a bold political position. After decades of prominence in Democratic politics, she became the chairman of Texans for Eisenhower. Her son, Bill, a student at Rice University, recalls going to his first precinct convention with her in their Houston neighborhood. It was at the Republican conventions that the Texas delegation started to move toward support for Eisenhower. The state convention that year was held in Wichita Falls. It was a raucous fight between delegates for Taft and Eisenhower. Oveta was there, working for Eisenhower. The Texas delegation did go for Eisenhower at the national convention—a pivotal point for his nomination. General Eisenhower picked up another prominent Texas Democrat, Governor Alan Shivers, who based his support on the refusal of Senator Adlai Stevenson to support Texas ownership of its tidelands, which had been a part of Texas's treaty with the United States when it entered the Union in 1845. General Eisenhower agreed to support the treaty, and that strengthened his support in Texas in 1952 and his success in carrying the state in the November vote.

Because Oveta Culp Hobby had been one of the new president's early and most influential backers, leading the efforts from the local precinct to the national campaign, he wanted her to be part of his administration. She was first appointed chairman of the Federal Security Agency. When that agency was reconstituted as the Department of Health, Education and Welfare in 1953, Oveta Culp Hobby became its first secretary and a member of Eisenhower's cabinet. As with the WAC, she now faced the bewildering task of creating order out of myriad responsibilities. In this case they spanned the life cycles of Americans from cradle to grave. Besides administering the Social Security funds that provide pension and health-care benefits to millions of disabled and retired people, the HEW secretary, as a *Time* magazine profile published a month after the formation of the department, stated,

> manages one of the world's greatest medical research centers, provides operations for harelipped children and blue babies, maintains hospitals for merchant seamen and dope addicts, an insane asylum and a leprosarium. Through the Office of Education, she distributes funds to land-grant colleges and administers the teacher-student exchange program with foreign countries. She is legally concerned with the problem of tapeworm control among Alaskan caribou, with cancer research, and with the attitude of Congress toward fluoridation of children's teeth. She prints Braille books, extends credit to deserving citizens, bosses the nation's largest Negro university (Howard, in Washington), and brings out new editions of the Government's most durable bestseller. (The Children's Bureau's *Infant Care,* which is published in eight languages, has sold 8,519,000 copies over the past 39 years.)

All in a day's work for the indefatigable Oveta, who, as one newspaper profile of her quipped, "[w]hen she learns her job, . . . may trim her week to 70 hours." During her thirty-one-month tenure as HEW secretary, she had little opportunity to relax. She oversaw the introduction of the Salk polio vaccine, a major expansion of the federal hospital and health-care infrastructure, an emergency plan to build new schools to meet the demand created by the postwar baby boom, the development of new forms of medical insurance, and a spurt in the number of people covered by Social Security. She resigned from HEW only when Governor Hobby, by then seventy-seven, became ill in Houston, and she wanted to be at home to help him recover and to pitch in to run the family business, the *Houston Post* and the radio and TV stations.

Besides becoming president and editor of the *Post* (her husband recovered and continued as chairman until his death in 1964), Oveta assumed a number of other prominent positions: first chairman of the board of directors of the Bank of Texas, first female trustee of Mutual of New York, member of the board of trustees of Rice University, and countless memberships on nonprofit and governmental commissions and advisory boards. One honor that especially pleased the woman who spent so many of her formative hours among the books in her father's law office was the dedication of the Central Texas College Library in her hometown of Killeen, as the Oveta Culp Hobby Library. President Lyndon Johnson did the honors. In the late 1990s, it was renamed the Oveta Culp Hobby Memorial Library.

In 1983, the Hobby family sold the *Houston Post.* The newspaper closed on April 16, 1995. On April 17, 1995, Oveta Culp Hobby suffered a severe stroke. She died at home in Houston on August 16, 1995, at the age of ninety.

The last time I saw this incredible woman was at the governor's inauguration in 1975, when her son, William P. Hobby, Jr., was beginning his second term as lieutenant governor of Texas. He served from 1973 to 1991, one of the longest-serving and most powerful lieutenant governors in Texas history.

His first election was the same year I was elected to the Texas legislature from Houston, so we served together in the legislature in 1973 and at the state constitutional convention in 1974. In 1975, we were both entering our second terms. Before the ceremony began that day, he had a few friends into his office for coffee. His mother was there. We had a wonderful visit. At the age of seventy, she was just as active and informed as ever, and had the bearing of a venerable personage. I thanked her for giving me an unprecedented opportunity six years earlier. She said she had watched my career and was proud of what I had been able to do. She left a legacy of service to our country and blazed trails that other women will follow, made easier by her stellar performance in every office she held.

The magnificent World War II Memorial in Washington, D.C., has quotes etched in granite from war leaders: Presidents Franklin Roosevelt and Harry Truman, Generals Dwight Eisenhower and Douglas MacArthur, and Admiral Chester Nimitz. The only woman so honored is Colonel Oveta Culp Hobby. Her quote: "Women who stepped up were measured as citizens of the nation, not as women. This was a people's war and everyone was in it."

Both her children followed their parents into public service: the aforementioned lieutenant governor, William P. Hobby, Jr., and his wife, Diana, who was associate editor of the academic journal *Studies in English Literature,* published at Rice University, for thirteen years; and Jessica Hobby Catto, who served with her husband, Henry Catto, from San Antonio, during his tenures as chief of protocol in the Nixon administration and as U.S. ambassador to Great Britain for President George H. W. Bush.

# Women of Today

OVETA CULP HOBBY broke barriers as CEO of a major media organization, turning a daily newspaper into a multimedia corporation with television and radio interests. She was also a leader in promoting and operating the women's effort in World War II, which was the forerunner to women being integrated into the armed services. She later became the first secretary of the Department of Health, Education and Welfare.

Half a century later, women were still breaking barriers in business and government. Carleton Fiorina became the first woman to head a Fortune 50 company; Muriel Siebert was the first woman to hold a seat on the New York Stock Exchange; Madeleine Albright served as the first woman secretary of state; and Condoleezza Rice became the first woman to serve as national security advisor to the president of the United States.

# CARLETON S. FIORINA

CHAIRMAN AND CEO of Hewlett-Packard, Carly Fiorina is the highest-ranking woman in business in the world today. She studied medieval history at Stanford, and her father, a law professor and federal judge, hoped she would become a lawyer, but after one semester in law school, she quit. While working as a corporate receptionist, she developed an interest in business, earned her MBA from the University of Maryland and a master's in science from MIT, both while working full-time.

## IMPORTANT TRAIT FOR SUCCESS

CARLETON FIORINA: I think it's actually two, both of which I learned from my parents. One is determination; the other is belief in yourself. And being true to yourself. My parents taught me, Never sell yourself, and it's stood me well.

## BIGGEST OBSTACLE

CF: I think the one many women unfortunately still face—in academic circles—they say we lack "the presumption of credibility and competence." Many people think you can't do it. That barrier where people don't immediately see you and say, "Well, obviously she's competent; obviously she's credible," but say instead, "I'm not sure she is competent or credible." It's a huge barrier. It's also a huge opportunity because in many ways it can turn into an advantage when people underestimate you. But in virtually every job I have ever taken, most people assumed I couldn't do it.

## BEST PREPARATION FOR ROUGH-AND-TUMBLE OF LIFE

CF: My parents had high hopes for me. They said, Your integrity and your reputation are everything. They said, There is no substitute for hard work and stick-to-it-iveness. Those things are so fundamental, and I have turned to those words in many tough times: Who am I? What do I believe? Am I doing the best I can? Am I doing the things I think are right? In the end, that's the best you can do.

I think, as well, the other thing I would say is, along the way, while there have been some who didn't believe I could do it, there have also been many people, both men and women, who believed I could—who gave me a chance, who gave me an opportunity, who believed in me. Those people, the fact that they believed in me, they gave me an opportunity, they were counting on me.

KBH: Name a couple of people who had faith in you and were a turning point for you.

CF: Let me start at the very beginning of my career. When I dropped out of law school, I had to pay the bills and I started working as a receptionist. I answered the phone, I typed, and I filed. One day two gentlemen in the firm that I worked for came up to me and said, you know, "We think you could do something bigger than that." That was a big deal.

They are the ones who really got me started thinking, well, maybe this business thing is something I could do.

Now I'll give you a more modern-day example. The board of Hewlett-Packard picked me to run the company. They believed I could do it. It was a very brave, untraditional decision and they backed me through an incredible fight. And so at the very beginning of my career and at a very highly visible time in my career—and there are lots of examples in between, of people who said, "We believe in you and we're counting on you."

## BEST NEGOTIATING STRATEGY

CF: Win-win negotiations, if they're possible, are generally always better. And I think win-win negotiations require finding common ground. By the way, there isn't always common ground. I mean, sometimes it's a knock-down-drag-out and one person wins and one person loses, but that, generally speaking, doesn't have to be the case. So, it's really trying to find where do we have common ground that we can build on, which is different from let's just all compromise so much that we're left with nothing that makes any sense. I think that finding real common ground requires listening very hard. It requires, in some cases, education, not negotiation. I think good negotiation always requires respect for the other person, the other side, the other point of view.

## HELPFUL CHILDHOOD MEMORY

CF: My parents gave me perspective. They exposed me to a broad range of things. And I think that's made a big difference. I remember, for example, going to the opera at four. Now, by the way, both of my parents came from backgrounds that didn't go to the opera, but they just decided that that was important. It was important for their children to be exposed to different things. I remember sitting at an opera at four and being terribly bored with most of it, and occasionally fascinated, but it gave me a different view of the world, a broader view of the world.

And I think because they always were making sure that I was exposed to different things, different experiences, different people, it taught me that there's something valuable in every person, every experience, every place. I think that's mattered a lot in my life.

KBH: It's so funny—I had such a similar experience. I grew up in a town of fifteen thousand, but my parents made such an effort to take me to Galveston to the symphony. I remember it. I was in elementary school. I remember being totally bored, but so appreciating later the effort they made to take me to something that they thought would broaden me, and it did later. One of the things I'm going to have to remember with my kids is to go ahead and do those things that you think are going to bore them because, when they start having a memory, they'll remember.

## BEST ADVICE

CF: Don't be afraid to fail. Be afraid not to try. I learned that there are worse things than failure, and that's important because if you think the worst thing in the world is failure, you cannot risk anything. My parents said, "Don't be afraid to fail, but do be afraid of selling your soul." Taking those two things together has been really important to me.

## Muriel Siebert

AN ARDENT SUPPORTER of recognition for women in business and government, Muriel "Mickie" Siebert is the chair of Muriel Siebert & Co., Inc., and served as New York State superintendent of banks from 1977 to 1987. After growing up in Cleveland, Ohio, Siebert dropped out of college in the 1960s, moved to New York City, and became a leading securities analyst with specializations in the aviation and entertainment industries. She founded her own firm in 1970 and took it public in 1996. In 1999, *Money* magazine recognized the firm as the number one discount brokerage firm.

IMPORTANT TRAIT FOR SUCCESS

MURIEL SIEBERT: A combination of hard work and a sense of humor . . . and luck.

BIGGEST OBSTACLE

MS: It was the fact that when you break a tradition that's a hundred and seventy-five years old, not everybody's going to love you, and that can be very hard because you have to realize that they don't dislike you personally. It's not a personal thing; they just like things the way they are.

BEST PREPARATION FOR ROUGH-AND-TUMBLE OF LIFE

MS: I can probably say I owe it to my mother and father. I have a mind that I see a page of numbers and they light up and they tell me a story. Don't ask me to spell, don't ask me to remember names, but I can remember numbers and ratios and I could analyze stocks. I could just see things.

KBH: How did your mother and father figure you into that, other than giving you—

MS: They gave me the genes.

## BEST NEGOTIATING STRATEGY

MS: You've got to put yourself into the other person's position. A deal has got to be a good deal for both of you, especially if you're buying something or convincing somebody to come work. It's got to be good for both people.

## HELPFUL CHILDHOOD MEMORY

MS: My mother's brother had been very successful. He was the oldest of eleven children, my mother was the youngest, and they were born in Hungary. They were a very well-educated family and well-off. My uncle Ben went to Cleveland, Ohio, because my grandparents and great-grandparents used to pay the way out of the army for the smart boys from their suburb of Budapest—and send them to America, and most of those people settled in Cleveland. So my uncle Ben went to Cleveland, and he made quite a bit of money, and then he lost it during the Depression. I remember one day driving with my parents in the car, and there was my uncle Ben pumping gasoline. He had opened up a gasoline station on Taylor Road in Cleveland Heights, which *Fortune* magazine later wrote up as the most successful gasoline station in the country. That was a lesson to me then. He was willing to do the physical work or whatever it took to make it back.

## BEST ADVICE

MS: I went to work for a firm and went on purely commissions. Now that was important, and I started to make a lot of money—based on just recommending the purchase or sale of the stocks that I really knew. I knew everything there was about them—anything that anybody could know. And I was doing very well, but I couldn't get a job in a major large firm. They just never had had women in the position, so I was a partner of three different small firms. I wanted to be with a firm that was larger than six or eight people. I asked Gerald Tsai, who was one of my clients—a legendary money manager, he started the Manhattan Fund, which he built from scratch—and I said, "Gerry, what large firm can I go to where I can get credit on the accounts?" And Gerry Tsai said to me, "Don't be ridiculous, you won't. Buy a seat. Work for yourself." And I said to Gerry Tsai,

"Don't you be ridiculous," and Gerald Tsai said to Mickie Siebert, "I don't think there's a law against it." I took the constitution of the New York Stock Exchange home and I studied it and felt I met the requirements. It never even dawned on me to buy a seat.

KBH: What year did you buy?

MS: Nineteen sixty-seven.

KBH: And when you did, was there real resistance to your getting the seat?

MS: Oh, sure. When I was putting the bid card in, they said they wanted a letter from the bank that said that in the event that the New York Stock Exchange accepts a bid card from Muriel Siebert, the bank stands ready to make the loan. And the bank said, "Buy the seat. We'll give you the loan." They had never had to write such a letter before, even though they had made similar loans. So I was in a Catch-22: the Stock Exchange wouldn't accept the bid card until I had the letter, and the bank said, "Well, get the seat; we'll loan you the money." I had securities I was going to pledge, and I told that to Chase Bank; I said, "I guess I'm not getting the seat," and in ten minutes I had the letter.

KBH: Is that right?

MS: Yep. I later regulated the bank that wouldn't make the loan.

KBH: So they made it for you.

MS: Yeah, and the first day I had the seat, they called me and they said they figured out the commissions to the penny that I was going to owe them that month in interest, and they said, "Well, here's an order. We have to make sure you don't go broke your first month."

## MADELEINE ALBRIGHT

BORN IN CZECHOSLOVAKIA in 1937, Madeleine Korbel was the daughter of a Czech diplomat who fled to England during World War II, returned to Czechoslovakia after the war, and requested political asylum for himself and his family while working at the UN in 1948. After graduating from Wellesley College in 1959, she earned a master's degree and Ph.D. in international affairs at Columbia University, where she became a specialist in Soviet studies. After working on the staff of Senator Edmund Muskie, she was invited by her former professor, Zbigniew Brzezinski, to join the National Security Council staff as a legislative liaison. In 1982, she began teaching international affairs at Georgetown University and became affiliated with the Center for Strategic and International Studies there. She served as adviser to several presidential aspirants, and was appointed U.S. ambassador to the UN by President Bill Clinton following his election in 1992. In 1996, President Clinton nominated her to become the first female secretary of state; she was unanimously confirmed by the Senate in 1997.

Dr. Albright recently published a memoir, *Madam Secretary* (2003). Her other books include: *The Soviet Diplomatic Service: Profile of an Elite* (1968), *The Role of the Press in Political Change: Czechoslovakia 1968* (1976), and *Poland, the Role of the Press in Political Change* (1983).

IMPORTANT TRAIT FOR SUCCESS

MADELEINE ALBRIGHT: Determination. Like so many women, I really did not have any kind of a straight path to what I became, but I really do think I was determined to have an interesting life and one in which I could make a difference. Whenever something was put in the way, positive or negative, in terms of diversions or issues, I just was determined to make it work. I was determined to combine my family life, which meant and means a great deal to me, with the ability to have an interesting career.

## BIGGEST OBSTACLE

MA: My biggest obstacle was that I was very much in a male field and there was always this question—no matter how many credentials I had (including a Ph.D.)—whether I really would be able to do whatever was supposed to be done in foreign policy. Could a woman do it? And even during the time I was secretary of state, the question was asked, Could a woman deal with foreign countries? Could an American woman deal with Arab leaders, for instance? So it was always that you had to prove you could rather than ever being given the benefit of the doubt.

## BEST PREPARATION FOR ROUGH-AND-TUMBLE OF LIFE

MA: I have had to adjust in many different ways. It has been the story of my life because I was not born in the United States. We traveled—when I was little, my parents were in exile in England and then my father was an ambassador and then we came here. So I think being able to absorb change and adjust to it probably helped me a lot. And also, I learned empathy toward other people, being a foreigner originally myself, and having spent a lot of time with people who come from different cultures.

## BEST NEGOTIATING STRATEGY

MA: First of all, try to get to know the person you're negotiating with. Know a lot about them before you go into the negotiation, and then try to establish some kind of human contact with them when you go in. I think—and this is an advantage for women—it is important to have some charm when you start and some human exchange, and then to be tough and tell it like it is. I used to say that when I traveled, I'd go someplace and I'd start with small talk; then I'd say, "I've come a long way so I must be frank." So I think the key is a mixture of human interchange, putting yourself in the other person's shoes, but not forgetting what your goal is in the negotiation. You can't become co-opted by the other side.

## HELPFUL CHILDHOOD MEMORY

MA: I am different from my American contemporaries because I actually lived through the bombings in London during World War II. What had the greatest impact on me was knowing the effects of war. We were in air-raid shelters. I was little, four or five, and would come out in the morning and see buildings bombed—London bombed. It had a huge effect on me, in realizing that we couldn't let that kind of thing happen ever again. The role of America—I don't want this to sound hokey, but it just happens to be true: America was not involved in the decision of Munich in September 1938 that really was the sealing of the fate of Czechoslovakia. Hitler marched in, and then when America entered the war, it turned the whole thing around. So for me, the concept of America being engaged and helping was just ingrained from childhood. I think it does make a difference when you've seen things up close.

## BEST ADVICE

MA: I got a report card when I was about seven years old in England, and it said "Madeleine is discouraged by first difficulties." My father took me aside when he saw this, and he said, "Nobody should ever be able to say that about you." My parents, especially my father, had an incredible influence on me, and that statement made a lifelong impression.

## CONDOLEEZZA RICE

BORN IN BIRMINGHAM, Alabama, in 1954, Condoleezza Rice graduated Phi Beta Kappa from the University of Denver, earned a master's degree at the University of Notre Dame, and returned to Denver for her Ph.D. in international studies. She studied with Dr. Josef Korbel, Madeleine Albright's father, who was one of her professors. She joined the faculty of Stanford University in 1981 and became provost in 1993. An award-winning professor at Stanford, 1981–1993, she has published numerous books and articles including: *Uncertain Allegiance: The Soviet Union and the Czechoslovak Army* (1984), *The Gorbachev Era* (1986) with Alexander Dallin, and *Germany Unified and Europe Transformed* (1995) with Philip Zelikow.

## IMPORTANT TRAIT FOR SUCCESS

CONDOLEEZZA RICE: I think I am pretty good at looking ahead, not back. And part of that is trying to be a problem solver—not constantly thinking over what the problem is, but trying to figure out what I'm going to do about it.

## BIGGEST OBSTACLE

CR: I never really had a sense of obstacles. My parents were—I had the best parents that God ever gave anyone. They were totally devoted to me, unconditional love, and they made me believe I could do anything. They really taught me not to think in terms of obstacles. Again, it's the problem-solving side.

If there was anything that ever got in the way, it was that I was interested in a lot of different things, and I had to learn to focus.

KBH: That's interesting. Whether you wanted to be a concert pianist or an advisor on national security or—

CR: Or do figure skating or whatever. I always knew I wanted to be a concert pianist, but I was probably not as dedicated and focused to one thing as a lot of people might have been. I tried all kinds of things. I was one of those kids who wanted to take this lesson and that lesson. It was a good thing, but it also meant that I did a lot of different things.

## BEST PREPARATION FOR ROUGH-AND-TUMBLE OF LIFE

CR: Being provost at Stanford. In an academic administration where you have fourteen hundred extremely smart people who are basically independent contractors, because (laugh) faculty don't believe they have a boss, I learned when it was necessary to persuade people and when it was necessary to inform or when it was necessary to demand. Learning to work in that environment was probably the most important thing, and learning how to be tough enough to deal with some very, very strong personalities.

## BEST NEGOTIATING STRATEGY

CR: Be absolutely certain of where you want to come out. Know what your true red lines are, and don't keep moving them. You have to be selective. You can't have ten red lines or you're never going to get anything done. So you really just have to know what is going to matter most and then decide essentially that everything else is negotiable. But you have to know what's nonnegotiable.

## HELPFUL CHILDHOOD MEMORY

CR: Probably throughout my childhood I was always performing in one way or another, piano and figure skating, and from the very early stages, I can remember doing Easter speeches at church. My parents were big believers in putting me out there. People would come to visit the house and my mother would say, "Oh, come play the piano for Mrs. Jones and her husband." So very early on I got comfortable doing that, so I'm not uncomfortable doing public speaking, I'm not uncomfortable being out in a public way, and I think it was really very important. It gives you self-confidence early because you have to learn to control the nerves, you have to learn to be on top of your brief, and whether it's playing a piano piece or knowing your skating program or knowing your Easter speech, you rely on the belief that you're going to do it and do it well. I just think my parents were very wise in having me do that from a very, very early age.

I founded a nonprofit in East Palo Alto, California, in a very poor school district, for after-school and summer programs for these kids. I absolutely insisted that we were going to have two performances a year. We were going to have an instrumental music band and they were going to have an opportunity to stand up in front of people and perform. I think it's an extremely important skill.

KBH: Absolutely. That's interesting. You know, I had the same experiences because I grew up ballet dancing, but I never thought of that helping me in my career.

CR: I'm sure it was key. When I was speaking at the Republican Convention in '92, the first time, my stomach got really nervous the night before. I had not been nervous in the whole run-up, but I had been over that day to see the auditorium and everything, and, of course, it was the Houston Astrodome, and I thought, "They play football in here." It was so huge, so cavernous. So I got home and I was actually nervous, and what calmed me down was I thought, "Well, at least I can't slip and fall or forget the piece." It just took me back to all those times from about age four that I had performed and survived it.

BEST ADVICE

CR: Don't let anyone else define your horizons. So many times people say you have to have a role model who looks like you. So if I had been waiting for a black female Soviet specialist role model, it would have been a while. I began to realize from people telling me, Do whatever it is that interests you. If that means being a Soviet specialist, then so be it. I think that that was really very important, and it was my parents who felt that so strongly.

# CHAPTER TEN

# WOMEN LOOK AT
# THE WORLD

## *Margaret Bourke-White*

AMERICAN WOMEN REPORTERS began covering World War I long before the United States joined the fray in 1917. The first American correspondent on the scene when Germany invaded Belgium in August 1914 was a woman, Mary Boyle O'Reilly of the *Boston Pilot*. Mary Roberts Rinehart, a successful novelist, sent the *Saturday Evening Post* an eyewitness account of the German use of chemical weapons in 1915, but the magazine refused to publish her report. After the United States joined the war, it barred women from the battle zones in Western Europe. Three resourceful Americans—Bessie Beatty, of the *San Francisco Bulletin;* Louise Bryant, a reporter for the Bell Syndicate; and Rheta Childe Dorr, of the *New York Evening Mail*—made their way to the east, where they were briefly able to cover the war from the Russian front.

During the course of World War II, some 150 foreign correspondents were women. Not all of them were allowed to report on the war from the front lines, and some of those who succeeded in doing so disobeyed military orders to evacuate dangerous areas or found a way around them—like Martha Gellhorn, who reached the beaches of Normandy on D-day by stowing away on a hospital ship. Two especially intrepid journalists who overcame the obstacles to obtaining military clearance to cover the war firsthand were Margaret Bourke-White, a photojournalist for *Life* who was the first female correspondent to fly on an American bombing mission, and Marguerite Higgins, the first American woman to enter the notorious Dachau concentration camp, in April 1945. Bourke-White's photo-essay gave millions of readers their first sense of what it was like to fly over an enemy target and drop a planeload of bombs. Later, she photographed the living and the dead at Buchenwald, indelible images that continue to haunt us today. Higgins, who was decorated for helping to liberate Dachau and accepting the surrender of German troops at the camp and nearby, led the way in lifting the veil of secrecy from the Nazis' "Final Solution."

Margaret Bourke-White's father, Joseph White, was an engineer and inventor whose many interests included photography, but Margaret was more interested in nature and animals. She wrote that she "hardly touched a camera and certainly never operated one until after he died." His death came in 1921, when she was just seventeen. The following year, already studying biology at Columbia University, she took a photography course with Clarence White (no relation) and bought a secondhand camera. She continued to pursue the sciences, however, first at the University of Michigan, where she got a job as a photographer for the yearbook, the *Michiganensian,* and then at Cornell, where she took her degree in 1927. Money was tight after Joseph White's death, so Margaret took photographs of the Ithaca, New York, campus and sold them to students and alumni. When the university's *Alumni News* used some of her photographs as covers, she got letters encouraging her to take up architectural photography.

After graduation, she settled in Cleveland, where her mother was now living, hyphenated her middle and last names, and set up as a freelance photographer. Two years later, Henry Luce hired Margaret as a photographer for the new *Fortune* magazine. She had caught his attention with her dramatic photographs of Cleveland's steel mills and other industrial settings, just the sorts of images Luce had in mind for *Fortune*. She fulfilled that promise and more, with photographs of the Chrysler Building, then under construction, and other subjects. Photographs of Margaret perched with her camera on one of the gargoyles that jutted out from the building's sixtieth floor, in order to capture unimpeded views of the surrounding cityscape, fed her growing reputation as a photojournalist who would risk anything for a stunning picture.

Her first trip to the Soviet Union, in 1931, was a great coup for Margaret and her magazine. On assignment in Germany, where she was photographing factories, she besieged the Soviet embassy in Berlin for six weeks and was finally granted a visa. Besides supplying photographs to *Fortune,* the trip also formed the basis for her first book, *Eyes on Russia,* the prototype for a series of volumes that combined her photographs with impressionistic essays and reportage. She repeated her Russian experiment in the United States, crossing the country to capture views of the drought in the Midwest and other images of the Depression. When *Life* made its first appearance as a magazine of news-cum-pictures, her report on the earthwork dam in Fort Peck, Montana, the world's largest, was the cover story.

For the magazine and in several books she continued her social reportage, from the United States and from Europe. The images and stories for *North of the Danube,* which documented the early stages of Nazi aggression, represented one of her collaborations with the fiction writer Erskine Caldwell, whom she married in 1939. In the spring of 1941, anticipating that Germany would soon invade the USSR, she asked to return to Russia. The Soviet embassy in Washington, D.C., advised her to enter Russia from the east rather than through Europe, so she and Caldwell flew to Hong Kong from Los Angeles and then spent another thirty-one days getting to Moscow.

On her previous trip to the USSR in 1932, she had photographed Stalin's mother, Ekaterina Dzhugashvili, at Tiflis. According to Margaret, Stalin's mother was puzzled about exactly what her son did. Hoping he'd become a priest, she'd sent him to study at a seminary and was disappointed when he joined the revolution and started robbing post offices. Margaret knew that photography was prohibited in the USSR, but

she'd gotten around the restrictions on previous trips and was sure she'd
be able to do so again. The Soviets had liked her photographs, which
contained echoes of Soviet style and ennobled industry. This time, the
presence of Caldwell, whose writings about discrimination—class and
racial—in the United States made him an admired writer, helped her cut
through the red tape, too.

As a journalist, Margaret was always drawn to stories that revealed
the everyday lives of people, rather than the official view. In Moscow, she
was surprised to find a church service in progress and was able to photograph inside the church. The government, she was told, didn't bother the
clergy or their parishioners. When the United States began to send supplies to the USSR that fall in return for Soviet guarantees of religious freedom, her photos became news and *Life* printed a twelve-page spread.

With the help of the Writers' Union, many of whose members admired Caldwell's work, and the Society for Cultural Relations with Foreign Countries, which knew Margaret's earlier Soviet photos, Margaret
and Caldwell were permitted to visit Ukraine and the Black Sea, both of
which were officially off-limits to Americans, including diplomats.

Germany crossed the Russian border on June 22, 1941, and Margaret and Caldwell rushed back to Moscow by train. At first it seemed
that the Nazi-Soviet conflict would be a short one; the Germans had destroyed over 1,800 Soviet aircraft on the first day and lost only 35. The
couple moved into a suite in the National Hotel, overlooking the Kremlin. Margaret photographed from her balcony, but first she had to get
permission to do so. No one was allowed to photograph; even having a
camera justified being shot. But Margaret was the only foreign journalist
in Moscow, and somehow she got permission to take pictures on July 15.

Four days later, the first bombs were dropped on Moscow. Since the
invasion had started, German troops had advanced more than four hundred miles. At first, Margaret and Caldwell followed orders and spent
the nights in the Moscow subways, so deep underground that no one
was injured in the bombardment. But Margaret soon decided not to
miss the chance to take photographs and went up to the American embassy roof. She called it "one of the outstanding nights of my life," and
wrote that "the opening air raids over Moscow possessed a magnificence
that I have never seen matched in any man-made spectacle. It was as

though the German pilots and Russian antiaircraft gunners had been handed enormous brushes dipped in radium paint and were executing abstract designs with the sky as their canvas." Her photographs, made at exposures of as long as twelve minutes, show the lines made by tracer fire and flares against a sky broken by the spires of the Kremlin.

When a bomb exploded nearby, shattering the windows of the embassy and other buildings, she took refuge in the basement. But as soon as the all-clear signal sounded, she went back upstairs to leave a note on the shards of window glass: "Please don't sweep up glass till I come back with camera." The photos, the first of the Moscow bombing that Americans saw, appeared in *Life* in September. She photographed nearly all of the twenty-two German bombing raids on Moscow, usually from the balcony or windows of her hotel suite. She stayed in Moscow until October, by which time even the Soviet government was evacuating to the east. Paralleling the scorched-earth policy Stalin had proclaimed with respect to agricultural products, factories were being dismantled and rebuilt in Siberia; and hydroelectric dams, such as the one on the Dnieper River that Margaret had photographed in 1930, were being blown up to prevent the Germans from profiting from the power they generated.

Harry Hopkins, Roosevelt's Lend-Lease administrator, came to Moscow in July 1941; Margaret hounded him to help her get permission to photograph Stalin. Through Molotov, permission was granted, and Margaret went to the Kremlin. After two hours of waiting, while Hopkins and Stalin conferred, she joined them in Office Number One. She had to communicate through an interpreter, but she tried to draw her subject into conversation, reminding him of the photographs she had made of his mother in 1932. "At this disclosure, the Kremlin interpreter exclaimed with astonishment, 'His very own mother! His real mother!' But Stalin spoke never a word. His rough, pitted face was as immobile as ice." Margaret couldn't get him to speak or even to sit down, and had given up trying "to make that great stone face look human" until her flashbulbs spilled out of her pockets and onto the floor. "The Kremlin interpreter and I went scrambling after them. I guess Stalin had never seen an American girl on her knees to him before. He thought it was funny, and started to laugh. The change was miraculous! It was as though a second personality had come to the front—genial and almost merry. The smile lasted just long enough for me to make two exposures, and then, as though a veil had been drawn over his features, again he turned to stone. I went away thinking this was the most determined, the most ruthless personality I had ever encountered in my life."

The pictures of Stalin that Hopkins took back to the United States with him appeared in *Life* in September. By then, unable to get to the front, Margaret was ready to come home. But her editors wanted her to stay and worked on the Soviet ambassador in Washington to persuade him that the coverage was doing the USSR good by improving its image in the American mind. Suddenly, Margaret and Caldwell were told on September 15 to prepare for a trip next morning. They and eleven other journalists—five British, six American—were taken to the front, Smolensk sector. She photographed at the plain of Yelna, where it was said that 50,000 German troops and 20,000 Soviet soldiers had been killed, and in a town nearby she photographed a family of four, minutes after they were killed by a bomb that stuck just outside her hotel.

"It is a peculiar thing about pictures of this sort. It is as though a protecting screen draws itself across my mind and makes it possible to consider focus and light values and the technique of photography, in as impersonal a way as though I were making an abstract camera composition. This blind lasts as long as it is needed—while I am actually operating the camera. Days later, when I developed the negatives, I was surprised to find that I could not bring myself to look at the films. I had to have someone else handle and sort them for me."

When a woman found her young daughter, dead, on the sidewalk, "[h]er desperate moans penetrated even my protective shell, and as I focused my camera on this vision of human misery it seemed heartless to turn her suffering into a photograph. But war is war and it has to be recorded."

In 1942, Margaret returned to Europe, this time to England, where she photographed Churchill and, more important, the American B-17 Flying Fortresses that could fly at high altitudes and were vital to plans to bomb military targets inside Germany in daytime. The planes flew over 1,500 sorties; only thirty planes were lost.

Margaret wanted to fly on one of those bombing runs. She had no fear of photographing from a rapidly moving open plane; as a commercial photographer in the 1930s she had taken shots of TWA and Eastern Airlines planes while strapped into a small craft that flew alongside them. But women weren't permitted anywhere near combat. Her chance to get to the war zone came when she was assigned to North Africa, sailing in a convoy carrying 6,000 British and American troops, 400 to 600 hundred nurses, the first five WACs to be sent to an overseas war zone, three women on General Eisenhower's staff—his secretary Jeanne Dixon, Elspeth Duncan, and Kay Summersby—and Margaret. She had somehow gotten wind of the fact that German U-boats were following the convoy, and she and two other journalists got permission to cover the action from the bridge in case they were attacked.

They did not have to wait long. Their ship, a former cruise vessel, was hit by a torpedo as it neared the coast of North Africa, and everyone lined up to get into the lifeboats, which were overcrowded and taking water dangerously. Margaret reported on the courage of two WACs who, as they were about to climb into their lifeboat, saw that it was already overloaded. They calmly stepped out of line and said simply, "Oh, of course, we can't all go." Once the boats were in the water, there was so little room, she wrote, "that we started singing, bending our bodies in rhythm to give the rowers room to move their arms." Yet as people floated up, clinging to flimsy rafts, the lifeboat took on more passengers, and in one case several nurses cradled a woman with a broken leg to give her a measure of protection from the violent rise and fall of the little boat in the rough sea.

Even when there was no room left in the boats, people handed cigarettes to men floating on the rafts alongside them. To spell the exhausted rowers, other passengers took turns, including Margaret and "splendid Elspeth Duncan," whom she called the best rower of all. As dawn approached and the seas calmed, Margaret climbed onto the gunwales and started photographing the others, using one of the two cameras she had salvaged from the ship. Before long, a destroyer reached them and plucked the survivors out of the water. They learned that only two lives had been lost. The good news restored a sense of normalcy, and they began to inventory what they had managed to save: Margaret's two cameras, Jeanne Dixon's prayerbook, and Kay Summersby's lipstick were among the items. By evening, they had docked in Algiers.

The experience is said to have been the basis for Alfred Hitchcock's film *Lifeboat*. Margaret, undaunted, soon resumed her efforts to accompany the crew of a B-17 on a mission. Eventually, General Jimmy Doolittle, commander of the Twelfth Air Force North Africa, gave Margaret permission to fly with the 97th Bomb Group if the commanding officer agreed. J. Hampton Atkinson didn't just give her permission, he fell in love with her, and she reciprocated his feeling (Caldwell had recently divorced her and remarried). When Atkinson was made a general, people at *Life* disparagingly referred to her as "the general's mattress," but that was unfair. Margaret was so good at cajoling people that she didn't need to use other means to gain advantages. Those who knew her believed they genuinely liked each other.

Margaret borrowed camera equipment from the Signal Corps and practiced on the ground techniques for photographing at the high altitudes and under the conditions of extreme cold that she would encounter in the plane. Her bombing run was on El Aouina airfield in Tunis, on January 22, 1943. After the Germans occupied Tunisia, the airport became the landing point for reinforcements from Sicily for Rommel's army as it retreated from Egypt. That morning, the German planes were to be on the ground for just half an hour before taking off again; the plan was to bomb the airfield within those thirty minutes. Margaret would be in the lead plane, piloted by Atkinson and Paul Tibbets, who later flew the *Enola Gay* on the mission that dropped the atomic bomb on Hiroshima. As soon as they were airborne she began photographing the crew.

Soon the B-17s were over their target and dropped their bombs on the airfield from 21,000 feet. Margaret observed plumes of white and black smoke rising into the air, sometimes punctuated by red flashes, but didn't immediately realize that they were the explosions caused by the bombs. Then she noticed "black spreading spiders, rather pretty, with legs that grew and grew." This turned out to be the antiaircraft fire, which slightly damaged the plane she was in and succeeded in disabling two of the other planes that took part in the raid. Over a hundred Luftwaffe aircraft were destroyed; the losses severely compromised Germany's capacity for bringing reinforcements to North Africa. The story that ran in *Life* showed Margaret, in flying gear, next to a B-17. She was, as the caption stated, "the first woman ever to fly with a U.S. combat crew over enemy soil."

In September 1943, Margaret returned to report on the fighting in Italy and Germany. Between Naples and Rome, she photographed the field engineers who did the unglamorous work of restoring roads and bridges blown up as the Germans retreated from the advancing British and American infantries. She also visited the Eleventh Field Hospital, where, she wrote, the nurses were "closer to the battle line than American women had ever worked in this or any other war." The hospital was just a string of tents arranged in a cross, their red cross symbols visible from above. Not long after she arrived on the evening of January 20, 1944, a German artillery shell scored a direct hit on the hospital's mess hall, flattening it and knocking out the hospital's electrical circuits. They were so close to the front that it wasn't clear whether the shell had been aimed at the hospital or simply gone off course. Throughout the night, many more shells screamed over the hospital, sending the medics and nurses—and Margaret—diving for cover.

While Margaret was in the area, the Thirty-sixth Division had been ordered to attempt to make inroads against a dug-in, fortified German position, as General Mark Clark strove to establish a bridgehead in the Liri valley. The Thirty-sixth was known as the "Texan," because most of its members were from Texas, and that night they took very heavy casualties while attacking the impregnable enemy positions: 56 percent of the riflemen and company officers were wounded. For most of them, the first medical attention they received was at this field hospital.

Margaret wrote about talking to one nurse, Wilma Barnes, who seemed to address all the patients by their first names. "'Do you learn all their first names?' I asked. 'Always when they come from Texas,'" she told Margaret. Wilma was from Abilene, and "the doctors just automatically call me every time they get a patient from Texas. It makes the boys pep up to know that somebody from their home state is taking care of them."

The doctors and nurses did their best to apply tourniquets, do surgery, and bandage patients while the shells passed overhead. Each time they heard the familiar scream of a shell, before ducking for cover themselves, the nurses would check that the IV needles in the patients' arms were secure.

At one point, the CO, Major Bonham, wheeled an oxygen tank into the operating tent and announced, "We're almost out of Type A blood. We're running out of blood citrates, which we need for all these transfusions, and now the oxygen is giving out." A little while later, Jess Padgitt, the corporal who had been assigned to escort Margaret, helped her move her camera into the operating ward. Then he asked, "Can you get along without me for half an hour, Peggy," and vanished. When he returned, she learned that he'd given a pint of blood; he was Type A, the blood Major Bonham most needed. All through the night of January 20, the hospital staff had been replenishing the supply with their own blood, and they'd gotten the truck drivers to do the same. Finally, even the artillery gunners from nearby positions had come down to the hospital, given blood, and then resumed shelling the German positions.

When she left the field hospital, Margaret felt a sense of completion. "I had my story now. I had completed my assignment. I had heroes, and I had heroines—ten of them. It was time to go home." Before she got back to New York, her editors cabled to tell her that as soon as the photos made it past the military censors, *Life* would run the story. She was already visualizing the spread in the magazine, with photo captions taken from her interviews with the medics, nurses, and wounded soldiers, and the book that would follow. When she reached *Life*'s offices, however, her editor, Wilson Hicks, told her that the package containing the hospital pictures had been lost. All they had were the "prosaic pictures taken back out of shell range, while the whole sequence of the heroic surgeons and nurses under fire was in the package that was lost." The magazine made do with the less dramatic pictures and ran the story anyway, but the images of the stoic heroism of Wilma Barnes, Major Bonham, and the wounded and dying soldiers were never found.

Before the global war had turned into the Cold War, Margaret was reporting on other troubled parts of the world. She visited India while it was struggling to shed its colonial status, photographed riots and violence, met with Gandhi shortly before his assassination, and reported on the partition that created India and Pakistan. A few years later she visited South Africa, where she became the first woman to witness first-hand the conditions of the black gold miners working as much as a mile below the surface of the earth. Her next journalistic encounter with a major war, however, came in Korea.

When Margaret arrived in Korea in 1952, the peninsula was already, in her words, "the most consistently raked-over news center in the world." The military and political stories had been told and retold, so she was determined to look at how war had affected the lives of ordinary South Koreans and to learn about the guerrilla fighters who were operating in the South. One of the Americans Margaret spoke to, Army Major Lewis Davis, an advisor to the Korean National Police, whose job it was to track down the guerrillas, told her the clandestine fighters were "as fast as rabbits, and as cautious as virgins." They were young South Koreans who had converted to the Communist cause during the period when the North Korean army occupied the entire South except for a tiny sector around Pusan. When the northern troops were forced to withdraw, the guerrillas established bases in the mountains of the South and continued operating from there, under the leadership of specially selected officers of the North Korean People's Army. They disrupted communications lines, terrorized villages, and occasionally staged surprise attacks.

Margaret wanted to know how the guerrillas managed to subsist in their mountain hideouts and why they had chosen to do so. She spoke to North and South Koreans who had been captured by the police and to some southerners who had surrendered after becoming disillusioned. She learned how they managed to publish newspapers on mimeograph machines hidden in caves, where they got the paper to print on, and how they looted food and cloth to sew uniforms. She also discovered that what convinced many of these young men and women to join the Communists was the promise of education and better lives for their families. One young woman told Margaret, "I was only a housemaid, but all my life I wanted to study. The Communist leaders pledged that all who joined would be taught to read and write. Also, they promised that I would have a position of increased dignity in the community. This was the first time in my life I was ever treated like a lady. It seemed such a good opportunity to get an education."

For a while, the guerrilla leaders delivered on their promises. Concealed in their mountain redoubts, the young recruits learned to read and write. That their textbook might be a *History of the Bolshevik Party* intended to indoctrinate them into Communist ideology mattered less to them than the freedom their newly acquired literacy represented. However, as the guerrillas' situation deteriorated, more of their time was devoted to finding food and avoiding capture, and the classes stopped. The young woman, who was a cook for her group and had to carry the kitchen utensils with her whenever they moved, grew demoralized and wanted to rejoin her family. She finally surrendered to the police.

While Margaret was reporting on the war from Korea in 1952, she began to feel pain in her left arm and leg. It would be six more years before her condition was diagnosed as Parkinson's disease, but meanwhile, her photojournalistic efforts slowed dramatically and soon ceased altogether. She underwent two brain surgeries intended to slow the progress of Parkinson's, which even today remains an incurable neurological disorder, and managed to write *Portrait of Myself,* her fascinating autobiography, which was published in 1963. She lived until 1971. She was sixty-seven when she died.

## *Marguerite Higgins*

M ARGUERITE HIGGINS, the first woman to win a Pulitzer Prize for international reporting, also cut her journalistic teeth on World War II. Born in Hong Kong in 1920, to an American businessman and his French wife, she grew up mainly in California, but her view of the world was, from her early years, a cosmopolitan one. Fluent in Chinese and French as well as English, she studied journalism at the University of California, Berkeley, and at Columbia University, where she managed to shoehorn herself into the already full journalism class just a few days before the opening of school in September 1941.

In Marguerite's view, being a first-rate war reporter demanded two qualities that reporters in other fields didn't need: "a capacity for unusual physical endurance and the willingness to take unusual personal risk." She possessed both in abundance and determined to use them to go beyond the usual assignments covering local news and politics. In California, she had already had her fill of that sort of journalism, both on the university's *Daily Californian* and as a reporter for small newspapers in the state where she worked during summer vacations. To convince the *New York Herald Tribune* to hire her straight out of journalism school, she managed to get into Madame Chiang Kai-shek's hospital room at Columbia Presbyterian in 1942 and came away with the only interview the Chinese president's wife granted while in New York for medical treatment.

Once at the *Trib,* she immediately requested assignment to Europe to report on the war. "I had known since childhood," she wrote in *News Is a Singular Thing,* "that if there was to be a war I wanted to be there to know for myself what force cuts so deep into the hearts of men." When the *Tribune*'s editor, Whitelaw Reid, refused, she went over his head to the publisher, the editor's mother, Helen Rogers Reid. She agreed to send Marguerite to the *Herald Tribune*'s London bureau in August 1944. From London, Marguerite made her way to recently liberated Paris, where she put her fluent French to excellent use. She not only read the Paris papers and wire-service dispatches in order to learn more about what was going on in France, but was able to follow up on stories by speaking directly to the French sources. Her own work for the *Tribune* catapulted her into the position of Berlin bureau chief early in 1945, when she was a mere twenty-five years of age.

From Berlin, Marguerite reported on some of the most dramatic moments of the war's final months. Less than two weeks before Germany surrendered, on May 8, 1945, Marguerite and Sergeant Peter

Furst, a German-born Jew who was a soldier and a reporter for the army newspaper *Stars and Stripes,* were the first Americans to enter the confines of the Dachau concentration camp, in Bavaria. Keen to be the first to reach the camp, they detoured their jeep around the continuing fighting north of Dachau and approached from the south. En route, they saw white sheets flying everywhere and encountered German soldiers who eagerly surrendered their weapons to the American journalists (Furst was, in fact, a soldier, of course). They piled the rifles and grenades into the jeep and continued on to the gates of Dachau.

While American soldiers from two other jeeps occupied themselves with the SS guards whom they found at the entrance to the camp itself, Marguerite and Furst headed for their first glimpse of the prisoners' barracks. Nothing could have prepared them for what they witnessed there. The inmates had gained control of that section of the camp the night before, when most of the remaining SS guards had fled. Unsure of whether German soldiers remained outside the barracks area, however, they stayed inside until Marguerite and her companion opened the gate of the enclosure and walked through. Others soon followed them in, and when the inmates realized that their visitors were Americans, "[t]attered, emaciated men, weeping, yelling and shouting 'Long live America!' swept toward the gate in a mob. Those who could not walk limped or crawled. In the confusion, they were so hysterically happy that they took the S.S. man for an American. During a wild five minutes he was patted on the back, paraded on shoulders and embraced enthusiastically by prisoners."

The excitement continued for over an hour. Afterward, the sole American prisoner, an air force major, conducted a tour of the barracks, where sick inmates lay dying; the torture chambers, which held 1,200 corpses; the crematorium; the spot in the camp where people who were to be executed were forced to kneel before being shot; and an open grave with 2,000 bodies the SS had not gotten around to burning before they fled. Adjacent to the camp, the Americans found a railroad siding with a line of "cattle cars in which prisoners from Buchenwald had been transported to Dachau. Hundreds of dead were still in the cars due to the fact that prisoners in the camp had rejected S.S. orders to remove them. It was mainly the men from these cattle cars that the S.S. leaders had shot before making their escape."

Marguerite's story, which appeared in the *Herald Tribune* on May 1, was the first revelation from inside Dachau that Americans read. The New York Newspaper Women's Club awarded her a prize for best foreign reporting for 1945, and the army presented her and Peter Furst with a citation for taking part in the surrenders in Augsburg and Dachau. After the armistice, Marguerite covered Maréchal Henri Pétain's treason trial, the Nuremberg Trials, and the blockade of Berlin. She continued as the *Tribune*'s Berlin bureau chief, with a focus on the countries behind the Iron Curtain. The devastation of the war had turned many of the countries of Eastern Europe into grim places, and Marguerite blamed the Soviet Union for extinguishing the spirits of Poles, Czechs, Hungarians, and others who were brought under the repressive Communist rule.

Her journalistic beat fascinated her, and when the *Tribune* assigned her to its Tokyo bureau in 1950, she was initially displeased. She changed her mind a month later, however, when North Korean troops crossed the thirty-eighth parallel into South Korea and paid no attention to the UN Security Council resolution demanding their withdrawal. Marguerite then flew into Seoul to cover the war. General Douglas MacArthur often invited the press to fly in his private plane. In Marguerite's case, he not only offered her a ride but took such a liking to her that he granted her an exclusive interview. This journalistic plum caused resentment among some of her male colleagues, who insinuated that her scoops were obtained by scheming rather than good aggressive reporting. Her first Paris bureau chief, Russell Hill, defended her. "She had a talent for getting difficult stories and getting them right," he wrote.

Marguerite's good relations with MacArthur proved useful when she returned to Korea a few weeks later. Except for nurses, no military women had been assigned to Korea, and Lieutenant General Walton Walker, commander of the Eighth Army, saw no reason to make an exception for a journalist. She was put on a plane back to Japan, but after she put her case to MacArthur, he cabled the *New York Herald Tribune:* "Ban on women correspondents in Korea has been lifted. Marguerite

Higgins is held in highest professional esteem by everyone"; and ordered Walker to allow her the same privileges as the male reporters. She returned to Korea in July, and in September reported on the Marines' amphibious landing at Inchon. For that story, she won the 1951 Pulitzer Prize for international reporting, the first woman war correspondent to capture that honor. The Pulitzer, which she shared with five of her colleagues on the *Tribune,* was one of the more than fifty journalism awards she collected in her first dozen years as a newspaperwoman.

By the time she landed in Asia, Marguerite had firmly committed herself to opposing Communism across the globe. She castigated Truman for not taking a firmer stand against the regimes that brought "deportations, incredible toil, terror, deplorable living standards and, in many cases, semi-starvation." In Korea, where in the war's early months she was the sole woman in a complement of over 130 foreign journalists, she suggested using nuclear weapons if the Chinese entered the peninsula. Shuttling back and forth between Berlin and Korea, she married Lieutenant General William Hall, an intelligence officer, with whom she moved to Washington, D.C., after the war, in 1955. A daughter born prematurely in 1953 had died when she was five days old, but the couple had two other children, in 1958 and 1959. During this period, she wrote a series of profiles of world leaders, in which she was inclined to be generous to anyone who was in the anti-Communist camp. She looked favorably, for example, on Spain's Francisco Franco, Marshal Tito of Yugoslavia, and the shah of Iran. She described the shah as a "progressive" and forthright leader.

Marguerite was no stranger to Vietnam when she arrived in 1963 as the *New York Herald Tribune*'s war correspondent. She made her first trip to the country, from Hong Kong, as a six-month-old, to recover from malaria in its mountains. In 1951, on her first visit as an adult, she interviewed Bao Dai, the emperor, and had a look at the French-Indo-Chinese conflict. Her seventh visit was in 1963. She knew Vietnam well and she spoke French and Chinese.

Marguerite interviewed Vietnamese from different geographic regions, social classes, and political groups—monks, peasants, tribal minorities, and political leaders—and also members of the American military, whose numbers had by then swelled well beyond 10,000. Her staunch anti-Communist views again came forward. She defended President Ngo Dinh Diem, who was beginning to lose support from his own people and the American military, as the best leader Vietnam was likely to get at the time. She conceded that Diem was not a democratic ruler in the Western sense, though he had been elected in nominally free balloting. She went so far as to concede that Vietnam was not a democratic state, but she considered Diem a credible Vietnamese nationalist who had gone to prison for opposing the French colonial rulers. The Buddhist opposition, she believed, was designed purely to convince the Americans that Diem lacked popular support and must be removed from power.

At the time, a number of Buddhist monks and nuns were protesting the Diem regime by setting themselves on fire in dramatic acts of self-immolation. Ostensibly, these were protests against the regime's religious repression, but Higgins spoke to Buddhists who told her that there was no religious persecution in the country. When she interviewed Thich Tri Quang, the monk who was leading the protests, she concluded that the demonstrations and suicides were staged to influence American thinking about the situation in Vietnam. Quang, mistaking Marguerite for a White House emissary, confided to her, "We the Buddhists have good information that President Kennedy sympathizes with our anti-Diem efforts . . . the time is coming when President Kennedy will have to be more outspoken because it would be hard to get rid of Diem without explicit American support."

Marguerite's analysis in the *New York Herald Tribune* on September 1 proved incisive and prescient. She wrote, "The State Department's apparent attempt to set the Vietnamese Army at the throat of the Diem regime in the middle of a war will be the subject of bitter controversy both inside this government and around the world." Two months later, Diem was overthrown and assassinated in a military coup that led not to stability in South Vietnam but to a series of seizures of power by generals who proved unable to guide the country's fortunes in the political arena or on the battlefield.

Marguerite became a columnist for *Newsday* in 1963. In her columns, she lamented the chaos precipitated by Diem's ouster, but she persisted in predicting that the Americans would eventually prevail. At the same time, she recognized the folly and ignorance that underlay the U.S. political program for a people she characterized as "Asians with a touch of French culture." Underscoring her conviction that countenancing Diem's overthrow had been a mistake, she wrote, "As the months, years, coup d'états and crises went by it became appallingly evident that the United States simply did not know who its friends were in that tormented country or how to distinguish them from its foes."

In November 1965, Marguerite developed a high fever that for weeks baffled the medical specialists at Walter Reed Army Medical Center. She was finally diagnosed with leishmaniasis, an extremely rare parasitic infection that is contracted from sand flies. Despite her illness, she continued to write her thrice-weekly *Newsday* column, "On the Spot," and even managed to sneak out of the hospital to appear on television in New York when her book, *Our Vietnam Nightmare,* was published. She did not cut back to one column a week until just two weeks before her death, in January 1966. As the wife of a U.S. Army general, she was buried in Arlington National Cemetery, one of just two women journalists so honored. The other, fittingly, is Mary Roberts Rinehart.

## *Women of Today*

THE WOMEN WAR CORRESPONDENTS overcame official and unofficial barriers to get to the front lines in World War I and World War II. They were true pioneers and won acclaim for their reporting and photography.

It was the entry of radio and television as communications media that began to make news much more available on a current up-to-the-minute basis.

At first, women were not regular correspondents. When I entered the field in 1969, it was the first time a local television station, in Houston, Texas, had a woman news reporter. I covered for both radio and television, but was once told that women's voices were not really suitable for anchor work, especially in radio.

Barbara Walters broke the barriers in national television. She co-hosted the *Today* show for NBC and was the first woman coanchor of a major network nightly news program for ABC.

Cokie Roberts was the first woman cohost of a Sunday-morning news interview show, *This Week,* with Sam Donaldson.

In the publishing field, there is one woman who is a global CEO, Jane Friedman, at HarperCollins Publishers.

## BARBARA WALTERS

THE DAUGHTER OF LOU WALTERS, a theater producer who owned the legendary Latin Quarter nightclub, Barbara Walters was born in Boston, Massachusetts, and grew up in New York and Miami. At Sarah Lawrence College (BA, 1953), she majored in English, but she began working at a local TV station in New York City before graduating from college. She was a producer at WNBC-TV, a writer for NBC's *Today* show, and became the show's cohost in 1974. Two years later, Barbara became the first woman network news anchor, on the *ABC Evening News,* and earned a place in the pantheon of TV journalism—and the first of a series of Emmy awards—with her interviews of Anwar Sadat and other prominent figures on the *Barbara Walters Special.* Since then, she has been anchor of *20/20* and the *ABC News Magazine,* among many other important appearances.

IMPORTANT TRAIT FOR SUCCESS

> BARBARA WALTERS: (After thinking a long time) I think intense curiosity . . . and perseverance and also the need to work. I couldn't just walk away. . . . I had to stick with it, through the hardships.

BIGGEST OBSTACLE

> BW: The fact that women couldn't do things men could do. [In 1961] I was a writer on the *Today* show—the only woman—it was a big deal when I was allowed to write for the men as well as the women on the show. When I was cohost with Frank McGee, he had an agreement that if we were in the studio I couldn't ask a question

until he had asked three. So if I got a big-name interview, like Henry Kissinger, I had to go off-premise and tape it in order to get the whole interview. It's taken a long time for women to have the same assignments as men, but now we never think about it. We have women war correspondents, women anchors, although there is still no woman anchoring an evening network news program.

KBH: But that may have been why you became so adept at nailing the big interviews.

BW: I had to. Otherwise I would have only been able to come in on the fourth question. Or I would have been doing just the lighter fashion shows, the celebrities.

## BEST PREPARATION FOR ROUGH-AND-TUMBLE OF LIFE

BW: I know that this will sound strange, but I think you have to have stability; a balance of some sort in your life that enables you to take the hard knocks professionally and not fall apart.

When I first came to ABC, which was now twenty-seven years ago, and I was the first female coanchor of a network news program, I was a terrible flop. My career, after all these years, was over, really over. I was drowning without a life preserver, and what saved me was a private life, friends, my child. My entire world was not wrapped up in my career. It's very easy to get so wrapped up in your career that if something bad happens, you just can't go on.

KBH: That's so interesting because to you that was, I'm sure, just devastating, but to the outside world, you just picked right up and started doing what you do so well . . . in-depth interview programs.

BW: Well, I think you have to. I think almost everybody faces a defeat or you get fired or something. It turned out to be the best thing that happened to me, although I didn't realize it, because I had to work my way back. And in working my way back, I could have a little faith in myself that it wasn't all just good luck. I don't suggest that everybody go through it, but it is a special experience.

BEST NEGOTIATING STRATEGY

> BW: When women, in particular, have said, "I don't have equality on the show" or "I don't make the same money," I have just said, "Work so hard that you become valuable. It really is the only way. You can't negotiate from weakness. Hang in there until you become so important that they really need you." To negotiate by whining or by saying, "She has it better"—

> KBH: Or my rights are being violated—
> BW: These are hard-nosed people. They don't care. You really have to say, "This is why you need me," and that takes time.

HELPFUL CHILDHOOD MEMORY

> BW: I had an older sister, a few years older than I was, who was borderline retarded. I always knew because of my family situation that I would probably have to take care of her. It was this sense of responsibility that I would have to work because I had someone whom I had to care for beyond myself.

> KBH: Did that come to pass?
> BW: Yes, it came to pass.

BEST ADVICE

> BW: Number one, you have to love what you're doing. If you do not love it, get out of it. Second, there's no substitute for hard work and homework. You've got to be the first one there in the morning and the last one there at night. And third, you must have a sense of balance in a private life. Otherwise, you wake up one day and say, "Was it worth it?"

# COKIE ROBERTS

AMONG HER MANY journalistic roles, Cokie Roberts is a senior news analyst for National Public Radio. For her NPR reporting, she won the Edward R. Murrow Award, and she is also the first radio or TV journalist to win the Everett McKinley Dirksen Award for her reporting from Capitol Hill. She was a regular contributor to the *MacNeil/Lehrer NewsHour* on PBS, for which she reported on the Iran/contra affair, among other major stories, and has won two Emmys, one of them for an ABC special, "Who Is Ross Perot?" She is a member of the Broadcasting Hall of Fame.

A former president of the Radio and Television Correspondents Association, Cokie has also made her mark in print. She writes a weekly syndicated column that appears in newspapers across the country, and has published three best-selling books: *We Are Our Mothers' Daughters* (1998), part memoir, part social history; *From This Day Forward* (2000), with her husband, journalist Steve Roberts; and *Founding Mothers: The Women Who Raised Our Nation* (2004). A native of New Orleans, Louisiana, daughter of Hale Boggs, who was majority leader of the U.S. House of Representatives, and Lindy Boggs, who succeeded her husband in Congress after his death and was U.S. ambassador to the Vatican during the Clinton administration, Cokie is a graduate of Wellesley College.

## IMPORTANT TRAIT FOR SUCCESS

COKIE ROBERTS: Of course, in the field that I'm in, curiosity is a tremendously important trait. But I would think in general it's discipline. I'm very disciplined. It allows me to get a great deal done that normally just seems impossible because of just the amount of stuff.

## BIGGEST OBSTACLE

CR: I did marry young and have children young, and finding a way to balance my family and work was an ever-challenging prospect. I don't feel that it was as much imposed on me from outside either by my family or by my workplace as it came from inside. I think that's something very important, again, for young women to understand. A lot of the pressures that they will feel are their own and they are appropriate pressures to feel.

KBH: Agree, and you were also chasing your husband's job.
CR: That's right. I was following him around the country and the world, but I liked doing that, if the truth be told, and I learned a lot doing that. Even though opportunities were closed to me because of that, other opportunities did open. I don't mean to sound like a Pollyanna, but that's true.

## BEST PREPARATION FOR ROUGH-AND-TUMBLE OF LIFE
CR: Fortunately, I grew up in politics, Louisiana politics, so I had some sense of rough-and-tumble. What I didn't really anticipate was the real and blatant discrimination that greeted me upon my graduation from college. It was 1964; the civil rights bill was passed that summer. I think that it is something young women really don't understand, which is that it made all the difference in the world to have the law on our side. And until then, men would say (even after then because it took a while for everybody to catch on), we don't hire women to do that. The help-wanted ads were white and Negro, male and female. That came just as a shock to me. It had never occurred to me that they wouldn't hire me to do something that I could do.

## BEST NEGOTIATING STRATEGY
CR: I guess I would say to listen and be willing to give some, but not all. Actually, my mother was the person who taught me this as a result of sitting on conference committees in Congress. She said, "You know, what will happen is you will be sitting in the room and you can win the room, and then you walk out of the room and realize you've lost the issue." Because of the dynamics of the room you're in, it seems like you've gotten something done. It's because the whole conversation gets framed in a different way sometimes, and so you think, "I've really gotten somewhere."

To give you an example, doing union negotiations once when I was the person negotiating at NPR, they came in and said, "All right, we're going to cut either your salaries or your pensions or your health plans." And for a while we were going along with that, and at some point when you came out of the room and said, "Okay, we've done this great job, we've only gotten a little bit cut from health plans," and everybody outside of the room says, "Hold on, why are our health plans being cut?"

So I think it's always important to remember what the goal is when you're negotiating, and not to give in on the basic goal, but to find ways that you can make the person you're negotiating with save face and feel that he or she has won on something.

## HELPFUL CHILDHOOD MEMORY

CR: I would say there were two things in childhood. One was my father took me seriously as a girl, and so did the nuns who taught me. And in the 1950s, that was quite remarkable. They always gave me the sense that what I had to say mattered, and that what I wanted to do mattered. All of that was unusual at the time. The flip side was also that the women in the family, and there were many of them, many generations, also told the stories and made the jokes and kept me laughing, and I kept them laughing, so that they really were the people who taught me about storytelling, which, of course, is basically what I do.

## BEST ADVICE

CR: I guess the best advice is listen to your mother. I can remember one day when I was about seven years old, and I remember it because I wanted to do two things that were conflicting, and it was frustrating me. And my mother said, "It's easy to be good if nobody ever asks you to do anything you don't want to do." That really is a life lesson: It's much harder to do the things you don't want to do. But you have to do them. You must do them.

## JANE FRIEDMAN

JANE FRIEDMAN, president and chief executive officer of HarperCollins Publishers, earned a B.A. in English from New York University in 1967. In February 2003, she was named chairman of the board of the Association of American Publishers, where she is only the second woman to hold that post in the organization's history. She serves on the boards of Literacy Partners, Yale University Press, Duke University Libraries, and Poets & Writers. She has been included on *Vanity Fair's* list of 200 Women Legends, Leaders and Trailblazers and was named one of New York's 100 Most Influential Business Leaders by *Crain's New York Business.*

### IMPORTANT TRAIT FOR SUCCESS

JANE FRIEDMAN: Decisiveness. I think focus, which is essential, and good people skills, which I think actually come from being a woman. The nurturing skills of most women are very important, and I think women make decisions faster, more clearly, more definitively than our fellow men.

### BIGGEST OBSTACLE

JF: I cannot say that I had an obstacle because I really don't talk in terms of obstacles. What I talk in terms of are challenges, and I believe that my biggest challenge was the balance of family and career, and there is no doubt that something's got to give. I feel very blessed— I have these four sons who are all okay, and I have a wonderful partner. We've raised these four boys together. Two were his, two were mine. But it is necessary to balance, and I think that to be a great success, you have to give twenty-four hours of your time. How do you give twenty-four hours to your career and also to your children?

KBH: Did you have children throughout your career?

JF: Yes, but I had a woman who came to help me, who planned to stay for three months and stayed for twenty-seven years. And that changed my life because she was a true mother surrogate—actually, in age, a grandmother. It was a wonderful balance, and I always shared with my children. I shared my travels, I shared my authors. My house was always full of writers, certainly full of books, full of adventure, and I shared it. So it was really the challenge of wanting my children to be happy and healthy and also interested and interesting. I also wanted to be a great success.

## BEST PREPARATION FOR ROUGH-AND-TUMBLE OF LIFE

JF: My background was very interesting. I was an English major, but I was always very good with numbers. When I graduated from college, I decided that I was either going to go to Wall Street or be a publisher. The summer that I graduated, I worked in a securities house and I hated it, and I then walked into Random House and got a job as a Dictaphone typist. In those days, there were still Dictaphone typists. So I am really the person who has gone from the proverbial mailroom to the CEO. I spent just under thirty years at Random House before I came to HarperCollins as CEO—global CEO. I was very fortunate in that I worked for a part of Random House called Knopf and I was able to absolutely learn every part of the publishing business by being in a small publishing house where I had my eyes open, my ears open—nothing was too demeaning to me. I opened mail, and I still to this day say to young women, "Open the mail and read it. You will learn so much. Answer the phone and ask if you can help." I started in publicity, but then I went into marketing, advertising, promotion, and publishing itself. I was able to just keep crafting as I went along. I was very fortunate. That is not something that everybody has, but it's also not something that everybody takes advantage of.

## BEST NEGOTIATING STRATEGY

JF: Honesty. Being completely logical. Keeping the company's best interests at heart. I just got off the phone calling an agent in London to say, "I know that my staff bid on this book today, and I know that you probably would have wanted more money. It isn't worth more money, but I am really for this book, and I will tell you that it will sell a lot of copies for us if you come with us." To me that's the honesty aspect. I've always been "what you see is what you get," and it's worked for me. I don't have any secret agenda or secret strategy. I really go in and say how I feel, and it works most of the time.

## HELPFUL CHILDHOOD MEMORY

JF: When I was in the sixth grade, which means I must have been ten, eleven, twelve, I had an English teacher who said to me at one time, "You think you're a big wheel, but I'm going to flatten your tire." I don't remember what caused her to say that to me, but I learned at that moment what arrogance is and what humility is, and that completely changed and formed my life.

KBH: How did you respond to that?

JF: Well, I was upset, of course. Initially I thought, "Oh, she thinks I've done something wrong," and I didn't. Then I thought, "Well, yes, I did." I mean, obviously I did something that was out of line, and it has stayed with me from that day.

KBH: Did you look at yourself and wonder what it was that turned her off or made her think you were arrogant, and then try to improve?

JF: Yes. Probably what I did is raise my hand to answer every single question. You know, there's always one person in the class who tries to answer every question, and probably at that moment I answered one too many. She would never say that I wasn't smart, but she obviously was a little annoyed that I was trying to dominate the conversation. And it has stayed with me, every time I feel like I may be going a bit too far. Children also help a lot with humility.

## BEST ADVICE

JF: My father was an artist, my mother was a model and a wonderful working mother. They said to me there was nothing I couldn't do. You know, everyone today wants to come from a dysfunctional family. I came from a functional family, and my parents were extremely supportive. The only thing they told me not to do was sing and that was because they said my voice was not up to that. (Laughs) But anything else, I could do. They really moved me forward.

# CHAPTER ELEVEN

# SETTING RECORDS, MAKING HISTORY

## *Mildred "Babe" Didrikson Zaharias*

MILDRED "BABE" DIDRIKSON ZAHARIAS started life in such poverty and obscurity in Port Arthur, Texas, that simple survival would have required a measure of luck and talent. Instead, this child of Norwegian immigrants Ole and Hannah Didricksen (Babe would later change the spelling of her name) became by general consensus the greatest female athlete of the first half of the twentieth century, and possibly of the entire century. Born in 1911 (she later claimed that the year was 1914 in order to make her early athletic achievements seem even more astonishing), she was an indifferent student but excelled in almost any sport as soon as she tried it. Babe claimed in her autobiography that she discovered her ambition of becoming "the greatest athlete that ever lived" when her father read news reports about the 1928 Olympics to her. If so, Ole Didriksen's interest was undoubtedly the result of the triumphs of Norwegian figure skater

Sonja Henie at that year's Amsterdam games. Babe's mother, Hannah, had herself been an accomplished skier and ice-skater in their native Bergen, Norway.

Babe was a largely self-taught, self-made champion in basketball, track and field, and—most notably—golf. As a young girl, she learned hurdling by jumping the hedges between her family's house and the corner grocery store. There were seven houses between the Didriksens' and the store. She could hurdle all of the hedges but one, which was much taller than the others, so "she just went along and talked to the neighbors, and asked them if they wouldn't mind cutting their hedges lower." To clear the two-foot-wide hedges without scraping her legs, she developed a style of crooking her left knee, an unconventional technique she retained throughout her competitive hurdling career.

Babe's father rarely earned enough to provide for his wife and seven children, so Babe started working when she was twelve, cleaning figs at the fig-packing plant and sewing potato sacks at the gunnysack factory. Most of what she earned she gave to her mother, a habit she would continue as long as her mother was alive. Hannah's devotion to her youngest daughter was the source of the nickname "Babe"—her mother's variation on "baby"—not, as legend has it, comparisons between her athletic prowess and Babe Ruth's. As often happens, more people know the legend than the truth. Providing for her parents, especially her mother, and her siblings was little short of an obsession for Babe and may help to explain a mercenary streak that was sometimes counterproductive. When she was young, she was indifferent to her own comforts, initially playing basketball barefoot, for example, because she lacked the proper shoes.

Popular but fiercely competitive, Babe had to win every game, even marbles, and her elementary school principal remembered, "She could outdo all the boys." At Beaumont High School, she was on the girls' basketball, golf, softball, swimming, tennis, and volleyball teams, and nearly talked her way into a position as place-kicker on the boys' football team, but the mores of the time prevented that scheme from coming to fruition. Bea Lytle, Babe's physical education instructor in Beaumont, recalled that in fifty years of teaching and coaching, "I never again saw the likes of her. Babe was blessed with a body that was perfect. I can still remember how her muscles *flowed* when she walked. She had a neuro-muscular coordination that is very, very rare."

In 1930, Melvin J. McCombs, impresario of the Employers Casualty Insurance Company's Golden Cyclones women's sports program, discovered Babe as he scouted the state for promising female athletes, whom he would hire as clerks at the firm if they joined one or more of its teams. The rosters included a number of all-Americans in basketball and two world record holders in track and field. He offered Babe a job in Dallas, to begin after she finished high school, but Babe was keen to start earning money and, already nineteen, perhaps eager to leave school. She countered with a proposal to start working right away and complete her graduation requirements later, which she would do after the national basketball tournament that year. McCombs agreed and Babe joined the ECC basketball, softball, swimming, tennis, and track-and-field teams. Her events included running, broad jump, 80-meter hurdles, javelin, and shot put. McCombs called her the "easiest to coach and hardest to handle of all athletes I have had."

When Babe joined ECC, women's basketball was an immensely popular sport with the press and the public. The reigning national champions were the Sun Oilers, archrivals of the ECC Cyclones. Babe's play brought the championship to ECC and made her an all-American from 1930 to 1932. Reliable statistics are scarce, but in the 1931 national tournament, which the Cyclones won, Babe scored a total of 106 points in five games, quite a feat when the team's average score was fewer than 40 points per game.

In the summer of 1930, McCombs took Babe to watch her first track meet at Dallas's Lakeside Park and taught her the rudiments of the javelin throw, high jump, hurdles, and other events. The company agreed to form a track team, and Babe, with typical bravado, announced that she would compete in all ten events. She reported winning all three weight throws—shot put, discus, and javelin—the broad and high jumps, and the 100- and 200-yard dash in one meet. She placed second in the 50-yard dash. The coaching Babe had received was minimal; she won thanks to a combination of talent and her tireless daily training sessions. McCombs often worried that she would overtrain.

Babe went to the combined Amateur Athletic Union (AAU) track-

and-field championships and Olympic tryouts held in Evanston, Illinois, in 1932, as a one-woman "team" representing ECC. She entered eight of the day's ten events—everything except the 50- and 220-yard dash. To allow her to rest between events, the officials sometimes held up the competition for a few minutes. She won six gold medals—shot put, baseball throw, javelin, 80-meter hurdles, high jump (tied for first), and broad jump—and set three world records. She failed only in the discus throw, an event she ordinarily didn't compete in, and 100-yard dash. Her world records included the baseball throw (272 feet 2 inches), javelin throw (139 feet 3 inches), and 80-meter hurdles (in one heat, her time was 11.9 seconds). In the high jump, Babe and Jean Shiley tied for first at 5 feet 3/16 inches, an AAU record. Her point total for the meet—30—was more than the 22 points amassed by the second-place Illinois Women's Athletic Club team, which had twenty or twenty-two members.

In the 1932 Olympics, there were seven track-and-field events for women, but individual athletes were limited to three events. The AAU promoted competitive sports for women, but many groups—including the influential Women's Division of the Amateur Athletic Federation—claimed that strenuous sports caused women physical and emotional harm and were unladylike. Team sports were considered particularly vulgar because they encouraged direct competition; women's basketball, for example, was absent from the Olympics until 1976, despite its wide popularity around the world. In Los Angeles, Babe chose her three best events from the Olympic tryouts: javelin, 80-meter hurdles, and high jump. She set new Olympic and world records in the javelin and hurdles, and she tied for first with her teammate, Jean Shiley, in the high jump but was awarded the silver medal in that event.

New Olympic records were set in all three of the events Babe competed in, but there was controversy over the outcomes in two of them. The javelin was a clear victory; Babe not only improved on her still-fresh world record by more than 4 feet, but she outclassed the German women, who had been expected to win. In the 80-meter hurdles, however, Babe was awarded the gold medal—and the world-record time of 11.7 seconds—after officials debated the outcome of a very close race with American teammate Evelyn Hall, who insisted even years later,

"My foot was over first, and I broke the tape first." She said the tape had left a welt on her neck. Similarly, in the high jump, in which Babe and her teammate Jean Shiley both cleared 5 feet 5¼ inches, Babe was penalized for diving over the bar instead of crossing it feet first. But later frame-by-frame studies of films suggest that her jump was in fact legal.

Young (and pretending to be younger), cocky but socially awkward, of medium height and powerful, Babe after her Olympic victories was scrutinized, anatomized, and criticized. She refuted suggestions that she wasn't feminine: "[W]hen I was little I would rather play with my Dad's hammer or hatchet than dolls. . . . Don't put that down as proof that I'm not feminine. I like to sew and knit, and I can cook pretty good, too."

With respect to marriage, she wrote, "They seem to think I'm a strange, unnatural being summed up in the words 'Muscle Moll,' and the idea seems to be that Muscle Molls are not people." She would explain that she wanted a home and children, but couldn't marry because of her three-year contract, or that she wanted to be independent before getting married.

The suspicions would not go away, in part because of questions about the sex of a number of famous track stars. Stella Walsh of Poland, who competed against Babe, was believed by many—including some of her rivals—to have been a man. Later athletes, like Dora Ratjen, a German high jumper, supposedly admitted to being a man named Hermann; Lea Caurla and Claire Bresolles, 1946 track-and-field stars, were Leon and Pierre; Sim Kin Dan of North Korea, women's 400- and 600-meter winner in 1964, was identified by a South Korean as the son who had disappeared during World War II.

An ad for Dodge cars with a photograph of Babe appeared in the *Chicago Daily Times* on February 1, 1933. The caption read "Dodge 5 is a real champion. Claims she owns one, her second Dodge. The Stuff That Makes Real Champions—Babe Didrikson." The southern branch of the AAU thereupon disqualified Babe from competing in amateur sports, and though Babe categorically denied having authorized the ad, the AAU declined to rescind its action or review her case. Babe and others suspected that the underlying motive for the AAU's suspension was to prevent her from competing in amateur golf. Then the province of the privileged, amateur golf was more restrictive than other sports. Touring players, for example, had to pay all their own expenses, in contrast to tennis players, who could accept reimbursement for their costs. Babe said bluntly, "[T]hey didn't want me to beat the rich dames." A magazine article put the case more politely: "[T]he AAU was determined to eliminate 'muscle molls' from its ranks. No official ever put it that bluntly, of course, but the decision was called 'for the best interest of the game.' "

Babe continued to proclaim her innocence, and her employer, ECC, announced that it was supporting her efforts to get reinstated. Meanwhile, she was officially suspended on December 14, and unless she was reinstated before December 27, she would be ineligible for the AAU's annual award to the best all-around athlete of the year. The AAU kept asking for documents to prove that Babe hadn't given authorization for the ad. At first she complied, but then she counterattacked by asking why the AAU had raised no objection to a similar ad involving a member of the Illinois Women's Athletic Club. In a denouement full of contradictions, Babe suddenly announced on December 21 that she was resigning from the AAU to pursue a professional career. Before the AAU's stewards had heard about Babe's decision, however, they made an announcement of their own: Babe's amateur status had been restored. There was no going back, especially after Babe had a field day with the AAU's arcane rules and sclerotic administration. "Being an athlete and being a member of the AAU are two quite different things," she said in an interview. "I'm not sure which is the more difficult." She preferred breaking records to memorizing the union's mazelike rules.

Its image tarnished, the AAU retaliated by excluding Babe from all amateur competition for a year. Avery Brundage, president of both the AAU and the U.S. Olympic Committee, told the *New York Times* that "the ancient Greeks kept women out of their athletic games. They wouldn't even let them on the sidelines. I'm not so sure but they were right." Brundage, who ruled over American and international Olympic competition for nearly half a century, later overrode the campaign for an American boycott of the 1936 Olympic Games in Berlin.

Babe had the last word. She criticized the AAU for having suspended her in the first place and suggested that their officials leave her alone to do "my best to attend to my own affairs." Chrysler had hired

308          KAY BAILEY HUTCHISON

her to promote the Dodge, the very car that had precipitated the scandal, and introduced her to an advertising executive who got her into a variety show at Chicago's Palace Theater, with further dates scheduled for New York City. Babe sang, played the harmonica, and stripped down to a track suit for a display of her athletic prowess. The public loved her, and so did the critics, but after a week she had had enough: "I don't want the money if I have to make it this way."

What she wanted to do was play golf. Playing golf, however, was one thing she couldn't do, at least not competitively. She was barred from amateur tournaments for one year, and it wasn't certain that she would be reinstated when the suspension period ended. Professional sports for women hardly existed at the time, and even men rarely got rich as athletes. Babe Ruth, the first professional athlete to sign a $100,000-a-year contract, was an exception. Golfers supported themselves as golf pros at country clubs; their winnings in tournaments merely supplemented their earnings. The exclusive clubs that could afford a golfer of Babe's stature were unlikely to consider a "muscle moll" for the position in 1933.

A brilliant self-promoter, Babe seized every opportunity to add to her own legend. Asked what sports she excelled in, she said, "I do everything best," not too great an exaggeration for someone who had single-handedly defeated every women's track-and-field team at the 1932 AAU championships. But such remarks revealed a different Babe from the one who said simply, "I'm tickled to be back home," when she spoke at the luncheon in Dallas honoring her after her triumphs at the Los Angeles Olympics.

When she needed money, the ECC was always happy to take her back as its spokesperson at $300 a month. But when her father needed surgery for a respiratory condition, Babe decided she needed more money to help her family financially while her father was unable to work. An Iowa promoter offered her $1,000 to $1,500 a month to join a touring basketball team, and she agreed. "Babe Didrikson's All-Americans," in Babe's words, "had a pretty fair bunch of basketball players." Her presence and the novelty of games against local men's teams attracted considerable press coverage, and that brought her back into the public's consciousness. After basketball season ended, Ray Doan, the promoter, arranged for her to pitch in exhibition games against minor- and major-league baseball teams and then tour with the famous bearded House of David traveling baseball team. They crossed the country for a rigorous schedule of over two hundred games, and Babe attracted much of the publicity, granting interviews and posing for photographs in everything from evening gowns to boxing trunks.

"I was an extra attraction to help them draw the crowds," Babe wrote. If the crowds came, she rose to the occasion. Grover Cleveland Alexander, the Hall of Fame pitcher who joined the House of David after retiring from the Philadelphia Phillies, said, "With a crowd, she'd really put out, but if there was no crowd, she wasn't worth a damn. And the bigger the crowd, the bigger Babe's performance." Otherwise, touring was a lonely existence for Babe. The House of David went all over the country for its games, and Babe wasn't permitted to travel with the team. She would drive from town to town in her own car, show up for the game, pitch the first inning or two, and then be on her own until just before the next game.

Baseball wasn't really her game, either. A fine hitter, "Babe wasn't really all that good a pitcher," according to Leroy Olive, who played for the House of David in 1934. "[W]e'd have her pitch one or two innings, but we'd fix it so the other teams wouldn't score against her." Even Babe herself admitted as much. In *This Life I've Led,* her autobiography, she told of a spring exhibition game in Florida, between the St. Louis Cardinals and the Philadelphia Athletics. Dizzy Dean had kidded the Athletics' Jimmy Foxx that the Cardinals would beat the A's with Babe pitching. "I always had pretty good control," she wrote, "[b]ut I couldn't seem to throw the ball past these major leaguers." The first three batters got hits, but then the Cardinals managed a double play, so with two outs it was Foxx's turn to bat. Dizzy Dean's brother Paul was in left field, with his back against the orange trees that lined the outfield, and Foxx hit a ball into the trees. According to Babe, Paul ran into the orange grove and emerged with the "baseball and about five oranges" in his glove. "That was how we made the third out. And that was enough pitching for me that day."

Among sports cognoscenti, Babe had plenty of supporters, notably the sportswriter Grantland Rice, who in 1933 made a short film of her playing twelve different sports. But in fact, her barnstorming and stunt-making had the net effect of cheapening the image of excellence Babe's 1932 Olympic performances had won for her. Golf—athletic and elegant—was the sport she would use to regain the lost luster. In the 1930s, it was one of a handful of sports—tennis and swimming were probably the only other candidates—in which a woman could compete without jeopardizing her femininity and respectability.

Babe played golf for the first time in 1927, but she took up the game in earnest in 1933. She moved in with a married sister in Santa Monica, California, and took lessons from a local pro named Stan Kertes, who became her mentor. When she was working, she would practice for three hours in the mornings before going to work and again in the evenings until it grew dark. On the weekends, she spent up to sixteen hours a day at golf and refused to stop even after her hands started bleeding. Kertes, whose clientele included Al Jolson, George Burns and Gracie Allen, and the Marx Brothers, tutored her at no charge. She had approached Kertes after watching him give an exhibition and asked whether he could teach her a good golf swing. "She was a warm and honest person and I liked her right away," he recalled years later, and of course he also knew who she was. Free lessons or no, her savings were gone by the end of the summer, and Babe returned to Dallas, and the job at ECC that she could always fall back on. She revered Kertes as a "great teacher" and returned to take lessons from him throughout her career.

The first goal Babe set for herself was the Texas State Women's Golf Championship. After she registered for the tournament, held at Houston's River Oaks Country Club in April 1935, another entrant, Peggy Chandler, commented, "We really don't need any truck drivers' daughters in our tournament." Chandler, a former champion and perennial finalist in the tournament, won the qualifying round of the match-play tournament. Babe probably didn't help her image by clowning her way through the driving contest and then easily winning it. She won the title on the thirty-sixth hole of a closely fought final round against Chandler and believed that she was finally on her way to stardom in women's golf. She had already filed her entry for the Women's Southern Amateur Tournament in May and hoped to become the national champion.

Two days later, however, the United States Golf Association (USGA) announced that it was looking into whether Babe was a professional under its rules, and in mid-May it advised the Women's Southern Golf Association to reject Babe's application to compete in the tournament on the grounds that she was a professional. The ruling was based on her touring and playing exhibitions for money in baseball, basketball, and billiards. Despite protests from Babe's many supporters in Texas—from the Beaumont Country Club, which she represented, and even the Texas Women's Golf Association—the national body declined to reconsider. In fact, it extended what had been expected to be a one-year suspension to three.

The USGA's three-year ban, followed by a two-year waiting period, probably made it easier for Babe to decide to turn professional. In May, she had said that she accepted the ruling but would apply to be reinstated as an amateur. When the longer term was made public in June, she made an agreement with P. Goldsmith Sons (which later merged with the MacGregor Golf Company) to endorse a new line of Babe Didrikson golf clubs and announced that she intended to play exhibitions. Exhibiting uncharacteristic restraint, she refrained from criticizing the USGA and in fact praised the association for enforcing the rules. Most likely she was hedging her bets in case she later decided to apply for reinstatement. Although there was a handful of open tournaments for women in 1935, women's golf remained an overwhelmingly amateur sport; to make a name for oneself as a serious golfer, it was necessary to win the prestigious amateur tournaments.

Babe's mild demeanor probably also owed something to Bertha Bowen's influence. Bowen, who energetically promoted amateur golf competition, had already helped shepherd Babe's entry into the Texas State Women's tournament in April, and more or less adopted the fiercely talented but awkward young woman. "I was just furious at those people who had been so cutting to her," Bowen said years later. "The fact that she was poor and had no clothes did not mean she had to be ruled a professional." Bowen and her friend Bea Thompson decided to make the Fort Worth Invitational into the Texas Women's Open, only the second open tournament for women in the country. As it turned out,

Babe did poorly in the tournament, but it was the beginning of the movement toward open tournaments that gave her the exposure she needed in her career.

Bertha and R. L. Bowen, president of the Community Public Service power company, became, in Babe's words, "like a godmother and godfather to me." The Bowens enjoyed her immensely. "We'd rather be with her than almost anybody, my husband and I," Bertha said. They took her on fishing trips, taught her to fly their plane, and—most important of all, perhaps—made sure that she got clothes that suited her new role as a golfing professional. Despite the fact that Babe had earned quite a bit of money in the early years of the Depression, most of it went to her family. "She was so poor it was pitiful. She'd have to wash out her one good dress every night," Bertha said. The rough edges disappeared only gradually, however, despite the Bowens' tutelage. At the Western Open in June 1935, Babe could still say in an interview, "They may as well wrap up the cup and give it to me now" (she didn't win). In October, when Babe was staying at the Bowens' house during the Texas Open, they got her a gown to wear to a formal party, but she thought it was too immodest. "We had to chase her all over the house before we could get that dress on her," Bertha Bowen recalled.

To earn money and improve her golf game, Babe toured with Gene Sarazen for two months during the summer of 1935. Sarazen, who won the Masters that year and was one of golf's premier professionals, later explained that during the Depression, "I was just out to make a few bucks," and Babe attracted the crowds. "People wanted to come out and see this freak from Texas who could play golf, tennis and beat everyone swimming up and down the pool." When he toured with Babe, they made a profit, but when he toured with Sam Snead, they lost money.

Sarazen acknowledged Babe's abundant natural talent, but what struck him most about her was her capacity for learning the sport. "She learned all her golf by watching. She'd stand ten feet away from me and watch everything I did. Then she'd go out and practice it for hours." And if she couldn't figure something out from observation, she would pepper him with questions. Even as she was learning, Sarazen recalled that they won about 80 percent of their matches, for which Babe gave him most of the credit. They played as a team in best-ball matches, where the player with the lowest score for each hole wins the hole. Babe wrote in her autobiography that she never won more than one or two holes in a round. "I wasn't a finished golfer yet. But I could give the gallery some laughs, and I could hit that long ball off the tee."

Babe, George Zaharias, and C. Parsee Erdman were assigned to play together in the 1938 Los Angeles Open. Since there were few women's tournaments she could compete in, Babe had entered the men's tournament in hopes of getting some attention and abetting her efforts to be recognized as the outstanding female golfer. Zaharias, a professional wrestler, was a passable golfer but had no chance of doing well in a tournament at this level; he had entered after some friends challenged him. Erdman was a Presbyterian minister who taught religion at Occidental College. Grouping them together was a publicity stunt devised by a local promoter.

The scheme worked. The photographers covering the Open were drawn to the trio like bears to honey. Zaharias had hoped to be grouped with male golfers who were contenders in the tournament, but he changed his mind as soon as the photographers began posing him with Babe. Known in the wrestling ring as "the Crying Greek from Cripple Creek" and "Gorgeous George Zaharias," Zaharias was strikingly similar to Babe in key respects: he was the child of immigrants, Gus and Demitra Vetoyanis (Zaharias had been a promoter's coinage), and had funneled a large part of his income into providing for his parents, helping relatives start businesses, and paying for his younger siblings' educations. The two of them were powerfully attracted to each other. George, much more strong-willed even than Babe, avidly pursued her, and soon they were doing their best to coordinate wrestling and golf exhibition schedules. In July, they announced their engagement, and in December, they married in a small ceremony at the home of Tom Packs, a St. Louis wrestling promoter.

Zaharias, who turned to promoting wrestling and other business ventures after leaving the ring, soon took over financial management of his wife's athletic career. Along the way, he made a number of shrewd decisions that benefited Babe. Their April 1939 "honeymoon" in Hawaii and Australia was actually a string of appearances for both of them. Babe's matches with leading male Australian golf professionals drew large crowds and inspired sportswriters to express in print their hope that she would be allowed to compete against the top women amateur players. Before that could happen, Babe would have to apply for reinstatement by the USGA. The five-year waiting period was scheduled to end in mid-1940, but even then there were no assurances that her petition would be granted. In any case, she could continue to play in open tournaments but would have to pass up any prize money that was normally available to professionals. In 1940 that included both the Women's Open, held that year in Milwaukee, and the Texas Women's Open in Fort Worth. She placed first in both tournaments and looked ahead to being allowed to enter the amateurs-only competitions as well, in order to prove that she was the best women's golfer in the world.

To pass the time, Babe took up two other sports with a vengeance: tennis and bowling. At the Beverly Hills Tennis Club, she took tennis lessons from Eleanor "Teach" Tennant. As always, Babe practiced at a pace that would have exhausted lesser mortals, wearing out countless pairs of shoes and socks and playing sixteen or seventeen sets a day. As she wrote in her autobiography, "When I go into a sport, I don't do it halfway." The cartilage tear she had suffered while throwing the javelin in the 1932 Olympics had healed naturally, so she could again extend her right arm fully while serving. Before long, she was outplaying her teacher, a renowned coach who had trained champions including Alice Marble and Pauline Betz (later, Maureen "Little Mo" Connolly became her star pupil). Then Babe graduated to playing and beating the club's top tennis-playing male movie stars, people like John Garfield and Peter Lorre, before moving up to the leading women tournament players, including Mary Arnold, Louise Brough, Pauline Betz, and Margaret DuPont, three of whom later won national singles championships. She and Brough were considering competing in tournament doubles until Babe discovered that organized tennis, like golf, considered her a professional and therefore ineligible. Having so recently gone through the same experience in connection to golf, it is surprising that Babe seems to have been unaware that amateur tennis was governed by similar rules. Her thirst for the chance to demonstrate her athletic dominance over first-rate competitors before the crowds who attended major tennis matches may have caused her to forget, momentarily, that it wouldn't be possible.

When the possibility of competing for titles and trophies was withdrawn, Babe lost interest and stopped playing tennis. For a while she tried bowling, partly, she said, because her husband enjoyed the sport, but also because the rules of bowling permitted her to compete as an amateur. During 1941 and 1942, she bowled for several teams in Southern California, one of which won its league championship. Both sports were only diversions, however, while she waited for the moment when she could compete in amateur golf. She played frequent practice rounds to keep her touch, entered the few open tournaments that existed, and appeared in exhibition matches with show business celebrities. The extroverted Babe enjoyed the opportunity to cut up for crowds in the company of figures like Bob Hope and Bing Crosby. Crosby was a serious golfer, whereas Hope, as usual, was more interested in the laughs. The comedian amused the spectators and his partner with lines like "There's only one thing wrong about Babe and myself. I hit the ball like a girl and she hits it like a man."

When Babe's amateur standing was finally restored in 1943, she was able to compete in tournaments in California, but the war made travel to more distant venues virtually impossible. As a result, many national tournaments were canceled during the war years, and travel was still difficult when they began to be resurrected in 1945. During that year's Western Women's Open in Indianapolis, Babe's mother, Hannah, suffered a heart attack in California. At first, Babe wanted to withdraw from the tournament to rush back to California, but George and her sister Nancy convinced her to continue playing. In any case, there were no seats available on trains and planes out of Indianapolis, so Babe stayed even after the news of Hannah's death arrived. "What kept me going was I felt I was playing for Momma now," she later wrote. After winning the tournament, she patiently made her way back to Los Angeles, on a series of flights that took her through Kansas City, Albuquerque, and Phoenix. At each airport, she would be bumped off her flight in order to make room for someone with a higher priority.

Hannah's death turned 1945 into a year of loss for Babe, who had constantly striven to lavish material comforts on her parents (her father had died in 1943). But it ended on a note of triumph. She was voted Woman Athlete of the Year by the Associated Press for the first time since 1932. The award was proof that Babe had regained her position at the top of her chosen field: women's golf. Over the next several years, she solidified that position and in the process changed the nature of the sport.

Her natural talent was responsible for her long drives off the tee—in her words, she "hit the ball instead of swinging at it"—and through endless hours of practice she perfected her short game. In the end, "her short game and her iron play were the strengths of her game," said Betty Jameson, winner of the U.S. Women's Open in 1947. Intensely competitive and focused, Babe shut out all distractions, and her confidence—some called it arrogance—unsettled her rivals, whom she wasn't above referring to as "spear carriers." At the same time, she loved the attention and adoration of the crowds that followed her around the course at tournaments, and she unfailingly kept them entertained. To one gallery that was pressing too closely around her as she approached her ball, she reportedly said, "I know I'm good, but not this good. I have to have room to hit the ball." The spectators obliged, and they loved it.

Babe's string of tournament victories in 1945 was the first act in a long-running domination of women's golf that continued into the early 1950s. In 1946, after announcing, "I want to establish the longest winning streak in the history of women's golf," she won thirteen consecutive tournaments, beginning with the Trans-Mississippi tournament, held in Denver in August. Her streak included a victory in the U.S. Women's Amateur, in Tulsa, Oklahoma, about which she wrote, "I was pointing for this tournament, all right. You could say I'd been pointing for it more than thirteen years, from the time I first took up golf seriously." The following year, 1947, she set her sights on a more distant goal, the British Women's Amateur golf championship, in Gullane, Scotland. No American woman had ever won this tournament, which was first played in 1893, but Babe wanted to enhance her reputation as Gene Sarazen and others had done by winning major tournaments in the birthplace of the sport. "I was trying to do the same thing—to show that I could beat the best on both sides of the Atlantic Ocean."

She was unprepared for the harshness of the Scottish climate—even in summer—and couldn't purchase new, warmer clothes because rationing was still in force in postwar Britain. Never reticent, she shared her problem with reporters, and soon what she called "Bundles for Babe" began to arrive at her hotel. Babe returned most of the garments, with thanks, but kept a "siren suit" worn by British air-raid workers and a pair of blue corduroys, which became famous as her "lucky slocks," in the Scottish vernacular. She wore the warm clothes whenever the weather turned chilly and in the process became a favorite of the public. The spectators turned out to see her in substantially larger numbers than they had for the British Men's Amateur championship two weeks earlier. In proper British tradition, they maintained a polite silence so as not to disturb the players, while Babe looked for ways to get them to respond the way American crowds did. Some of the stodgier fans were offended by her clowning, but Helen Holm, a former British Women's Amateur champion herself, defended her. "You're speaking of the finest woman golfer that has ever been seen here," she said simply.

Babe returned to the United States a champion and within a few months decided to become a professional. She had proved herself the finest women's golfer, almost certainly the finest ever; now she intended to cash in on her talent and her fame. There were still not enough professional tournaments to support a touring pro, even if she won all of them, but there was money to be made from exhibitions and endorsements, and in her case there were even rumors of a series of golf instruction films for which she would be paid the then astronomical sum of $300,000. The fee turned out to be one of Babe's self-aggrandizing flights of fancy, but she did ultimately make three short films for Columbia Pictures for a comparatively modest fee. She also signed on to promote personalized models of clubs and other golfing gear, helped design a line of women's golf clothes, produced *Championship Golf,* a book of advice about playing the game and choosing the right equipment, and endorsed other products. She even contracted for a syndicated column of advice about the game aimed at women, to be called "The Babe Says—." The title aimed to capitalize on Babe's celebrity, but the columns were to be written by a less well-known professional, Betty Hicks, who was a capable writer as well as golfer. The arrangement was canceled when George Zaharias, after reading the first few columns, complained, "The writing don't sound like Babe." Hicks's response was, "I thought that was the whole idea!"

In order for the product endorsements made by Babe and other women golfers to be valuable, they had to sustain their reputations as athletes, but with only a handful of tournaments open to them, this was a Herculean task. Equipment manufacturers, agents and entrepreneurial managers like George Zaharias, all had a vested interest in building the women's professional circuit into a newsworthy series of events, as the men's tour had already become. It was probably L. B. Icely, president of Wilson, who proposed to Fred Corcoran, promotional director of the Men's Professional Golf Association and also the agent for Babe and other athletes, the formation of a circuit for women golfers. It was christened the Ladies' Professional Golf Association (LPGA), because a moribund organization called the Women's Professional Golf Association refused to give up the rights to the name.

Sponsors were found for a few tournaments. To entice top-flight players to turn pro, however, it was essential to have a number of tournaments that offered sizable prizes. But to convince potential sponsors to commit large amounts of money to tournaments, a sufficient number of players had to exist. Women's sports continue to experience these growing pains even today. Building the critical mass for women's professional golf in the late 1940s and early 1950s was an uphill struggle. In 1950, there were still only eleven charter members of the LPGA. Hicks wrote an article for the *Saturday Evening Post* describing four months on the tour in 1953. Among the statistics she reported were: prize money, $3,750; expenses, $3,335; miles driven, 40,000. In the middle of one 1948 tournament, Babe threatened to walk out unless the prize money was raised before the next round of play.

For the exceptional figures—primarily Babe—substantial exhibition fees handsomely supplemented her tournament winnings and endorsement money. In 1950, she won two-thirds of the LPGA's tournaments and earned almost $15,000 in prize money. Of course, there weren't yet ten events on the tour. But by playing two hundred or so exhibitions per year, she earned a very respectable income. *Time* nicknamed her "Big Business Babe" and estimated her total annual income at a quarter of a million dollars. Still, despite the money, publicity, and constant adulation, Babe and other members of the small contingent of touring pros were wearying of the monotonous, exhausting routine. For

Babe, the role of teaching pro seemed an attractive alternative to the grind of constant travel. For part of 1950, she was the pro at Grossinger's, a resort in New York's Catskill Mountains. Later that same year, she moved to Sky Crest Country Club near Chicago, and finally she talked George into buying a country club in Tampa, which they renamed the Tampa Golf and Country Club.

As Babe's marketability increased, so did the friction between her and her husband. A number of people who knew them both well credit George with helping Babe cash in on her celebrity, but in the early 1950s his role shifted from someone who made Babe's career possible to an impediment to it. Babe was getting tired of the interminable grind of going from one tournament to the next, but George kept pushing her not to miss the chance to compete as often as possible. Prize money was a pittance on the women's tour, however; Babe estimated that the grand total for 1949 was less than $15,000, although by 1951 things had improved to the point where Babe herself broke the $15,000 mark in tournament winnings. That year Babe won seven of the twelve tournaments in which she competed (although she lost the U.S. Women's Open to Patty Berg by one stroke, after a thirty-six-hole playoff), and was elected to the LPGA Hall of Fame. She had already won seventy-four tournaments.

For an athlete of Babe's stature, the money came from guest appearances and exhibitions. During this period, Babe played upward of two hundred exhibition rounds a year at $500 to $600 per appearance. Increasingly, she was able to negotiate these without George's assistance and wanted to make her own decisions about where to appear. This shift threatened him. He enjoyed his role as the behind-the-scenes orchestrator of Babe's material success—"a grunting grizzly bear of a man, with a deep vein of tenderness permitted to surface only if it did not interfere with a business objective." By now George had become, at four hundred pounds, a swollen caricature of his former self—in Bertha Bowen's words, "an unattractive, big, fat Greek wrestler, and Greek wrestlers weren't members of country clubs." He continued to represent stability in Babe's life, but he was no longer the emotional support he had been.

A more flattering version of the manager-superstar relationship, which took the Zahariases as its point of departure, was George Cukor's

1952 film, *Pat and Mike,* starring Katharine Hepburn as a gym teacher whose pro career in tennis and golf is orchestrated by her devoted and charming manager, played by Spencer Tracy. Babe played herself in the film, as did professional golfers Beverly Hanson, Betty Hicks, and Helen Dettweiler, in a cinematic version of the Women's National Match Play Championship. Babe and Hepburn face off in the finals, which Hepburn was originally scripted to win. But Babe refused to go along with the plot—either because she didn't like Hepburn or because she couldn't stand to lose even in the make-believe world of film—and prevailed on the director to write a one-stroke, eighteenth-hole victory for herself. According to Jim Backus, who played a golf pro in *Pat and Mike,* Hepburn was nonplussed by Babe. "What teed Hepburn off above all was that Babe was completely unimpressed by her. Hepburn did everything to get her attention."

Golf scores aside, the film's stars were of course Hepburn and Tracy, whose characters sparred affectionately about their mutual dependence: "What'd happen if I ever dropped you?" Hepburn asks. "I'd go right down the drain," Tracy/Mike admits. And after a pause, he adds, "And take you right down with me, shorty."

For affection and support that mirrored the bantering tenderness of Pat and Mike, Babe increasingly turned to Betty Dodd, a golfer twenty years younger than Babe herself, whom she met at a Miami tournament in 1950. Within a year, the starstruck Dodd was living with the Zahariases in Tampa. As the daughter and granddaughter of army generals, her ostensible reason for moving to Tampa was to work on her golf game under Babe's tutelage. Babe, however, was no teacher, and in fact, Dodd did not win a professional tournament as long as Babe was alive. But she rapidly supplanted George as Babe's chief emotional support. From 1951 onward, Dodd was her friend, her companion, and, after her surgery for colon cancer in 1953, her nurse.

Beginning in 1948, Babe had experienced a recurrent pain and swelling in her left side. As long as the pain was bearable and the symptoms subsided, Babe ignored them. As she put it in her autobiography, she'd tell herself, "I should see a doctor about this, but I'm too busy right now. I'll have to put it off for a while." Whether George pressured Babe to remain on the tour despite her pain is a matter of dispute, but in

May 1952, in excruciating pain, she phoned her Beaumont physician, Dr. W. E. Tatum, and flew to Texas, where she was found to be suffering from a strangulated femoral hernia, which cut off the blood circulation in her leg and might have been fatal if left untreated.

The hernia operation was successful, and within a few months, Babe returned to the tour. Her tournament record in 1952 was far below her average, however; she won only four tournaments out of twenty-four. The next year she experienced constant fatigue and did not win a tournament until April, at the Babe Zaharias Open in Beaumont. On the final hole, she scored a birdie to win by one stroke over Louise Suggs. The next day she was back in the Beaumont Hospital Hotel Dieu. She went to a specialist in Fort Worth, who performed a biopsy, and she learned that she was suffering from cancer of the colon.

Babe opted to have her colostomy performed in Beaumont by Dr. Robert Moore, a surgeon from the University of Texas's John Sealy Hospital in Galveston, with Dr. Tatum's assistance. Although the surgery itself was successful, the cancer had already spread to the surrounding lymph nodes, and at the time there was no treatment for this form of malignancy. Moore advised George and Dodd not to tell Babe that the results of the surgery were merely palliative and had not cured her cancer, a common practice in the 1950s and one they opted to follow. Following her release from the Hospital Hotel Dieu, Babe convalesced at the Beaumont home of her brother Louis and sister-in-law Thelma. From that point on, it was Thelma (and Dodd, after Babe went home to Tampa) who assumed the responsibility for Babe's care, including daily colostomy irrigation.

Less than a hundred days after her surgery, Babe returned to tournament golf. By ordinary standards, the fact that she was able to compete was itself a triumph, but to Babe, 1953 was a failure. She won only two tournaments, and she was desperate to prove that it was possible to resume a normal life after cancer—not merely for herself, but for other cancer survivors. Long a supporter of the Damon Runyon Cancer Fund, Babe became a highly visible, outspoken advocate for cancer education and research. During the week of June 22–28, 1953 (timed to coincide with Babe's June 26 birthday), nearly two thousand golf courses all over the United States donated their revenues to the fund.

In 1954, Babe succeeded in what she had to do the previous year. She won five tournaments, including the coveted U.S. Women's Open, which she won by twelve strokes over Betty Hicks. Hicks graciously described herself as having "the dubious distinction of going into the USGA record books as the most out-distanced runner-up in USGA history." Had Babe still been the braggart who ran roughshod over her opponents' feelings, Hicks could not have been so gracious in defeat. But cancer had humbled Babe. She still wanted to win, but she began to devote as much time to charity work as to competition. She kicked off the 1954 Cancer Crusade at the White House (where, she reported, President Eisenhower, in an aside, told her, "I'll see you later, Babe. I want to talk to you about this game of golf"), did radio and television spots for the American Cancer Society and the Damon Runyon Fund, and visited cancer patients in the cities where she played tournaments. As Babe explained in her autobiography, she persevered in her golf career "because every time I get out and play well in a golf tournament, it seems to buck up people with the same cancer trouble I had."

Brave to the end, when Babe wrote those words in 1955, her cancer had returned. She continued to compete in tournaments, and even won the Tampa Open, the Serbin Women's Open, and the Peach Blossom–Betsy Rawls Open that year, but she relied on prescription drugs to dull her constant pain. Because the doctors at John Sealy Hospital were slow in identifying the recurrence of her cancer, her physicians suspected that she had become addicted to the narcotics and tried to wean her from them. Fortunately, Dr. Grace Jamison, a psychiatrist at the hospital, talked to Babe and realized, as she told Dodd afterward, "She's no more addicted to drugs than I am. That girl is in pain." Jamison then badgered Babe's doctors until they agreed to resume the painkillers. In August, the doctors finally found signs of Babe's cancer after minutely examining her X-rays and began radiation therapy. But her condition continued to deteriorate, and for the next year she would be in and out of the John Sealy Hospital. Just before she was discharged on September 14, 1955, Babe and George announced that they were establishing the Babe Didrikson Zaharias Cancer Fund at the hospital, to provide diagnosis and treatment of cancer patients who lacked the means to pay their own medical costs. Babe's choice of Sealy acknowledged not only her own treatment there, but also her father's. Ole Didriksen, Sr., had been a cancer patient at Sealy in 1943. She died at the hospital in Galveston on September 27, 1956, three months past her forty-fifth birthday.

# Althea Gibson

I F BABE ZAHARIAS'S EFFORTS to gain acceptance in the genteel world of golf were an uphill battle, Althea Gibson's integration of another genteel sport, tennis, can be described as an epic siege. A sharecropper's daughter who grew up tough and wild in Harlem during the Depression, she was as unlikely a candidate for the task as one could imagine. In 1930, when Althea was three years old, her parents sent her north from Silver, South Carolina, to live with her aunt Sally in New York City. Depending on which version of the story you believe, Aunt Sally earned her living selling bootleg liquor or did it as a sideline. Before Althea was ten, she was reunited with her parents, Annie and Daniel, a brother, and three sisters, in a tenement apartment on West 143rd Street in Manhattan. She preferred playing games and going to the movies to attending school, and took to staying away from home, often riding the subway all night to avoid being punished for her truancy.

In her 1958 autobiography, Althea remembers being a profoundly uncooperative kid, but not a bad one. Although she grew estranged from her family, she didn't blame her mother for trying to force her to stay at home or her father for beating her when she refused. "I gave him a whole lot of trouble," she wrote. Eventually the Society for the Prevention of Cruelty to Children took her in, after she showed them the welts raised by one of her father's whippings, and tried to reconcile her with her parents. They finally worked out a deal: she would work during the day and attend night school.

She quickly stopped going to classes, but she worked at a series of jobs and actually enjoyed one of them, as a mail clerk at the New School in Greenwich Village. But she lost that job after skipping work to go to a Sarah Vaughan concert with some of her girlfriends. When she admitted the reason she'd been absent, her supervisor praised Althea's honesty but explained that she had no choice but to fire her. The welfare department then found her a room with a family and gave her an allowance while she looked for a new job. Instead of job hunting, however, Althea hung out on the streets.

A summer program sponsored by the Police Athletic League closed off a section of Harlem thoroughfares for sports and games. One of the Play Streets activities was paddle tennis, and almost as soon as Althea discovered the game in 1941, she became, in her own words, "the paddle tennis champ of 143rd Street." The program supervisor was Buddy Walker, a part-time bandleader. Walker himself wasn't much of a tennis player, but he bought Althea a used racket and convinced her to try the game at the nearby public courts. Her tennis education began in earnest at the Cosmopolitan Tennis Club, the only black tennis club in the still-segregated city. Fred Johnson, the one-armed pro, showed Althea the continental grip that he used, and began teaching her the fundamentals. Some of the Cosmopolitan's members offered to buy her a membership and pay for rackets and balls, shoes and tennis whites. According to some accounts, Althea worked at the club—chasing balls, laundering towels, and the like. If she did, her cooperativeness suggests that she was enjoying her new surroundings and her new status as black tennis prodigy.

Johnson taught Althea as much as he could. Desmond Margetson, captain of the New York University team when he was a student (ironically, intercollegiate tennis was integrated, at least in the North, but amateur tennis was not), saw Althea on the court soon after she arrived at the Cosmopolitan Club. He knew immediately that she was an extraordinary athlete, but he also understood that there were limits to how far she could get on sheer talent. "There were no truly great teachers, or places to go to get a first-class tennis education, with [all] due respect to Fred Johnson," he later said. For the moment, though, what she lacked in technique she made up for in natural ability; she was quick, she ran down every ball with her long strides, and she hit the ball hard.

Of course, tennis in the 1940s was as much a ceremony as a sport, and the street-smart teenager had at least more to learn about court etiquette than she did about ground strokes and volleys. She would retain her edginess for years, but it was through tennis that Althea started to learn how to behave. "After a while, I began to understand that you could walk out on the court like a lady, all dressed up in immaculate white, be polite to everybody, and still play like a tiger and beat the liver and lights out of the ball." It was Rhoda Smith who volunteered for the daunting task of trying to "civilize" Althea. A member of the tennis club, Mrs. Smith had lost her own young daughter, and she more or less adopted the Cosmopolitan's unruly phenomenon. Althea complained that her mentor was picking on her. "I guess I was, too, but I had to," Mrs. Smith remembered many years later. "When a loose ball rolled onto her court, she would simply bat it out of the way in any direction at all instead of politely sending it back to the player it belonged to, as is done in tennis. But Althea had played on the street all her life and she just didn't know any better."

Barely a year after her first lesson with Johnson, Althea entered the New York State junior girls' (under eighteen) singles tournament sponsored by the American Tennis Association (ATA), the black counterpart to the USTA. She won the tournament, held at the Cosmopolitan Club, easily, winning the final against Nina Irwin, one of the club's few white players. That summer she also played in the finals of the national tournament, at Lincoln University, near Philadelphia. This time her opponent was a black girl, Nana Davis, and this time Althea lost. Davis later described Althea as a "crude creature." The final was Althea's first ATA tournament loss, and she was rarely gracious in defeat.

The ATA nationals were canceled in 1943, as were many tennis tournaments during the war. When the tournament resumed in 1944, Althea, a bit older and a great deal better, won easily, and she repeated her victory in 1945. That same year she reached her eighteenth birthday, making her eligible to compete in the women's bracket. She also moved in with the family of her friend Gloria Nightingale, one of the members of the Mysterious Five, a basketball team on which Althea also played. She lived on the money she earned waitressing, paid rent to Gloria's grandmother, and learned to balance her independence and newfound sense of responsibility.

Bowling was another of Althea's passions, one that she shared with Gloria. At the bowling alley one winter night in late 1945 or early 1946, Gloria introduced Althea to her friends Sugar Ray and Edna Mae Robinson. With customary bravado, Althea told the great prizefighter that he was just a welterweight contender, while she was the reigning ATA champion in the girls' eighteen-and-under category. Robinson was taken with the brash but awkward teenager; in fact, he and his wife became another pair of Althea's surrogate parents. Edna Mae Robinson remembered that Althea "was unhappy. She had a gaunt build, and she felt that she was the least good-looking girl she knew. She had insecurity and went into herself. She used to talk wild. I tried to make her feel she could be something." Sugar Ray, who was only months away from winning the welterweight championship when they met, bought Althea a saxophone when she said she wanted to learn to play one, and paid for a trip to Detroit (where she stayed in Joe Louis's hotel suite) so she could take lessons from famed tennis teacher Jean Hoxie in Hamtramck, Michigan.

The 1946 ATA women's national tournament was Althea's first taste of major (albeit blacks-only) competition. In the final, she lost to the older, more experienced Roumania Peters, a Tuskegee Institute coach and teacher and the top ATA player among the women. Althea believed that what cost her the championship was her lack of tournament savvy; in the deciding third set, she lost her poise and her game fell apart. But among the spectators were Hubert Eaton and Robert Walter Johnson, two black physicians who were also avid tennis enthusiasts. They knew about Althea, of course, and had probably seen her play in the girls' division at earlier ATA tournaments. When they saw her in the women's final, they were confident that beneath the nervous eighteen-year-old on the court lay the makings of a great tennis player, and decided to talk to Althea about her future after the match ended.

There are two versions of that first meeting. It's impossible to say which is correct, but each one contains more than a kernel of truth about what tennis meant to Althea's future and what she meant to the future of tennis. In the first, it was the tall, dignified, fatherly Eaton who approached Althea to say that he could help her get a tennis scholarship to Tuskegee or another black college. Althea's reported response must have shocked Eaton, who had graduated from the University of Michigan Medical School: "That would be great, except I never even been to high school." In the other version, it is Johnson, an effervescent former football star known as "Whirlwind," who walked over to the disappointed girl after she had lost to Peters and asked her whether she'd like to play in an even bigger women's tournament, the U.S. Nationals at Forest Hills. "Of course I'd like that," Althea is said to have replied. "But you know that's impossible."

"It is impossible now," Johnson told her, "but if you are willing to work hard enough, I believe you are the key to unlock the door."

The two doctors invited Althea to move to Wilmington, North Carolina, live with the Eatons from September to June, attend Williston High School, and practice on the private tennis court next to the house. She would spend the summers at the Johnson's home in Lynchburg, Virginia, making the rounds of the tournaments in Johnson's Buick. Althea was grateful, but she wasn't sure she wanted to leave the excitement of Harlem for the sleepy, segregated South. According to her, it was Sugar Ray Robinson who talked her into going. "You'll never amount to anything just bangin' around from one job to another like you been doin'," he told her. "No matter what you want to do, tennis or music or what, you'll be better at it if you get some education."

Right after Labor Day in 1946, she took the train to Wilmington, was picked up at the station by Dr. Eaton's chauffeur, and was immediately absorbed into the doctor's household. Althea wrote that Mrs. Eaton greeted her "as though I were her favorite niece," and a few minutes after Eaton came home from his clinic, the two of them were on the tennis court.

Althea called her three years with the Eatons "the first real family life I had ever known." Already nineteen, she was optimistically placed in tenth grade and applied herself to finishing high school in three years. Academics were difficult for Althea, who hadn't seen the inside of a classroom since sometime in junior high, but getting along with other people and living by their rules posed even more serious challenges for the fiercely independent and unruly girl. The Eatons treated her as well as they treated their own children, but they also expected her to behave like one of theirs. Adjusting took time. According to one account, Althea had to take her meals in the kitchen until her table manners improved to the point where Mrs. Eaton would allow her to join the family in the dining room.

Althea chafed at the rules imposed by the Eatons and the restrictions of their segregated community. The closest they came to a real crisis was the night she took one of the family cars out for a drive without permission. A neighbor saw her and told Dr. Eaton. As she had done when she was working at the New School, Althea didn't deny her culpability, and afterward she resolved to repay the Eatons' faith in her. In town, she accepted the injustices in silence. In Harlem, she always sat in the balcony at the movies, but "I never really enjoyed a movie all the time I was in the South because I *had* to sit in the balcony."

Althea's twin focuses were school and tennis; in the former she did well, and in the latter she shone. She outplayed everyone she was matched against on Dr. Eaton's court. In addition to blacks, who flocked to one of the few courts in the area open to them, some whites who wanted to compete against the better black players also turned up. None of them was able to challenge Althea. Eaton was as interested in helping her learn to be generally more disciplined and less erratic as he was in raising the level of her tennis. His rules for tennis were those he had absorbed from his teacher, Dr. Charles W. Furlong. "I played a controlled game of tennis," he recalled, "as I had learned to live a controlled life. Dr. Furlong taught me to place the ball carefully, to be consistent, and to wait for my opponent to make a mistake."

Absorbing principles that relied on patience and control would be difficult for Althea throughout her life. At Williston High, she persisted in being her nonconformist self, wearing slacks and T-shirts rather than dresses, playing baseball and football with the varsity boys, quitting choir because the others laughed when the director put her in with the tenor boys (she did have a tenor singing voice). She was probably more comfortable during the Lynchburg summers, under the irrepressible

Johnson's more carefree supervision. Like Eaton, Johnson had a tennis court behind his house, where Althea practiced with the Tom Stowe Stroke Developer, a machine that shot tennis balls at her, and played with anyone willing to face her from the other side of the net. Throughout the summer, there were tournaments every weekend. For years, Johnson had been ferrying a car full of promising young black athletes to one tournament after another; starting in 1947, Althea squeezed into the Buick along with four others. That first year, she played in nine tournaments, winning all the singles and eight mixed doubles, with Johnson as her partner. In the ATA nationals, she beat Nana Davis, 6–3, 6–0, the first of ten straight victories in the tournament. "For what it was worth," Althea wrote about the years before she was finally allowed to compete in U.S. Lawn Tennis (USLTA) events, "I was the best woman player in Negro tennis."

In the summer following Althea's graduation from Williston High School in June 1949, Eaton told her that efforts were under way to make it possible for her to play in the U.S. Nationals at Forest Hills. She had already become the first black woman to compete in a USLTA event: the Eastern Indoor Championships, in New York City, in the winter of 1949; Reginald Weir had broken the USLTA color barrier a year earlier, in the same tournament. At the Eastern Indoors, she got as far as the quarterfinals before losing to Betty Rosenquest, 8–6, 6–0—not quite earth-shattering, but "[a]t least I hadn't been disgraced." The National Indoor Championships, also in New York, right after the Eastern, invited her to compete; again she lost in the quarterfinals, this time to Nancy Chaffee.

Althea could be sensitive to slights—racial or otherwise—throughout her life, and she had testy relations with quite a few of the players on the tour, but her memories of the reception she got on her first outings were overwhelmingly positive. "In both the USLTA tournaments I played in that winter—my first experiences as the only Negro in an otherwise all-white draw—I was made to feel right at home by the other girls. It wasn't just that they were polite; they were genuinely friendly, and believe me, like any Negro, I'm an expert at telling the difference." She made strong impressions on a number of the players. Sarah Palfrey Cooke, who was soon to grow into one of Althea's strongest allies, noted her speed and power: "She can hit like a boy," she wrote, "and cover the court with huge cat strides."

Nancy Chaffee, her quarterfinal opponent, said, "She was very light on her feet. It reminded me of Alice Marble," a flattering comparison to one of the sport's greatest figures. Marble retired that year, at thirty-six, with eighteen singles and doubles championships at Forest Hills and Wimbledon alone, tennis's two most prestigious tournaments. Althea had actually seen Alice Marble in an exhibition match at the Cosmopolitan Club in 1944. She later wrote, "I can still remember saying to myself, Boy would I like to be able to play tennis like that. . . . [I]t was the aggressiveness behind her game that I liked. Watching her smack that effortless serve, and then follow it into the net and put the ball away with an overhead as good as any man's, I saw possibilities in the game of tennis that I had never seen before."

Indoor tennis, played on hardwood courts, was considered a poor relation to the important grass-court tournaments. Few people were aware, at the time, that discussions about opening Forest Hills and other prestigious tournaments to black players had been going on behind the scenes for several years. As early as 1946, ATA officials Bertram Baker and Arthur Francis lobbied their USLTA counterparts about the possibility. Many of the figures at the top of amateur tennis's governing body at the time were, of course, snobbish. But there were exceptions, notably Harold Lebair, who as a Jew was familiar with the polite, insidious face of discrimination. The USLTA chairman of umpires, he had set a precedent by appointing women as umpires for Forest Hills matches, and he wanted to integrate tennis at its top levels.

Meanwhile, Althea was anticipating her future. Florida A&M, a black school in Tallahassee, had offered her a scholarship and invited her to spend the summer there playing tennis. Two days after graduation, she left Wilmington. Althea was deeply grateful to the Eatons, but she was nearly twenty-two and eager to be on her own again. There was no women's tennis program at Florida A&M, so she practiced with the men's team and continued to play in tournaments. During the winter, she played on the women's basketball team and amazed her schoolmates with her versatility. Carrie Meek, who attended the school at the same time, said, "We'd had a strong women's athletic program, but when

Althea came, she was the entire program wrapped into one woman. She was so outstanding, so skilled in every form of women's sports, she was the epitome of what you would call a superstar."

Students were subject to a host of restrictions, some necessitated by segregation and others a product of a strict philosophy of proper conduct. A student judiciary committee held hearings in cases of violations and meted out punishments to the guilty. "One year, believe it or not, I was the chairman of the committee," Althea wrote. Perhaps she was, but that hardly meant that she herself was a paragon of virtue. Althea was at least four years older than almost all her classmates, street-savvy, and still cocky. Basketball teammates report that she was continually at loggerheads with coach Julia Lewis. "She would break curfew and she would smoke, and some of the girls would go tell the coach," according to Edwina Martin. "Coach Lewis could hardly manage her, because she always had an answer back. Althea was a very strong person that way."

In tennis, her record kept improving, though the crack in the exclusive USLTA veneer didn't get any wider. At the 1950 National Indoors, Althea made it all the way to the finals, before losing, again to Chaffee, 6–2, 6–0. When she got back to Tallahassee that winter, the school marching band was waiting, the acting president welcomed her, and a big sign proclaimed "Welcome Home, Althea!" Despite the attention she attracted on campus, there was nothing but silence from the all-important gatekeepers of tennis. "I don't consciously beat the drums for any special cause," Althea later wrote, "not even the cause of the Negro in the United States, because I feel that our best chance to advance is to prove ourselves as individuals. . . . I had the notion that, having done so well in the Indoors, I would almost as a matter of course be invited to play in the summer grass-court tournaments, the big ones. But nothing happened. The USLTA acted as though I wasn't there."

Everyone, of course, knew that she was there, however, and as the clock ticked down to the late August opening of the U.S. Nationals, the sense of expectancy increased. The press began to wonder out loud why a player of Althea's quality was kept out of tournaments. Writing in *American Lawn Tennis,* Howard Cohn praised her withering serve and powerful forehand, "when she has it under control," and pointedly observed, "Miss Gibson obviously needs more competitive experience."

That was Althea's dilemma: her tennis had reached a point where she would continue to get better only if she played in the tougher tournaments, but until she was admitted into at least one of the grass-court tournaments, it was impossible to demonstrate that she deserved to play in the others, much less at Forest Hills. The Indoor Championships were easy to discount because they weren't played on grass. When Althea or another black player submitted an application to a tournament in East Hampton, for example, it invariably came back marked "Refused. Insufficient Information." This coded response meant that in the view of the tournament officials, the applicant did not have enough tournament experience at the right level to qualify. It might also mean that the tournament was held at a country club that did not permit blacks to play even as guests and saw no reason to change its policy. The USLTA might adopt a more liberal posture, but it could not compel the private clubs that hosted the tournaments to relax their restrictive—even discriminatory—rules.

Arguments about grass versus hardwood surfaces aside, Althea was already a force in the USLTA indoor tournaments that allowed her to play. In the 1950 Eastern, she won easily, and in the Nationals she lost in the finals because she choked in her match against Nancy Chaffee. ATA members and officials, people like Eaton, Johnson, and Baker, wanted to get Althea into more—and more prestigious—USLTA tournaments sooner rather than later, so she could use the competition to improve her tennis game in the crucible of competition. Many of the players favored allowing her to play because they agreed with Althea that tennis tournaments should be tests of talent, not skin color. And Althea's talent and record had earned her the right to compete.

The tide began to turn when Alice Marble, one of the greatest women players in American tennis, published an open letter in the July 1950 issue of *American Lawn Tennis*. Recently retired from tournament play, Marble still commanded respect in the world of tennis. "On my current lecture tours," she wrote, "the question I am most frequently expected to answer is no longer: 'What do you think of Gussie's panties?' For every individual who still cares whether Gussie Moran has lace on her drawers, there are three who want to know if Althea Gibson will be permitted to play in the Nationals this year." When Marble asked the question of a USLTA committee member, he told her that Althea's showing in the National Indoors failed to prove that she was worthy of an invitation to the U.S. Nationals because the field at the Indoors was a poor one. Marble disagreed with that assessment: "It is my opinion that Miss Gibson performed beautifully under the circumstances. Considering how little play she has had in top competition, her win over a seasoned veteran like Midge Buck seems to me a real triumph."

Marble stopped short of predicting a place in the tennis pantheon for Althea. She reminded her readers that many exciting young players don't live up to their early promise of greatness. "Whether she can achieve championship status here or abroad depends no more on her lovely strokes than on what Althea Gibson finds within herself when the chips are down." What was important, Marble insisted, was that she be tested on the court, not "in the inner sanctum of this committee, where a different kind of game is played." She rejected the Catch-22 logic and hypocrisy that required Althea to prove her merits by making good showings in invitational tournaments that refused to invite her, thus making it impossible for her to qualify for the ultimate invitation— to compete in the U.S. Nationals in Forest Hills.

Marble was writing only a few years after Jackie Robinson became the first black player in major-league baseball, and she was undoubtedly mindful of the symbolic difference made by the integration of that sport at its highest level. She obviously had a similar role in mind for tennis, when she concluded her argument with this exhortation: "If the field of sports has got to pave the way for all of civilization, let's do it. At this moment tennis is privileged to take its place among the pioneers for a true democracy, if it will accept that privilege. If it declines to do so, the honor will fall to the next generation, perhaps—but someone will break the ground. The entrance of Negroes into national tennis is as inevitable as it has proven to be in baseball, in football, or in boxing; there is no denying so much talent. The committee at Forest Hills has the power to stifle the efforts of one Althea Gibson, who may or may not have the stuff of which champions are made, but eventually she will be succeeded by others of her race who have equal or superior ability. They will knock at the door as she has done. Eventually the tennis world will rise up en masse to protest the injustices perpetrated by our policy-makers. Eventually—why not now?"

Reading Marble's words more than half a century later is still a moving experience, but the immediate response to her letter was silence and inaction. After the July issue of *American Lawn Tennis* appeared, Althea's application to the New Jersey State Championships in Maplewood was refused. But then, Althea—and tennis—got a lucky break. The Eastern Grass Court Championships were held at the Orange Lawn Tennis Club (OLTC) and Jack Rosenquest's house was across the street from the club. Jack's daughter, Betty, had played Althea in the 1949 Eastern Indoors; now, he persuaded the OLTC officials to invite Althea to enter their tournament. She lost in the second round, but at the National Clay Court Championships in Chicago, she advanced to the quarterfinals before being eliminated by Doris Hart, who would be the number one–ranked woman player in the world in 1951. After Althea's more than creditable showing in two major tournaments, the USLTA quietly sent word to Bertram Baker of the ATA that if she applied to the U.S. Nationals, she would be accepted.

For any player, a first appearance at Forest Hills is a daunting experience; for Althea, who would be the first black person in the U.S. Nationals, just walking into the West Side Tennis Club was truly intimidating. She asked her friend Sarah Palfrey Cooke, two-time U.S. Women's champion, to arrange for them to practice on one of the courts before the tournament began.

Althea decided to compete in mixed doubles as well as women's singles and was paired with Torsten Johansson of Sweden in the doubles. During the tournament, she stayed at Rhoda Smith's in Harlem; the two of them commuted to Forest Hills by subway, and Smith tried to help shield Althea from the crush of reporters and photographers eager to capture the history-making debut. Despite Smith's best efforts and those of Forest Hills officials, the photographers crowded around Althea throughout her match, popping one flashbulb after the other. Nevertheless, Althea began play with an efficient straight-set victory over Barbara Knapp, a British player. Althea wrote in her autobiography that after her first-round match, she was so relaxed that she thought about going to the movies, but decided against it out of fear that she might strain her eyes.

It was her second-round match—against Louise Brough, the current Wimbledon champion—that attracted widespread attention. Brough had also won the U.S. Nationals, in 1947, and was by any measure a formidable opponent. Clearly nervous, Althea lost the first set, 6–1, but she got herself under control and evened the match with a 6–3 victory in the second set. In the third, deciding set, Althea was leading 7–6 when a sudden downpour forced a suspension of play. The match would be completed the following day.

With an entire night and morning to fret over the outcome against an opponent of Brough's caliber, and with relatively little experience of the sort of pressure that accompanies a national championship, Althea went to pieces. In her words, "By the time I got through reading the morning newspapers I was a nervous wreck." Back at Forest Hills, she warmed up with Sarah Palfrey Cooke but found it impossible to relax. She showed up at the court nineteen minutes after the 1:45 start time, claiming that she had had trouble getting through the crowds. Whatever the reason, she was not the same player who had a day earlier battled the Wimbledon champion point for point. In just eleven minutes, Brough won the game, 9–7, and the match.

Depending on one's point of view, Althea's brief appearance at the 1950 U.S. Nationals was either a personal disappointment for her or a signal achievement for black people. American tennis had been integrated at the top. But Althea consistently claimed that she was interested purely in her individual success or failure. Seven years later, after she won the singles championship at Wimbledon, she told a *Time* magazine reporter, "I tried to feel responsibilities to Negroes, but that was a burden on my shoulders. If I did this or that, would they like it? Perhaps it contributed to my troubles in tennis. Now I'm playing tennis to please me, not them."

Alice Marble seemed to side with Althea in a second open letter to *American Lawn Tennis,* this one addressed to Althea Gibson. Marble expressed sympathy with the twenty-three-year-old who had to shoulder the burden of "making history." She complimented her play: "You also played some remarkably good tennis, considering that you had only played on grass three times previous to Forest Hills." Most important, she cautioned against letting too many people attach themselves to her as "managers" and "advisors." Marble apparently noticed that Althea had attracted an instant entourage, and advised her to listen only to those who were with her before she became famous. About the others, she said, "They weren't willing to go out on limbs to help you achieve what you've done, but now that you have become a national figure, they'd like to get in on the ground floor where a little of the glory might reflect on them."

Now that Forest Hills had opened the door, Althea had her pick of tournaments. Of course, since tennis was still an amateur sport, she didn't necessarily have the means to get to distant venues. When she and the ATA's Bertram Baker met with Hollis Dann of the USLTA to discuss the possibility of her playing at Wimbledon in 1951, she was told that she had the association's approval but could not expect money for her travel expenses. They did suggest that she return for more instruction from Jean Hoxie in Hamtramck, Michigan. While she was in Detroit, members of the black community there collected money for her expenses in England, and Joe Louis offered to pay for her flight to London.

When Althea went to Miami for the Good Neighbor tournament, she became the first black player to compete in a racially mixed tournament in the Deep South. "I felt as though I were on display, being studied through a microscope, every minute," she wrote. She didn't enjoy the feeling. After a single night at the Admiral Hotel in Miami Beach, where all the players had been billeted, she moved to the Mary Elizabeth, a black hotel in the city of Miami. "I was lonesome at the Admiral," she wrote, "all by myself. I'm an authority on what it feels like to be the only Negro in all-white surroundings, and I can assure you that it can be very lonely."

In the summer of 1951, Althea competed at Wimbledon for the first time. Several years later, she wrote about that first tournament, "All I got was more experience." By most accounts, she played erratically. Beverly Baker, who was then the fourth-ranked American, eliminated Althea in the second round. Althea, Baker recalled, "was a very confident person, but she made a lot of errors on the court. No matter how well she might be playing, you were never out of a match with her." Another player was even less charitable. At the time, he said, her tennis skills were almost nonexistent. "Her serve was pretty big for a woman and she could volley and move, she could run, but it was just athleticism, nothing more."

One British player, John Barrett, who later turned to writing about the sport, was impressed by the very qualities that others were prone to dismiss. When he watched her serve for the first time, he initially thought she was a man. He wasn't blind to the flaws in her technique, but, he said, her aggressiveness "wowed me. She was a very good athlete at a time when there weren't many good athletes playing. She had her own shots, her own strokes, her own way of hitting the ball, but champions find a way of making those shots work for them. Given time, I felt certain that she, too, would find a way to make them work."

It would be a while before Althea managed to get her tennis game to work well enough to become a champion. Not that she had no success. Her national ranking rose—to number nine in 1952 and seven in 1953—only to drop to thirteen in 1954. And as Althea wrote, "[Y]ou can't call that progress."

One reason Althea's tennis had stopped improving was that she had no one to learn from. Her peers may have been, as she claimed, "genuinely friendly," but Althea wasn't. As she wrote in her autobiography, "It's always been a fault of mine that I don't let many people get close to me, and not many of those people had any way of knowing what I was really like or what made me that way." Her demeanor may have been a defense mechanism, but what the other women saw was an overaggressive, arrogant opponent who refused to observe the common courtesies of their sport. As Betty Rosenquest Pratt remembered, "You were lucky if you caught her hand after a match, and things like that can irk you into competitiveness." Many women formed doubles partnerships with players they would practice and discuss strategy with, even when they were competing against one another in singles. Margaret duPont, whose doubles partner was Louise Brough, said, "Louise and I were against the world. Shirley Fry and Doris Hart [their principal rivals in doubles] were our great enemies—but also our dear friends." Not so with Althea. With the possible—and impermanent—exception of the British player Angela Buxton, she never formed a genuine friendship with another player and never seemed to understand that it could be mutually beneficial.

Several people deserve a share of the credit for helping Althea transform herself from a tennis also-ran in 1954 to the world's best two years later. One was Sydney Llewellyn, a tennis teacher in Harlem who had been her mixed doubles partner in 1950. By 1955, the two of them were out of touch. When she wasn't playing in tournaments, Althea was earning a pittance teaching physical education and coaching the men's tennis team at Lincoln University in Jefferson City, Missouri. A friend of hers there, an army officer who directed the school's ROTC program, had convinced her to join the WAC, which would guarantee her security and a decent income. She had all but given up on succeeding in tennis, although she was still winning the occasional minor tournament. In fact, Llewellyn and Althea met at the Red Rose tournament in Lancaster, Pennsylvania, where Althea won both the singles and mixed doubles titles. Llewellyn offered to coach her, insisting that she could be the greatest woman player since Helen Wills. Althea, who was waiting to hear from the WAC, agreed to work with him, but even as her game picked up, she insisted, "If I was any good, I'd be the champ now. But I'm just not good enough. I'm probably never going to be."

Llewellyn set out to rebuild Althea's game from the ground up. First he got her to switch from the continental grip, which she'd learned from Fred Johnson, to the eastern, to add power and control to her strokes. He also taught her to think more strategically about shot selection and court position. Llewellyn called his ideas "the Theory of Correct Returns." Briefly stated, he believed that there was a single optimal way to play every ball.

Althea went along with Llewellyn, and occasionally she won a big match. But she wasn't winning tournaments, and success meant everything to her. As a result, her heart wasn't in tennis, even when Forest Hills rolled around in September. At the U.S. Nationals she lasted until the third round, when she lost to an old nemesis, Beverly Baker, with a new name, now that she had married John Fleitz.

Despite Althea's disappointing showing at Forest Hills in 1955, her presence there led to a turning point in her career. She was invited to join a goodwill tour of Southeast Asia with three other American players: Ham Richardson, Bob Perry, and Karol Fageros. The State Department had specifically asked to have Althea on the team, probably to give the impression that the United States was a racially open society. She was never given a script to follow if she was asked about race; she was told only to "remember that I was representing my country."

Several things about the tour made it important to Althea. The first was that she enjoyed herself immensely. As the only person of color among the players, Althea was the center of attraction, a position she hadn't been in since she stepped out of the world of ATA tournaments into the competitive environment of the USLTA. People were not only amazed that a black woman could play tennis so well; they were proud of her, and that restored her self-confidence. Second, she was playing tennis all the time, and after the tour ended she made her way back through Asia and Europe playing in one tournament after another. The constant tennis was exhausting, but it also sharpened her game and her competitive edge. Finally, she and Ham Richardson became friends.

Richardson, an acutely intelligent tennis player who won the 1956 U.S. Nationals men's doubles title with Alex Olmedo, discerned how incredibly talented Althea was. She was faster than her opponents, had a better serve, and was stronger, but she made too many mistakes. As a result, she lost matches she should have won. "She just had to learn how to win," Richardson said. From Llewellyn she had learned to think strategically about individual shots; Richardson taught her to think strategically about an entire match. He helped her understand why some points (30–40 or 40–30, for example) were more important than others, so she stopped trying to overpower opponents on every point. He taught her volleying strategy, when to attack off her ground strokes, when to take chances, when to try to control the point, and when just to keep the rally going.

Thanks to Richardson, Althea now had a perspective on the game of tennis that few players or coaches could have revealed to her. She wasn't entirely cured of her tendency to lose patience and control, but she started to win. Her first major title was the 1956 French Open; she was the first black player to win the singles in any major tournament: Australian, Wimbledon, Forest Hills. At Wimbledon, she suffered a lapse— "I wanted to win so badly that I pressed"—and lost to Shirley Fry in the quarterfinals. Fry won Wimbledon that year, but she told reporters, "If [Althea] had crowded me at the net like I expected her to, she [would] have won."

Althea and Fry were to face off a number of times in 1956 and 1957. In the first year, Fry defeated her two more times, at the National Clay Courts Championships in Chicago, and at Forest Hills, where the only two sets Althea lost were in the finals, to Fry. The following year, the two of them continued their rivalry in Australia. They split four tournaments, though Fry won the Nationals, the Australian leg of the Grand Slam. "When I lost, it was because I made all the errors and she played a steady, waiting game, the game for which she is famous," Althea wrote. "When I was on my game I didn't have much trouble with her."

Nineteen fifty-seven was the year Althea captured her dream. At Wimbledon, she defeated the local favorite, sixteen-year-old Christine Truman, in the semifinals and breezed past Darlene Hard for the championship, before a crowd that included Queen Elizabeth. Back in the United States, there was no royalty to present the trophies, but Althea continued her winning ways, both at the National Clay Courts in Chicago and in the Whiteman Cup team competition against England, where she won her two matches. At Forest Hills, it was Louise Brough, the player who had won the rain-delayed match in Althea's first U.S. Nationals tournament in 1950, who succumbed in the finals in straight sets.

Nineteen fifty-eight featured repeat performances at Wimbledon and Forest Hills, against different opponents in the finals: Angela Mortimer in London and Darlene Hard in New York. Now at the pinnacle of women's tennis, Althea announced that she would turn professional. At the time, there were no open tournaments and no prize money, so Althea's plan was to tour with the Harlem Globetrotters basketball team, playing tennis exhibitions before the games. Her preferred touring partner, Shirley Fry, opted to stay home with her infant son, so Althea's friend Karol Fageros signed on. The hypercompetitive Althea was unwilling to borrow a page from the Globetrotters' playbook and make the matches entertaining. She won 114 of 118 games, and the Globetrotters opted not to renew her contract for a second year. Althea invested everything she'd earned from the Globetrotters in another tour, but this one was a failure, and she was broke again.

Althea had been awarded the Babe Didrikson Zaharias Trophy as the outstanding woman athlete of 1958, but with no clear career path for women athletes in the late 1950s, she was at another dead end. A column under her byline for the British daily the *Evening Standard* (actually written by Richard Evans) during the 1959 Wimbledon matches failed to lead to a regular column, and a tennis club wasn't a success, either. With a $25,000-a-year contract to endorse Tip-Top Bread her only regular source of income, Althea decided to try a new sport, the one in which Babe Zaharias had made her fortune: golf.

Golf, unlike tennis, already had a pro tour for women, under the aegis of the LPGA. Althea had played while in college, and with her usual confidence was convinced that she could duplicate her tennis successes in her new sport. When she qualified for membership in 1963, she became the first black professional female golfer. The other golfers supported her trailblazing efforts even more emphatically than the tennis players had. As Alice Dye, who competed against Althea in the National Amateurs in 1962, said, "We all appreciated that [Althea was starting over], and tried to help her however we could." Help included refusing to play if Althea was barred from a club where an LPGA event was held. Discrimination persisted at hotels, however, so Althea often had to settle for separate accommodations.

From 1963 to 1978, Althea played in 171 pro tournaments without winning a single one. She was a creditable golfer, averaging less than 76 strokes per round for two of her playing years, but she never came closer to winning a tournament than in the 1970 Buick Open. Her total winnings were just $24,437.

Personal happiness also eluded Althea. In 1965, she married for the first time. Her husband was Will Darben, brother of her close friend Rosemary Darben; he had been pursuing her for years. By most accounts, Althea never paid much attention to him, and they divorced in 1973. She lived a peripatetic life on the golf tour throughout that period and seemed unable to settle down. She married a second time, even more briefly, in 1984. Again her husband was someone she had known for a long time—Sydney Llewellyn—and she later described the relationship as "a marriage of convenience." Its purpose may have been to help Llewellyn, who was originally from Jamaica, obtain American citizenship. In any case, they never lived together and divorced within a few years. She started seeing Darben again in the early 1990s. "She found out she really loved him," Rosemary Darben said, but others said Althea and Will were probably just friends. By that time, Darben was suffering from complications of diabetes and lived in a home for senior citizens. He died in 1997.

Billie Jean King had idolized Althea from the time she first saw her, which was when, as Billie Jean Moffitt, she was a thirteen-year-old tennis prodigy. In 1968, she and her husband organized a small professional tennis tournament in Oakland, to which the top current players were invited, and also Althea. By then Althea was on the golf circuit and hadn't played tennis seriously for ten years, but she gladly participated. She lost all her matches but told her hosts that she would like to be included in any future tournaments. A few years later, prize money in women's tennis finally amounted to more than token amounts, and Althea—at forty-four—attempted a comeback. Bowing to reality, she competed only as a doubles player, with Gardner Mulloy, a former partner; Arthur Ashe, the first black man to win a major tournament; and Darlene Hard. In every tournament, she lost in the first round.

There was by this time an air of desperation about some of Althea's efforts, but they were also signs of her unquenchable competitiveness. Billy Jean made her own participation in the 1975 ABC Women's Superstars competition contingent on the organizer's agreeing to invite Althea. When they did so the following year, Althea actually placed second in bowling and basketball and won over $4,000, probably the biggest sports paycheck of her life. Somehow, though, she had never managed to find a way to earn a livelihood from sports after her tennis triumphs. In 1995, broke and in failing health, a despondent Althea phoned Angela Buxton, the former British tennis player and close friend whom she hadn't been in touch with for a decade. It's not clear why Althea reached back into a more hopeful period to call Angela, who by then was living in Florida, but in fact she made a shrewd choice. Angela created the Althea Gibson Foundation and staged a campaign that raised enough money for her old friend to live on comfortably for the rest of her life. Then the once-intimate pair lost touch again. When Althea died in September 2003, they hadn't spoken in at least five years.

# Women of Today

BABE DIDRIKSON ZAHARIAS dominated women's athletics for the first half of the twentieth century. She was the first woman to be considered a great all-around athlete—track-and-field Olympic gold medalist and champion golfer.

Althea Gibson came along at midcentury and broke the color barrier in women's tennis, the first African American to compete at Wimbledon and the national championship tournament at Forest Hills . . . winning both.

The late century produced more opportunities in women's sports, more teams, and more emphasis. And it produced even more incredible feats, by Jackie Joyner-Kersee and Nadia Comaneci.

## JACKIE JOYNER-KERSEE

DESPITE AN EAST ST. LOUIS, Missouri, childhood so impoverished that she described the house she grew up in as "little more than paper and sticks," Jackie Joyner-Kersee ultimately won more Olympic medals in track and field (six, including three gold) than any other American woman and was named *Sports Illustrated for Women* Female Athlete of the Twentieth Century. She excelled in basketball and the long jump in high school, won a basketball scholarship to UCLA, and quickly became the NCAA and U.S. champion in women's track and field's multievent heptathlon. Her accomplishments are even more remarkable when one considers that she struggled against injuries (a pulled hamstring that began troubling her in 1983), an asthma condition, and the death of her mother at the age thirty-seven, the person who was Jackie's inspiration in her climb out of poverty.

A true scholar-athlete, Jackie majored in history at UCLA, and when she graduated in 1985 was named the country's outstanding female college athlete. In 1986, she set a world heptathlon record at the Goodwill

Games in Moscow, and the following year she tied the world record in the long jump. Her years of triumph at the Olympics were 1988, 1992, and 1996. Among her six medals, the three gold were in the heptathlon (twice) and the long jump. Even more impressive is her 7,291-point, world-record performance in the seven-event heptathlon at the Good-will Games in 1998, when she was thirty-six years old. She retired that same year and started a foundation that raised $12 million to build a haven for children in her old neighborhood in East St. Louis.

## IMPORTANT TRAIT FOR SUCCESS

JACKIE JOYNER-KERSEE: Generosity. I would just have to say that re-specting myself allows me to respect others in what I do and not to be judgmental of others, to have an open mind.

## BIGGEST OBSTACLE

JJK: Probably my biggest obstacles were dealing with the loss of my mom at the age of seventeen and being an asthmatic and trying to compete in athletics.

KBH: Who stepped in when you lost your mom at seventeen to be-come the closest person to you?

JJK: I would say my aunt, but being a teenager and being at UCLA so far away from home, the coaches really made it easier for me. If I was having a difficult time in any situation, their doors were al-ways open for me if I just needed to talk. Before I married my husband, he was one of those individuals that stepped forward and said, "If you need someone to talk to, to get some things off your chest, I'm there as well as my teammates." My family was supportive as well.

## BEST PREPARATION FOR ROUGH-AND-TUMBLE OF LIFE

JJK: Growing up in East St. Louis, Illinois, not having a track or being able to run in a park, living across the street from a tavern or a liquor store and just seeing a lot of bad things going on, prepared me. I was exposed early in life to seeing people struggle, seeing peo-ple shot as well as killed. But through it all, I always felt that there were good people in my hometown of East St. Louis. And because of that, when I went to California to go to school—not knowing if I was going to make it to the Olympic team—I didn't think there was really anything in sports that could frighten me.

KBH: Yeah, after what you'd been through. (Laughs)
JJK: So, you know, all I had to do was stay focused on what my dreams were and what I believed I could do on the athletic field and not let any distractions become obstacles.

BEST NEGOTIATING STRATEGY
JJK: Always go in there with a game plan; know what outcome you want. If someone wants to work with you or wants you on their team, go in knowing exactly what you want, and you'll get what you want or close. For example, I always wanted to long-jump twenty-three feet; that was a milestone. But I would always come up with twenty-two-ten or twenty-two-eleven. So I started thinking to myself that I probably need to say twenty-three-five or twenty-three-six, and then maybe twenty-three feet will come. And when I started doing that— I know it sounds crazy, but beyond twenty-three started coming.

And it's the same way, really, in business when we're negotiating. Sometimes you just have to know what you want and what you're trying to achieve. And don't let someone change your mind, because that's why it's called negotiation.

HELPFUL CHILDHOOD MEMORY
JJK: I would have to say my mom encouraged all her kids to make something of their lives and—well, athletics wasn't high on my mother's list for me. She was a young mom and she knew how difficult it was for her to find a job, so she really wanted me to be a good student and become a teacher or a physical therapist. I began to realize how much my mother saw in the future and what she wanted for her kids. When I lost her at the age of seventeen, I really had to reflect back on the things that I was being stubborn about and not listening to. It really gave me the strength to go on and become, I believe, the person I have become.

KBH: That's amazing. Her death really made you stronger because you listened to what she had said, which you hadn't really done before.

JJK: Right, because when I was growing up, she was constantly saying, 'Read the paper, know about current events.' She said, "The reason I want you coming home is because I don't want you to think that you can't be snatched from the street." And at the time, it was "Yeah, okay, Mom." But the reality of it was that she had really tried to prepare me for life, and being the oldest girl, she wanted me to set the example for my two younger sisters. It didn't make sense until after she was gone, because she would always tell me, "Don't say what you want to do tomorrow; take advantage of today. Enjoy today because tomorrow might not come." And I never really quite understood that until I was in college. I had told her I wouldn't be home until the summer—you know, "I'll see you during the summer"—but the summer never came because she passed in January.

BEST ADVICE

JJK: When I was a senior in high school, I was at a dinner and a man said to me, "Win when you can win." I didn't quite understand what he meant by that, but it all made sense to me when I made my first Olympic team in 1984. Even though I had a hamstring injury and the injury wasn't really that bad, I focused so much on the negative and never thought about the positive. I was picked to win the gold medal, but mentally I just wasn't there. And it wasn't until years later that I realized exactly what he meant by that. It was, Never doubt yourself. When you have an opportunity to win, take advantage of it because those opportunities will never come again. By missing the gold medal by three points, I realized after the event—not to take anything away from the girl that won the gold medal—that I didn't believe that I could win. It all made sense some eight years later.

# NADIA COMANECI

THE FIRST WOMAN to score a perfect 10 in women's gymnastics in the Olympics, Nadia Comaneci, at the age of fifteen, won three gold medals, one silver, and one bronze in the 1976 Olympics. In the 1980 Olympics, she won two gold and two silver. Born in Romania in 1961, she started training at the age of seven and won her first international competition at the age of ten. From age twelve to eighteen, she lived in training camps away from home. She defected to the United States in 1989, married U.S. Olympics star Bart Conner, and has become a U.S. citizen.

## IMPORTANT TRAIT FOR SUCCESS

NADIA COMANECI: Hard work. My parents worked so hard and dedicated everything they had to help us as kids. What I got most from my father and my mom was the idea that you can accomplish everything in your life if you work very hard.

## BIGGEST OBSTACLE

NC: When I was a kid, at the beginning, it was difficult to stay away so long from my parents because we had to live in a training camp during the week. When you are young, you mostly wake up every day with your parents next to you, so there were some things you had to give up.

KBH: From what age were you having to live in a training camp?
NC: Twelve to eighteen.

## BEST PREPARATION FOR ROUGH-AND-TUMBLE OF LIFE

NC: The mental preparation of being ready to deal with whatever comes up. Even if you're good in training, you have to deliver the best routine in competition, and you have only one try. I think the mental preparation was what helped me get through. I tell a lot of little gymnasts that I wasn't perfect from the beginning of my career.

I made mistakes and I fell down on beams a couple of times. They need to know, if they get disappointed when they make some mistake, to remember that everybody makes mistakes but in the end you try to make it better.

## BEST NEGOTIATING STRATEGY

NC: I don't do the negotiations for anything I do. I've got somebody else to do that. I think that's something that doesn't look good on me. I'm not a good negotiator. (Laughs)

## HELPFUL CHILDHOOD MEMORY

NC: I was probably about eight and I left home in the morning to play with the kids in the neighborhood. I ended up with some friends playing a little farther than my neighborhood and, you know, you start to play and you forget that your parents are worried about where you are. I left in the morning and I was coming home really late when it was getting dark and my father was worried about me, and my mama and he told me to never do this again. Then he put me on cracked nutshells, on my knees, for three hours. I had to stay there.

KBH: Oh, my gosh. For three hours?

NC: Yeah. (Giggles)

KBH: My gosh, you did remember that.

NC: Yeah, I never did that again.

## BEST ADVICE

NC: Follow your dreams. Never give up when it's tough. That's what people tend to do. When it's getting harder, it's easy to give up. For somebody who wants to succeed in life, the most important moment when you shouldn't give up is when it's getting tough.

# AFTERWORD

When I was in elementary school, each semester we had to read a certain number of books in the library from each of three categories—fiction, nonfiction, and biographies. I used biographies for all my nonfiction *and* biography requirements. By the time I entered the sixth grade, I was unable to fulfill the biography assignment because I had already read every biography in the entire library.

I was inspired by reading about the lives of people who became great contributors to our country. I think this early immersion may have been a reason I always thought I could do whatever I dreamed of doing. Even though I was a girl, and not particularly encouraged to be ambitious, these biographies taught me how people made themselves better—by failing and persevering . . . by overcoming obstacles of poverty or lack of education or death of a parent at a young age.

Most of the ones I remember were about the Founding Fathers—Washington, Jefferson, Adams, Franklin. The only one I recall about a woman was Betsy Ross.

As my world expanded, of course, I became aware of the many women who contributed to the building of our nation. This book attempted to focus on a few. There were so many others.

Because I was inspired by biographies, I hope other boys and girls, men and women, can find nuggets of wisdom in both the pioneer stories and contemporary interviews. I have made some general observations. The women who strove for a cause or for success in the nineteenth and early twentieth centuries worked incredibly hard, got little or no encouragement, wore themselves out, and mainly didn't believe they had made it to their goal. Some died before their prime, most died thinking they had failed, and some even showed signs of mental instability. But they did succeed in so many ways and paved the way for those who came along in the mid-twentieth century. The early women did break down resistance to women's achievements and recognition.

The independent streak that drove these strong women to survive in the harsh new world clearly had a role in shaping our nation. American women created educational opportunities, spoke out forcefully, and were true partners in the evolution of our democracy, even without a vote, which they did not obtain until the Constitution was amended in 1920.

The mid-twentieth century brought forth a generation of women who had many of the same characteristics, and some of the same obstacles, as those pioneers who helped forge our nation. The difference is, they have realized their success. They have broken the last barriers. Women now head some of America's Fortune 500 companies, are elected to the U.S. Senate and governorships, excel in athletics, and have equal opportunities in the highest professions. The only political offices not yet held by a woman in America are president and vice president. But the pipeline is now full. In ten years or less, it will happen.

It occurs to me now that this is the last generation about which this type of book can be written. The wall has come down; the glass ceiling is shattered. Will there still be issues and problems for future generations to address? Of course. But in very short order, it won't be gender discrimination.

I remember giving a speech to a group of young women fresh out of college a few years ago. I was giving my *Raiders of the Lost Ark* speech, talking about the dodging and weaving I had to do in my career. I thought they looked nonplussed. It finally occurred to me that these young women had gone to college and graduate school experiencing no discrimination. While I was one of thirteen in a class of three hundred ninety in law school, these young women were 50 percent of their graduate business and law classes.

This is the fulfillment of my dream. I have often said, we will know we have succeeded when there are no more stories about the first woman anything, when the stories are about the great performance of a company whose chief executive officer just happens to be a woman, not about the fact that she is CEO.

What a fabulous time in our country's history I have been able to witness. In the early sixties, my father took me out of high school for two hours to go see a U.S. senator who was visiting our small hometown of La Marque, Texas. No one remembered a U.S. senator ever coming there before, so Dad thought it was important for me to see. But it certainly never occurred to him, or anyone else (including me), that this wide-eyed girl would ever aspire to be one, too.

America is the best place on earth to be a woman. Even before I learned about other cultures that degrade women or treat them as less than full citizens, I knew that women could work hard and achieve their dreams, in our country. We have been allowed to contribute to our communities in exponentially increasing ways. And by using the brainpower of all our citizens more and more, America has captured the leading edge in world competition.

The creativity unleashed by including women in business, the professions, community leadership, and government has given America the advantage—economically and culturally.

My hope in writing this book is to increase the awareness of the impact women have had—and are having—on our country.

# SUGGESTIONS FOR FURTHER READING

## *Mary Austin Holley*

One full-length biography of Mary Austin Holley has been published: Rebecca Smith Lee, *Mary Austin Holley: A Biography* (Austin, TX: University of Texas Press, 1962). Mattie Austin Hatcher includes a long biographical introduction to *Letters of an Early American Traveller, Mary Austin Holley, 1784–1846* (Dallas, TX: Southwest Press, 1933), a collection of Holley's letters that also reprints *Texas: Observations, Historical, Geographical, and Descriptive, in a Series of Letters Written During a Visit to Austin's Colony, with a View to a Permanent Settlement in That Country in the Autumn of 1831* (originally published in 1833). Also see Marilyn M. Sibley's introduction to her reprint of Holley's 1836 history, *Texas* (Austin, TX: Texas State Historical Association, 1985).

James Perry Bryan edited *Mary Austin Holley: The Texas Diary, 1835–1838* (Austin, TX: University of Texas Press, 1965). There is a collection of manuscript sources, the Mary Austin Holley Papers, in the Eugene C. Barker Texas History Center, the Center for American History, University of Texas at Austin.

## Ann Raney Coleman

C. Richard King wrote a biographical introduction to his edition of Coleman's journal, *Victorian Lady on the Texas Frontier: The Journal of Ann Raney Coleman* (Norman, OK: University of Oklahoma Press, 1971). There is also a short biographical essay, "Ann Raney Coleman," pp. 29–47, in Jo Ella Powell Exley, ed., *Texas Tears and Texas Sunshine* (College Station, TX: Texas A&M Press, 1985).

## Jane Long

Jack C. Ramsay, Jr., *Texas Sinners and Revolutionaries: Jane Long and Her Fellow Conspirators* (Plano, TX: Republic of Texas Press, 2001), connects Jane's life with those of other early Texas patriots. Martha Anne Turner, *The Life and Times of Jane Long* (Waco, TX: Texian Press, 1969), is the only book-length study. The earliest biographical essay is by Anne A. Brindley, "Jane Long," in the *Southwestern Historical Quarterly* 56 (October 1952): 211–38.

## Adina De Zavala

There is no book-length biographical treatment of De Zavala. Richard R. Flores prefaces his reprint of De Zavala's privately published *History and Legends of the Alamo and Other Missions in and around San Antonio* (Houston, TX: Arte Público Press, 1996; originally published 1917) with an essay about her life and work. L. Robert Ables incorporates many of the facts of De Zavala's life into his essay about the controversy over the preservation of the Alamo, "The Second Battle for the Alamo," *Southwestern Historical Quarterly* 70 (January 1976): 372–412. Ables's "Adina De Zavala," in *Keepers of the Past,* ed. Clifford L. Lord (Chapel Hill: University of North Carolina Press, 1965), pp. 203–14, focuses on De Zavala's historical contribution.

Because De Zavala has become so closely identified with the Alamo, the study by Susan P. Schoelwer, *Alamo Images: Changing Perceptions of a Texas Experience* (Dallas, TX: DeGolyer Library and Southern Methodist University Press, 1985), also sheds light on her many years of involvement with the Alamo's history and buildings. There is a collection of documents, the Adina De Zavala Papers, in the Eugene C. Barker Texas History Center, the Center for American History, University of Texas at Austin.

# Clara Driscoll

Martha Anne Turner wrote a book-length biography, *Clara Driscoll* (Austin, TX: Madrona Press, 1979). A pamphlet by Jack C. Butterfield, *Clara Driscoll Rescued the Alamo—A Brief Biography* (San Antonio, TX: Daughters of the Republic of Texas, 1961), includes an introduction by DRT member Mary Lasswell, "Clara Driscoll Sevier As I Knew Her." There are also biographical essays, "Savior of the Alamo," in Ann Fears Crawford and Crystal Sasse Ragsdale, *Women in Texas* (Burnet, TX: Eakin Press, 1982), pp. 176–89, and "Clara Driscoll" in *Notable American Women: A Biographical Dictionary* (Cambridge: Harvard University Press, 1971), I: 523–24.

# Elizabeth Seton

The earliest biographies of Elizabeth Seton were published in the second half of the nineteenth century, both in the United States and in France. The best modern treatments are Joseph I. Dirvin, *Mrs. Seton: Foundress of the American Sisters of Charity* (New York: Farrar, Straus & Cudahy, 1962), and Annabelle M. Melville, *Elizabeth Bayley Seton, 1774–1821* (New York: Scribner, 1951). Dirvin has also compiled a "biography" out of selections from Seton's writings, *The Soul of Elizabeth Seton* (San Francisco: Ignatius Press, 1990).

The first two volumes of *Elizabeth Bayley Seton: Collected Writings* have been edited by Regina Bechtle and Judith Metz (Hyde Park, NY: New City Press, 2000, 2002). A one-volume work, *Elizabeth Seton:*

*Selected Writings* (New York: Paulist Press, 1987), has been edited by Ellin Kelly and Annabelle Melville.

Seton's letters, manuscripts, and other documents can be found in a number of collections. The largest is the Archives of St. Joseph Provincial House, Emmitsburg, Maryland. For a listing of all the archives, see http://www.famvin.org/seton/index.htm. There are also Elizabeth Seton materials among the Robert Seton Family Papers in the University of Notre Dame Archives, Notre Dame, Indiana. Robert Seton (1839–1927) was Elizabeth Seton's grandson.

# *Mary Baker Eddy*

The standard life of Mary Baker Eddy is the three-volume biography by Robert Peel: *Mary Baker Eddy: The Years of Discovery* (New York: Holt, Rinehart & Winston, 1966); *Mary Baker Eddy: The Years of Trial* (New York: Holt, Rinehart & Winston, 1971); and *Mary Baker Eddy: The Years of Authority* (New York: Holt, Rinehart & Winston, 1977). Many other biographies have been published, including Cynthia Parsons, *The Discoverer: Mary Baker Eddy* (Chester, VT: Vermont Schoolhouse Press, 2000); Gillian Gill, *Mary Baker Eddy* (Reading, MA: Perseus Books, 1998); Richard A. Nenneman, *Persistent Pilgrim: The Life of Mary Baker Eddy* (Etna, NH: Nebbadoon Press, 1997); and Martin Gardner, *The Healing Revelations of Mary Baker Eddy: The Rise and Fall of Christian Science* (Buffalo, NY: Prometheus Books, 1993).

The Mary Baker Eddy Library in Boston, Massachusetts, houses a huge trove of manuscripts and other artifacts related to Eddy's life. The Longyear Foundation in Brookline, Massachusetts, has materials as well.

# *Mary Shindler*

The first book-length biography is in preparation by Linda Sundquist-Nassie, *The Life of Mary Shindler: The Poetess of Song*. Although Shindler never wrote a memoir, she did publish an account of her personal experiences with spiritualism, *A Southerner Among the Spirits* (Boston: Colby & Rich, 1877).

Many of Shindler's letters, journals, and other manuscripts are included in the Shindler-Palmer Family Papers at the East Texas Research Center, R. W. Steen Library, Stephen F. Austin State University, Nacogdoches, Texas.

# *Emma Willard*

Two twentieth-century biographies have been written, both by Alma Lutz. *Emma Willard: Daughter of Democracy* (Boston: Houghton Mifflin, 1929) is the more comprehensive treatment; the shorter, *Emma Willard: Pioneer Educator of American Women* (Boston: Beacon Press, 1964), focuses more on its subject's pedagogical work. The earliest biography of Willard was John Lord, *The Life of Emma Willard* (New York: D. Appleton, 1873).

*Journal and Letters, from France and Great-Britain* (Troy, NY: N. Tuttle, printer, 1833) brings together the diary and letters Willard wrote during her European tour in the early 1830s. There are collections of this prolific writer's papers in the Amherst College Library, Amherst, Massachusetts; in the libraries of the Emma Willard School, the Rensselaer County Historical Society, and Russell Sage College, all in Troy, New York; and in the Blackwell Museum, Northern Illinois University, DeKalb, Illinois.

# *Clara Barton*

Elizabeth Brown Pryor, *Clara Barton: Professional Angel* (Philadelphia: University of Pennsylvania Press, 1987), covers the Red Cross founder's entire life. Another study, Stephen B. Oates, *A Woman of Valor: Clara Barton and the Civil War* (New York: Free Press, 1994), focuses on the seminal experience of Barton's life.

There are many biographies of Barton. Percy Epler, *The Life of Clara Barton* (New York: Macmillan, 1915), was the earliest. William E.

Barton, *The Life of Clara Barton, Founder of the American Red Cross,* 2 vols. (Boston: Houghton Mifflin, 1922), includes selections from the subject's correspondence. Other noteworthy works include David H. Burton, *Clara Barton: In the Service of Humanity* (Westport, CT: Greenwood Press, 1995); Ishbel Ross, *Angel of the Battlefield: The Life of Clara Barton* (New York: Harper, 1956); and Blanche Colton Williams, *Clara Barton: Daughter of Destiny* (Philadelphia: J. B. Lippincott, 1941).

Clara Barton's papers are located at the American Antiquarian Society, Worcester, Massachusetts; Duke University Library, Durham, North Carolina; the Manuscript Division of the Library of Congress, Washington, D.C.; the Huntington Library, San Marino, California; and the Sophia Smith Collection, Smith College, Northampton, Massachusetts.

# Sarah Winnemucca

The most exhaustive study of Winnemucca's life is also the most recent: Sally Zanjani, *Sarah Winnemucca* (Lincoln, NE: University of Nebraska Press, 2001). Earlier biographies include Gae Whitney Canfield, *Sarah Winnemucca of the Northern Paiutes* (Norman, OK: University of Oklahoma Press, 1983), and Katherine Gehm, *Sarah Winnemucca: Most Extraordinary Woman of the Paiute Nation* (Phoenix, AZ: O'Sullivan Woodside, 1975). All studies of Winnemucca's life are indebted to her memoir, Sarah Winnemucca Hopkins, *Life Among the Piutes: Their Wrongs and Claims* (New York: G. P. Putnam's Sons, 1883; repr., Reno: University of Nevada Press, 1994).

# Elizabeth Palmer Peabody

Bruce Ronda has published the first comprehensive biography, *Elizabeth Palmer Peabody: A Reformer on Her Own Terms* (Cambridge: Harvard University Press, 1999), and edited a collection of her correspondence, *Letters of Elizabeth Palmer Peabody: American Renaissance Woman* (Middletown, CT: Wesleyan University Press, 1984). Ruth M.

Baylor, *Elizabeth Palmer Peabody: Kindergarten Pioneer* (Philadelphia: University of Pennsylvania Press, 1965), devotes particular attention to Peabody's fostering of early childhood education.

A collection of Peabody's papers is housed in the Berg Collection, New York Public Library, New York City.

## Mary Cassatt

The most recent—and most authoritative—biography is Nancy Mowll Mathews, *Mary Cassatt: A Life* (New York: Villard Books, 1994). Other notable treatments include Nancy Hale, *Mary Cassatt: A Biography of the Great American Painter* (Garden City, NY: Doubleday, 1975), a portrait with both Victorian and psychoanalytic overtones; and Frederick Sweet, *Miss Mary Cassatt: Impressionist from Pennsylvania* (Norman, OK: University of Oklahoma Press, 1966), the first three-dimensional, human portrayal of the artist. These authors and others were indebted to Louisine Havemeyer's posthumous memoir, *Sixteen to Sixty: Memoirs of a Collector* (New York: privately printed, 1961; repr., New York: Ursus Press, 1993).

Mathews edited *Cassatt and Her Circle: Selected Letters* (New York: Abbeville Press, 1987). The Smithsonian Institution Archives of American Art, Washington, D.C., has letters, manuscripts, and other material by and about Cassatt and many of her friends and contemporaries.

## Marian Anderson

Allan Keiler, *Marian Anderson: A Singer's Journey* (New York: Scribner, 2000), is a thorough biography, complete with appendices listing the singer's repertory and recordings. Anderson published *My Lord, What a Morning: An Autobiography* (New York: Viking) in 1956. It has been reprinted many times, most recently with an introduction written by her nephew, the conductor James DePriest (Urbana, IL: University of Illinois Press, 2002). Her accompanist, the Finnish pianist Kosti Vehanen, told Anderson's story from a musician's perspective in *Marian Anderson, a Portrait by Kosti Vehanen* (New York and London: Whittlesey House, 1941).

The Marian Anderson Papers are in the Annenberg Rare Book and Manuscript Library of the University of Pennsylvania Library in Philadelphia. The holdings have been described in depth in Neda M. Westlake and Otto W. Albrecht, *Marian Anderson: A Catalog of the Collection at the University of Pennsylvania Library* (Philadelphia, PA: University of Pennsylvania Press, 1981).

## Selena Quintanilla

Standing out from several biographies rushed into print after Selena's tragic death is one by music writer Joe Nick Patoski, *Selena: Como la Flor* (Boston: Little, Brown, 1996).

## Amelia Earhart

The records of Earhart's copiously documented life begin with her own memoir of her historic transatlantic flights, *20 Hrs. 40 Min.: Our Flight in the Friendship. The American girl, first across the Atlantic by air, tells her story* (New York: G. P. Putnam's Sons, 1928); and her dispatches from her attempted circumnavigation of the globe, *Last Flight* (New York: G. P. Putnam's Sons, 1937), arranged by George Palmer Putnam. Jean L. Backus collected some of Earhart's correspondence in *Letters from Amelia* (Boston: Beacon Press, 1982).

Biographies by Earhart's family members include the volume by her husband, George Palmer Putnam, *Soaring Wings: A Biography of Amelia Earhart* (New York: Harcourt, Brace, 1939); and two books by her sister, Muriel Earhart Morrissey, *Courage Is the Price: The Biography of Amelia Earhart* (Wichita, KS: McCormick-Armstrong, 1963); and *Amelia, My Courageous Sister* (Santa Clara, CA: Osborne, 1987), written with Carol L. Osborne.

Among the noteworthy recent examinations of Earhart's life by other writers are Susan Butler, *East to the Dawn: The Life of Amelia Earhart* (New York: Da Capo Press, 1997); Doris L. Rich, *Amelia Earhart: A Biography* (Washington: Smithsonian Institution Press, 1989); and Mary S. Lovell, *The Sound of Wings: The Life of Amelia Earhart* (New York: St. Martin's Press, 1989).

Theories about Amelia Earhart's disappearance have proliferated ever since her plane vanished in 1937. Investigations into the mystery have been published by a number of writers, among them Elgen M. Long and Marie K. Long, *Amelia Earhart: The Mystery Solved* (New York: Simon & Schuster, 1999); Randall Brink, *Lost Star: The Search for Amelia Earhart* (New York: Norton, 1994); James A. Donahue, *The Earhart Disappearance: The British Connection. A Story about the Disappearance of Amelia Earhart and the Cover-up Which Followed* (Terre Haute, IN: SunShine House, 1987); and Fred G. Goerner, *The Search for Amelia Earhart* (London: Bodley Head, 1966).

The largest trove of documents and memorabilia is the George Palmer Putnam Collection of Amelia Earhart Papers, in the Archives and Special Collections Division, Purdue University Library, West Lafayette, Indiana. Other collections—manuscripts, photos, and memorabilia—of Amelia Earhart and her family can be found in the Smithsonian National Air and Space Museum Archives, Washington, D.C.; the Schlesinger Library at Radcliffe College, Cambridge, Massachusetts; the Medford, Massachusetts, and Atchison, Kansas, public libraries; and the Headquarters of the Ninety-Nines in Oklahoma City.

## *Jacqueline Cochran*

Jacqueline Cochran's biography has yet to be written, but she told her own story in a pair of memoirs, *The Stars at Noon* (Boston: Little, Brown, 1954), written with the help of her husband, Floyd Odlum; and *Jackie Cochran: An Autobiography* (New York: Bantam Books, 1987), with coauthor Maryann Bucknum Brinley. Leslie Haynesworth and David Toomey recount Cochran's exploits with the WASP, as well as before and after, in *Amelia Earhart's Daughters: The Wild and Glorious Story of American Women Aviators from World War II to the Dawn of the Space Age* (New York: William Morrow, 1998).

## Margaret Chase Smith

Of the many books about Margaret Chase Smith's life and career, the most recent and most informative are Janann Sherman, *No Place for a Woman: A Life of Senator Margaret Chase Smith* (New Brunswick, NJ: Rutgers University Press, 2000); Patricia Schmidt, *Margaret Chase Smith: Beyond Convention* (Orono, ME: University of Maine Press, 1996); and Patricia Ward Wallace, *Politics of Conscience: A Biography of Senator Margaret Chase Smith* (Westport, CT: Praeger Publishers, 1995).

Marlene Boyd Vallin has collected a number of important speeches in *Margaret Chase Smith: Model Public Servant* (Westport, CT: Greenwood Press, 1998). The Northwood University Margaret Chase Smith Library in Skowhegan, Maine, is the repository for the Margaret Chase Smith Papers.

## Oveta Culp Hobby

No full biography of Oveta Culp Hobby has been written. There is a limited-edition collection of biographical material, *Oveta Culp Hobby,* compiled and edited by Al Shire (Houston, TX: W. P. Hobby, 1997). Some details of her life can be found in James A. Clark, with Weldon Hart, *The Tactful Texan: A Biography of Governor Will Hobby* (New York: Random House, 1958); and in Nancy Brinton Shea, *The WAACs* (New York: Harper & Brothers, 1943), to which Hobby contributed a foreword. There is also a biographical essay, "Mrs. Secretary," in Ann Fears Crawford and Crystal Sasse Ragsdale, *Women in Texas* (Burnet, TX: Eakin Press, 1982), pp. 248–59.

Important collections of Oveta Culp Hobby's papers can be found in the Woodson Research Center, Fondren Library, Rice University, Houston, Texas; in the Manuscript Division, Library of Congress,

Washington, D.C.; and in the Eugene C. Barker Texas History Center, the Center for American History, University of Texas at Austin.

## Margaret Bourke-White

The authoritative biography is Vicki Goldberg, *Margaret Bourke-White: A Biography* (New York: Harper & Row, 1986). Theodore M. Brown, *Margaret Bourke-White: Photojournalist* (Ithaca, NY: Cornell University Press, 1972), makes the case that Bourke-White's life is most accurately reflected in her work. The study lists her publications and extensively reviews her career. Susan Goldman Rubin, *Margaret Bourke-White: Her Pictures Were Her Life* (New York: Abrams, 1999), takes a similar approach.

*Portrait of Myself* (New York: Simon & Schuster, 1963) is Bourke-White's version of her story, written when Parkinson's disease had forced her to stop taking photographs. The Margaret Bourke-White Papers are in the Special Collections Research Center, Syracuse University Library, Syracuse, New York.

## Marguerite Higgins

There is just one full-dress biography, Antoinette May, *Witness to War: A Biography of Marguerite Higgins* (New York: Beaufort, 1983). The Special Collections Research Center, Syracuse University Library, Syracuse, New York, is the repository for the Marguerite Higgins Papers.

## Mildred "Babe" Didrikson Zaharias

The two most authoritative biographies are Susan E. Cayleff, *Babe: The Life and Legend of Babe Didrikson Zaharias* (Urbana, IL: University of Illinois Press, 1995); and William Oscar Johnson and Nancy P. Williamson, *"Whatta-Gal": The Babe Didrikson Story* (Boston: Little, Brown, 1977), based on the authors' exhaustive series of articles. Zaharias also

composed her own memoir, with the help of writer Harry Paxton, in
*This Life I've Led: My Autobiography* (New York: A. S. Barnes, 1955),
written while she was battling cancer.

A collection of Zaharias's letters to newspaperman William "Tiny"
Scurlock and his wife, Ruth, is in the Special Collections Division, John
Gray Library, Lamar University, Beaumont, Texas.

## Althea Gibson

Bruce Schoenfeld, *The Match: Althea Gibson and Angela Buxton* (New
York: Amistad, 2004), is the first biographical treatment of Gibson intended for adult readers. The two volumes of Gibson's memoirs, *I Always Wanted to Be Somebody* (New York: Harper & Brothers, 1958) and
*So Much to Live For* (New York: Putnam, 1968), originally intended for
young readers, are nonetheless absorbing, frank accounts of her often
troubled life and career.

# PHOTOGRAPHY CREDITS

CHAPTER ONE: PIONEERS AND PRESERVATIONISTS

Mary Austin Holley: Courtesy of the Center for American History, University of Texas-Austin
Ann Raney Coleman: Courtesy of Duke University
Jane Long: Courtesy of the Center for American History, University of Texas-Austin
Adina De Zavala: Courtesy of the Center for American History, University of Texas-Austin
Clara Driscoll: Courtesy of the Center for American History, University of Texas-Austin
Anne Legendre Armstrong: Courtesy of Anne Armstrong


CHAPTER TWO: WOMEN OF FAITH

Elizabeth Seton: Courtesy of AP Photo
Mary Baker Eddy: Courtesy of the Mary Baker Eddy Collection
Mary Shindler: Courtesy of Senator Hutchison
Marj Carpenter: Courtesy of Marj Carpenter

## CHAPTER THREE: EDUCATION FOR EVERYONE

Emma Willard: Courtesy of the Emma Willard School
Lynne Cheney: White House photograph by Tina Hager
Ruth Simmons: Clark Quin / Brown University
Rosalyn Yalow: Courtesy of the Bronx Veteran Administration
    Hospital

## CHAPTER FOUR: SAVING LIVES

Clara Barton: Courtesy of the Clara Barton Birthplace Museum
Elizabeth Dole: Courtesy of Elizabeth Dole
Bernadine Healy: Courtesy of the Cleveland Clinic Foundation
Antonia Novello: Courtesy of the New York State Deptartment
    of Health

## CHAPTER FIVE: THE VOICE OF HER PEOPLE

Elizabeth Palmer Peabody: Courtesy of the Concord Free Public
    Library

## CHAPTER SIX: A WOMAN'S ART

Marian Anderson: Courtesy of AP Photo
Selena Quintanilla: Courtesy of AP Photo
Beverly Sills: Don Purdue

## CHAPTER SEVEN: CONQUERING THE SKIES

Amelia Earhart: Courtesy of AP Photo
Jacqueline Cochran: Courtesy of AP Photo
Sally Ride: Courtesy of Sally Ride

CHAPTER EIGHT: PUBLIC LIVES, PUBLIC SERVICE

Margaret Chase Smith: Courtesy of the Margaret Chase Smith Library
Geraldine Ferraro: Courtesy of Geraldine Ferraro
Sandra Day O'Connor: Dane Penland, Collection of the Supreme
    Court of the United States

CHAPTER NINE: RENAISSANCE WOMEN

Oveta Culp Hobby: Courtesy of Getty Images
Carleton Fiorina: Courtesy of AP Photo
Muriel Siebert: Courtesy of Muriel Siebert
Madeleine Albright: Portrait by Timothy Greenfield-Sanders
Condoleezza Rice: White House Photo

CHAPTER TEN: WOMEN LOOK AT THE WORLD

Margaret Bourke-White: Courtesy of AP Photo
Marguerite Higgins: Courtesy of Getty Images
Barbara Walters: Yolanda Perez/ABC
Cokie Roberts: Photograph by Lynn Goldsmith
Jane Friedman: George Lange

CHAPTER ELEVEN: SETTING RECORDS,
MAKING HISTORY

Mildred "Babe" Didrikson Zaharias: Courtesy of AP Photo
Althea Gibson: Courtesy of AP Photo
Jackie Joyner-Kersee: Courtesy of AP Photo
Nadia Comaneci: Courtesy of AP Photo

# INDEX

Numaga (Young Winnemucca), 130,
131

Oberlin College, 80
O'Connor, John Jay, 246, 248
O'Connor, Sandra Day, 243, 247–49
  background of, 246–47
  on women's issues, 247–48
Odlum, Floyd, 200, 206
Odlum, Jacqueline Cochran, 199–200,
  201–2, 203, 204, 205–6, 207
Olds, Robert, 200
Old Stone Fort, xiv
Olivares, Antonio de, 25
Olive, Leroy, 309
Olmido, Alex, 339
Olympics, 302–3, 305–6, 307, 343, 346,
  347
O'Neill, Thomas P. "Tip," 245
opera singers, 183, 184, 189–90
O'Reilly, Mary Boyle, 275
Ormsby, Lizzie, 129
Ormsby, Margaret, 129
Ormsby, William, 129, 131
Oytes (Paiute), 135, 138, 139, 142, 143,
  144, 147, 149

Packs, Tom, 313
paddle tennis, 323
Padgitt, Jess, 284
Page, Blin, 212, 213
Page, Ed P., 212
Paiute Joe, 141
Paiutes:
  culture of, 127–28, 130, 136, 140,
    153
  education of, 136, 155–58
  on reservations, 131–40, 147–51, 152
  white conflicts with, 128–31, 140–47
Pakistan, creation of, 284
Palm, Nancy, 251
Palmer, Benjamin, 56, 60
Palmer, Bertha Honoré, 174
Palmer, Jane, 56, 58
Palmer, Keith, 56, 59
Palmer, Mary Bunce, 56
Paris Salon, 167, 168

Parren, Thomas, 217
Parrish, Annie, 136
Parrish, Samuel, 134–36, 137–39, 145,
  148
Partridge, Emma Dot, 212
*Pat and Mike,* 320
Patten, Ronald, 214
Patterson, Daniel, 51, 52
Patterson, Mary Saunders, 181
Payne, Frederick, 232
Peabody, Elizabeth Palmer, 151–58
Peabody Indian School, 155–58
Pearson, Drew, 204
Pennsylvania Academy of Fine Arts,
  164, 177
Pennsylvania Railroad, 177
Perez, Chris, 187
performing arts, 179–90
  films, 185–86
  racial discrimination in, 181, 182,
    183
  singers, 179–84, 187–90
Perry, Bob, 338, 339
Perry, Emily Austin, 5, 24
Pétain, Henri, 289
Peters, John, 211
Peters, Roumania, 326, 327
Phelps, Timothy, 1
phrenology, 95
physicists, 89, 207
Physick, Philip Syng, 47
Pierce, Franklin, 51
Pisarro, Camille, 169, 172
Pittman, Ira, 199
Pittman, Mary, 199
Pius XII, Pope, 205
*Plan for Improving Female Education,
  A* (Willard), 73, 74
poetry, 57–63
Polk, James Knox, 22
Postimpressionists, 178
Pratt, Betty Rosenquest, 329, 334, 337
Presbyterian Church, 63, 64
Price, Hiram, 155
Price, Leontyne, 184
Princeton University, 86
prisoners of war, 92, 105, 110

Spanish Governors' Palace, 33
SPARs, 202, 219
spiritual healing, 53–54, 55
Stalin, Joseph, 277, 279–80
Stanford, Leland, 155
Stanford University, 207, 246, 271
Stanton, Elizabeth Cady, 82
Stephanopoulos, George, 64
Sterling, Ross, 254
Stetson, Augusta, 55
Stevenson, Adlai, 234, 259
Stewart, Potter, 247
Stimson, Henry, 203, 256, 257
stock brokerage, 266, 267–68
Stone, Elvira, 102–3
Stratton, Dorothy, 202
Streeter, Ruth, 202
Suggs, Louise, 321
Summer, Charles, 103
Summersby, Kay, 281
supersonic flight, 205–6, 207
Supreme Court, U.S., 243, 247
surgeon general, 124
Suydam, Peter, 100
Swayze, Patsy, 161

Taft, Robert, 229, 259
Taliban, 216
Tambiago, 141
Tatum, W. E., 321
Taylor, Anna Mary, xiv, 15–16, 56, 61
Taylor, Charles S., xiv, 14–15
Tejano music, 187–88
television journalism, 250–51, 292–93, 296
Tennant, Eleanor "Teach," 314
tennis, 207, 314–15, 323–43
    racial integration and, 323, 324, 325, 329, 330–34, 339, 340, 342, 343
Teresa, Mother, 126
Terrell, Kate, 16, 18
Texas:
    American settlers in, 5–22
    1836 War of Independence in, 14–17, 19–20, 27–28
    historical preservation efforts in, 23, 24–34

slavery in, 8–9, 11, 13, 14
statehood obtained by, xiv, 13, 20, 22, 259
Tejano population of, 23, 32, 34
tidelands of, 259
Texas, Republic of, xiv, 14, 20–21, 22, 23–24, 25, 66–67
Texas, University of, 67, 250
Texas A&M University, 38, 67
Texas Historical and Landmarks Association (THLA), 32–33
Texas (Holley), 8, 9, 10, 14, 20
Thacker, Charlie, 148
Thatcher, Margaret, 126
Thich Tri Quang, 291
This Week, 293
Thomas, John, 16
Thompson, Bea, 311
Thoreau, Henry David, 154
Thye, Edward, 230
Tibbetts, Paul, 282
Tito (Josip Broz), 290
Tobey, Charles, 230
Tocqueville, Alexis de, xiii
Today, 293
Toscanini, Arturo, 180, 183
Tower, John, 242–43
track-and-field competition, 303, 304–6, 343, 345
Tracy, Spencer, 320
Trafton, William, Jr., 234
Transcendentalist Club, 154
Transylvania University, 2–3
Travis, William, 30
Troy Female Seminary, 76–80, 82
Truman, Christine, 340
Truman, Harry, 205, 222, 224, 227, 262, 290
Tsai, Gerald, 267–68
Tuboitony (Paiute), 131
Twain, Mark (Samuel Clemens), 55

Umapine (Cayuse chief), 145, 146, 147
Union of Soviet Socialist Republics (USSR), German invasion of, 277, 278–79, 280

United Nations, 259, 269
  Commission on Human Rights of,
    244
United States Golf Association
  (USGA), 311, 314, 322
U.S. Lawn Tennis Association
  (USLTA), 329, 330, 331, 336, 339

Valet, Mathilde, 179
Van Fleet, James, 232
Vassall, Bernard, 101
Vassall, Irving, 109
Vassall, Sally Barton, 93, 94, 95, 109,
  111, 113
Velez, Lupe, 185
Verrett, Shirley, 184
Vietnam, conflicts in, 239–40, 290–92
Vincent de Paul, Saint, 42, 45
Vinson, Carl, 217

WAAC (Women's Army Auxiliary
  Corps), 202, 220, 256–57
WAC (Women's Army Corps), 202,
  219, 220, 221, 257–58, 281
WAFS (Women's Auxiliary Ferrying
  Squadron), 201, 202
Wagner, Henry, 133
Walker, Buddy, 324
Walker, Walton, 289, 290
Walsh, Stella, 306
Walters, Barbara, 292–95
Walters, Lou, 293
war correspondents, 275–76, 277–92
WASP (Women's Airforce Service
  Pilots), xv, 202–4, 205, 206
Waterford Female Academy, 74, 76, 77
WAVES (Women Accepted for
  Voluntary Emergency Services),
  202, 219, 220, 221
Wayne, John, 32
Wayne, "Mad" Anthony, 104
Webster, Daniel, 79
Weir, Reginald, 329
Weis, George, 43
Wellesley College, 269
WFTD (Women's Flying Training
  Detachment), 201–2

Wharton, Edith, 178
Wharton, William, 13
Whistler, James McNeill, 163
White, Clarence, 276
White, Joseph, 276
White, Juliana, 46
White, Rose Landry, 42, 44–45
White, Wallace, 212–13, 222
Whittier, John Greenleaf, 152
Wilbur, James, 134, 148, 149, 150–51
Willard, Emma Hart, xiii, 68–83
  background of, 68–71
  on democracy, 81–82
  schools managed by, 71–72, 73,
    76–80
  as teacher, 70, 71–72
  on teacher training, 74–75, 78, 81
  on women's education, 71, 73–76,
    80, 82
  writings of, 79, 81, 82
Willard, John (father), 69, 71, 77
Willard, John (son), 70
Williams brothers, 130
Wills, Helen, 338
Wilson, Charles, 232
Wilson, Henry, 102, 103, 109
Wilson, Woodrow, 211
Winnemucca, Lee, 131, 135, 142, 143,
  144
Winnemucca, Mattie, 144, 145, 146
Winnemucca, Natches Overton, 131,
  133, 141, 143, 146–47, 148, 150,
  155, 158
Winnemucca, Sarah, 127–51
  Bannock War and, 141, 142–44, 145,
    146–47, 148, 151
  on Indian/settler conflicts, 130, 143,
    148
  as interpreter, 129, 131, 132, 133,
    134, 135, 140, 144–45, 156
  marriages of, 145, 151
  memoirs written by, 127, 152–53,
    155, 158
  as public speaker, 148, 153
  on reservation system, 131–33, 137,
    139, 140, 148–49, 150, 152
  as schoolteacher, 136, 155–58